Liberating Lawrence

Liberating Lawrence

Gay Activism in the 1970s at the University of Kansas

Katherine Rose-Mockry

UNIVERSITY PRESS OF KANSAS

Published by the University Press of Kansas (Lawrence, Kansas 66045), which was
organized by the Kansas Board of Regents and is operated and funded by Emporia
State University, Fort Hays State University, Kansas State University, Pittsburg State
University, the University of Kansas, and Wichita State University.

Library of Congress Cataloging-in-Publication Data

Names: Rose-Mockry, Katherine, author.
Title: Liberating Lawrence : gay activism in the 1970s at the University of
Kansas / Katherine Rose-Mockry.
Description: Lawrence, Kansas : University Press of Kansas, 2024. |
Includes bibliographical references and index.
Identifiers: LCCN 2023057811 (print) | LCCN 2023057812 (ebook)
ISBN 9780700637355 (hardback)
ISBN 9780700637362 (ebook)
Subjects: LCSH: Lawrence Gay Liberation Front. | Gay college
students—Political activity—Kansas—Lawrence—History—20th century. |
Gay liberation movement—Kansas—Lawrence—History—20th century. |
Student movements—Kansas—Lawrence—History—20th century. | Gay
rights—Kansas—Lawrence—History—20th century.
Classification: LCC LC2575.5.K2 R67 2024 (print) | LCC LC2575.5.K2
(ebook) | DDC 378.0086/64—dc23/eng/20240418
LC record available at https://lccn.loc.gov/2023057811.
LC ebook record available at https://lccn.loc.gov/2023057812.

British Library Cataloguing-in-Publication Data is available.

Printed in the United States of America

That is how you spark a revolution. You shift the frame,
you change the lens, and all at once the world is revealed,
and nothing is the same.

Nadine Burke Harris, The Deepest Well

This book is dedicated to all the courageous LGBTQ pioneers at the University of Kansas and beyond, including those who shared their powerful stories with me. They dared to travel the difficult, sometimes daunting path and push the boundaries to change the culture. They sparked a revolution.

Their stories of determination and persistence provide hope to future generations for a more equitable world. In addition, they remind us that it is essential to keep fighting to eradicate a culture of intolerance so all may live freely and authentically without fear.

Contents

List of Photographs   *xi*
Preface   *xiii*
Acknowledgments   *xix*
About the Identity Terms Used in This Book   *xxiii*
List of Abbreviations   *xxv*

Introduction   1

Chapter 1 "The Times They Are A-Changin'": Setting the Stage in the 1960s   11

Chapter 2 "Out of the Johns and Into the Streets!": Creating the Framework and Getting the Group Started (1970–1975)   41

Chapter 3 From Vision to Reality: Launching the LGLF (1970)   65

Chapter 4 Lawsuits and Leadership: Gaining Traction and Influence (1971–1973)   119

Chapter 5 "There Are a Lot More Homosexuals at the University Than We Thought": Challenging Attitudes and Anchoring the Foundation (1975–1979)   162

Chapter 6 "We Are Here and We're Not Going Away": The 1980s and Beyond   192

Conclusion   202

Appendix A: Key Individuals Who Appear in This Book   *223*
Appendix B: The Power of Connections: Lawrence Lesbian Communities in the 1970s   *228*
Appendix C: Gay Activism on Other Campuses across the State in the 1970s   *261*
Notes   *279*
Bibliography   *329*
Index   *337*

Photographs

1. Michael Stubbs and John Bolin recover after being attacked   93
2. Venus house   93
3. Vietnam antiwar protest November 8, 1970   94
4. Police officers handcuff a student, summer of 1970   94
5. Protesters block traffic during the Days of Rage   95
6. Funeral procession for Rick "Tiger" Dowdell   95
7. International Women's Day, February 28, 1971   96
8. LGLF founder David Stout   96
9. John Bolin   97
10. John Steven Stillwell   97
11. Michael Stubbs and Richard Linker   98
12. Reginald "Reggie" Brown   99
13. Reginald Brown, Joe Prados, and friends   99
14. Steven Weaver at Pooh Corner   100
15. LGLF's first official meeting, August 30, 1970   100
16. Members of the New York, Boston, and Philadelphia Gay Liberation Fronts visit Venus   101
17. "Keep the Scene Clean" work day   102
18. Women's Coalition sponsored dance poster   103
19. William Kunstler, LGLF's attorney   104
20. William Kunstler speaks to reporters   105
21. "Hot to Trot"   106
22. "Too Hot to Stop"   107
23. Todd Zwahl and Ruth Lichtwardt give a class presentation   108
24. Leonard Grotta and Reginald Brown pose with the Jayhawk   108
25. LGLF Halloween dance   109
26. LGLF members speak at a panel at "51 Years OUT"   110
27. Women's community members speak at a panel at "51 Years OUT"   110
28. Women's Music Collective at "51 Years OUT"   111

29. Early LGLF friends reunite at "51 Years OUT" 111
30. Lawrence Women's Music Collective performs at a concert   112
31. Julia Deisler (Julie), Holly R. Fischer, Susan Davis, Deb Holmes   112
32. The group Suffrage   113
33. Dean Emily Taylor coaches a women's softball team   114
34. Molly Laflin, a member of the Holy Cow Creamers softball team   115
35. Holy Cow Creamers members   115
36. Holly R. Fischer and Susan Davis, Women's Music Collective   116
37. Janean Meigs, Susan Davis, and Toni Cramer at Womanspace   116
38. South Farm   117
39. Martha Boyd   117
40. Kathryn Clark and C. Lathrop   118
41. Stephanie K. Blackwood   118

Preface

It was the fall of 2010, and I was excited (and relieved) to have just passed my doctoral exams. I was looking forward to beginning the next step: writing my dissertation. But I needed to settle on a topic. I had entered the program with a topic in mind but decided to change course. As luck would have it, one of my advisors, Lisa Wolf-Wendel, came to me with an opportunity. A University of Kansas (KU) alumnus had just contacted her. His name was David Stout. He was looking for a doctoral student to research the Lawrence Gay Liberation Front, an organization he spearheaded in 1970. It was the first gay rights activist group at KU and in the state of Kansas. He had created a grant to make sure KU's place in the national gay liberation movement was researched and documented while he and other activists were still around to share their stories.

I didn't remember hearing about the Lawrence Gay Liberation Front (LGLF) when I was a KU undergraduate in the mid-1970s. I had transferred to KU for my senior year and was heavily involved in the music department, so I wasn't always aware of general campus activity. However, my husband and friends of mine, who were at KU in the early 1970s, remember LGLF's presence. As I considered taking on this project, I needed to find out what this group was about. I started investigating and was inspired. David Stout must have possessed considerable determination and courage to have taken such a bold step, especially in 1970 when many who were not heterosexual were targeted and lived in fear. How many students today would go head to head with the chancellor, regents, and lawmakers, risking confrontations with the police and their family's rejection? The more I learned about the organization and its founders, the more excited I was to take on this project. I was convinced that this was a story that had to be told.

In my many years directing a women's center at both UCLA and KU, I had dealt with gender, gender identity, sexual orientation, and related issues on a daily basis. In addition, I was prepared through my academic studies (counseling, higher education) and had a connection to the organization in question, whose office was down the hall from mine (with a different name). I would say, though, that the most compelling reason for my strong interest was my deep professional and personal relationships over the years with many in the LGBTQ communities, including close family members. The stories that people shared with me about the inequities they had experienced as well as their joys and triumphs underscored the need to share them with others. I jumped at the opportunity to research this important topic and submitted a writing sample to be considered with other interested researchers. I was delighted to hear back a short while later that I had been selected.

There were no specific parameters given for the ways in which this research should be conducted. After my introduction to the group's history, which included a review of David Stout's impressive collection of information on the LGLF, I decided to speak with those who were at KU and in Lawrence during that era. I planned on interviewing former members, students, administrators, and faculty to get a multilayered, personal perspective of the times and the group's place in these times. I was concerned, however, about my ability to find enough people. It had, after all, been over forty years since the group began, and many had moved out of the state and were difficult to locate. But my research and David's remembrance of early members put my fears to rest. In addition, I was introduced to the strength of the "gay grapevine."[1] Almost every interview led to the interviewee asking me, "Have you thought about speaking with these people? Here's their contact information. And I'll let them know you'll be calling." Not only did my interview list grow quickly, but soon I was on the verge of having more names than I knew what to do with. I was starting to catch on that this was a really special group, one that had lasted well beyond the members' years at KU.

I identified 199 individuals to contact. Of these, I was able to find contact information for sixty-two, and thirty-five accepted. Ultimately, thirty were interviewed. Close to half (sixteen of thirty) were interviewed by phone. Interviews were recorded and transcribed. The wide range of interviewees with different vantage points (e.g., group members, faculty members, community members) provided a broad perspective and enhanced the validity of the study. I also ensured reliability by, among other things, verifying the accuracy of information provided in interviews. In addition, I researched newspaper, magazine, and journal articles, books, LGLF writings and publications, and other archival materials. It is interesting to note that while over forty years had gone by, there were very few discrepancies in the information I received when compared to historical documents. The level of recall likely indicates the importance of the group and the times to those with whom I spoke.

I was very moved by people's willingness to open up to me and share some very personal stories: stories of victory and joy, loss and pain. As I continued, it became clear to me that the stories were not just the tools for conducting this research; they were the heart of this research. This seemed fitting since stories play an essential role in bringing to light historical injustice and promoting progress and change. They can capture the meaning and significance of the life experiences of those whose histories have been ignored and devalued and whose identities have been marginalized.[2] By making these histories visible, they can become integrated in current conversations and contribute to what historians Martha Howell and Walter Prevenier call "the new cultural history," challenging outmoded boundaries and welcoming other identities in the discourse.[3] Telling one's story can be a subversive act, giving a personal face to power, struggle, and privilege, illuminating the impact of inequity on individuals' lives.

During the course of my research, David Stout and I discussed organizing an event to recognize and celebrate the group's fifty-year anniversary in 2020.[4] I was excited to pursue this and, with his blessing, set aside the remaining grant funding for this purpose. Discussions began in 2018, three years after I completed my degree, and became serious in 2019. KU colleagues and the community agency, Watkins Museum of History, joined in (details about this event are included in the conclusion). It was fortuitous that a former LGLF member who had a major role in the group and in KU 1970s activism, Michael Stubbs, saw an event announcement and reached out to those of us organizing the event. When we spoke, he filled me in about his role in gay organizing and the radical contingent within the LGLF. This brought a new perspective and depth of understanding to my research. He also connected me with additional LGLF members, some of whom had been hesitant to speak with me, an unknown entity, and were key to the history of the group.

I discovered in my research that, while the LGLF was conceptualized as gender inclusive when the group began, it evolved during the 1970s to be a primarily male group. Given this, an important part of the story was missing: that of lesbian communities at KU and in Lawrence. Scholar Beth Bailey addressed some of the actions that lesbians and feminists took to challenge the pervasive sexism and misogyny of the time;[5] however, much of the history is underground, known only within the ranks of women who were part of this community, and has not been formally preserved. I was fortunate to connect with many of these women to find out about this little-known history and have included it here. This history is essential in understanding the impact and scope of this community more broadly and provides a more complete picture of LGLF and the times (see appendix B).

I conducted thirty-seven additional interviews after deciding to write this book, following up on additional contacts I had received. This expanded the total number of those interviewed to sixty-seven. The stories, like the ones I had heard earlier, were powerful. They brought me to tears and made me laugh out loud. I became even more resolved to share these with others. My original fear of not having enough material turned out to be far from the actuality; in fact, I had collected more stories than could be included here. The depth and vibrancy of these stories are a testament to this rich history.

This book, in addition to being about stories, is also about connections. These connections were the strength of LGLF and the women's community. Interviewees frequently commented on how central these relationships were to their burgeoning sense of self as a gay or lesbian person, and their ability to survive the college experience. And for many, these connections have continued through the years.

The connections that LGLF members formed with each other were important, but equally so were the connections they formed with those in the broader community. They developed a web of support across the state, pushing up against widespread resistance and providing a toehold to other campuses to advocate for gay and lesbian students at their institutions (see appendix C). LGLF members' impact was due not only to their actions, but also to the ways in which they carried out their actions. They used affirmation and humor rather than hostility to get their message across as they invited others in. This was not the norm for similar groups across the country. Their desire and ability to form connections and draw in "the other" expanded their base of support and broke down barriers.

I got to experience this connection firsthand. I recall my first interview with group member Lee Hubbell. I met Lee at his house, my digital recorder and list of prepared questions at the ready. Interviewing was not a new experience for me; I had conducted numerous interviews for graduate and doctoral classes and for work as well. It didn't take long, though, before I felt like I was speaking with an old friend. And so it continued with each new interview. Interviewees' openness, honesty, and trust made me feel connected to them in a way I had not anticipated. They were not subjects in a research project but people I came to think of as friends.

In the fall of 2021, the big moment arrived. I finally got to meet many of these early pioneers at the fifty-year anniversary celebration event. As I watched them dance the night away in the ballroom, I was transported back to their legendary dances in the 1970s, and I could see their close-knit connections firsthand. That same youthful energy and passion to change the world was still present all those years later. There was no doubt in my mind that these people were the movers and shakers who had the skills to change an institution and the minds and hearts of a society who had been taught to fear them. What began as a project for me evolved into a passion.

A final comment: this is a carefully researched and documented history but not a complete one. There are people who were involved in this history that I did not speak with. There are stories that are not included here. My hope is that others who were there and were part of this memorable time will document this history for KU Archives. Current and future generations need to hear these stories. It has been my pleasure to document and preserve this history, and it is my honor to share it with you.

Acknowledgments

The 1970s were a unique time—a time of dismantling old norms to create a new world. A hallmark of the time, as well as a theme throughout this book, is the power of community in achieving this goal. This book, true to its 1970s spirit, relied on the involvement and collaboration of many to capture this largely unknown history, a history that needs to be shared. I would like to thank them for their efforts.

First, a special thank-you to those who shared their stories with me. They are the heart and soul of this book, providing a very personal glimpse into the challenges and victories that those who were gay and lesbian experienced during this important time in history. Interviewees' candid recollections provided richness and dimensionality to the understanding of the meaning of this organization and have brought this history to life. Their honesty must be commended, for even though many advances have been made, the current climate for those who are LGBTQ cannot be described as totally safe and accepting. Additionally, the willingness of those who are straight allies to provide unvarnished, sometimes un-flattering stories about the reality of the time was also courageous. I am deeply indebted to them for their generosity and contributions.

I am grateful to many in the group who, in the spirit of community, have spent considerable time and energy beyond their interviews, providing me with important, little-known details, connecting me with others, sending me information and photos, and helping me fill in gaps and clarify discrepancies. Their wisdom and support have meant so much. Michael Stubbs and John Bolin provided information and history not available anywhere else, offering their time and expertise to ensure that this important history will not be forgotten. Others who provided their time and talents include Reginald Brown, Deb Holmes, Martha Boyd, Kathryn Clark, Molly Laflin, Stephanie Blackwood, and Susan Davis.

I also thank LGLF founder David Stout, who generously funded my dissertation research through the KU Center for Research. David, driven by his desire to preserve this history, shared with me his remarkable gift for interpreting and articulating his experience. He was the catalyst for this project and opened the door to my research. He went out of his way to provide me with invaluable information, support, and encouragement, which helped me give shape and meaning to the large amount of information I acquired. He has my deep admiration and appreciation.

My wholehearted thanks to my dissertation advisor, Dr. John Rury. I have learned a tremendous amount from John about the true meaning and value of research and holding oneself to high standards in the process. His ongoing encouragement and guidance strengthened and reinforced my resolve to meet those high standards. I am indebted to John for letting the University Press of Kansas know of my research, to be considered for possible publication. He has my utmost appreciation and respect. I also thank my dissertation committee, including Lisa Wolf-Wendel, Susan Twombly, Jennifer Ng, Dongbin Kim, and Jeff Moran, for their insightful feedback that strengthened the organization and presentation of my material.

As this is my first book, I have come to realize the importance of having top-notch editors in your corner to help navigate through the process. Many thanks to University Press of Kansas senior editor David Congdon, who has guided me along the way, providing creative, insightful, thoughtful feedback that has refined my writing and improved the flow of the book. I appreciate his commitment to my project and the many ways he has worked with me to advance the important message of this book. And a big thank-you to Kelly Chrisman Jacques and Lori Rider for their excellent editing—their eagle eyes and attention to detail have been invaluable. I am also grateful to the University Press of Kansas leadership for their willingness to take on my project as well as their flexibility during COVID as we all "rolled with the punches" during this unprecedented time. I also thank manuscript reviewers C. J. Janovy and Patrick Dilley for their careful review and analysis of my manuscript draft. As recognized authorities in the field, their expertise and broad perspective helped frame their observations and suggestions. Their comments helped me tighten up the manuscript and expand its scope.

Librarians provide an invaluable service to researchers. I greatly appreciate the KU Spencer Research Library Archive librarians, who in addition to helping me access materials and resources, also answered questions I didn't know I had and led me to materials I would not have located without their help. Thanks to Letha Johnson, Shelby Schellenger, Kathy Lafferty, Elspeth Healey, Caitlin Donnelly Klepper, and Molly Herring for the care they took to make sure I got what I needed.

Nicki Rose is a special person in my life. Nicki was a student assistant during my tenure as director of the Emily Taylor Center for Women and Gender Equity. Her sharp intellect and unwavering work ethic led me to call on her while I was carefully balancing the demands of my position while also finishing my dissertation for my doctoral program. She spent many hours in the libraries hunting down newspaper articles and materials I had identified, as well as picking up work tasks so that after my workday was done, I could focus on completing my research. She was wise beyond her years and supported my research—an invaluable contribution.

Another special person in my life who generously offered help without hesitation or a second thought is Erik Tyler. Erik, a talented author, lent his incomparable graphics and technology skills in order for me to adjust some of the photos included here to publication standards.

And last but far from least is my family—my husband Lynn, sons William and Stephen, and daughter-in-law Gabby. Words cannot describe my appreciation. They have been my tireless supporters and have cheered me on, served as my sounding board, and encouraged me to keep going on those days when I could not see the light at the end of the tunnel. Their belief in the importance of this work has bolstered me, inspired me, and helped me move forward. They have my endless love.

A special thank-you to my son William, a gifted, insightful writer. He spent countless hours reading and providing feedback that was immeasurably helpful. I often called on his impeccable grammar skills and consider myself fortunate to have had him as a resource. How often does a parent get to thank their offspring for becoming their teacher? Thank you, William—I am proud and grateful.

Parts of my article "A Place I Could Be Myself: A History of Gay Activism in the 1970s at the University of Kansas," in *Embattled Lawrence*, vol. 2: *The Enduring Struggle for Freedom*, edited by Dennis Domer (Lawrence: Watkins Museum of History, 2023), have been used here with permission, courtesy of the Watkins Museum of History, Douglas County Historical Society.

About the Identity Terms Used in This Book

Throughout the years, the language used to refer to those who are not heterosexual has evolved. Since this book focuses on the 1960s and 1970s and language use has changed since those times, I am listing the terms that will be used in this book. In my writing, I was careful to use historically correct language that is contemporary to the time period.

"Gay" and "lesbian": The term "gay," considered somewhat radical in the 1960s and early 1970s, was used to refer to gay men, but it was also used as an inclusive term, referring to both gay men and lesbians (e.g., "gay community"). By the mid-1970s, however, the term had evolved to refer more specifically to gay men. Lesbians sometimes used the term "gay" to refer to themselves and each other, but more often they used the terms "lesbian" or "lesbian feminist."

"Homosexual": This term was commonly used at the time to describe those who were nonheterosexual.

"Bisexual": This term was used infrequently in the 1970s since bisexuals were often not acknowledged or recognized, either in the LGBTQ community or in society at large. Bisexuals often felt ignored and excluded from the gay community, having to justify and defend their sexuality in a climate that was oftentimes disregarding and sometimes hostile. Unfortunately, this continues in current times and is referred to as bisexual erasure or bi erasure.[1]

"Queer": This term was generally considered derisive when used by the straight community but was reclaimed by those within the community with pride and some amount of defiance. Some LGLF members used this term to define themselves. It is used here primarily in quoted text.

"Transgender": This term evolved in the early and mid-1970s and was only infrequently used during that time.[2] Transgender individuals were

not usually welcomed or acknowledged within the gay community or the population at large, and typically remained deeply closeted and invisible.[3]

"LGBTQ": There are many versions of this acronym, such as "GLBT" and "LGB." The term "LGBT" began to be used in the 1990s, and eventually people began adding the "Q." In 2016, GLAAD recommended that the "Q" be added officially to the acronym.[4] The initials stand for Lesbian, Gay, Bisexual, Transgender, and Queer. Many commonly include a "+" to indicate that this is not a fixed grouping and other categories may also be represented as the nomenclature continues to evolve. I will be using the acronym "LGBTQ" without a "+" for ease of reading with the understanding that it is intended to be all-inclusive. It will be used as appropriate in this book when relating to current times since this term was not used in the 1970s.

Using the terms "gay" and "lesbian" together in a sentence: Writing in a manner that is inclusive and nonsexist while also being clear and succinct can be a challenge. When both lesbians and gay men are mentioned in a sentence together, I had intended to vary the order of the terms to communicate gender equality but found this to be visually confusing and cumbersome. I made the decision to consistently use "gay men and lesbians" with the understanding that this does not imply that gay men are more important in the discourse.

Other Language Notes

In a few cases, small technical changes were made to grammar or spelling in quotations to enhance readability and accuracy without changing meaning (e.g., adding a hyphen or comma). These changes were minute, not calling for an in-text notation (e.g., *sic*).

List of Abbreviations

ACLU	American Civil Liberties Union
CSW	Commission on the Status of Women (KU student organization)
FHSU	Fort Hays State University
FREE	Fight Repression of Erotic Expression (student organization at the University of Minnesota)
GAA	Gay Activist Alliance
GLF–NY	Gay Liberation Front–New York (original group)
K-State	Kansas State University
KSTC	Kansas State Teachers College (name for Emporia State University in the 1970s)
KU	University of Kansas
LDJW	*Lawrence Daily Journal-World* (name changed to *Lawrence Journal-World* in December 1993)
LGBTQ	lesbian, gay, bisexual, transgender, and queer—a term used to refer to the spectrum of nonheterosexual identities
LGLF	Lawrence Gay Liberation Front (also referred to by locals as GLF and Gay Lib). Other names in the 1970s: Lawrence Gay Liberation, Inc. (LGL Inc., LGL); Gay Students of Kansas (GSOK).
LJW	*Lawrence Journal-World*
ROTC	Reserve Officer Training Corps
SDS	Students for a Democratic Society
SGD	Center for Sexuality and Gender Diversity (KU)
UDK	*University Daily Kansan*
UFM	University for Man, Manhattan, Kansas (changed to UFM Community Center)
WC	Women's Coalition (KU student organization)
WSU	Wichita State University

Introduction

There is a theory that revolutions don't happen when
things are at their worst. The revolution comes later,
on a tide of rising expectations. And I think that tide of
rising expectations happened at the University of Kansas
because there had been a civil rights movement and
there was a women's movement, and that was making a
revolution in expectations of gays and lesbians, that
they too would be treated as full human beings. That
created the revolution. The revolution has to happen
in one's own head before it can happen on the streets or
in the offices of the Student Union.
*Kathy Hoggard, former University of Kansas graduate student
and Information Center director*

Leonard Grotta had an inkling that he was gay before he came to the University of Kansas (KU) in 1970.

> I had spent my whole life in a public library looking in the indexes of books under "H" for homosexuals, and the prevailing wisdom was it was a phase I was going to grow out of. By the time I went on to high school and hadn't grown out of it, I was beginning to wonder about that and, of course, you know, even then, growing up in Wichita, Kansas, you're smart enough to not let anyone know about that.[1]

Growing up during the 1950s and 1960s in what he referred to as a "Pentecostal fundamentalist family," Grotta remembered his "horrible childhood" and the "toxic, anti-gay" sentiments that predominated. "You grew up thinking you were the only one in the whole world," he recalled, "and there's a whole lot of shame there because you go to church and then, just kids talk on the playground. It's sinful, it's shameful, it's disgusting, and you think you have this deep dark secret." In addition to the feelings of shame, there were other serious consequences of being open about one's sexual orientation. A person could be ostracized, harassed, or worse—including being arrested for having gay sex, which usually resulted in their name being published in the paper with the likelihood they would lose their job.

In the middle of his first year at KU, Grotta saw an article about the Lawrence Gay Liberation Front (LGLF) in the KU student newspaper, the *University Daily Kansan* (*UDK*). It caught his attention. After all the secrecy when he was growing up, he was surprised to see that there was a group for gay KU students to get together and meet other gay people. They were meeting not in the bathrooms nor in secret but in the open, with the purpose of building a community.

He was intrigued, but his internalized shame and fear won out. He didn't go. Still, knowing of this group's existence gave him something to think about. It took him until his second year of college before he finally took the brave step of showing up at a meeting. "After having a secret your whole life, to actually admit who you are, it was exceptionally frightening. But I thought, even at that young age, I either have to do this or I'll be afraid the rest of my life." Once he made this important decision, he experienced a sense of liberation and belonging. "Being part of a group, knowing that there were other people like you out there . . . it gave you a real sense of connectedness and a sense that you were part of a whole." This brought about a newfound sense of confidence and pride. Looking back, he described it as "the best experience of my whole life."

Words like "connectedness" and "confidence" that Leonard Grotta and others have used to describe their experience with the Lawrence Gay Liberation Front were not often associated with being gay in the 1970s. John D'Emilio, one of the foremost scholars in the country on LGBTQ history, characterized this as "the worst time be queer," observing that "there were powerful institutions that promoted oppression. It was a period of gay witch hunts like we'd never seen before and haven't seen since."[2] During this time of great social and cultural upheaval, those who were gay and lesbian had become tired of hiding and living in fear. The unrest and growing anger led to a tipping point, and gay men and lesbians joined forces to challenge this oppression and demand their civil rights.

It is here that this story begins. In 1970, a small group of gay and lesbian students at the University of Kansas began a revolution. They formed the Lawrence Gay Liberation Front, the first LGBTQ campus organization in the state and one of the earliest in the country.[3] Not only did members take a courageous stand by organizing, but they were also courageous in their response to the opposition they received. No more than two months after their first meeting, they went head to head with the chancellor about their right to be recognized as an official campus organization. The registration procedure, normally a quick, routine administrative process, turned into a ten-year protracted battle with the university. This battle was about far more than the granting of recognition to a student organization. It exposed the antigay climate and homophobic attitudes of the time. It also set the stage for the radical actions and advocacy that the group spearheaded to challenge repressive norms, advance gay rights, and create a more welcoming climate for gay men and lesbians, despite resistance from the university administration, state lawmakers, and some conservative members of the community.

This book chronicles the early, formative years of the LGLF from 1970 to 1979 when members laid the foundation for what was to come in their ongoing fight for gay rights. As members organized, they had no mentors, role models, or road map to provide direction. They instead charted their own path, energized by their shared passion, guided by their personal knowledge and experience, and strengthened by the connections they had established with other LGBTQ communities across the country.

The lawsuit that LGLF members brought forward against the university was perhaps the most visible of the group's actions. The case received both local and national attention in newspapers and other media. The visibility of this controversial case grew when the group engaged prominent civil rights attorney William Kunstler, who had a national reputation for taking on high-profile cases, including the Chicago Seven and the Freedom Riders. Group members' ability to bring a renowned legal powerhouse on board to argue their case spoke to their influence and impact.

Yet the lawsuit wasn't the only way the group left its mark on the campus and the Lawrence community. For years to come, community members recalled the impact of the LGLF's initiatives. The importance of LGLF dances in the Kansas Union Ballroom cannot be overstated. They were a unifying event that brought in people from all over the region, at times drawing in more than a thousand participants. The group also developed a range of educational programs designed to challenge harmful myths and assumptions while normalizing the gay and lesbian experience. In addition, they established counseling services that helped countless LGBTQ students who were struggling and felt isolated. For some, these services were lifesaving. And the group's activism that challenged inequitable, exclusionary cultural norms and campus policies inspired many, both gay and straight, to get involved, take a stand, and speak out in ways they had not done before. Most of all, members recalled the "space of comfort and welcome" and sense of community and pride that the group generated.[4]

A Brief Review of Selected Key Works Related to the Topic

Very little was written about LGBTQ history prior to the late 1980s, despite the historic events that were unfolding. As the cultural climate began to shift on the heels of the civil rights and women's rights movements, the widespread discontent, rejection of the status quo, and sense of urgency that was brewing in the 1960s and 1970s fueled the rise of the gay liberation movement. This brought about a newfound visibility, leading to a growing recognition of the importance and value in examining and documenting this history. A scholar of this early history, Sharon Sievers, commented on its significance: "This is no small achievement, given the obvious (and continuing) barriers to historical research in a field still in its infancy."[5]

Three of the pioneering scholars who brought this important history into the foreground and have contributed to the emerging knowledge base are John D'Emilio, Jonathan Ned Katz, and Genny Beemyn. D'Emilio was one of the earliest academics in the country to explore the economic, political, and social underpinnings of gay and lesbian history, as well as its intersection with the broader area of sexuality (in collaboration with Estelle Freedman). Beemyn brought to light the gay and lesbian communities before Stonewall in urban centers such as Boston, Chicago, New York, and San Francisco, affirming that gay communities were widespread, existing in numerous cities throughout the United States. Katz introduced the concept of sexual orientation as a social construction in the early 1970s, pushing up against the mythology at the time that homosexuality was an anomaly, a sickness to be cured. This early research generated conversations that advanced more equitable treatment, providing leverage for groups such as the LGLF to move forward and organize.

Much that has been written on early LGBTQ activism tends to focus on large metropolitan centers such as New York, Chicago, Miami, and San Francisco, where there were political organizations, community resources, and support for early grassroots organizers. The Midwest has often been overlooked for its role in this activism, but in fact it was a major player in the push for change. Research on the unique contributions of the Midwest to these efforts has taken on greater interest, filling in gaps and clarifying our understanding of the ways in which regional dynamics, perspectives, and experiences broadened and diversified the gay rights movement as a whole and led to the evolution of the Prairie Power movement. Robbie Lieberman's book *Prairie Power* is a compelling read about 1960s and 1970s student activism that drove this effort.[6] This important movement, of which Lawrence was a part, was based on the radical ideology of the New Left and Students for a Democratic Society (SDS). Students mobilized across the middle of the country and relied on their own resources and tight-knit communities in their grassroots organizing efforts. Prairie Power was an inclusive, wide-ranging movement that included but was not specific to LGBTQ issues.

C. J. Janovy filled that gap with *No Place Like Home: Lessons in Activism from LGBT Kansas*.[7] She explored midwestern LGBTQ activism from a personal perspective as she traveled through the state of Kansas. Interviewing "everyday activists" and allies who were shaped by midwestern sensibilities such as populism, conservative values, community, and roll-up-your sleeves determination, she compassionately presented their stories and experiences. She compiled these stories to identify ways in which midwestern values influenced these Kansans' approaches to navigating opposition, locating support, and advocating for their rights. Janovy's book brought a journalist's perspective to this history by focusing on local, personal stories that shed light on the behind-the-scenes efforts to challenge conservative opposition, ultimately leading to hard-fought wins. In addition, her book's later time frame—from 2005 to 2016—reveals what had and had not changed politically and culturally since the 1970s. It also supports the important influence of LGLF members' actions throughout the state as they took the lead to get the wheels turning.

Other significant books that have been introduced to the literature include Mary L. Gray, Brian J. Gilley, and Colin R. Johnson's *Queering the Countryside: New Frontiers in Rural Queer Studies*; Colin R. Johnson's *Just Queer Folks: Gender and Sexuality in Rural America*; Will Fellows's *Farmboys: Lives of Gay Men from the Rural Midwest*; and Samantha Allen's *Real Queer America: LGBT Stories from Red States*.[8] Looking not only at regional influences but also at urban and rural differences, these authors have argued that rural queer life is neither "less than" nor the same as the urban experience. They have supported the growing interest in exploring the many voices within LGBTQ communities, acknowledging their diversity and richness.

Voices that have lagged behind in this historical research are those in LGBTQ college student organizations. Beemyn attributed this omission to LGBTQ historians overlooking "the importance of college groups to gay liberation."[9] There is a need for further research in this area to rectify this oversight and highlight students' importance in the movement.

Books by Patrick Dilley and Beth Bailey are particularly relevant in this regard, both in terms of their review of student activism during that time period and their specific recounting of LGBTQ history at KU and in the region. Patrick Dilley's research on the experiences of gay college men led him to create a typological theory on gay male student identity development that has been critical to the field. His books, *Queer Man on Campus: A History of Non-Heterosexual College Men, 1945–2000* and *Gay Liberation to Campus Assimilation: Early Non-Heterosexual Student Organizations at Midwestern Universities* have substantially contributed to efforts to form a base of knowledge that was heretofore lacking.[10] Focusing on the college experience, he also documented Midwest LGBTQ student history, including the KU LGLF, as he examined the institutional, social, and cultural factors that both hindered and facilitated change.

Beth Bailey's trailblazing book *Sex in the Heartland* addressed the importance of the gay liberation movement to the sexual revolution of the 1960s. Centering on Kansas as the "quintessential heartland state" and specifically Lawrence, which "represents the antithesis of bicoastal sophistication . . . the ultimate not-New York,"[11] she examined some of the actions taking place at KU that helped change the local and regional climate for those who were gay and lesbian. She provided a snapshot of the LGLF and lesbian communities with an eye to the broader topic, arguing that issues occurring in a small city in Kansas captured and reflected the larger gay liberation movement, including New York. She also discussed KU's reputation as a "hotbed for radicals" and the "Berkeley of the Midwest."

Another important resource to mention is Tami Albin's collection of oral histories titled "Under the Rainbow: Oral Histories of Gay, Lesbian, Bisexual, Transgender, Intersex and Queer People in Kansas."[12] This collection of interviews, conducted between 2009 and 2019, features Kansans throughout the state, some of whom had been students at KU and other Kansas colleges in the 1970s.[13] Albin's interviews provide insight into what it was like to be gay or lesbian in Kansas during this time, supporting the findings discussed in this book. Albin examined people's experience as Kansans, and some of those interviewed spoke about their time at KU or in Lawrence. While some have characterized the state as having few LGBTQ residents, Albin's interviews challenge this stereotype and reveal the communities and sense of connection that have developed among LGBTQ people throughout the state that the LGLF worked so hard to promote.

Although Bailey, Dilley, Albin, and others have explored aspects of the LGLF story, this book goes a step further by centering the organization as the focal point. Its aim is to delve deeply into the creation and evolution of the LGLF to illuminate the significance of this group on both an individual and institutional level. The book relies on more than sixty-five author interviews conducted specifically for this project with people from this era. It explores the group's tactics and approach that advanced gay rights, created a more welcoming campus climate for KU LGBTQ students, and laid the foundation for building a gay community.

In addition, this book includes two topics that impacted the LGLF and contributed to building the LGBTQ community at KU, in Lawrence, and in the state in the 1970s: lesbian communities, and activism occurring at other campuses throughout the state (see appendices B and C). It is strongly recommended that readers not overlook these appendices—they are critical in understanding the thesis of this book from a broader perspective and are topics that are not covered at length elsewhere.

The unique focus of this book—telling this history from the eyes and hearts of people who were there and lived it—offers a fresh perspective on the LGLF and on gay student organizing during a transformational time in LGBTQ history locally and nationally. This book follows the stories and experiences of a small group of students in a midwestern college town, augmented by faculty, staff, and community remembrances, to paint a picture of the significance of their actions to the campus, town, broader community, and movement as a whole.

This book captures the frustrations, fears, and triumphs that gay and lesbian students at KU encountered. The stories are unique to these students, but they also reflect a common experience shared by other gay liberation student activists across the country. Focusing on a singular institution to understand the broader culture provides an opportunity to examine these issues close-up and in depth in order to translate them to a broader context. The powerful stories in this book help us understand the cost of this inequity and the very personal ways in which it was experienced as well as the role we all can play in challenging it.

An Overview of Book Chapters

This book examines the history of the LGLF at KU from a chronological perspective. Chapter 1 provides a snapshot of the time that led up to the beginnings of the national gay liberation movement and the birth of the Lawrence Gay Liberation Front. This chapter explores prevailing attitudes about homosexuality, both personal and public, during the 1960s, examining ways in which those who were gay and lesbian connected prior to groups and communities such as the LGLF coming into being, and the climate on the KU campus in the midst of this turbulence.

Chapter 2 (1970–1975) details the beginnings of the LGLF, including how the group got started and members' early organizing efforts. In addition, it discusses group members' mission, goals, and philosophical underpinnings. It also discusses philosophical splits that emerged, and ways in which members found common ground.

Chapter 3 begins in 1970 as the group applied to be an official campus organization. This chapter discusses what followed and also outlines the many projects, educational presentations, and activist efforts the group undertook as they were getting started.

Chapter 4 (1971–1973) covers the escalating conflict that LGLF members were facing with campus administration, particularly related to the lawsuit that the group filed against KU for denying them recognition as an official campus organization. This chapter also reviews the many initiatives LGLF members introduced or expanded during this time, just one year after they were founded. This includes creating the first LGLF dance and the Gay Counseling Service.

Chapter 5 (1975–1979) examines the changing campus culture and its effect on gay rights nationally, locally, and at KU. This chapter delves into the issues the group tackled and the tactics they employed in the latter half of the 1970s to advocate for change as students were less politically engaged, including challenging campus affirmative action policies as well as KU student organization registration policies and processes.

Chapter 6 looks ahead to the next era and beyond as the group had become an established presence on campus. It highlights some of the key challenges the group faced in the 1980s and 1990s following its designation as an official campus organization during a time of AIDS in a changing climate. It also reviews the evolution of current LGBTQ services provided at KU.

Many people are mentioned throughout the book who had a connection with the LGLF as (1) members; (2) student activists, allies, and leaders; (3) faculty; and (4) community members. Appendix A provides a listing of some of the key individuals who had a role in moving the organization forward and helps clarify their affiliations for readers. This list is by no means comprehensive; there are many others who were involved who are not included here. This in no way minimizes their contributions and/or importance.

Appendix B broadens the scope of the book to bring in the voice of the thriving lesbian feminist community on campus and in Lawrence. While some lesbians were involved with the LGLF, a majority formed their own communities in the 1970s. This important history, not well known outside of the circle, is essential to fully understand the evolution of the gay and lesbian culture and community in Lawrence and beyond. It also illustrates some of the gender differences that fostered and maintained this division, including men's and women's priorities, needs, organizing approaches, and methods of connecting.

Appendix C explores the LGBTQ activism and support taking place (and in some cases, not) at public colleges across the state. Comparing LGLF members' efforts and experience on the KU campus with what was happening at other campuses across Kansas during the 1970s provides a context for understanding the importance of LGLF members' boldness, courage, and leadership as role models for other Kansas campuses. It also illustrates the role of campus culture, administrative philosophies, and regional differences in LGBTQ acceptance across the state, requiring each campus to respond to their unique culture to bring about change.

A half century has passed since gay liberation took off across the country, energizing and mobilizing those who were gay and lesbian to demand equitable treatment. This gives rise to the inevitable question—why is this history important now? In transitional times, it is critical to look back at the hard battles fought and victories won for LGBTQ people to understand how far society has progressed and what still needs to be done. Progress can be precarious and must be carefully guarded and maintained. The old maxim "Knowledge is power" is relevant to the conversation. By understanding the hostile climate that existed for LGBTQ people not so long ago in the 1970s, we can gain knowledge from these early stories to identify current-day strategies to continue to fight the battle. These pioneers' creative strategies to push through opposition, form strong connections, and persevere can guide current and new generations as they work to protect the advances that have been made while they continue to advocate for equity.

1

"The Times They Are A-Changin'"
Setting the Stage in the 1960s

The Lawrence Gay Liberation Front (LGLF) formed on the heels of great social change in America. In the 1960s, students at KU and across the country began rising up in unprecedented numbers to challenge the inequitable treatment of those who were historically excluded.[1] As Bob Dylan proclaimed in his 1964 song, the times indeed were changing. This fanned the flames and led to what historian John Skrentny identified as the "minority rights revolution."[2] The numerous social issues raised during this time and their interrelation created a climate of questioning and challenge, priming society for the significant cultural shift that was to come.[3] The lessons learned and victories won of the civil rights, women's rights, and antiwar movements contributed to a collective consciousness of dissent, opening doors for those who had previously been silenced. This emboldened those who were gay and lesbian to take action to address issues that had previously been taboo.[4] As they watched other historically excluded groups fight for their freedom, it became clear that the time for an LGBT revolution had arrived. This chapter will explore some of the cultural forces contributing to the atmosphere of rebellion and change that influenced the creation of the LGLF.

"The Sordid World": Public Perceptions of Being Gay in the 1960s

Homosexuality was rarely talked about in the public sphere in the 1960s. It was therefore surprising when *Life* magazine, often found on coffee tables in homes throughout America, featured a series of articles titled "Homosexuality in America" in 1964.[5] This was one of the early public statements about homosexuality in popular media, but it was "far from an affirmation," reflecting the homophobia of the times.[6] It began by referring to the "gay world" as "sad and sordid," claiming that "only a tiny minority would ever beat the drums so sensationally for their way of life. Far more of them regard their homosexuality as an affliction."[7] Despite this dismal portrayal, there was concern about gay men "openly admitting, even flaunting, their deviation." Pulling on the public's heartstrings, raising the unspoken fear related to the indoctrination of children into this "sordid world," the article continued: "This social disorder, which society tries to suppress, has forced itself into the public eye because it does present a problem—and parents especially are concerned." The negative, fearmongering tone of the piece reflected the discomfort some straight Americans were feeling as gay activism was gaining traction, apprehensive that homosexuality would infiltrate "their" communities. Writer Will Kohler speculated that "[this] probably tells us more about society's revulsion towards gay people [during that time] than it does about gays themselves."[8]

Despite the negativity of the piece, it was important to many who were gay. It was one of the few acknowledgments in popular culture that homosexuality existed.[9] John Bolin, a member of the LGLF in the 1970s, remembered when this article hit the newsstands. On a trip to San Francisco with his family, his mother, after reading the article, would not allow him and his brother to wear "wheat jeans" while in the city (the gay men were pictured wearing wheat jeans, light-colored jeans that were popular at the time). Nonetheless, despite the stereotyped, negative portrayal, Bolin was "thrilled to see photo documentation of visible gay men congregating—it showed that I was not alone. At this time there was no representation on television, [and] homosexual content in movies was buried under oblique references." He commented that "many gay men in my generation were aware of this article and affected by it." He also pointed out that lesbians were not mentioned, which was "very telling of the time."[10]

A few years later, in 1969, another article was published, but this time from a very different perspective. The article, "The New Homosexuality," ran in the men's magazine *Esquire*. It approached the topic from a radical, unapologetic perspective, interviewing gay men who were out, proud, and refusing to buy into the "guilt and shame" culture. According to the article, the effeminate image of a fashion-conscious gay man with an "uncertain mouth, wet basset eyes, a Coppertone tan and a miniature Yorkshire" had "expired with a whimper to make way for the new homosexual of the Seventies, an unfettered, guiltless male child of the new morality in a Zapata moustache and an outlaw hat, who couldn't care less for Establishment approval." Celebrating this new, empowered image, an interviewee in the article commented, *"That's* what has died—this homosexual feeling of being isolated from the straight world by guilt." Other comments indicated that the tide was beginning to turn: "Nobody has to be one thing or the other anymore." "Why should I pretend to be something I'm not?" "How can you live a lie, man? That's not living."[11] As with the *Life* article five years earlier, the *Esquire* article got the attention of many who would become involved with the LGLF, providing visibility and encouragement.[12]

"It Was Much Easier to Lead Two Lives": Being Gay in the 1960s

Considerable research exists regarding the oppressive, homophobic culture for those who were gay and lesbian across the country during this time.[13] Anthony D'Augelli, a nationally known scholar and writer on LGBTQ development, stated that the "hidden curriculum" of heterosexism is taught to children at a very young age, perpetuating the belief that other forms of sexual expression and identity are abnormal and unacceptable. These "destructive mythologies" become imbedded in one's self-view, making them particularly difficult to "untangle" and confront as one grows up.[14] In contrast to those who are heterosexual, those who are gay and lesbian must create their identity through struggle and rejection of the norm. College students are particularly affected since developmentally they are at a stage in their lives where they are figuring out who they are and how they connect with others.[15] These "destructive mythologies," fueled by oppressive cultural norms of the 1960s, were toxic for gay and lesbian college students. KU students experienced this firsthand.

Some denied who they were. This gave rise to feelings of confusion,

low self-esteem, alienation, depression, and fear of being found out.[16]
LGLF member Bob Friedland struggled with this denial: "Despite my
attraction to men, even at age twenty, I had no idea that I was gay." Chris
Caldwell, who did not identify as gay until after he graduated from KU,
provided some insight on this denial: "What was it like to be gay in the
seventies? Miserable is probably the word I would use. [Laughs.] Miserable and closeted for the vast majority of people who were gay." Trip
Haenisch, who knew he was gay but was not out when he attended KU,
agreed, describing the feelings that kept him closeted: "Just that fear and
that shame, the shame was enormous. . . . Yeah, and I just kind of ran. I
just ran." Chad Leat, who did not identify as gay until after he graduated
from KU, discussed gay individuals' need at that time to adopt straight
and gay identities depending on the situation and environment: "In those
years I didn't take the risk of having myself publicly identified as a queer.
It was much easier to lead two lives."

Leading two lives was not uncommon for gay men and lesbians, particularly for those in subcultures that valued propriety and conventional
norms, most notably the Greek system. KU Greek members recalled that
any conversations about homosexuality were underground and not held
openly. Sororities were noted for being careful to keep up appearances of
respectability and present themselves as straight organizations despite
the presence of many lesbians among their ranks.[17] Fraternities were
described as hostile toward those who were suspected of being gay or
were viewed as effeminate. It was no secret that there were a number of
closeted gay men in fraternities; yet in the midst of a climate that was described as homoerotic, these issues were not talked about. This presented
a double bind for those in the system who were gay—they could speak
up, raising suspicion, or remain silent, feeling like a "fraud." Chad Leat
attributed some of the long-standing fraternity traditions to maintaining
this culture: "At [one of the fraternities], they used to have a damn fire
chief award, which was getting completely naked and taking a metal ruler
that had sat on a piece of ice and [using it to] measure people's penises."
Members learned to navigate the system to protect their image and avoid
detection. Haenisch commented: "I felt like coming out would've been
like social suicide for sure."[18]

The fear of being exposed created ongoing stress and restricted the
ability to be authentic and open.[19] Professor emeritus of social welfare

Dennis Dailey provided support and therapy to gay KU students during this time. Dailey spoke of the concerns that students who "played it straight" shared with him about being outed and feeling vulnerable and unsafe. Trip Haenisch, who "invented" dates with women as a cover when talking to his friends and parents, described the double bind: "There was this self-hatred that goes with telling a lie." He admitted that the duplicity created feelings of shame and lack of integrity: "That's hard. And then when you finally come out, you kind of feel like you were a phony. I felt kind of dirty. I felt like a liar. I hated that and I hated myself for that but I don't know how else I would've survived those years even now thinking back."

Many, especially those who grew up in small, rural towns, had to carefully guard their secret for fear of being ostracized and rejected within their hometown communities. The fear of being discovered coupled with the inability to gain information and speak with others led to feelings of isolation and being different. Ron Gans explained, "I mean, logically, you couldn't be the only one, but really, what do you know? You know nothing." Coping with this was challenging: "Well, the isolation is very difficult, and everybody finds their own way of dealing with it and somehow come to terms with it. Or not. Some end up in jail or [consider] suicide or something. . . . But you [could] deal with it, sort of find a way to swim through these unfriendly waters in a way, and just hope something didn't pull you down."

Gay and lesbian students often had to deal with the disapproval and/or lack of acceptance from family and friends when they disclosed their sexual orientation. D'Augelli commented that the probability of rejection was exceedingly high for those who came out to their family.[20] Students preparing to go home for breaks and summer vacation wrestled with how they would manage the awkwardness, stress, and deception.

Martha Boyd, who was involved in the lesbian community at KU, provided counseling through the Dean of Women's Office as a graduate counseling psychology student. She recalled first-year women students who had fallen for another woman and were considering telling their parents at an upcoming break. Boyd would ask, "What do you think is going to be the outcome of that?" The student's response was often, "Oh, they'll probably not give me any more money for tuition." Boyd would probe further: "And then what's that going to do?" The student answered, "I probably can't go back to school." This led to the inevitable follow-up question, "And then what's that going to do?" Boyd would often end the conversation with "Okay—how about if you put coming out to your parents on hold right now and you and I are going to work on this a little bit."[21]

Additionally, for those who were out on campus but had not revealed their identity to their family and home community, there was a concern that others would spread the word through tight-knit community grapevines. LGLF members David H. Stout and Lee Hubbell, who were from small, religious towns in Kansas, decided to share the news with their parents before a news story for which they had been interviewed was released nationally. Stout had come out to his parents six years earlier when he was eighteen but suspected that they thought it was a passing phase. He attempted the conversation two more times but lost his nerve. He was able to follow through on the third try. When both Stout and Hubbell had "the talk" with their parents, the response was less than positive, as they had expected. Hubbell shared what happened: "The love was there. It was just exceedingly difficult for my family to accept. Really, the agreement was, 'You live whatever life you want to live in Lawrence but don't bring it to the hometown.' They just could not, and basically hardly ever talked about it."[22]

John Bolin shared a story about how far-reaching this nonacceptance could be. When Bolin's brother began searching for colleges in the late 1970s, Bolin commented that "[our parents] didn't allow him to go to KU because of the shame that might be brought on him by my behaviors and activities. [It was] a decade later and he had a different last name! They would not let him go to the better school just because someone might remember what I did while I was there."[23]

Another negative outcome of this hiding and lack of self-acceptance was its impact on the ability to form positive, authentic relationships. "A lot of times you would need liquor to have the nerve to do anything or try anything," Haenisch recalled. Thinking of going into a gay bar created feelings of panic when he was sober. "I can remember going into these bars in Kansas City, and kind of sneaking in and staying on the periphery and trying to see who was there and just being very, very nervous. Then after a few drinks you get more comfortable. But I was always on like kind of high alert." While fear of rejection and the use of alcohol as a social lubricant can be considered common experiences for gay and straight students alike, there was a greater likelihood of negative consequences for those who were gay.

This affected Haenisch's relationships. "We would kind of hook up. ... We were just like really excited and really nervous and then afterwards he just couldn't even talk, would run away, wouldn't talk to me for like a week until he got horny again and then he would come back." This left Haenisch feeling disconnected: "It was just that kind of twisted. ... I wanted [the] more affectionate part of it. ... There was no intimacy. It was just like this act and then you were made to feel like you were doing something wrong, or it was dirty, or what did I do and the person hates me now. I don't know. It was just kind of confusing and sad."

This could have serious consequences, including thoughts of suicide, as some LGLF members recalled. For some, the feeling of despair from having to remain hidden became unbearable. Bob Friedland shared that he went through "terrible times," referring to himself as "presuicidal" during that time. For others it was the isolation they experienced. Ron Gans disclosed that he considered suicide, "not from abject misery, but because—I was still very lonely and found no way out of it." David Stout wrestled with feelings of guilt, shame, and despair, prompting what he referred to as "suicide gestures" on a number of occasions. He attempted suicide twice when the feelings became overwhelming.[24]

Others fought their internalized homophobia when they could no longer deny their true identity. "I never even knew I was gay," Barry Albin revealed. "I had been doing things sort of off and on most of my young life but I had no idea what those were." After an encounter with another man in a bathroom, Albin went back to his dorm room "absolutely mortified. Here I was barely eighteen and we got a dictionary and I read what it meant to be homosexual." He struggled with the realization "because it was just so challenging to be gay then."

Many gay men and lesbians experienced interactions that made them feel devalued and invisible. Trip Haenisch recalled that those who were gay were ignored in general conversations: "It was just like 'Can we talk about something that matters?'" Microaggressions often went unrecognized and were not acknowledged. Haenisch talked about the use of the phrase "you fag," often used as a put-down in conversations: "You could say whatever. Nobody corrected anybody. I don't ever remember anybody ever saying to somebody, 'Don't say that. That's hurtful,' or, 'Why would you talk like that?' Never."

Given the homophobia that existed, one would expect this to also result in harassment and bullying. While this certainly occurred, it was not reported as a common experience. Martha Boyd shed some light on this. Recognizing that gay men and lesbians were invisible to a majority of the population, she commented, "It's hard to harass something you don't see. Or doesn't have value."

Some talked about experiences they encountered when holding hands with a partner in public. When Bob Friedland was harassed on the street in Emporia, where his boyfriend went to school, he recalled that they "were holding hands, and somebody yelled out something from a car, and I might have yelled out like, 'Fuck you! Just get out of your car!'" Surprised by his own response, he thought to himself, "Whoa! Was that me? I'm not a big fighter. . . . What was going on inside of me?" He talked about the pride he felt going from a place of tremendous fear to becoming a person with a voice.

Richard Linker shared another occurrence: "One night, as my boyfriend and I walked down the street [on Jayhawk Boulevard in the center of campus] holding hands, a bunch of young guys drove past and threw full cans of beer at us. I was struck by the amount of hatred and fear they must have felt to throw away good beer." He continued to explain: "They actually threw full cans of beer. They weren't open. We didn't get wet. Yeah, they grazed me. They hit John [his boyfriend] right square in the middle of his back, and he had a bruise from it, actually. And then they yelled probably, 'Faggot.' I don't remember exactly. But they *were* yelling at us."[25]

Another source of harassment was police outside of Lawrence. Officers in town were described as "tolerant."[26] This was not necessarily the case, however, when going beyond the city limits. LGLF member Joe Lordi shared a situation that occurred when he and friends were driving around Kansas City: "A lot of cruising was done in the Plaza [an upscale shopping district in Kansas City]. . . . So the cops knew there were a lot of gay people there." And those who looked to be students were particularly suspect. He recalled the prejudice he and some out-of-town friends encountered when he was showing them around the city: "The cops stopped us, made us get out of the car, put us up against a wall with our hands up. They were basically harassing us."

Gender played a central role in this harassment. As the women's movement was gaining momentum, traditional conceptualizations of gender and power were being challenged.[27] Central to the conversation were the stereotyped definitions that were being perpetuated, and ways in which femininity was devalued for both men and women. Martha Boyd commented that gay men were more frequently bullied and harassed for deviating from the masculine stereotype. She reflected: "Come on—you got a guy . . . makeup and high heels in 1975—they [the straight community] didn't like that." Women were often afforded more latitude in their gender expression than were men, particularly in rural communities. "You [lesbians] could run around in a flannel shirt and corduroys and they'd say—'they probably work on a farm, rural kid.' It wasn't the same. It wasn't the same at all." Boyd observed that, for lesbians, "the harassment wasn't there. The prejudice certainly was." Sexism and inequitable treatment were serious problems for women, making it far more likely that lesbians who were harassed or bullied were targeted due to their gender rather than their sexual orientation.[28]

This was particularly salient for gay men who were perceived as "effeminate," who were far more likely to be treated with disdain and hostility. John Bolin shared a poignant example: "In high school I was maligned as being effeminate. My stepbrother and his friends referred to me as his sister. In a student assembly there was a skit about a radio station and the Four Seasons song 'Walk Like a Man' was dedicated to me." This perception affected his precollege opportunities as well.

> In [my] junior year I applied to the American Field Service, the international cultural exchange program. My mother had previously been the faculty sponsor where she taught, [and] we were hosts one year. In my interview in a room of adult committee members, I was questioned about my blonde hair, if it was dyed (it was not). Other inquiries [were made] that were code for homosexual. I was not accepted into the program.[29]

These personal reflections paint a picture of some of the challenges that gay and lesbian students in the 1970s faced. Given the stigma that existed during that time related to being gay or lesbian, it is important to consider the effects this had on a student's college experience. Research, in fact, indicates that gay and lesbian students are often at a disadvantage in adjusting to the college environment as they counter homophobia and cultural norms centering on heterosexism, making it more difficult to resolve developmental tasks necessary for thriving and succeeding.[30] Institutional services that were sensitive to the needs of gay and lesbian students were unheard of during this time, pointing to the critical role of other sources of support. That was the role that was filled by the Lawrence Gay Liberation Front.

"A Very Open Community": Making Connections and Navigating the Lawrence Scene

Long before the LGLF came into being, many gay men and lesbians had found ways to connect despite the hostile, homophobic climate that existed. Most connections were clandestine and underground. An organized gay subculture did not emerge in the United States until the late 1960s in response to the systematic targeting and harassment that escalated during the McCarthy era.[31] The Mattachine Society, the first contemporary gay rights organization, relied on nonconfrontational, reformist tactics to bring about change, working within systems to educate and raise awareness.[32]

All this changed on June 28, 1969, when those in the gay community had had enough and rose up in revolt against police targeting and violence in a bar raid at the Stonewall Inn in New York City. This is one of the most widely recognized acts of gay defiance, but it was by no means the first. Momentum had been building prior to the Stonewall uprising, leading researchers Elizabeth Armstrong and Suzanna Crage to observe that the Stonewall story was "an achievement of gay liberation rather than a literal account of its origins." San Francisco was a center of rebellion, with a large-scale uprising in 1965 related to a raid at a New Year's Eve ball and a riot in 1966 at Compton's Cafeteria.[33] Other actions were happening across the country. This included the founding of FREE (Fight Repression of Erotic Expression) at the University of Minnesota in 1969. FREE engaged in what activist Michael McConnell referred to as steampipe politics to "get people to pay attention" by "keep[ing] the pressure on" and organized the first nationwide gay conference in 1970.[34] This momentum created a sense of urgency and was a catalyst for the creation of the Gay Liberation Front–New York (GLF–NY) shortly thereafter.

Closer to home, the climate for gay men and lesbians in Kansas prior to 1970 exacerbated feelings of fear and isolation for many. They could be the target of hate crimes, denied housing, arrested, fired from their place of employment, or expelled from school. Lawrence, reflecting its relative diversity as a college town, had had a long history of liberalism and progressive politics, which, at times, had been at odds with the state's conservative politics and values.[35]

This clash could also be felt within the city in the 1960s. Richard Linker, a countercultural activist who became a member of the LGLF, commented that when he moved to Lawrence in the late 1960s, he was "surrounded by and part of a community of people who saw a new vision of how we might change the world for the better." He observed there were many with progressive attitudes, "but there was the other side too. Restaurants with signs in the window showing a peace sign and labeling it 'Track of the American Chicken,' [and] cops who hassled hippies." The city's reputation as a liberal oasis in a conservative state was tempered by the serious discrimination and conflict that existed within its boundaries, particularly related to race.[36] Some were tired of the violence, upheaval, and hippie drug culture that they attributed to local radical and historically excluded communities. As a result, they did not support efforts to address the problem. Rusty Monhollon, a scholar of American and Lawrence history who graduated from KU, reasoned that some had bought into what he referred to as a "Free State narrative," believing that "the town has paid its dues to the cause of justice and equality" in its early battles against slavery and discrimination.[37] These residents, in essence, had their metaphorical blinders on, neither seeing nor desiring to see the inequity that continued to exist. So despite an overriding sense of liberalism, there also existed conservative factions that created friction within the city.

Homosexuality was not widely acknowledged or accepted in Lawrence, as was common throughout the Midwest and the country at large. As a result, those who were gay and lesbian kept a low profile, and it was not discussed outside the inner circle of these tight-knit underground communities.[38] Lee Hubbell, who attended KU in the 1960s and later became an LGLF member, described it as a "Don't Ask, Don't Tell" mentality that allowed homophobic, discriminatory attitudes to remain unchallenged. But it also provided some protection to those who were gay and lesbian, since many who were not accepting would look the other way rather than openly protest.

KU professor emeritus of religious studies Timothy Miller, who has written about the 1960s and was a KU student during that era, recalled the challenge that this emerging gay activism had on the Lawrence community: "The whole idea of gay liberation was a real shock to a lot of people. . . . It couldn't even be talked about." As gay men and lesbians were becoming more visible and vocal, Miller observed that many in town were "shell-shocked. . . . Not so much hostility as just, 'Wow, this is a wrenching change from everything we've learned.' And I think any kind of social change takes some time."

Progressive community members had a strong presence in the city, shaping the overall climate. Their push for policies and practices that were inclusive contributed to the city's reputation as a safe haven for gay men and lesbians. Barry Albin, a KU student during that time who later joined the LGLF, recalled Lawrence as "a very open community" in which residents "were willing to allow things to happen underneath the horizon."

As community members looked the other way, some gay men and lesbians found ways to gather together in small, informal groups of friends in living rooms and local pubs.[39] Professor emeritus of theater and dance Paul Lim, who arrived at KU from the Philippines as a student in 1969, recalled the many dinner, dance, and cocktail parties that gay students and faculty members attended in people's homes. These groups ranged from mainstream to radical and political to social, yet they did not generally connect or overlap, inhibiting the formation of a coherent gay community.[40] As Steven Weaver, a gay rights activist who later became an LGLF member, remarked, "We knew our own worlds, but not necessarily what was going on outside them." Michael Stubbs, an antiwar advocate who also became an LGLF member, described the scene: "There were definitely two 'strains' of gay people developing a gay consciousness at the same time in Lawrence between 1968 and 1970. As far as I can tell, the counterculture gays and the traditional gays . . . didn't acknowledge each other's existence until the spring of 1970." He also commented that there was no interaction between these two strains.[41]

Lawrence was part of the grassroots Prairie Power movement, fashioned after the New Left movement as well as the national radical organization Students for a Democratic Society (SDS), which had a strong presence in Lawrence.[42] It was also home to many activist groups with national ties.[43] Sharon Mayer, a KU student in the late 1960s who was involved with the LGLF, described the communal atmosphere: "Most of the people we knew lived in the Oread neighborhood because that was kind of 'it.' And most of us didn't have cars, or TVs, or even phones. We'd just walk to each other's house. And it was really a lot of fun. It was a great period."[44] Many eschewed personal possessions as a way of renouncing middle-class values contributing to economic disparities.[45] Out of this came discussions about pressing topics of the day, from the Vietnam War to getting by on a student budget. Said activist C. J. Brune, who discussed the vibrancy of the Lawrence activist scene: "We were all in it together. Whether you were gay or lesbian or not, it didn't matter. These were the same people you had rubbed shoulders with for the last five years. . . . And you were going to jump in and support their cause."[46]

Activists were drawn to what civil rights organizer Robert Pardun described as the "mixture of direct-action politics and cultural rebellion" that the movement promoted.[47] Lawrence was a place "where young activists not only lived and breathed social justice, but also worked to create a radical alternative to virtually everything around them," leading some to call KU "the Berkeley of the Midwest" and a "mecca" for radicals.[48] This could sometimes prove to be a challenging balancing act for activists. Former KU student Kathryn Clark explained: "At night, we might be with people who were planning political actions, and in the daytime, I might be serving sandwiches [at her Woolworth's lunch counter job] to people who were saying they were going to go shoot up those hippies." David Awbrey, KU student body president from 1969 to 1970 and award-winning journalist and author on education and social issues, characterized the Lawrence movement as having two branches, the "hippie sixties" and the "radical politic sixties." He commented that the latter had strong antigay sentiments within their organizations. This may have contributed to the lack of visible gay and lesbian organizing in Lawrence during those early years.

Finding Shared Identity: A Gay Commune Is Born

In the late 1960s, one of the most pressing issues on activists' minds in Lawrence and across the country was the Vietnam War.[49] Groups such as SDS, SNCC, and SPU drew in large numbers of KU students. The overriding focus on ending the war, paired with the absence of gay organizing locally and nationally, led many who were gay or lesbian to direct their activist energies to antiwar efforts.[50] Two of these students were John Bolin and Michael Stubbs.

Bolin, an Oklahoma native who spent summers in Los Angeles with his father and stepmother, began college at Washington University in 1967.[51] He liked the school and students' progressive attitudes, "but not the debt I was incurring." This led him to transfer to KU the following year, where he majored in art education. He credited the strong women in his family and their liberal, democratic influence as well as his summers in Los Angeles for providing him with a broad, activist perspective. Early on at KU, he became involved with the campus antiwar movement, which drew him in from "both [a] principled and practical self-interest." Many male college students like Bolin, who were exempted from the draft while they were enrolled, were concerned about being called for service after they graduated.

During his first year at KU, Bolin met fellow antiwar activist Michael Stubbs and they quickly connected. Stubbs, like Bolin, identified with the counterculture "freaks," a term used with pride among those within the counterculture community.[52] As their connection intensified, so did their radical leanings. Stubbs and Bolin recounted an experience in the late 1960s when they engaged in a "sly challenge" to the antigay, heterosexist attitude that dominated the "radical politic" movement mentioned by Awbrey. After attending a presentation at KU by Yippie cofounder and icon Paul Krassner, John Bolin recounted that Stubbs "asked Krassner to autograph his ass in front of the audience. There was an awkward pause. Michael pulled down the back of his jeans a bit, [and] Krassner reluctantly wrote his name with a Sharpie."[53] Stubbs's action was a power move, calling out Krassner and the Yippie movement on their disrespectful attitude and behavior aimed toward gay liberation activists. In another incident, they joined members of their commune in heckling Bob Dole for his backing of the Vietnam War.[54]

Their shared politics and beliefs led them to begin dating, and their relationship lasted for the majority of their years at KU. Bolin identified with this new group, commenting:

> Almost all of our friends were straight freaks, brought together by the counterculture. I was comfortable in my skin at last. . . . I was no longer judged for being gay. [I] found acceptance in my tribe. Don't know how else to say this, [but I] felt like a man equal to other men. [I] recall little ostracism for being a homosexual specifically, more generally about an outlier to society norms. The derogatory "hippie fags" was leveled at my straight friends too—we were all put in the same category.[55]

Bolin was drawn to working on gay issues at KU from a broad social justice perspective: "My move to gay identity politics came primarily from the groups already seeking equality—people of color, women. It was a natural progression."[56]

Stubbs was referred to by most LGLF members as the most radical and politically engaged in the group.[57] His early "ugly experience" growing up in Topeka influenced his activist leanings. He recounted a memory about the parents in his neighborhood when he was fourteen: "[They] ostracized me, wouldn't let their kids hang out with me" once they discovered that he was gay. One of these parents was Henry Bubb, who lived down the street from Stubbs's family. Bubb was an influential business leader and a Kansas regent from 1961 to 1977. He was well known for his animosity toward left-wing and gay students, particularly at KU.[58]

Stubbs began at KU in the fall of 1968. He moved off campus with Bolin the following semester. Early on, he became involved in radical campus, local, and national organizations, including the Black Panthers. In the 1970s, his political involvement would intensify, including being arrested in the spring of 1970 following a confrontation with the National Guard in Lawrence (prior to the Kent State massacre).

He also traveled to Cuba as one of seven members of the first openly gay contingent to participate in the Venceremos Brigade in the late summer of 1970.[59] The Venceremos Brigade is an organization that was founded in 1969 by the SDS in collaboration with Cuban government officials. It brought together student volunteers to work side by side with Cuban workers to show solidarity while harvesting sugarcane in Cuba.[60]

The efforts of Stubbs's contingent led Beat poet Allen Ginsberg to comment: "I think the confrontation between the Venceremos Brigade and gay lib showing the Cuban mental block on the subject of homosexuality was one of the most useful things gay lib did on an international scale."[61]

In October 1969, Bolin and Stubbs attended an event in Kansas City known as the Urban Plunge.[62] They were joined by other antiwar activists from KU and Lawrence, including Rick Moody, Fred Lipper, Julie Highfill, John Naramore, and Rod Grey. This national project evolved from pioneering work by Chicago and Los Angeles churches and was sponsored and supported by various ecumenical groups.[63] The Urban Plunge immersive weekend consisted of presentations, in-depth discussions, and visits to inner-city sites that exposed participants to the experience of urban life. The Kansas City Urban Plunge was sponsored by the KU Wesley Center as part of the University Christian Movement. This event was a radical step considering the conservativism embedded within many religious denominations at that time.

The event was titled EROS Plunge (EROS was an acronym for *E*xposure to *R*epression, *O*ppression, and *S*uppression).[64] The aim of the weekend was to "Plunge, Study, and Confront," centering on interpersonal development, sex positivity, and community building.[65] Bolin explained that this occurred by "getting in touch with feelings, [and the] ability to dialogue without ego [about] feminism, racism, homosexuality, anti-materialism."[66] Stubbs added that participants got "a heavy dose of what it was like to live as the 'other' in the United States, to live on the margins."

The Kansas City Plunge followed the Los Angeles model, featuring workshops, discussions, field trips (including Skid Row, gay bars, and drag bars), and a visit to the house of a gay couple.[67] Bolin mentioned that bisexuality, which was rarely discussed, was one of the topics included. He also recalled that he and Stubbs were the only participants who were openly gay.[68] Stubbs was particularly moved by a presentation led by a gay man who was out, describing it as intensely emotional. As a result, Stubbs and Bolin were moved to "re-examine our lives and our personal politics" as they "began creating an identity around gay liberation."[69]

Stubbs also witnessed this occurring with the women who attended.[70] Barbara Taylor, a KU first-year student, wrote an article in the KU underground newspaper, *Reconstruction*, about her Urban Plunge experience.

She recounted her reaction when the Plunge group visited a local bar that welcomed both gay and straight patrons: "The tenderness and love. So very touching. And these people have to repress their sexuality because of the system. SHIT. People need people. People need love." She concluded: "WOW. My mind is really blown!! Blown by the Plunge."[71] The weekend changed people's lives. It also motivated Stubbs and Bolin to take their activism to the next level and work to advance rights for gay people.[72]

Excited to share their Plunge experience and begin their work, Stubbs and Bolin informally began having these new conversations with friends in activist and counterculture communities. They also joined with other Urban Plunge participants to form a commune. A few months later, in the spring of 1970, the group left the commune and started a new political collective at 1219 Ohio Street. While Stubbs and Bolin were the only gay residents, they were building a base of straight allies.[73]

These communes were important in the activist and freak communities, providing a way for like-minded people to strategize and easily engage in political activism. This connected burgeoning gay liberation efforts with other counterculture communities, communicating a radical presence.[74] The communes were primarily in the Oread neighborhood near campus, referred to as the "hippie haven," and were known for being run-down and in poor repair.[75] Many of these houses were owned by landlord Daniel Ling, who owned a substantial number of properties in the Oread neighborhood and had a reputation as a slumlord.[76] In the spring of 1971, articles about the substandard conditions of these properties ran in the campus newspaper, the *University Daily Kansan* (*UDK*). Ling countered that the problem was not the dilapidated condition of the houses themselves or his neglect but the "bad living conditions of the people living there."[77]

In the end, having an uninvolved landlord was an advantage for the gay and lesbian community. Kathryn Clark, who was a KU student in the early 1970s, lived in eight places while in Lawrence. Five of the eight were Ling properties. Noting the importance of these properties to the development and growth of activist and gay communities in Lawrence and their affordability for students, she commented that "certain houses became known as part of the gay community."[78]

One of the most notable hippie houses/communes that was formed in

the late 1960s was the Body Shop. Most were called by their street numbers, but the Body Shop was one of the first "named" houses.[79] Located at
924 New Hampshire Street, it began as a random group of residents and
evolved in 1969 and early 1970 as a house for gay students.[80] While both
gay and straight students lived there, it was referred to as the "unofficial
gay Greek house" and served as a gay hangout and hub.[81]

The origin and first use of the name is not known, but resident and
LGLF member Peter Felleman speculated that it was in reference to "the
sexual orientation of gay men in those days. It was a sexual revolution."
David Stout, who founded the LGLF, agreed, and quipped: "The name
'Body Shop' certainly carried the 'whore house' reputation, but this was
the era of hippies and free love."[82] It had an important role in the formation of the LGLF in the summer of 1970. Those interested in getting the
group started joined house residents to meet and plan, and the first official meeting of the LGLF was held in Stout's room. Albin stated, "It was
definitely the seminal place in which the ideas that ended up in being the
Lawrence Gay Liberation Front came from."

In September, shortly after many of the radical early LGLF founders
moved in, residents decided to change the name of the house.[83] Felleman
commented that they felt a need to align the name with their political
perspective at the time: "I think that 'Body Shop' was just simply *way*
too butch. . . . To me, 'Venus' was a better fit with what I would call our
radical feminist perspective." Richard Linker agreed, commenting, "We
didn't like the sexual connotation of 'Body Shop.' That was another one
of our goals in a sense: to desexualize the common notions of who gay
people are."[84] Linker and Felleman recalled that the name "Venus" was
chosen because of the 1958 movie *Queen of Outer Space* staring Zsa Zsa
Gabor, which took place on Venus.[85] Stubbs added that Venus was the
"Roman goddess of love, sex, beauty, and fertility. She was the Roman
counterpart to the Greek Aphrodite. It was a very gay choice."[86] Member
Chuck Ortleb (who did not live in the house) commented that this new
name, Venus, embodied the feeling of the LGLF and generated a sense
of community while also making a statement about oppressive norms
related to sexuality and gender.[87]

In August 1971, the group moved from Venus.[88] They found another
house at 1244 Tennessee and kept the "Venus" and movie themes going, naming it "Bride of Venus" (after "Bride of Frankenstein," Linker

recalled).[89] Felleman remembered the vibe of the house: "We were getting campy." Residents included students, nonstudents, LGLF members, and residents not affiliated with the group. During this time, they held many social events and parties, drawing in large numbers.[90]

Venus's physical presence in the community was important, becoming a touchpoint and way station for gay students, a "magnet" and a "social center."[91] The house functioned like a clearinghouse and support network for the LGLF, with a resource and counseling phone line and drop-in counseling.[92] It was also a known drop-in spot for gay radicals traveling across the country.[93] Creating a house for those who were gay and lesbian was quite revolutionary.[94] It asserted residents' sense of pride and legitimacy. It is likely that it also provided protection from antigay targeting and harassment. It fostered discussions among residents that promoted a sense of shared identity and community that had not happened so openly before. They pushed the envelope on social norms related to gender expression and sexuality and were able to get people's attention in their everyday experience.

That same summer in 1971, Stubbs heard from a friend about a thirteen-year-old guru from India, Prem Rawat.[95] He had become an American sensation and was featured in national media. Intrigued, Stubbs traveled to Boulder, Colorado, where Rawat had been speaking. Stubbs returned to Lawrence in the fall after a stay at Rawat's ashram (a spiritual retreat). Inspired by his experience, he shared it with Bride of Venus friends Bolin and Linker, and Plunge friends Rod Grey and Rick Moody. Shortly thereafter, they all boarded a plane to India.[96] The group's sudden departure created tension with the remaining resident, Peter Felleman, particularly as their portion of the rent went delinquent. Felleman explained: "I held down the fort on my own, but I left the house not long after everyone got back. Not having the same spiritual inclination and feeling some resentment, I moved on."[97]

Bolin, Stubbs, and Linker returned to Lawrence and Bride of Venus after their adventure at the end of 1971, transformed by their experience. Stubbs commented that "it changed the direction of my life."[98] After they returned, however, numbers in the house continued to drop. Linker and Bolin brought in new roommates, but conflict arose, and Linker and Bolin left the house themselves shortly thereafter. "What broke up the remaining Venusians, was probably just shifting priorities and interpersonal dynamics," Felleman reflected. Staying in one place for a length of time was not the norm for 1970s students, so Bride of Venus dissolved as a result of these changes. Sharon Mayer commented, "We all still saw each other but didn't all live together anymore."[99]

A Place for Us: Informal Hangouts

Hippie houses and communes were one of the ways that some gay and lesbian students fostered a sense of community and belonging. They also found other informal ways to connect. Many of these spaces became fairly well known through the informal gay and lesbian grapevine. Gay men and lesbians generally hung out and socialized separately since their connecting styles and interests tended to be different. Gay men held social gatherings, meeting up at people's houses and local establishments such as the Rock Chalk Café, a local bar.[100] They often went out together to bars, particularly in Kansas City, and hung out together at LGLF picnics.[101] Lesbians hosted wine and cheese socials and women's dances. They also had feminist and lesbian softball teams and the Women's Music Collective, to name a few.[102] It was not uncommon for faculty and students to socialize together. When asked if this posed awkwardness or conflict-of-interest challenges in relating in both arenas, Paul Lim commented: "It really wasn't an issue. Being the close community that it was, I think people were fairly protective of each other."

In the mid-1960s, there were active underground groups of gay people in Lawrence. Renowned gay activist Michael McConnell, who with his partner Jack Baker shook up the country by becoming the first gay men to marry in the United States, lived in Lawrence during this time. Prior to connecting with Baker, McConnell lived in Lawrence with another man, Bob, who was his first gay partner in the mid-1960s. Bob got a job at the University of Kansas libraries, and it was during this time that McConnell found "this whole secret society of gay people." He described the group as quiet and secretive but well connected. The hangout in Lawrence was the Rock Chalk Café, which was still "the" spot in 1968 when McConnell returned to Lawrence with Baker. He observed that "people kind of knew there was this gay subculture, but nobody talked about it."

David Awbrey added that he had also heard of one of these informal networks while chatting with a professor who was gay but closeted. The professor talked about a gala event that took place one entire day every year in which "upper elite" professors received the "secret dog whistle" to "converge on the Eldridge [a historic hotel known for its elegance] for like the greatest gay Oscar Wilde." This reinforced Awbrey's speculation that there had been a "very strong gay underground in Lawrence for apparently decades."

In the later 1960s, local hangouts such as the Bierstube pub, the Gaslight Tavern, and Tansy's Bookstore were popular with the radical crowd, which included many gay men and lesbians, and many who would become early LGLF members. These were places to meet, listen to poetry, and engage in intellectual conversations.[103] Abington Bookstore, another popular spot, featured gay and lesbian poets and writers such as Allen Ginsberg, Denise Levertov, and Robert Duncan, whom owner John Fowler invited to come to Lawrence. Lawrence resident and 1960s activist Jim McCrary, who was contributing editor of *Grist* magazine, commented that there was a definite gay and lesbian presence in town in the 1960s.[104] Some bars in town also were known to be gay-friendly.[105] The most notable was Louise's, which had an area in the back where gay customers would gather.[106] Later in the evening, Louise was known to clear the bar for her gay patrons. Joe Lordi remembered: "What happened is about eleven o'clock at night, she'd throw all the straight people out, and it would become like a gay bar. . . . That's definitely where a lot of the gay people went."

In addition, there were gay social hangouts. One that was off the beaten path was an area on the periphery of a small lake in the nearby state park called Lake Henry. Lim commented that "it was kind of like a nudist camp" that was a popular congregation spot for gay campus and community members. Stout also remembered this spot, agreeing that it was a popular place for gay people to socialize that was frequented by LGLF members.[107]

There were also places that had a reputation as "cruising spots," most notably in the Kansas Union and by the Campanile.[108] The Union also served as a gay hangout, as Richard Linker shared: "All of us would go up there from time to time, and often it was just a gang of us sitting up there talking and having fun." This created some misperceptions and hostility with Union staff, however. Linker recounted a time when he was in the

Union, "reading until it closed and walking out with a bunch of other guys who were gay and who were probably in the bathrooms, frankly, and having the man who was in charge of the building who was locking it up yelling at us as we walked out, 'Get out of here, you fucking queers!' Which especially offended me because I was up there reading that night."

When asked about how gay people got connected, Lim talked about the "code" that enabled them to recognize each other while remaining undetected by outsiders: "They talk about gay-dar, and I think that you somehow know, and you pick up hints. People drop hairpins. . . . It's a very close community, and once you meet one or two people, then socially you get invited. And then your circle of friends grows."[109] Incidents that occurred not but a decade earlier in Lawrence, however, reminded members of the gay community that they had to be ever watchful when they gathered. KU professor emeritus of English Ed Grier recalled a gay dance in the 1950s held in a barn on Fifteenth Street. "The Dean of the College took it upon himself to raid it. . . . They found a couple of assistant professors there, who were fired on the spot."[110]

For many at KU who were gay, bars were their social connection. The fear of being discovered led many to seek out the relative anonymity of gay bars in larger towns outside of Lawrence. Many knew of these gay bars, particularly in Kansas City, but they existed "on the margins." They provided a place for people to be themselves without fear of reprisal despite concerns of being raided.[111]

One that was frequently mentioned was the Terrace Lounge in the nearby city of Topeka. Typical of the time, it was camouflaged in a surreptitious location, only known to those who had gotten the inside word about its existence. Local gay activist and leader Keith Spare commented that it was in a nameless building next door to a business with a sign, the "Mirror Store." He recalled that the entrance was an unmarked door east of the store near the capitol building.[112] Ron Gans, remembering the hiddenness, but also a door sign and "fogged-over" windows, recalled a sign that said, "Private party tonight." Guests were greeted by a "stern-looking, unfriendly" woman at the door, who Gans recalled asking guests: "What do you want?" She let in those who identified themselves as gay. Keith Spare's experience was slightly different. He recalled her asking those who were wanting to enter if they were homosexual, and if they answered yes, she let them in. He described her as imposing, taking her role of protecting patrons seriously but making those she knew feel welcome. It was common for police to come around, making checks. Gans commented, "They actually called ahead to make sure everyone was seated down and nothing was improperly going on." There were rumors that the Menninger Foundation influenced the relaxed attitude of police toward gay people in Topeka, but this seems unlikely given the agency's views about homosexuality.[113]

The bigger draw was Kansas City. Group member Joe Prados commented that "those bars had better music, were better bars. I'm sure they were mafia run. . . . And of course, down there we would meet fellow students who were in the bar, obviously were gay. You would meet another KU student and 'ta-dah!' And so that's part of how the network was operated, see?" Bars such as the Bank (which was an actual bank that was converted), the Tent, Arabian Nights, and Redhead were mentioned as hangouts. The Jewel Box, which was known for its highly popular drag shows, was a Kansas City icon. It featured performers from all over the country and drew in both gay and straight patrons. Albin recalled an advantage of going to bars in Kansas City: students could be anonymous and not as easily detected. Socializing in Lawrence could be intimidating since "there was no way you could stay in the closet. The vast majority of the people didn't want to be out. They didn't want anybody to know. They didn't want their parents to know. They didn't want their friends to know. They certainly didn't want their fraternity brothers and sorority sisters to know. So they kept it a big secret."[114]

There was one bar in Kansas City, Pete's, that was named after the owner, a lesbian. It was considered a key hangout among lesbians at KU. Similar to the Terrace Lounge, it was a nondescript building with no indication of its actual function. To enter, patrons needed to know the system. Martha Boyd described how this worked when her spouse, Sandra, went for the first time: "She didn't know how to get in because there was no neon, no signage, no nothing. So she was standing there, and a woman behind her said, 'Well, have you pushed the doorbell?'" That did the trick. Pete screened people at the front door, requiring ID from those she didn't know, but "she knew most everybody." Boyd explained, "Talk was that Pete had to pay money under the table to the police department so they wouldn't raid the place. Because if they would raid it, they took everybody's name, and they got published in the *Kansas City Star*. And you had doctors and lawyers and teachers and all kinds of people going to Pete's."[115]

Women would also go to Kansas City for women's music concerts as well as for clubs and bars. Christine Leonard Smith, who was involved with the Lawrence women's community in the 1970s, recalled: "When we would go to Kansas City, we would go and see Willie Tyson or Sweet Honey in the Rock and then we would stop by these clubs. The one I remember, the upstairs was kind of men's disco-y, lights flashing, and then downstairs there was a women's area. And so that was a way to meet people."

But these places outside of Lawrence left a gap; many were wanting a safe home base. Smith observed: "The Gay Liberation dances eventually became a way to meet other gay people. . . . That's what they were for, and without that whole bar scene kind of feeling to it." Prados agreed, commenting that that was one of the goals of the LGLF. Hubbell added that they wanted Lawrence to be their social home base, but the lack of anonymity and options in Lawrence motivated them to look to Kansas City. Hubbell credits the LGLF members' creativity in establishing dances and programs with turning this around.

Another popular spot was a Kansas Union cafeteria alcove where gay and lesbian students congregated.[116] It was not easy to locate—but that was the point. Stout elaborated on why the spot was chosen: "It wasn't just one of the inconsequential corners in the great big cafeteria hall. It was actually in a smaller separate room with no more than six or eight tables accessed from the main cafeteria. . . . This smaller room just off the main hall felt more isolated, more secluded, more private—a nest, a gay Jay's nest, and the larger corner table was perfect for a small group." Finding the space was only half the battle. Being welcomed into the group took a little effort. Stout began hanging out at lunchtime, "eventually working up the courage to even sit inside the alcove. Not knowing anyone though, breaking into the group proved to be somewhat difficult." Eventually, group members reached out and invited him in. But Stout commented that "being invited to join a group at a table in a cafeteria doesn't mean one is automatically inducted into the clique."[117] In time, he worked his way into the in crowd.

For Bob Warren, who became an LGLF member, this cafeteria connection was particularly important. He had transferred to KU from Pittsburg State University in 1970, having served a stint in the military. "I didn't have a lot of free time—I never went to the places to drink beer, or beer holes, I guess they called them then." He talked about the ways that this group opened up his world: "So in the afternoon, between classes, quite a few gay people would collect down there, and that got to be a little bit of a clique, and that's where I discovered other gay people. . . . And I went, 'Wow, this is pretty cool!'" He met gay people with diverse backgrounds and career aspirations, normalizing and turning around his preconceptions about being gay.

These informal ways of connecting with others who were gay provided many things, including fun, excitement, friendship, and a sense of identification with the culture, yet they did not necessarily provide the sense of affiliation and belonging people were needing. The many informal ways that people connected were not enough to build a community. The efforts had to be intentional, formalized, broad-based, and coordinated. That was the role of the soon-to-be-formed LGLF.

Interestingly, there has been a reference to an earlier gay student group at KU prior to the LGLF. David Awbrey, who was student body president in 1969–1970 during the first year of the newly created Student Senate, remembered this earlier group. A student approached Awbrey in 1969 about forming a student branch of the Mattachine Society on campus. Awbrey supported the request, and the group was formally recognized. The student, in fact, purchased office supplies with the Student Senate funding he received. Awbrey continued, "That's really the end of it because the guy never showed up in the fall to take over his organization. . . . This is the spring of '69. Stonewall didn't happen until July of '69. We were 'KU Student Government [is] for Gay Rights' before there were any gay rights." There is no other documentation about this group's existence. But Awbrey's recollections may indicate that in the late 1960s, the wheels were slowly and quietly beginning to turn, contributing to the creation of the LGLF.

A Time of Turmoil: KU during the Protest Years

The grassroots organizing taking place in Lawrence brought together the community and campus. It was bolstered by New Left activism and the growing unrest nationwide while also fueling radicalism on campus. To understand how this unfolded, it is important to provide a snapshot of the campus at the time and review significant events contributing to the campus culture of rebellion.

KU was typical of many public universities in the Midwest in the 1960s. As an open admissions campus, the majority of students hailed from towns throughout the state from a wide range of backgrounds. In addition, it attracted students as well as faculty and researchers from other states and countries. KU's total enrollment in 1966 was 14,697 and increased to 18,134 in 1972 as baby boomers entered college in unprecedented numbers, ushering in a time of growth and expansion. Students were largely undergraduates, predominantly white, with more males than females.[118] The university was central to the economy of the community and made up close to 40 percent of the city's population.[119]

Many KU students, propelled by the national student unrest and calls for change, were speaking out and challenging KU administration and the established order. The unrest and protest sparked an atmosphere of tension and distrust between KU students and administrators. To add to the tension, state lawmakers, the regents, and the general public had grown weary of the dissension. They began to question the value of higher education to the state and its residents. Rusty Leffel, a prominent KU student leader in the 1970s who established the campus group Students Concerned about Higher Education in Kansas, had witnessed this change, in which university administrators were caught between the competing factions. Students "were polarized between the far right and the far left," and student government leaders had lost students' confidence in their ability to represent their needs and concerns.[120] John H. McCool, in his article "Cause for Concern," commented that there had been "deep state budget cuts, loss of prominent faculty, and perilously low morale" with no solutions in sight for these short- and long-term problems threatening the future of higher education in the state.[121] It was a time of turmoil.

KU had its share of conflict in the 1960s, as did many campuses across the country. The years between 1965 and 1970 at KU were stormy ones. It is helpful to highlight some of the significant events that occurred during this time to provide a context for the creation and development of the Lawrence Gay Liberation Front. A series of events paved the way for what was to come, influencing campus and community reactions to the fledgling group.

In 1965, a time in which civil rights was at the center of national attention, a campus group called the Civil Rights Council led a sit-in protest outside Chancellor W. Clarke Wescoe's office to protest the treatment of African Americans on campus.[122] Chancellor Wescoe's refusal to meet with the group or issue an executive order responding to their demands led students to take over his office suite and lead a peaceful march in front of the chancellor's residence. Many were jailed for their involvement. It received national attention and caused considerable concern among administrators.

This protest was of particular significance in that it brought the issue of discrimination close to home, heightening awareness of its existence at KU. It was not just an issue "out there" but was present and pervasive in KU's backyard.[123] It was likely a wake-up call for KU administrators, who underestimated the undercurrents of discontent as well as students' ability to effectively mobilize. As they were figuring out their strategy to manage this discontent, they were challenged with competing interests. On one hand, campuses were expected to foster free speech and civic engagement. On the other hand, there was also an expectation that students' actions should not jeopardize the university's standing with state leaders. KU was at odds with the regents and legislators who were questioning KU's liberalism and the effect it had on the growing dissension on campuses throughout the state. This would become a significant issue in the 1970s under Chancellor Laurence Chalmers's leadership. Chalmers's liberal attitudes and student-centered philosophy raised the ire of state officials, who felt that he did not do enough to control campus unrest.[124] This directly affected his response to the LGLF as they began to organize. This protest also demonstrated students' ability to come together to effectively organize. This group's success in drawing in substantial numbers and gaining the attention of the KU administration, resulting in most of their demands being met, may have provided a model for other KU groups to follow. Much more was on the horizon.

In the mid-1960s, a growing number of KU and Lawrence community members joined in opposing US involvement in the Vietnam War. Antiwar sentiment among KU and community members continued to get louder and more forceful with protests and speak-outs. Timothy Miller recalled the impact on campus: "The war kind of took over as the main focus of protest activities. It really was front and center. I think the war really became the dominant social issue for six or eight years, and certainly had the biggest following. Civil rights had a constituency, but the war was the thing here. You have a march down Jayhawk Boulevard—there'd be thousands of people [who would] show up for it."

As antiwar sentiments continued to dominate the campus, a 1969 demonstration on campus exacerbated the tension between student activists and administrators. On May 9, approximately three hundred students disrupted the annual Chancellor's Review of ROTC cadets in Memorial Stadium.[125] Administrators tried to maintain order but to no avail. Fearing the worst after some protesters brought bats and other club-like items, local police, sheriff's deputies, Kansas Highway Patrol, and Kansas Bureau of Investigation officers were brought in to keep the protest from escalating. Despite the governor's belief that the event should go forward, Chancellor Wescoe canceled it.[126]

Taking their lead from their earlier experience in 1965 with the civil rights protest, Wescoe and his administration acted quickly and tracked down the names of all those who participated in the protest. Close to half (thirty-three) were suspended.[127] Wescoe, who was preparing to leave his post in May, was reported to be visibly shaken by the event and expressed extreme disappointment that the disciplinary board did not sanction more students.[128] He warned that this would jeopardize the university's ability to respond to campus unrest in the future.[129] The Student Senate stood firm in renouncing the disciplinary measures, including the chancellor's call to impeach the student body vice president, who had participated.[130] In the end, the student voice won out.

Many on campus questioned Wescoe's harsh sanctions. Professor emeritus of American studies William (Bill) Tuttle, an expert on civil rights history, commented on Wescoe's ongoing apprehension about "things going wrong and violence erupting," which exacerbated the situation. Tuttle speculated that this incident evolved into a big issue due to Wescoe's punitive treatment of students and his rigid disciplinary approach. Wescoe's response may have also been linked to his sense that this protest was unlike earlier ones. Compared to the 1965 protest, this one was more confrontational and engaged tactics used by militant groups. It was also more disruptive, shutting down a university event. The threat of violence was also more real with the heightened anger regarding a war that was considered unjust. This angrier, more aggressive, and potentially more violent tone set the stage for what was to come just one year later.

In 1970, unrest on the KU campus mirrored the turmoil nationwide. A *UDK* article described the tense atmosphere: "Second only to Quantrill's Civil War Raid, the summer of '70 perhaps marked the darkest period in Lawrence history and fueled a hatred so intense that most residents cringe at its remembrance."[131] Anger related to US involvement in the Vietnam War continued to rise, and racial tension had reached an all-time high. Monhollon pointed out that many white members of the community, fed up with years of violence, found it easier to blame external sources for this tension. They placed the onus on the counter-culture radicals and hippies rather than examining issues closer to home, specifically attitudes and policies in the city and state that contributed to racism and inequality.[132]

In mid-April of that year, a number of racially motivated incidents occurred in Lawrence, prompting John Spearman, president of the KU Black Student Union, to encourage African American students on cam-pus to arm themselves for self-protection.[133] Tension mounted in the city as well, resulting in protests and violence. African American students at the local high school led a highly charged walkout, which was sup-ported by parents and members of the African American community. A few hours after the walkout, the Kansas Union on the KU campus was in flames. It had been vandalized and firebombed. It took over three hours to get the fire under control.[134] The motive and identities of those respon-sible were never discovered, but speculations ranged from agitated stu-dents of color to Lawrence's radical leftist groups.

The worst was yet to come. As the unrest and tension continued, townspeople grew increasingly apprehensive and fearful.[135] Police pres-ence increased, clashing with the counterculture activists. This contrib-uted to what was already a difficult situation, adding to the distrust of and hostility toward each other, and leading to what is referred to as the Days of Rage. The city issued a curfew and arrested those who did not abide by it.

On July 16, 1970, two people in Lawrence received nonfatal gunshot wounds. [136] There were differing accounts of who fired the shots, with some blaming the activists and some the police. The police investigated, identifying two suspects. A chase ensued, and after losing control of the car and ending up on the sidewalk, suspect Rick Dowdell got out of the car and ran down the alley. Officer William Garrett pulled his gun and fired the fatal shot, killing Dowdell.[137]

Anger was at a fever pitch. The following day, African Americans in the community presented a petition to city officials demanding the sus-pension of Officer Garrett. They also insisted on a thorough investigation of the incident. Later that evening, police were called to check out a report that "four to five Negroes" were involved in firing shots downtown. Police arrived to face an angry crowd of more than forty armed African Americans and violence erupted.[138] It spread to the "Hippie Haven" close to campus. Fires burned in the streets, and police were pelted with rocks and bricks.[139] A group of students marched to the chancellor's residence and threw objects through the window when Chancellor Chalmers failed to come to the door.

More violence was to come. The evening of July 20, police were called to investigate a crowd gathering at the Rock Chalk Café, which was a block from campus. When they arrived, they were showered with rocks, bricks, bottles, and tomatoes. Police contained the crowd and left. A few hours later, however, they were called back to the café to find an overturned Volkswagen and students with matches threatening to ignite the gasoline that had spilled out. The tension from days of unrest had put the police on edge and they fired tear gas at the crowd. A few, in addition, fired their weapons. A fleeing student, Nick Rice, was struck in the head with a bullet and died at the scene. Those who sided with the activists were shocked and outraged. Some townspeople, who were fed up with the ongoing violence, believed the shootings were justified. The formal investigation conducted by the Kansas Bureau of Investigation found no wrongdoing on the part of the police who were involved. Many were furious, calling the report a cover-up.[140]

This lack of closure and sense of injustice and upheaval was a backdrop to the birth of the Lawrence Gay Liberation Front. KU professor of law and university attorney in the 1970s Charles Oldfather stated that the LGLF emerged during a time on campus when "everything was being questioned."[141] This atmosphere provided a framework and impetus for the courageous acts that were to follow.

"Out of the Johns and Into the Streets!"

Creating the Framework and Getting the Group Started (1970–1975)

The activism that started in the late 1960s by Michael Stubbs, John Bolin, Richard Linker, John Steven Stillwell, and others provided the momentum for the next step in the creation of the Lawrence Gay Liberation Front (LGLF). Stubbs commented on the national push fueling this momentum:

> Gay liberation was a grassroots movement. No one person was responsible for starting it, and it didn't start in any one place. Those of us who were gay and lesbian and involved in the counterculture, the antiwar movement, and the women's movement were like dry prairie grass ready to be ignited. . . . The spark was Stonewall and the New York GLF formed within hours. There had been other rebellions before, but for the first time the anger and pain of an oppressed people was harnessed and turned into the joy of coming out and creating a sustainable, inclusive movement. That dry prairie grass was soon a verdant springtime green.[1]

David Stout entered this picture in 1970, turning the momentum into an organized campus group.[2] Stout's story reflects the experience of many of those growing up on farms in Kansas and other places in the Midwest and of many gay and lesbian youth who would come to KU during this time.

Stout did not know in the spring of 1970 that a research project he conducted for one of his classes would begin a sequence of events that would lead to the creation of the LGLF. On the day of the first meeting, a small group of dedicated activists got together, generating the momentum to move forward. They were unaware of the significance of their actions as they forged ahead and developed a mission and goals, created an organizational structure and approach, and began the process of establishing the group with the intention of becoming a recognized student organization.

The Group's Beginnings

David Stout learned at a very young age how to hide. Growing up on a farm in the small town of Rolla, Kansas, in the 1950s and 1960s,[3] he knew that being gay wasn't something a person talked about. He was aware, coming from what he termed a semireligious family, that acknowledging he was gay would violate all the values and core beliefs held by both his family and community. And not ever meeting a gay person (that he knew of) added to his feelings of isolation and fear of being found out. Stout had no choice but to keep his sexual orientation a secret. This created what he described as the "agony I would soon be going through with the conflict between my newly emerging Christian identity and my never-healed queer core."[4]

When Stout entered the University of Kansas in 1963, he did poorly due to his struggle with academics and self-doubt about his sexual orientation: "In spite of the problems with grades and money, the number one problem on my mind needing fixin' was this damned homosexuality." Seriously depressed and confused, he considered suicide. Instead, he decided to seek the help of prominent religious leader Oral Roberts, asking him to heal him of his homosexuality. In a state of turmoil and with faltering grades, Stout left KU.

Over the next few years, Stout struggled to find himself and come to terms with being gay. "I was recognizing who I was, and I recognized who I was was taboo—I was queer. I resisted knowing who I was, I resisted acknowledging who I was, I denied who I was." In considering the repercussions of this denial, Stout reflected: "When we are forced to live in secret, when we are forced to live our lies, we live in constant fear of being discovered." He explored many directions, including jobs in health care and the ministry. After a summer working at a youth home for boys and coming to terms with some "demons" resulting from years of denial of his identity (including a second suicide attempt), he realized that it was time to change directions. It was time to give KU another try and finish his degree, which he had put on hold. In 1968, he returned to KU with a new sense of purpose and self-acceptance, committed to living an authentic out life.

Stout's first semester back at KU, he decided to find out how to be an openly gay man on campus. He was introduced to Mike Shearer, a writer for the *UDK* who had written quite possibly the first article that explored homosexuality at KU.[5] Shearer had interviewed a student who was gay. The article, interestingly, was on the front page directly above an article about electing the committee to select the new chancellor, one of the most visible places in the paper. This suggests that this story was of enough value and interest to be placed in this coveted spot.

Stout's interest was piqued. He contacted Shearer. They met for dinner and, on discovering Shearer himself was gay, Stout shared with him that he believed society needed to evolve in its treatment of gay people, using the term "tolerate" to describe the outcome he was seeking. Stout recounted, "Shearer jumped on my choice of the word 'tolerate.' For him, tolerance wasn't good enough. He said, 'I don't want to be merely tolerated. I expect to be accepted.'" Acceptance was a long way from the guilt, shame, and denial with which Stout grew up. This changed Stout's perspective. He began asking around and seeking out other gay and lesbian students on campus, forming new connections. He did not realize it at the time, but this newfound acceptance would also inadvertently lead him to the next steps that would result in the creation of the LGLF.

Unlike his earlier KU experience, Stout was thriving. For one of his social work classes in the spring of 1970, he researched the gay communities in Lawrence, Topeka, and Kansas City. He interviewed a group of over one hundred gay and lesbian people. Among them was a Lawrence High School student. After the semester ended in May, this young man followed up with Stout about the findings, asking, "What now?" Stout responded by telling him that he planned on graduating the following year and would use the information from his research in his work. The young man was not satisfied. "But it's such a waste," he said. "You've met everyone in town, in Kansas City and in Topeka. You know everyone. You need to get us all organized like the other gay liberation groups starting up all over the country." Stout again explained that he did this for his class and had no plans to go further with this assignment.

The young man would not take no for an answer. Stout recalled, "Like me in 1968, he didn't like what gay life had to offer him in 1970. He wanted something more, something better." A short while later, he showed up again—this time not to repeat the original request but to tell Stout that he had created flyers and posted them all over KU, especially in the gay hangouts. They said: "Out of the Johns and Into the Streets! Get out of the johns and find a meaningful quality existence as a gay person. Call Gay Liberation at [Stout's personal phone number]." This flyer reflected the pressing need for organizing. When asked how gay men connected at KU, Barry Albin replied, "It was called the bathroom, dear. [Laughs.]" Cruising was common on the KU campus at places such as the Kansas Union restrooms, the Campanile, and the Trophy Room at the Union.[6]

This fostered a culture of secrecy and shame, which was exacerbated by the intense monitoring by the dean of men, Donald Alderson. Alderson was known for his disapproval of homosexuality, keeping detailed records of those whom he suspected were gay and harshly disciplining students for behavior he considered inappropriate.[7] Group member Lee Hubbell commented: "You couldn't talk to the dean of men. We knew that he was not for us. He didn't want anything to do with us." Barry Albin was subjected to Alderson's discipline firsthand: "[Alderson] called me in and reamed my ass one day and made me scared to death I was going to get thrown out of school . . . very antigay. And very upsetting." After this meeting, Albin said he believed that Alderson sent people from his office to keep an eye on his activities. He felt like he was being followed.

Stout knew from his research and personal experience that there was a serious need to bring those who were gay together to break through this shame and secrecy, form positive, healthy connections, and identify resources to challenge a campus that could be unwelcoming and inequitable. But what to do next since he had not planned on starting a group? He conferred with his good friend Elaine Riseman, whom Stout described as an out lesbian who was involved in the feminist community. She encouraged him to choose a time and location for the meeting and told him she would be there to support him. Numerous people called to express interest, but on the day of the meeting, only seven attended. Ironically, the Lawrence High School student who got the ball rolling was not one of them.[8]

In early June 1970, Robin Burgess, John Bolin, Richard Linker, Elaine Riseman, and Laurie Stetzler joined David Stout in his room in the Body Shop for this meeting. They talked about the experience of being gay—the challenges, triumphs, and visions for change. Explaining his inability to recall the specific date of this first meeting, Stout stated that "not realizing we were making history, nobody paid any attention." There was not unanimous agreement about the seventh member at this meeting, but it seems likely that it was John Steven Stillwell.[9] Stillwell, described by former boyfriend Steven Weaver as a "trailblazer," a "sincere radical," and "one of the most intellectual people I have ever met," took on an important leadership role in the group. As a film studies graduate student involved in the campus film studies organization, he introduced many films to the campus that challenged heteronormative and gender stereotypes. The group joining Stout represented diverse experiences. Riseman and Stetzler were feminists from the Kansas City area; John Bolin and Richard Linker, who was a community member and teacher at the Lawrence-based Lorean School, were counterculture radical freaks from out of state; and Robin Burgess was an army medic in the Vietnam War, described as "cerebral," "with flair," and "highly articulate on issues of racism, sexism, and homophobia," who was attending college on the G.I. Bill.[10]

At this time, tensions were high in the community and students were not feeling supported or understood by those in positions of power. The fatal shootings of two KU students just a few weeks earlier, with one outside of the Body Shop in the New Hampshire Street alley, exacerbated their distrust and fear. David Stout recalled the day after the shooting of Rick Dowdell: "We went out to look at my car and found the blood under my back bumper."[11] Four days later, member Reginald Brown (Reggie) was only a few feet away when Nick Rice was gunned down outside the Gaslight Tavern, with a bullet grazing Brown's ear as both ran from the police.[12] The incidents reminded those in the room that life-and-death consequences could result from activist actions and paints a picture of how close to home this came for many in the group. To gather to talk about the controversial issue of gay activism was risky and courageous, particularly in the tense, distrustful, divided community.

Breaking New Ground: Early Organizing

The late 1960s and early 1970s were unique times for student activism and organizing. Tonda Rush, a former KU student who was involved in the women's community, explained: "We lived in a time where young people had begun to really use their voices in ways that our parents' generation thought were pretty shocking and in a lot of ways unwelcome. I think this idea that everybody deserved a path, and everybody deserved a voice, was the lodestar for almost all of us in that time period." The time was marked by students' feelings of agency and empowerment—in Susan Davis's words, "a very hopeful, high time."[13] Activists, challenging the status quo and old models of leadership, did not look to what had come before for guidance but were finding their own way.

Kathy Hoggard, who was involved in the activist community during the 1970s as a KU student and as director of the KU Information Center, described how it worked: "Those were the days of, 'Let's put on a conference and we'll be the speakers.' [Laughs.] 'And we'll lead the workshops.' . . . We were not looking to experts of the past because they didn't know about the world. . . . It's happening here and now. We're inventing it." These KU activists were figuring it out as they went, confident that their collective vision would provide the answers. LGLF member Sharon Mayer explained: "I don't have to know how this will happen for it to happen."[14]

This first informal meeting in the summer of 1970 laid the foundation for what would become the LGLF.[15] Early on, members were exploring the meaning of gay liberation in their lives and did not feel a pressing need to structure the meetings.[16] These early discussions took on a political focus, integrating values and goals of the first Gay Liberation Front in New York (GLF–NY). "The slogan back then was 'the personal is political,'" recalled Steven Weaver. "And that was very key to understanding what was going on." Richard Linker commented that "most of the [LGLF] founders never abandoned a political approach to the issue. . . . Most of us in the founding group were committed to liberation politics in general and a sort of leftist/socialist slant. To that end we had political reading groups and consciousness-raising sessions."

As the group continued, they decided it was time to figure out where they were going and take a step toward becoming official. The group, which had grown from seven members to ten, worked through a long evening to put together the following statement to communicate their vision, which included both a political and an educational component:

> In formulating a statement expressing our reasons for desiring official recognition of existence, we, of the Lawrence Gay Liberation Front, offer this statement as an expression of what we feel to be representative of our thinking. It is our realization that:
>
> I
> Homosexuality exists as an incontestable fact. That this condition can be changed is a point questioned by the sociological, psychological, and medical disciplines. However, we assert that the choice to attempt change should be the result of individual free thought and not the result of social pressure.
>
> II
> Inseparable from the freedom to be homosexual is the freedom to participate in homosexual activities. In a society that professes the freedom of the individual, moral and sexual legislation has no valid place. Therefore, to recognize our right to exist is to recognize our right to engage in homosexual acts. We know that we are entitled to this recognition.
>
> III
> In order to bring about the changes in the social atmosphere under which our right to exist is free from repression, a program of educational and legislative action must be established and maintained. The success of this program depends, in part, upon the cooperation and assistance of the community and university in their fulfillment of their roles as social institutions.[17]

The language of this statement communicated members' political, civil rights focus, reflecting the radical New Left influence on emerging gay activism that called for direct action and confrontational tactics.[18] But the LGLF statement also included a focus on education to bring about change, which was not always a priority in New Left circles. The group's statement was a rebellious act—an early iteration of the slogan "We're here, we're queer, get used to it" coined by the New York activist group Queer Nation.[19]

Group members saw their mission as broad-based and transformational, demanding recognition, equal treatment, social change, and support from the community. Lee Hubbell summed it up: "We're real, we're
people, we exist, and we're not going to let you run over us like that.
You're not. We have rights too." By explicitly identifying the responsibility of both straight and gay members of the larger community in contributing to this change, they shifted the conversation from an "us versus
them" to a "we're in this together" proposition. This communicated a
different tone from other gay liberation movements that operated from
an identity politics framework, which had the potential to be polarizing.
Stout commented that the group was committed to "expand[ing] the individual and collective consciousness in both gay and straight society."[20]

While the statement as a whole took a powerful, affirming stand, Article I, "the choice to attempt change should be the result of individual free
thought and not the result of social pressure," reflects the internalized
homophobia that evolved from the repressive attitudes of the times. It
began as an assertion of the rights of those who were gay. The statement,
though, took a turn by suggesting that conversion or reorientation is acceptable in any context. Stout commented that he expected that group
members would rewrite this section if they were to reconvene in current
times.[21] Yet it was a progressive statement for the time, asserting that
those wrestling with their identity had a right to determine their own
course rather than being influenced by social pressure.

The group also communicated their educational and political vision
through handouts and flyers that they produced. Not only did these promote the newly formed group, which by the end of August had grown to
between eighty and one hundred members, but they also educated the
campus about being gay from an affirming perspective.[22] This was a radical departure from common messages that predominated. The handouts
asserted that homosexuality was healthy, positive, and normal. They
confronted devaluing and derogatory language, such as the use of the
term "queer." While many gay men and lesbians used this term among
themselves with pride, it was commonly used by straight society as an
insult. They stated: "Providing a strong alternative to being 'queer' is
the purpose of this Gay Liberation Front, and will allow us to join with
others, and others with us, in the declaration of our individual dignity
and freedom."[23]

Members' goal of working in collaboration with others to achieve their ends was a central, recurring theme. They also reiterated their focus on political action and rejection of heterosexist norms: "We see political organizing and collective action as the strategy affecting this social change. We declare that we are healthy homosexuals in a sick sexist society." Richard Linker elaborated, "The general atmosphere of revolution and liberation always informed us politically." These statements also emphasized their solidarity with other campus, community, and national civil rights organizations. It was common at the time for groups to copy the language used by other radical groups who had drafted similar statements. Group members borrowed from these documents intentionally and liberally to communicate their allegiance.[24]

Philosophically, members were committed to promoting justice for people of all historically excluded identities, not only those who were gay and lesbian. To that end, they also produced flyers supporting actions affecting other underrepresented campus populations, particularly women and African American students. [25] For instance, articles appeared in the LGLF newsletter calling for support of African American residents who were encountering racism in Cairo, Illinois, and campus antiwar protesters who were challenging Chancellor Chalmers and "his opposition to the free expression of our mutual desires to promote the dignity and sanctity of human life."[26] Their intersectional focus was evident in the solidarity statement they issued in the fall of 1970 to support the Black Student Union, protesting the firing of KU staff and Black Student Union member Gary Jackson.[27] Said Reginald Brown, "just like the Gay Liberation Front here in New York, it wasn't just about queer things, it was about all of the things that were wrong: the war, about sexism, all of these things." Many group members also found time for other countercultural work, particularly antiwar activism and the women's movement.

Specific group goals were drafted early on as the group was defining its purpose and structure. Richard Linker elaborated: "Our chief goal was to educate people about gay people. I remember one of our talking points was 'we're just like you.'"[28] These goals were later outlined in a *UDK* letter to the editor on October 14, 1971, submitted by member Joe Prados. It included some language changes that more closely communicated the group's purpose as educational, aligning with equity and social justice outcomes. This suggests that members were aware of the importance of convincing administrators and the campus community of the group's legitimacy and political agenda to push for change. The goals are listed below, and the later additions are italicized:[29]

- securing for homosexuals the rights and liberties established for all people by the word and spirit of the Declaration of Independence and Constitution *of the United States of America.*
- equalizing the status and position of the homosexual by achieving equality *under the law, equality of opportunity,* and equality in the society of his or her fellow men *and women.*
- informing and enlightening the public about homosexuals and homosexuality *by alleviating adverse prejudice, both private and official.*
- assisting, protecting, and counseling homosexuals in need.
- providing an atmosphere where homosexuals *can feel free to* enjoy each other's company and develop friendships; *thus securing for the homosexual as a human being the right to develop and achieve his or her full potential and dignity, and the right, as a citizen, to make his or her maximum contribution to the society in which he or she lives, and to mankind.*

John Bolin elaborated: "My lofty definition of GLF would be about 'intersectional battles of race, class, and sexuality.'"[30] He identified the priorities of the group: (1) promoting self-affirmation, pride, sex positivity, and consciousness raising; (2) providing counseling; (3) creating community; (4) advocating for equal protections, particularly tenant and employment rights; (5) advocating for the elimination of laws criminalizing sex between persons of the same sex; (6) providing education and outreach; (7) providing social opportunities and resources, including organizing events and being a clearinghouse for activities and services; and (8) identifying safe spaces.

The group's vision was to provide a comprehensive service, having a broader purpose beyond the scope of a typical student organization in the spirit of a grassroots movement. Said Prados: "We were talking about how some schools might have a gay office, an office for gay students. Well, we were, in effect, that." This was not uncommon across the country. Before colleges offered formal gay and lesbian services, groups such as the LGLF often took on this role and stepped up to fill this gap.[31] The dearth of services, support, and gay community presence throughout the state and region made the LGLF's efforts more critical and significant. They were truly the one safe haven in the entire area for those who were gay and lesbian. For some, it would be their first encounter with affirmation and acceptance. Reginald Brown summed it up: "We were working on just establishing a space where people who were queer could come and be. Could come and have an identity, a space where they could come and feel safe, and come and be around people of their own kind."

Brown (who uses they/them pronouns) understood the need for a safe haven. Growing up in Kansas City, Kansas, they were popular in school and involved in many activities. They were also known as a gifted dancer. Having to hide their identity was stressful, however. Brown recalled this experience: "I spent my entire life, childhood, doing things to make other people comfortable about myself, and psychologically, that took a lot of energy. A lot of energy, and [it] just made me very good at lying and hiding." When Brown started at KU and discovered the LGLF, they had a revelation, commenting, "'You know what? I now have a reason, I now have impetus, somebody to look up to, that I don't have to live this way anymore. I have a choice now, so what am I going to do about it?' So that's what I chose. I said no matter what happens, I'm not going to live the way that I have lived all my life anymore. I'm just not going to do it."

Being gay and African American, there were additional issues to consider. Brown explained: "Some of the other Black gay people were uncomfortable being around me. Because I was so out. Doesn't mean I was flamboyant, doesn't mean that I was being anything, but the fact that I was not afraid to be who I was." Brown discussed the rejection they received from other African American students, not only due to being gay, but also in response to Brown's decision to center on their gay rather than their racial identity. Recalling that the pushback came not only from African American students but also from the Black Student Union (BSU), they tried to understand the reaction: "They [BSU members] could not understand why I would choose to be with white people, [people] other than them, and they just couldn't understand the fact that I could be queer. I could be queer and Black. And I could not be Black and queer.... So I was really just considered an outsider by them." This conflict led to Brown being physically threatened by BSU members. LGLF member Bob Friedland, who had accompanied Brown for a presentation, was struck by a comment that Brown made during the talk: "'I've had more acceptance by the gay community for being Black than I have by the Black community for being gay.'"

Paul Lim, professor emeritus of theater and dance, commented on what it was like being gay and Asian during that time. "One of the problems that I had was that here in mid-America the young gay people who were socializing, they tended not to be terribly accepting of people of color because they were thrilled to be discovering other people like themselves, so they tended to be very cliquish. Black people, Asians, Latinos were kind of an oddity, a curiosity so that you were twice the outsider." Gay people in historically excluded communities were often ignored and absent from discussions; therefore, much gay activism organizing that took place reflected white values and perspectives.

Acknowledging this disparity, Brown and other LGLF members of color, including Joe Prados, a Puerto Rican, and Robin Burgess, an African American, took a step in breaking through the color barrier as visible role models. This was particularly important on a majority-white campus in a majority-white community and state. Brown concluded that gay people of color needed to "see somebody like me in order to do things . . . and that gave them permission or the incentive to be themselves." This need for visible role models was certainly on the mind of the Lawrence High School student, who was both gay and African American, when he approached David Stout. Stout commented that this intensified this student's sense of urgency to create a group due to the double stigma he experienced.[32]

As members strategized, they recognized that academic buy-in would be critical to their success. Their first step was to reach out to the academic community to gauge interest, support, and backing. Many schools and departments were on board, including religion, social welfare, law, psychology, English, sociology, and human development.[33] They also met with staff from the campus mental health clinic, United Ministries in Higher Education, and local churches and religious organizations.[34] Some organizations were reticent, but many offered their support. The United Ministries in Higher Education, a space that housed some campus religious organizations, was one of the first to offer public support by providing the group a meeting space and some staff support. With these important alliances to protect them, members felt bolstered. In addition, members reached out to student organizations for collaboration and backing.[35]

Campus faculty and administrators played an important behind-the-scenes role in supporting the group. Gay and lesbian faculty and administrators, who could face hostility and repercussions if they were discovered, provided support quietly and carefully. Straight faculty and administrators, however, often had the power, privilege, and influence to push forward conversations and challenge discriminatory policies and practices. Both the quiet and the outspoken allies provided an internal base of support that allowed LGLF members, in turn, to reach out and form additional strategic alliances with people from diverse communities.[36]

Understanding the origins of the group's name sheds additional light on its political philosophy and vision. The strongest influence was unquestionably the Stonewall uprising one year earlier, in the spring of 1969. Earlier groups such as the Mattachine Society and Daughters of Bilitis adopted names that would not be easily recognized by straight society to provide protection to members and facilitate organizing. After the uprising, however, there was a new sense of anger and impatience. Gay activists wanted to assert their identity, push forward their cause, and be seen and heard. The new organization they formed, the Gay Liberation Front, reflected their radical sensibilities and affiliation with revolutionary civil rights and antiwar movements. Many campus and community gay rights groups that began forming followed their lead, adopting the "Gay Liberation Front" name to communicate their alignment with these values.[37]

The KU group took a while to arrive at a name.[38] As the Lawrence group members considered their purpose, "We wanted to say we were a revolutionary organization. We were doing things that were new and different and we wanted to make change. We wanted to liberate people."[39] Graduate student member David Radavich recalled that there had been some wrangling over the name early on and several options were considered.[40]

While most agreed with the final choice, it was not without controversy. Some were concerned that the name was off-putting or too closely connected with radical political ideologies.[41] Members as a whole, however, were not swayed by these concerns. They consciously wanted to get people's attention, raise some eyebrows, and communicate their activist orientation.[42] Patrick Dilley's research on identity typologies that were predominant in different eras for nonheterosexual college men found that during the late 1960s and 1970s, there were two primary categories: "homosexual," in which gay individuals acknowledged their feelings but sexuality was considered a private matter, and "gay," in which individuals publicly recognized their sexuality and were engaged politically to challenge oppressive policies and institutions. Dilley characterized the LGLF, whom he wrote about in his book, as collectively aligning in this more radicalized camp.[43] This puts into context the radical statement that LGLF members were making in intentionally using the term "gay" in their name.

In addition, the word "liberation" was central in the message the group wanted to convey, echoing the sentiments of GLF–NY founders that "our liberation is tied to the liberation of all peoples."[44] This is clearly identified in the LGLF statement that ran in the underground student newspaper, *Vortex*, in 1970: "We assert our strong belief that gay liberation is not an end in itself, but merely one of similar means aimed toward ultimate, unconditional liberation; toward active respect for all men: and to love without fear."[45] Radavich pointed out, "The campus in 1970 . . . liberation was in the air. And I think this was a way to connect gays and lesbians with the general liberation movement." And of course, one cannot forget the seed that was planted by the Lawrence High School student who distributed the flyers calling for gay liberation.

Moving the Agenda Forward: Group Structure and Organization

The LGLF continued to grow, and the influx of new members with new ideas encouraged Stout and other group leaders to institute some structure so the group would not turn into a free-for-all and members could move their agenda forward. Stout also wanted to institute some checks and balances to control membership to avoid being infiltrated by those looking to undermine the organization.[46]

The group began meeting on a regular basis at the United Ministries in Higher Education (UMHE) building every Monday evening.[47] The UMHE board voted to support the group by twenty-one to one. Former student Richard Crank commented that "it was likely one of the first times that there had been a public acknowledgement and support of the gay/lesbian community in Lawrence."[48] The group held two types of meetings: those that focused on business and those that were social or educational in nature. This ensured that the group operated efficiently but would draw in those who did not have an interest in operational details of the group. Steven Weaver recalled the difficulty of this seemingly straightforward task: "Looking back on it, I can remember trying to figure out how to structure the group. Because the freaking thing's called Gay Liberation Front, right? Sounds pretty radical. It wasn't really. It was only as radical as it could be in Kansas, let's face it." Weaver's comment gives a sense of the challenge in introducing this structured approach to a group of people who embraced radical ideology, which was more free-form and spontaneous in nature. The free-form approach was in fact the norm for other gay groups across the country.[49]

Another one of these checks and balances was a two-tiered membership system. All who were interested could be a member and participate in group activities, but to be a voting member, individuals had to register their name and pay dues. Organizers reasoned that someone who was straight would not want to be publicly listed as a paying member of a gay organization. At a time when other gay rights groups across the country were developing mechanisms to protect the anonymity of members, the Lawrence group took a different approach. Voting members did not express discomfort in having their names on a publicly accessible list.[50]

Group members had a legitimate reason to be careful, though. They had encountered attendees they considered suspicious, including Kansas Bureau of Investigation representatives and a man who claimed to be an antiwar, civil rights activist who urged members to purchase guns. Group members suspected that he was a mole, trying to incite violence.[51]

David Stout recalled another incident in the summer of 1970 when the group heard a rumor that the sheriff's department was planning on raiding the next meeting. "The paranoia ran rampant." Members decided not to cancel their meeting but take precautions, including asking all minors not to attend and contacting the local chapter of the American Civil Liberties Union to determine their rights and obtain some protection. Stout commented: "Incidentally, the raid never came off at all, apparently being no more than a mere rumour."[52]

There were other suspicious encounters. Ron Gans recalled talk of

someone named Tommy the Traveler, an FBI agent and undercover officer
who was reported to have surreptitiously gained access to radical groups
to disrupt and expose them: "I'm not sure he even existed . . . so we were
always a little paranoid about being infiltrated and careful about that."
In fact, the stories about Tommy the Traveler were true, although Tommy's infiltrations took place in New York, and he is not known to have
ever visited Kansas.[53] This illustrates, however, the constant fear that was
present and members' continual heightened vigilance.

Group registration served another purpose. Those who were gay were
announcing their gay identity not only to themselves but to others. By
being publicly out, members were confronting homophobic attitudes,
proclaiming their right to be equal citizens without having to hide. For
many, this was a source of pride, but it could also have some negative repercussions. For those who were closeted, questioning, or hesitant, this
registration policy may have been off-putting or intimidating. In an era
when gay students could be denied internships, professional licenses,
and job offers, being identified could be harmful on many levels. Leonard
Grotta, mentioning that this generated debate among members, explained
the dilemma that this caused for those considering professional fields
such as law or medicine: "Both of those professions in that day and age, if
you weren't of 'good moral character,' they would take away your license
or not give it to you." He concluded, "I think people were very brave to
plow ahead despite knowing that those things were hanging out there." It
doesn't appear that the registration requirement lasted very long.

Another important aspect of the group was the way in which decisions were made and the leadership was structured. In the early days,
the group followed a traditional structure adopting a majority-rule
decision-making model. Leadership was designed to be shared between a
gay man and a lesbian, who served as co-coordinators. David Stout and
Elaine Riseman were chosen for these roles when the group started.[54]
Later on, as the fall semester progressed, the group moved to a consensus
model, in which decisions had to be supported by all voting members
prior to moving forward. This framework, which was popular among
countercultural groups, centered on member involvement and shared
power in decision-making.[55] The group opted for this less-differentiated
model in the spirit of a collective. "Of course we didn't believe in 'leaders,'"
explained Steven Weaver. "So everything had to be done by consensus.

That was just the way that we approached things because we were radicals." This collective approach and the shared leadership models also clearly communicated the group's desire to embrace feminist philosophy and incorporate a leadership structure that modeled gender equity, which was not the norm for New Left or gay rights groups across the country.[56]

LGLF members, feeling empowered through their organizing, were raising awareness on campus about their existence, much to the consternation of campus administrators. Their public presence gained attention, leading Lee Hubbell to comment, "LGLF members were never 'anonymous.'" Members had a policy of not outing people. Yet they also strongly believed in the value and importance of being openly gay. Richard Linker explained that back then "we wanted everybody to be out. And I'm afraid I don't remember a lot of compassion or understanding. I don't remember that we attacked them or anything. But we just felt, 'You need to be out. You need to be out regardless.'" Linker commented that in current times he has a different perspective: "Each person has to make what his or her own best decision is and do it at their own pace."[57]

Being out was seen as essential in normalizing the gay experience, communicating pride, and raising awareness.[58] Nationally, gay organizations pushed for those who were gay to come out to promote self-acceptance and build the movement.[59] One student summed it up: "You either come out or you sort of die."[60] "I think it's kind of central to everything," Steven Weaver elaborated. "And that belief was that if everybody would just come out of the closet, it would change everything. And lo and behold, when people started coming out of the closet, it did change everything. It was exactly the process that happened. And it started with us, and people in all parts of the country, but then it went from us to . . . the next level."

Members understood the power of the media in advancing their cause and worked closely with the mainstream newspapers, the *University Daily Kansan* and the *Lawrence Daily Journal-World*. They depended primarily, however, on the campus underground newspapers—the *Oread Daily*, *Vortex*, *Reconstruction*, and others—to get the word out and draw in like-minded students.[61]

In July 1970, as the LGLF was beginning to form, the *Oread Daily*, a Lawrence underground newspaper begun in June 1969 by the Lawrence Liberation Front, a community organization, in an "effort to create a collective spirit of people working for change," provided visible support.[62]

That summer the paper featured announcements for a gay rap taking place on July 14 in the KU Student Union organized by the fledgling LGLF, as well as a meeting at Potter's Lake on July 15. In addition, there was a piece labeled "Purple Power" that advocated for the group and its goals: "In San Francisco the 'Purple Fist' are marching in militant action. Here in Lawrence the gay liberation group is forming. Get out of your head fears and realize we are in the same revolution."[63]

Another important underground newspaper was *Vortex*, which began in September 1969 and was steadily building a strong readership base of those interested in radical, counterculture issues and activities.[64] LGLF members knew that these readers were far more likely to be in alignment ideologically with the LGLF and more interested in its activist agenda than their mainstream counterparts. Taking advantage of the platform to educate, members John Steven Stillwell and Steven Weaver took the lead in writing articles for these papers.[65] Members Michael Stubbs, John Bolin, Laurie Stetzler, and others also submitted articles on current issues and events in addition to writing candidly on the challenges and joys of being gay.

The group's philosophy was also reflected in the language that it used in the media. It echoed the language members used in their official statements, flyers, and publications. One of the first statements that the LGLF published in *Vortex*, taken from GLF–NY leaflets, is an example:

> The new sexuality is helping to free men and women from the restrictive roles and repressive institutions of Amerika. We are letting go of these securities in an effort to grab ahold of our lives and know who we are. Gay men and women are coming out into the open to help shape this new sexuality. We are being confronted by an uptight, authoritarian, racist, sexist Amerika. So the Gay Liberation Front joins other oppressed brothers and sisters of Amerika and the Third World to struggle against the nightmare and create one world of people living together.[66]

Some of the more mainstream members in the group did not embrace some of this radical rhetoric nor identify with the countercultural, militant image. Nonetheless, the group was characterized by most members as "very clearly on the left-hand side of the political spectrum."[67]

Which Way Forward? Philosophical Splits

As the group continued to grow, conflict surfaced between the radical and the more mainstream members regarding the philosophical orientation of the group. The members of the 1969 radical group didn't always see eye to eye with the members who joined in 1970. "Counterculture gays were a minority within the minority," John Bolin recalled.[68] Many of the early organizers wanted the group to be more confrontational and radical in its approach, focusing on broad political and systemic issues. For other, newer members, however, many were still figuring out how they wanted to express their gay identity and were looking for opportunities for self-exploration and forming connections with others. For these members, simply attending meetings and rap sessions was a radical statement in and of itself. Bob Warren explained:

> It seemed to me that there were three factions within the organization. There were the, for lack of better terminology, the hard-core politicals who were going, "Okay, we've had enough of this shit. This is us. We're here now, and we're queer. Get over it and get on with it." And then there was kind of a midstream or a middle zone. It's like, "Yeah, I'm gay, but I'm not going to stand up on the pulpit. I'm not going to get up in front. I'm not going to be proactive and push this at other people." And then there was the third faction, who were like, "Oh my God, I can just barely sit here myself with myself . . . but this is going to take me a little while, and I don't know where I'm going to fit into this organization." . . . Some were just kind of seeking—to me, it felt like—seeking social relief in the sense that "I'm not totally alone." And I always felt like I was one of the ones in the middle. I didn't want to be out there where some of the others were on the very front lines with the flag, wearing it on their shoulder or whatever. But I wasn't back in the dark corner going, "Oh my God, I don't know how I'm ever going to get out of [the closet]."

Conflict surfaced not only within the group as a whole but also within the radical faction. Michael Stubbs, who passionately advocated for radical political action, was periodically at odds with other radical members. His intensity generated friction in the group as others felt their radicalism and involvement were "not enough" by Stubbs's standards. Stubbs's "very traumatic childhood" being gay in a nonaccepting community motivated him to find his voice and speak out against this oppressive experience, engaging in political action as soon as he entered college. He remembered it being "liberation in a sense. And so I was very passionate, and I guess I kind of expected people to be as passionate as I was, and so that created friction."

Stubbs commented on this in a letter he wrote to John Bolin in 1970. He was living in Los Angeles with members of the New Adult Community, organizers of the Urban Plunge, after being told by local authorities that he had to leave Lawrence following his arrest for a curfew violation during the Days of Rage. While in California, he became a member of the Venceremos Brigade.[69] He speculated that his passion and intensity were misinterpreted to mean that in order to be a "good enough radical," members must enact their activism as Stubbs had: "If Rick and Phil and Peter [group members and another friend] did not have the definition of 'radical gay' or 'high gay consciousness' hanging over them, if they were free to define themselves, I'm sure things would be a lot better. I think I intimidate, inhibit growth because they see me as political. . . . They think to be political they have to give something they hold dear up."[70]

Finding common ground and meeting the needs of all those involved was a challenge. Sharon Mayer, an early group member who started out as a KU student but later dropped out and became active in the community, explained: "People had different opinions about what the group was, of course. People were there for different things. . . . Some people were very conservative. And they wanted other people to act very conservatively, not the acting out, like out in public. . . . And some people thought that that was just fine. And that was who they were, and they wanted to be free to do that." Talking about different comfort levels with speaking out on issues and being visible, she commented: "A lot of people were still very afraid to be out. They didn't want to lose their jobs, have a lot of people know. A pretty wide range of how that was manifested in people's personal lives."[71]

These conflicts were not only an issue for the LGLF but also common problems for student and community gay rights groups across the country that were trying to get off the ground.[72] Differences in ideology and organizing strategies played a major role in this conflict. The tension and polarization that developed affected group dynamics and functioning. Many groups were not able to move forward, and as a result they reorganized, disbanded, or formed subgroups and spin-off organizations. Michael Stubbs commented: "Lawrence was fortunate in that it didn't succumb to the factionalism that eventually took place in many other communities. People of color, gay men, lesbians, and trans people remained together in the fight for equality."[73]

The Gay Liberation Front–New York (GLF–NY) started off as a "volatile coalition" of people unified by a common cause—to fight oppression.[74] It was organized shortly after the 1969 Stonewall uprising by many Mattachine Society "defectors" with a large focus on countercultural ideology, political action, and youth involvement. D'Emilio referred to the prevailing attitude as "audacious daring."[75] Early on, the group began experiencing a split among its members. Continual conflict regarding the group's structure and disagreement over its philosophy led dissatisfied GLF members to leave after only four months, creating an alternate organization, the Gay Activist Alliance (GAA). GAA members chose to concentrate on action over ideology and eschewed political endorsements and focus, functioning as a single-issue organization devoted solely to gay liberation, rather than advocating for other organizations. Both the GLF and the GAA had great impact but were short lived. The GLF disbanded in 1973 and the GAA in 1981.[76]

Michael Stubbs recalled the wisdom of transgender activist Sylvia Rivera, whom he met and connected with in New York, when considering these clashes as early groups formed: "Sylvia talked about it a lot before she died about how in the very beginning . . . we were all just joyously coming out, and nobody was putting down anybody, women, men, the whole bit, but then when the politics and the factions started evolving, and the different goals—that's why gay lib in New York only lasted a short time."

Understanding these organizing roadblocks with his social work background and training, Stout worked with social work student Elaine Riseman and the other LGLF founders to balance these diverse viewpoints in order to create cohesion and avoid the fallout that other groups encountered.[77] Structural features that enhanced functioning included separating the structured business and relaxed rap meetings; establishing interest subcommittees so members could be involved on the level and style of their choosing; establishing a regular weekly meeting time; and sharing leadership responsibilities. The group was described as having two circles of involvement: "inner circle" members who attended meetings and participated in activities, and "outer circle" members who attended social functions but had few other connections with the group.[78]

As the LGLF continued to form over the summer of 1970, Stout, who was co-coordinator of the group, grew concerned that the influx of new members, the philosophical split, and the surge of campus unrest had the potential to affect the focus and orientation of the group, making it difficult to coordinate. He commented: "I was hearing concerns from both ends of the political spectrum—conservative (and scared) gay kids who were concerned that the LGLF would endanger what little gay life we had, then on the other end of the continuum, radical leftists who thought we should burn down Strong Hall (or at least mount opposition rallies in front of the chancellor's office). Consequently, I took the middle ground."[79] The conflict between the members who aimed to work within systems to bring about change and the members who aimed to overthrow the system by creating a new paradigm was not only a common theme within gay rights organizations across the country but also surfaced within the LGLF.

Stout began to question his ability to lead the group and considered stepping down, but a friend in the group, Body Shop resident Riley Austin, convinced him to stay. His concern grew as the weeks went on and the tension between the radical and moderate cliques escalated. This tension also filtered down to group members. Said Joe Lordi, "Yeah, it was a lot of in-fighting. 'You don't understand this,' and 'You don't understand that.' 'It's not easy being a woman.' 'It's not easy being a gay man.' I stopped going, quite frankly, because it was just easier to ignore them all. I gave support whenever I could."[80]

In mid-September, some of the more radical members confronted Stout about wanting to take the group in a different direction. Tensions were high and Stout left the meeting feeling shaken up. The timing was less than ideal. News outlets across the state were covering the LGLF's conflict with KU administrators related to the denial of group recognition. Shortly before this conflict, Stout had come out to his parents who expressed their disapproval. They were unhappy and embarrassed by the publicity related to his involvement in the LGLF. Following this, he had a confrontation with a coworker over his role in the LGLF, causing him to leave his job.

Feeling demoralized and depressed, Stout attempted suicide. He realized that he needed to take some time off. Stout stepped down from his role in late September 1970 and left campus. Co-coordinator Elaine Riseman took over the leadership role. In his last meeting, Stout urged members to "give plenty of support to those of us who were willing to put our necks in the news" since "we, the leaders, were the ones taking the risks . . . going where no fairies had flown before, and it was damn scary for us to fly so high."[81]

The struggles of the LGLF reflect a common conundrum related to gay rights organizing and leadership: namely, determining the most effective means of change. This struggle has played out in gay activism nationally, resulting in conceptual clashes, membership instability, group splintering and closings, and difficulty in moving forward on an agenda.[82] Researchers Kristen Renn and Patrick Dilley pointed out that one's self-definition and identity related to being gay can result in very different views of the world and how to make change within it. This, then, has the potential to create tension in gay rights groups as individuals with different self- and worldviews try to find consensus in approaching and addressing social systems.[83]

Despite the ideological differences, members were able to work through them due to their commitment to each other and the cause. "When I went to my first GLF meeting, I was so relieved to be in a room where I did not have to explain myself," remembered Reginald Brown.

> I had never ever in my life been in a room of people who were queer and weren't trying to hide it. . . . The meetings were meetings, and we would go discuss stuff, and we disagreed, but you know what, we liked each other. . . . We felt relieved to be around each other. Like I said, when I walked into the room that was full of queer people, I thought, "Wow, I'm not the only one. I'm truly not the only one."

These differences may have, in fact, strengthened the group. The diversity among members generated a range of initiatives in which members could channel their energies and draw in new members and a wide base of supporters. As Hubbell explained: "We accepted each other; and looking back on it, [it] was a real strength to that organization early on. I don't think we could have done what we did without that diversity in our group."

From Vision to Reality
Launching the LGLF (1970)

more space

Over the summer of 1970, the newly formed LGLF continued to meet in Stout's room in the Body Shop.[1] As the group continued to grow and plans began to crystallize, members talked about finding a larger meeting space and becoming an official campus organization. This would provide many benefits, including obtaining space for meetings and events and the ability to request funding. The most important benefit, however, would be the legitimacy and institutional support that would come from this designation.[2] Stout speculated that the benefit of recognition was of greater importance to the LGLF than other campus student groups "because recognition of a gay organization would have political repercussions shattering the closets that gays must hide in, breaking open their ghetto, and freeing them to be whole human beings."[3]

While most members saw the value in seeking group recognition, some did not support the idea. There were concerns that the additional visibility might increase surveillance of group meeting spots, making members more vulnerable to harassment and arrests. Others in the group were more interested in addressing larger-scale social issues and felt that pursuing recognition fed into supporting archaic "establishment" rules and would deflect the group's energy.[4] Michael Stubbs recalled, "I remember this tension manifesting when it came time to pursue recognition with the University. Initially, we 'revolutionaries' didn't see the importance of university recognition in the same way more conservative gays did. We were focused on stopping the war and exposing racism and sexism and all of the other struggles of the time."[5] Nonetheless, the group decided to go forward.

Starting the Registration Process amid Resistance

In July, group members went to the Dean of Students' Office to fill out the necessary paperwork, generally a simple, straightforward process. Frank Shavlik, assistant dean of men, got them the forms and told them, "That's all that it'll take." But that was not to be the case. A short while later, Dean of Men Donald Alderson summoned Shavlik to his office, advising him to "tread lightly and walk carefully with this." He commented that "it's not going to be as easy as it usually is," foreshadowing the opposition that was to come. Their request for recognition was put on hold. In evaluating this turn of events, Shavlik sensed that most of the concern seemed to be coming "further up the pole" from senior administrators and the regents.

Stout and Elaine Riseman, unaware of this new development, headed over to the Kansas Union Reservations Office to request meeting space for the growing group. Expecting a call back from the scheduling secretary, they were surprised to receive a call from Vice Chancellor of Student Affairs William Balfour. Balfour was a well-respected professor of biology who was appointed as dean of students in 1968 and became the first vice chancellor of student affairs in 1970.[6] He was described as liberal, well liked, and an advocate for students. Balfour oversaw the group registration process. The group's request had stirred things up among the administration, and he wanted to meet.[7]

Stout met with Balfour, who began the conversation expressing his concerns related to the group's radical orientation. As they continued to talk, Balfour raised a question that was on campus administrators' minds: "'Do you think if your group is successful it will help to reduce the activities going on in and around the men's restrooms at the Student Union?'" Stout reassured Balfour that this new group would reduce the problem of bathroom cruising through its outreach and activities, serving as a benefit to both the group and the administration.[8]

The Student Union bathrooms were a known hot spot on campus. For many who were gay, years of hiding obscured more positive ways of connecting. David Radavich elaborated: "I had a friend named Brian. . . . He was sitting in the stall of one of the bathrooms and trying to pick somebody up or whatever. And the guys from Gay Liberation Front, they climbed up on the wall to this stall and they looked down and they said,

'Come out. You don't need to do this. Be friends with us. Talk to us.'"
While their approach could be considered invasive, Brian's friends were
putting into action the slogan on the flyer that led to the group's first
meeting: "Out of the Johns and Into the Streets." They let Brian know
that he had other choices, particularly the LGLF.

After learning about the purpose and goals of the group, Balfour offered his support. Stout remembered, though, that Balfour expressed
doubt that the group's request would actually be approved. Yet Balfour
painted a different picture when he told an *LDJW* reporter that he saw
"no reason that LGLF could not qualify for recognition."[9] This contradiction between his comments to Stout and to the press left members
puzzled but hopeful. Balfour explained to Stout that since the LGLF was
not currently a recognized student organization, there would be a fee. He
would, however, allow the group a free pass for their first meeting.[10]

The controversy surrounding the LGLF's application was hardly a
surprise, mired in the heated politics of the times related to the civil unrest on campus and the regents' displeasure with Chancellor Laurence
Chalmers's response. The regents had voted on a proposal a few months
earlier to request the chancellor's resignation due to their belief that he
had not taken adequate measures to keep the conflict under control.[11]
Chalmers was spared when the motion to fire him failed by one vote,
but he was shaken and in a precarious position. He needed to watch his
step.[12] KU professor emeritus and historian Bill Tuttle pointed out that
Chalmers had faced opposition throughout his tenure despite his ability
to keep further violence at bay. Dolph Simons, the politically conservative publisher of the *LDJW*, was one of the most vocal in his criticism,
frequently expressing his lack of support for Chalmers in his opinion
columns.[13]

The last thing the governor and regents wanted was another political
controversy, and they had made it clear that they did not support gay
liberation or radical ideology on any of the college campuses across the
state. The LGLF was now on their radar.[14] A letter from Senator John
Crofoot expressed the disapproval that was shared by many when he
cautioned the field director of the Alumni Association following a *University Daily Kansan* article about the LGLF: "Things like this damage the
image."[15] In addition, a Kansas sodomy law aimed specifically at gay men,
adopted in July 1969, had gone into effect just one month after the LGLF

was formed, in July 1970.[16] This contributed to the heightened concern and negative sentiment related to homosexuality at the state level.[17] KU associate professor of philosophy Arthur Skidmore, who was an alternate legal advisor for the LGLF, shared in an interview that the governor "had zero tolerance for gays, and that his position on 'sexual proclivities' was nothing but a last-minute concoction."[18] Francis Heller, who was a KU professor of law, served as chief academic officer in 1970 and knew the political climate well.[19] In a 1995 *UDK* article, he stated: "[Chalmers] was trying to protect his rear because the Board of Regents was trying to get rid of him." He continued: "You had public opinion out there that said that anyone who admitted that they were gay didn't deserve to live."[20]

This created a climate in which the administration was bound to publicly oppose the LGLF. Behind the scenes, however, Vice Chancellor Balfour continued to provide his quiet support to the group, which group members recognized and appreciated.[21] Concerned that the group could face roadblocks in moving their request forward, Balfour asked the Student Senate Executive Committee to review the request prior to the LGLF formally submitting an application.[22] Changes had just taken place with the student governance structure the previous semester, increasing students' role in campus policies, fiscal affairs, long-range planning, and the university's role in public affairs.[23] This newly formed Student Senate provided students with an increased voice in decision-making from the previous governing body and had greater authority in advocating for students.

The first leaders of this new organization, President David Awbrey and Vice President Marilyn Bowman, were elected in April 1969 to assume office in the fall of 1970. Awbrey described the way they approached their position: "We were the radicals. We were very much a women's rights thing, all the antiwar stuff." He commented that in this new structure, "students really did have real power." The Student Senate took on a liberal tone, challenging the administration and supporting student initiatives. Bill Ebert, KU student body president from 1971 to 1972, agreed: "We were definitely a left-leaning organization—the whole campus was left-leaning then so you take a cross-section of kids and you're going to be left of center, even in Kansas."[24] This liberalism predisposed the Student Senate to be supportive of the LGLF's request.

The Student Senate Executive Committee unanimously approved

the request and recommended that Balfour "recognize the Gay Liberation Front as a student organization on this campus." Bill Ebert mentioned that there had been an investigation into the legality of a group for gay people and it was permitted, leading him to state, "There is no basis for discrimination."[25] Ebert's findings are important to emphasize since the legitimacy of the organization and its right to exist were challenged for many years to come. Bolstered by Student Senate Executive Committee support and preliminary approval by the Office of Student Affairs, LGLF members then went forward to submit their application on August 1, 1970.[26]

Group members were notified by the Office of Student Affairs that their application had been received but they needed to identify a faculty advisor for their application to be considered.[27] After the *UDK* reported on their situation, faculty members came forward offering to take on this role. Group members selected Michael Maher, associate professor of physiology and cell biology, who was described as "fairly radical."[28] Having an advisor on board fulfilled all the application requirements. First-year law student and group member Barry Albin refined the application and the group's constitution to create a stronger, more compelling document, and group members quickly resubmitted their improved and complete application in August before the semester began.

Meanwhile, taking advantage of Balfour's free pass, LGLF members held their first campus meeting in the Kansas Union on August 30, 1970, and approximately thirty attended.[29] The meeting featured a group of Gay Liberation Front organizers from Minnesota who were traveling around the country to help groups who were getting started. They included Jim Chesebro, the chair of the National Gay Liberation Alliance and coordinator of the organization FREE, the University of Minnesota gay liberation group; Jack Baker and Michael McConnell, a trailblazing gay couple who challenged the Minnesota courts in their efforts to obtain a marriage license; and Jim Meko, editor of *MPLS Free*, a gay liberationist newspaper published monthly by the Minnesota FREE.[30] LGLF members had already formed networks with other fledgling campus and community gay rights groups across the country, including the evening's speakers.

This first campus meeting covered important ground and was meant to spur campus activists into action, speaking of the importance both locally and nationally of launching the LGLF and embracing gay pride, pushing for equal rights to achieve an identity "not established by straights."[31] Said Joe Prados about their impact, "At the time, they were mind-blowing for me. I was, then, completely new at this whole expanded way of being out that the LGLF was about, and here are people from maybe two dimensions beyond in outness."[32] The organizers advised LGLF members to begin by working within institutional bounds, but if that was not successful, to go forward to "expose the bigotry and hypocrisy within the system."[33] They also asked to meet with the president of the Lawrence chapter of the American Civil Liberties Union (ACLU), Floyd Horowitz, to provide information on legal precedents that had the potential to help with the LGLF's case.

"We Are Not Persuaded": Recognition Denied

Shortly thereafter, on Saturday, September 5, 1970, a press release was issued announcing the chancellor's decision that "official recognition as a student organization at the University of Kansas has been denied to the Lawrence Gay Liberation Front." The press release stated that this decision was reached "since we are not persuaded that student activity funds should be allocated either to support or oppose the sexual proclivities of students, particularly when they might lead to violation of state law."[34] The objections were devised to give an appearance of legitimacy to the homophobia motivating the decision but were in fact spurious. The group was not promoting illegal sexual activity at events and had clearly communicated its educational focus: "In order to bring about the changes in the social atmosphere under which our right to exist is free from repression, a program of educational and legislative action must be established and maintained."[35] It is important to note that this announcement was released over the Labor Day weekend, increasing the likelihood that it would not be seen or receive much attention.

This announcement was not a surprise to the group. Prior to the release of the statement, Balfour let Stout know that the chancellor had overridden the Student Senate's vote to approve the LGLF's request and had denied recognition to the group. Balfour suggested that group members call the ACLU for assistance after listening to their frustration about being blocked from moving forward. Balfour placed a call on their behalf to President Horowitz, who was also a professor of English and computer science. Horowitz had anticipated this call, having gotten a heads-up from Jack Baker. Balfour advised the group to lay low since the chancellor had shared with him that the time was not right to push for recognition. Recalling this meeting and Balfour's advice to wait, Stout quipped: "Our response? 'When do we come out?' 'How long do we put ourselves down so we don't upset someone?'"[36]

Balfour did not approve (or deny) the LGLF's request when he received it, as was the role of his office, but instead forwarded the request to the chancellor with no decision.[37] This action was not expected, given his earlier assurances to group leaders. One possible explanation for this noncommittal response is that Balfour was actually advocating for the LGLF by avoiding taking a direct stand, reasoning that it would protect both the group and the campus from backlash from disgruntled campus and community members. In fact, shortly after Balfour's comments appeared in the paper in 1970, he received the following from KU alumnus Karl E. Johnson: "I was shocked to read your statement . . . that . . . an organization of homosexuals is entitled to official recognition by the University of Kansas. . . . I cannot in good conscience give moral or financial support to an institution that tolerates such activities."[38]

It is likely, however, that Balfour was straddling the fence to avoid the conflict that was surfacing. In addition to forwarding the LGLF's recognition request, thereby avoiding a decision, he also stated that he understood "the group had made arrangements to advance its purposes through means other than achieving recognition by the university."[39] This response baffled group members since they, in fact, had not made other arrangements. They knew that their request might be denied, and they might need to prepare a backup plan, but "advancing their purposes through other means" was a last resort since they were committed to becoming a recognized campus organization. Given the animosity held by the regents, state lawmakers, and the public, Balfour may have decided to play it safe to appease both sides as the battle had begun. But by all appearances, he was feeling the heat.

And the heat was indeed rising. In addition to Chalmers's precarious standing and the general climate of unrest, Stout had been told that the regents were "incensed" with the LGLF's request. This led the chancellor to ask a member of the board of regents to check with Kansas attorney general Vern Miller to determine the legality of a gay liberation group on campus. As student body president Bill Ebert had stated, the existence of a gay group was determined to be legal. Stout confirmed this, commenting that "the Attorney General's opinion was that gay liberation was completely within the law and completely within their rights to be doing what they were doing. The Governor of Kansas was also advised of this. But of course, all of this was off the record and word of this never reached the people of the state."[40] In fact, in 1980, Executive Vice Chancellor Del Shankel reiterated to Chancellor Dykes that in 1973, "the Attorney General has told us that the matter is for us to decide." This confirmed that the administration would not be in violation of the state law if they were to "recognize the group and permit them to apply for funding from the Student Senate."[41]

The regents, concerned about the community's reaction to the group, were looking for ways to build a case against it, so this information was disregarded. Balfour had shared this in confidence with Stout to help guide the LGLF through the political quagmire.[42] Group members pushed Stout to share this publicly, but he refused, honoring Balfour's request that this information remain private.

Balfour, meanwhile, continued to counsel the group, and he raised the issue of the group's name. He suggested that members consider a name that he deemed less confrontational, such as the Homophile Study Group. Stout reported that members in attendance stifled their laughter in response to this "antiquated" suggestion. Group member Jon Blevins respectfully and diplomatically replied, "We would like to identify with all the other groups across the country which have displayed their courage by leading the rest of us to this point." Stout said further that "Balfour understood the futility of pushing his point and graciously accepted Blevins' rationale."[43] Members also did not heed Balfour's advice to lay low and instead planned a press conference to bring the chancellor's decision to light. As they moved forward, they followed up on Balfour's recommendation to contact ACLU president Floyd Horowitz to get help in challenging the decision.

On September 10, 1970, a day after the press release about the denial hit the papers, Stout and LGLF members held their press conference. The goal was to educate the campus, and particularly administrators, about the purpose of the group to "clear up improper assumptions that now stand."[44] Stating that the purpose of recognition was "not to receive University funds, but to establish that the Front and gay people do exist," he criticized the administration: "Although the function of both Gay Liberation and the University is to educate, the University is making us pay for the right to educate people." He cited as support the fact that twenty-eight other American universities had given official recognition to gay groups.[45]

The group was backed by the Student Senate, which drafted a resolution denouncing the decision as "indefensible."[46] They argued that the activity fee supported other groups that dealt with "sexual proclivities of students," including the Women's Coalition (WC) and the Commission on the Status of Women (CSW). Both were recognized student organizations that hosted seminars, projects, and programs in which sexuality was discussed frankly and openly.[47] Many, including Steve Leben, KU student body president in the late 1970s, observed that the term "sexual proclivity," which was a derisive term aimed at the gay community, was intended to target and exclude gay students. During the press conference, Stout called on the regents to reconsider their decision to deny recognition to the group and stated that the group was prepared to move forward and take the issue to the federal courts.[48]

Behind the scenes, however, the LGLF was divided. While the group presented itself as a united front to the outside world, Stout described the group as on shaky ground. He reflected that "it was probably at this point that the movement came closest to dying than at any other time because it just did not have the internal cohesiveness necessary to produce a unified reaction to the chancellor's statement."[49] The group's rapid growth brought energy and momentum but also created a divide between those who opted for working within the structures of the system and those who advocated for more radical approaches. Stout, on the advice of friends in the group, chose to challenge the chancellor through established methods such as conferring with the ACLU, holding a press conference, and citing research and data to challenge the chancellor's decision. Others in the group, however, did not support his approach. Stout recalled the reaction of Robin Burgess and some of the more radical group members in the room: "They were visibly and audibly displeased with my statements, feeling I was being too measured, too restrained. They wanted my tone to be more confrontational. Be that as it may, for the time being, my more moderate approach was the tone I set for the Lawrence Gay Liberation Front."[50]

The LGLF withstood the conflict. As the 1970–1971 academic year was underway, the group continued to grow, drawing in an estimated eighty to one hundred at meetings during the fall semester.[51] Stout stepped down from his position and left the campus in mid-September 1970, and Elaine Riseman, co-coordinator of the LGLF, took over the leadership role. Still not formally recognized, the group went forward nonetheless to establish itself and create an identity and presence in a campus culture embedded in antigay bias. They were ready to take their commitment to the next level and devised an action-based plan. This included educational programs, activism and advocacy, community engagement, social events, and support.

Learning and Unlearning: Early Educational Programs

The LGLF had barely gotten off the ground yet had already come head to head with KU administrators and the regents. Members knew that they needed to engage students in the fight, helping them understand that the battle was not just about gay rights but about civil rights more broadly. The resistance that the LGLF was experiencing in its efforts to become an official campus organization made it clear that educating the campus was a critical priority. Education was a cornerstone of the LGLF's mission. As the group's position paper stated: "In order to bring about the changes in the social atmosphere under which our right to exist is free from repression, a program of educational and legislative action must be established and maintained."[52] Members quickly developed a series of educational programs to get their movement off the ground.

Members agreed that one of the first steps in their education plan was to bring out in the open thoughts about being gay that, until now, had been unspoken. Their early conversations in meetings and at local hangouts focused on gaining a better understanding of the impact that being gay or lesbian had had on their lives. To embrace their identity and become empowered, gay men and lesbians needed to unlearn the negative societal messages that they had absorbed throughout their lives and start identifying as "non-heterosexual."[53] Self-awareness was key in this process.[54]

Consciousness-Raising Groups

Created by feminists in the late 1960s, consciousness-raising groups were embraced by gay liberation groups across the country in the 1970s.[55] Participants gathered in small groups to talk about their personal experiences, relating them to the broader systemic inequities and oppression they encountered. Listening, reflecting, and creating a climate of trust and safety were essential to the process. These groups were a central feature of the Gay Liberation Front in New York (GLF–NY).[56] Nikos Diaman, an early member, explained: "More than any other activity, they provided the foundation which supported the public actions we engaged in."[57] Gay and lesbian organizers followed the lead of the GLF–NY, forming local consciousness-raising groups.[58] As participants began sharing their individual experiences, they were no longer "the only one." These conversations would have an important role in developing a blueprint for moving forward when there were many risks for doing so.

Consciousness-raising and rap sessions were a very popular feature of LGLF gatherings and were also embraced by the counterculture activists in the Lawrence community, springing up in people's living rooms and over a beer at popular hangouts like the Bierstube and Rock Chalk Café. LGLF members used both terms somewhat interchangeably, but the term "rap session" appeared to refer to discussions that were more free-form and politically focused. Some took the form of political reading groups.[59] These sessions were described as "enlightening," "challenging," "transformative," and "life-changing," leading to a sense of pride and empowerment as well as broader political awareness and engagement, hallmarks of the consciousness-raising movement.[60]

These sessions drew in members and were identified as a catalyst for organizing and moving the group forward.[61] Prados captured the impact of these groups, commenting that they were "absolutely fabulous." He remembers that, as members got together and talked about their lives, he had the realization that "wow, people might have a different feeling about things than I do, and those feelings maybe I should consider. . . . It was just a fantastic thing for me to be exposed to all of that." Richard Linker attested to the significance and importance of these conversations: "They were an important part of making me who I am today, honestly."

Consciousness-raising sessions were popular as the group began but faded into the background as the requests for educational presentations continued to rise. Members missed the opportunity for self-exploration and reflection, so in the fall of 1974, they again became a feature of the group. Stout concluded that in their efforts to educate others, members had sidelined their own needs.[62]

The LGLF was not the only group on campus that provided consciousness-raising sessions. The Gay Women's Caucus, which began in the fall of 1972 as a subgroup of the Women's Coalition, began offering consciousness-raising discussions once a month for lesbians on campus. The caucus focused on the double oppression of being both gay and female. This core group of ten women was identified as being part of the LGLF but decided to branch off to focus more specifically on their needs and interests as lesbians. They continued to support the LGLF, occasionally collaborating on programs and projects.[63]

Speakers' Bureau

Educating themselves was only one part of the group's plan; educating others was also a high priority. With this in mind, members created the LGLF speakers' bureau. They provided workshops and presentations to organizations about the experience of being gay, relying on research and personal experience. Education was an essential first step in their strategy to bring about change. Lee Hubbell explained: "We knew we first had to get . . . you don't get acceptance. Acceptance comes after tolerance. Tolerance comes after recognition and awareness. And at that point, we were just trying to be recognized."[64] Reginald Brown agreed: "I was more interested in getting the story out that this is what queers look like and that there are probably people [like] that in your life that you probably don't even know [are gay]. Could be your mother, your father, your uncle, your sister . . . The whole point was to start to say: We are everywhere."

They also were sending a message to those who were gay in the audience that they were not perverted, pathological, or deviant, and that there were safe havens available, including the LGLF, to provide support. David Radavich recalled the impact of having gay program presenters tell their stories: "Just the willingness of people to be open and upfront about who they are . . . People would just talk about their experiences and expertise, and from different walks of life." He emphasized the normalizing effect of these presentations.

A broader political goal of presentations and events was to challenge the fundamental way in which gender was conceptualized and enacted, which perpetuated homophobic attitudes. Stout stated: "Gender is not the dictator of length of hair or fingernails, who wears skirts, pants or make-up so do what you desire and fuck your gender."[65] Members wrote articles for underground campus newspapers, identifying their rejection of gender stereotypes as central to their gay identity: "We reject strict role definitions for men and women . . . because we want to relate out of our total beings whether that essence is at times called feminine or masculine by straight society."[66] They accomplished this by overturning traditional expectations about gender expression and encouraging people to be their authentic, true selves.

The speakers' bureau quickly became an established feature of the group and continued to grow. Only two months after the first LGLF meeting, the group already had requests from three organizations for presentations.[67] As the year progressed, requests increased and LGLF members provided presentations to campus classes and organizations as well as two high schools (Lawrence and Topeka High Schools).[68] In 1971 and 1972, the LGLF continued to receive numerous presentation requests and also were asked to speak at campuses across the region.[69] By 1973, group members were reported to have provided at least two educational workshops per week in Lawrence and continued to provide presentations, trainings, and assistance to other colleges in the state.[70] The speakers' bureau was an ongoing feature of the group for decades.[71]

When asked about the reactions to their presentations, members reported that participants were generally curious and interested. Linker reported that "there was often puzzlement and even distaste from some of the audience but never anything ugly or violent." His observations led him to conclude that the presentations opened people's eyes and changed minds.

The group thrived on "teachable moments." During this time, they spoke to a number of fraternities, who were known for their antigay attitudes, despite having many closeted gay members. David Radavich explained that they periodically received harassing crank calls from fraternities, which he suspected was connected to pledging. He talked about how the group handled these: "We said, 'Oh, we're sorry that you have this concern, and we would be happy to come to your fraternity and give a presentation.' . . . Within the month that ended that kind of harassment." In light of some of the resistance they received from the Greek community, LGLF members created some novel ways of educating fraternity members in addition to the presentations they provided. John Bolin spoke of a cultural exchange that the group hosted in which members of a campus fraternity invited LGLF members to their house to spend the weekend there with them. Bolin explained that the Greek leaders who invited them were "wanting fraternity members to just be more comfortable, get to know more about our experiences."

The speakers' bureau was known on campus and beyond but also worked in tandem with a campuswide task force, the Human Sexuality Committee (HSC). KU administrators and faculty recognized the need to get in front of conversations and questions related to sex and sexuality that were circulating in the early 1970s on the heels of the profound cultural shift taking place in the midst of the sexual revolution. The HSC educated the student body about sexuality from a positive, affirming perspective. Sexuality was presented as a range of behaviors on a spectrum, and the words "normal" and "abnormal" were never used.[72] Presenters included staff, faculty, and students who were knowledgeable and equipped to handle discussions with sensitivity.[73]

Often speakers were a gay man and lesbian paired together.[74] There were twenty to thirty trained speakers who gave presentations, and the large number of requests often exceeded this pool. Deb Holmes recalled her first presentation with the HSC at a sorority her first year at KU: "That was memorable. . . . And one of the things I remember was that somebody told me that they would have known looking at me that I was lesbian because I wore the waffle-stomper shoe." When asked if she knew that a designated outfit existed, she answered jokingly, "I did not. And I probably also had on a flannel shirt." Clearly the need to challenge stereotypes began at the ground level.

Members also provided training to those in professional therapeutic fields, often by invitation, and included the Menninger Foundation (Topeka), KU Medical Center (Kansas City), and the local crisis center,

Headquarters Counseling Center.[75] This was critical since there were no established counseling or medical services in the region with specific expertise in treating gay and lesbian clients, and many providers approached the issue from a "mental illness" framework. David Radavich described their approach, as illustrated by a presentation that he, David Stout, and Elaine Riseman gave at the KU Medical Center. Since homosexuality was regarded as an illness at that time, they countered this myth with information:

> We said that homosexuals are no more likely than anybody else to have psychological problems. But that because of what we now call homophobia—we didn't call it that in those days—and the social pressures and all, they would add burdens to gay people and lesbians. . . . Our goal all along was to get people to a healthy place . . . and coming out was obviously part of that.

He went on to describe a humorous moment when speaking to a room of doctors: "One of them said, 'Well, have you ever slept with a woman?' [intending the question for the gay male presenters] and Elaine said, 'I have!' Everybody cracked up, and it was a nice moment."

Humor, in fact, was an important aspect of LGLF members' approach in getting their points across, as this anecdote depicts. Leonard Grotta, Reginald Brown, and a few additional LGLF members traveled to Emporia State Teachers College to do a presentation for a group of students. A female audience member who grew up in Kansas City asked Brown, who also was from Kansas City, when they had their first gay sexual experience. Brown replied, "In your father's Boy Scout troop!"[76] Helping participants understand that gay and lesbian people existed in the same circles but were not necessarily known to them challenged assumptions and provided a sense of normality in a nonthreatening way.

Presentations could challenge attitudes in unexpected ways. Reginald Brown shared a compelling story about the power of confronting ignorance with education. One day in third grade while walking to elementary school in Kansas City, Kansas, a group of older boys had surrounded and taunted Brown with names such as "sissy," "faggot," and "smarty pants." Brown was terrified but refused to be intimidated. Many years later, after joining the LGLF, Brown was startled to see these same bullies in the audience of an LGLF presentation they did at Emporia State Teachers College. Brown recalled, "I was able to walk in that room and not be afraid for the very first time in my life looking at these people. It was just a life-changing thing for me. . . . Walking in and seeing those boys and not having fear—that had changed my life. That was definitely the turning point when Reggie was no longer Reggie but became Reginald." When asked about the bullies' response when they saw Brown, "In fact, I went up to them. . . . They had nothing to say. It was like they literally had nothing to say."[77]

The value of these presentations in challenging attendees' attitudes and normalizing the gay experience was clear. Equally important was the effect they had on those who were presenting. It allowed presenters to publicly confirm their identity and speak with pride about who they were. Bob Warren described the experience of fielding questions from those in the audience, many of whom had not met someone who was out. Students wanted to know how Warren and other presenters knew they were gay and how they got to a point of acceptance. Warren admitted that he didn't know the answers and commented: "That helped me quite a bit in my own self-discovery and in going back within the group for our own internal discussions."

The consciousness-raising groups and speakers' bureau filled a large gap, generating new conversations on campus. Hubbell's assertion that awareness is the first step in working toward acceptance underscores the importance of these programs in providing a more positive sense of gay identity and improving the climate for those who were gay and lesbian. Focusing on education as a tool to bring about change, however, challenged the New Left confrontational focus of the GLF–NY. It reflected the competing agendas within the national movement related to the importance of promoting awareness versus engaging in militant action.[78] An argument can be made that explicitly challenging the institutional structures that define knowledge and truth, of which higher education is at the forefront, is in fact a political action.[79] Therefore, by educating the campus, LGLF members were engaged in political action, positioning themselves to transform the culture. By leveraging their authority and gaining a foothold on campus, members began a larger-scale discussion about being gay that helped advance their activist agenda.

Forming Alliances and Taking Action:
Early LGLF Initiatives

Educating the KU and Lawrence community was only one of LGLF members' goals. Another important goal was to ally themselves with gay rights movements locally and nationally to facilitate social change. These discussions led to LGLF members getting involved in political actions to bring this about. From the beginning, the LGLF was involved with the national gay liberation movement as well as other civil rights causes through their participation in key events, advocacy for public policy change, and connections they established. Some of the members of the group who were part of the radical contingent got their political start in antiwar and civil rights organizing, with Michael Stubbs and John Bolin leading the way. These organizations had an important role in gay rights organizing.[80] In March 1969, San Francisco journalist and radical gay activist Leo Laurence, editor of the Society for Individual Rights' newsletter, *Vector*, called for those who were gay to become more militant and form alliances with the Black Panthers, antiwar organizations, and other radical groups.[81]

A spark was ignited in 1969 when Stubbs and Bolin joined other Lawrence activists that November at one of the largest antiwar protests in the country's history, the Moratorium March in Washington, DC.[82] The following year, Stubbs and Bolin attended the People's Constitutional Convention, organized by the Black Panthers, further reinforcing their commitment to activism.[83] An aim of the convention was to ratify a new version of the US Constitution, aiming to bring other activist organizations to the table in these efforts. Ratifying the draft did not occur due to, among other things, problems in finding meeting places and the arrest of key leaders; Stubbs and Bolin were able to meet with other gay attendees, however.[84] Segregation and hostility toward gay liberation activists, a problem in many New Left organizations, was evident in this meeting.[85] Michael Stubbs reported: "I can remember all these Black women yelling 'Faggots' at us. 'What are you faggots doing here?'" Taken aback by such open hostility toward the gay community within the activist ranks, Stubbs, Bolin, and other KU gay activists felt frustration, determination, and a sense of urgency to organize.

These early regional and national political experiences gave KU activists a voice and expanded their grassroots organizing experience while also forging important relationships and connections with other gay liberation organizers.[86] In the summer of 1970, some of those who were instrumental in getting the LGLF started took a trip to Chicago to get some ideas. Gary Kanter described the sequence of events that led to this taking place. It started with the *Rolling Stone* cover story in the spring of 1970 about a gay campus group that had formed on the Circle Campus of the University of Chicago. Kanter shared the article with Stout, whom he had heard was trying to get the LGLF organized. Stout followed up and contacted the Chicago group.[87] That summer, John Bolin, Robin Burgess, Elaine Riseman, and Gary Kanter piled into Stout's old white Chevy, and made their way out to meet with the group's founders.[88] Kanter summed up the outcome of the meeting: "We returned to Kansas filled with enthusiasm for starting our own campus organization. It was a time for political awareness and social change."[89] Their initiative and resourcefulness were key in helping move the LGLF forward.

Later that fall, several KU students attended the First National Gay Liberation Convention, held in Minneapolis on October 9–11. This ambitious undertaking was the first of its kind and involved groups from all over the region and both coasts. It was spearheaded and organized by the University of Minnesota student organization, FREE (Fight Repression of Erotic Expression), one of the earliest gay rights student organizations in the country, established in 1969 prior to the Stonewall uprising.[90] From its inception, the convention faced difficulties. The University of Minnesota withdrew its support late in the planning, leaving student organizers to scramble for venues and funding at the last minute. After the event began, deep, contentious divisions developed between the radical and more mainstream contingents and mirrored divisions within the movement as a whole, particularly related to sexism and racism. As a result, the event was "marred by chaos" as conflict erupted among groups and attendees.[91] In addition, Michael McConnell commented that the convention "had been infiltrated, we found out years later, by the FBI, who was there to stir up as much dissention as possible." Despite this, the convention was a landmark event for the city and the nation. It was important in beginning conversations about strategies and tactics for organizing and increasing visibility of the developing gay liberation movement. It also provided the opportunity for groups attending to cultivate relationships with each other and provide support.

Steven Weaver, John Steven Stillwell, and John Bolin drove out together for the event and met up with the other ten Lawrence participants. Bolin, who wrote an article for *Vortex* about his experience, commented that "the division in us paralleled the division in all political organizations—we were all gay but with vast life style [*sic*] and political differences." Early on, challenges to the convention agenda highlighted these divisions and did not reflect the interests of the KU contingent. Bolin commented that the agenda "read like consciousness raising workshops for the Kiwanis club." Bolin joined efforts with the other like-minded radical "freaks" to reconstruct it. "Before the night was over, the group threw out the entire [FREE] agenda. Instead raps were set up about general feelings within the group—racism, sexism, plus city reports and plans for the Panthers' Constitutional Convention."[92] The leadership of Bolin and other KU attendees positioned KU to have a voice in future organizing efforts.

Reporter Lars Bjornsen stated in an article in the *Advocate* that this political split within the group created a hostile environment in which "the delegates spent the weekend trying to 'outradical' one another."[93] The clash was a microcosm of the larger problem within the emerging gay liberation movement and reflected the frustration people felt related to the power differentials that sidelined some voices over others. Bolin noted that the disregard of women within the gay rights movement was raised as a serious issue, with the small number of lesbians in attendance as a testament to the problem.[94] In an act of protest to the "chauvinism of an all-male dominated group," a majority of the women at the convention splintered off and formed their own group.[95] The Lawrence contingent, who embraced lesbians and feminist ideology, gave their voice to the call for greater inclusion of women and people of color within the movement.

Another issue raised that resonated with the KU group was "big city chauvinism." Bolin explained, "It was hard for the city people to relate to the hassles of a small town. It is easier to be open about your sexuality in a city because you can still be fairly anonymous. In Lawrence everyone knows pretty quickly. Also Lawrence has not had any place for gays to meet until GLF."[96] A Lawrence attendee commented at the conference that Lawrence "was not a united effort yet." Bolin agreed, stating that "there is no felt gay community."[97] This revelation and the challenges the Lawrence contingent encountered during the weekend strengthened their resolve to build up the newly formed LGLF to counter the lack of community at KU.[98]

An important connection that evolved as LGLF was getting organized was an alliance that members formed with activist Jack Baker. Baker was a central figure in FREE at the University of Minnesota. Soon after joining FREE, Baker assumed the role of president. He made waves in 1971 when he was elected as the first openly gay student body president at the University of Minnesota and in the country. He made more waves when he was elected to serve a second term.[99] Baker was known for taking on difficult fights. In 1970, he and his partner, Michael McConnell, filed for a marriage license, which was soundly denied. After a string of legal battles, Baker and McConnell officially married in Mankato, Minnesota, in 1971, becoming the first same-sex couple in the country to do so.[100]

Some LGLF members did not view the issue of same-sex marriage as important to their cause, mirroring conversations taking place among radical activists nationally. Michael Stubbs commented: "In the beginning of gay liberation, we wanted to shed all heterosexual norms, preconceptions about relationships and sexuality. If we were starting anew, we were starting fresh, so we could invent our own lives and modes of behavior." Jim Pettey asked: "Why would anybody want to be married? That's so heteronormative. And the whole thing was: Gay liberation, not assimilation." Bolin identified the political issues at play: "Marriage was a tool of religion and society to control people, [to] subjugate women." Michael McConnell had a different perspective on the benefits of marriage for same-sex couples: "It's a legal institution that is created for the distribution of wealth and privileges, and if *they* [heterosexuals] can take these wealth and privileges, *we* can join this same institution, and *we* can define our relationships. *They* don't define our relationships. *We* define our relationships."[101]

Baker provided guidance and support to the LGLF over the next few years. His 1970 visit to KU with other LGLF organizers helped prepare LGLF members to mount their case against the university. Baker and McConnell had ties to Lawrence, living there together for a year until Baker left for law school at the University of Minnesota in 1969. McConnell moved to Kansas City for a year, where he served as acquisitions librarian at Park College. Baker returned to KU to speak about gay liberation in 1972 when he was invited by Student Union Activities for the Minority Opinions Forum on May 4.[102]

Baker's fearlessness in challenging the courts may have helped encourage the LGLF to challenge the Kansas legislature in 1973. They lobbied against a bill that was introduced to prohibit marriage between couples of the same sex in Kansas. Regardless of which side of the issue members were on, this was viewed as a civil rights violation. David Stout and Barry Albin, who at that point was an attorney, presented a statement to the House Judiciary Committee in March 1973.[103] As an incorporated group, a designation they applied for and received in 1973, the LGLF was prohibited from engaging in lobbying and influencing legislation, but this did not keep Albin and Stout from making their statement.[104] Their involvement was not challenged and proved to be critical to the outcome. The *Hutchinson News* reported, "Two days after they [legislators] sat stunned in the presence of gay libbers the committee voted to kill the bill."[105]

LGLF members continued to be a presence at conferences, strengthening their connections with others in the region and providing ideas about creating a Big 8 Gay Federation. This early vision would be pursued through the second half of the decade. While this federation ultimately did not come to pass due to concerns on the part of senior KU administrators, LGLF members' leadership was recognized by other campuses regionally and nationally, and the group was sought out to provide guidance to other campuses in the region who wanted to establish gay rights organizations.[106]

National publications were another way that LGLF members created a presence regionally and nationally, helping put the LGLF on the map. Richard Linker talked about the group's connection to the national publication *Rural Free Delivery* (*RFD*), a journal of gay men's writings put together by Radical Fairies, a national gay movement with a rural slant. Each issue was organized and produced by different groups across the country. Linker and LGLF member John Steven Stillwell put together one of the issues. Linker commented, "That was probably part of the way we spread the word about our existence. We [LGLF] were well known." Another publication that got the word out about the LGLF was *Gay Sunshine*, a radical gay underground newspaper out of Berkeley that was distributed nationally.[107] Michael Stubbs commented that due to this visibility, when promotion for the Austin conference ran in the paper, "the contingent from Philadelphia, Boston, and New York went to it, and they came through Lawrence on their way."

The LGLF was gaining a reputation as a hub for gay liberation activists all across the country. Venus, the house where many LGLF members lived, had become a way station in the middle of the country for not only Austin conference attendees but also gay people traveling back and forth. Many of these visitors were gay liberation leaders, including Kiyoshi Kuromiya and Earl Galvin, who were nationally known as civil rights pioneers. Kuromiya and Galvin were two of the founders of the initial Gay Liberation Front of New York City.[108] Being located in the middle of the country had its advantages.

Michael Stubbs's attendance at numerous conventions and radical events played a role in the group's widespread recognition. Peter Felleman said of Stubbs: "Michael was off to various things. Events. Or concerts. Radical social feminist conferences or socialist whatever. Planning for the revolution. And he met a lot of people along the way." Felleman shared a humorous story about some of the people Stubbs had met who stopped by Lawrence. As Felleman walked past the campus library, a car of strangers pulled up. One put his head out the window and inquired, "'Do you know where Michael Stubbs lives?' [Laughs.] . . . They had me typed right away. . . . I said, 'Oh, sure,' and hopped in the car." Felleman directed them to Venus. He was amazed that they had reached out to him, a stranger, with the assumption that Michael Stubbs was so well known that a random "radical on the street" would know of his whereabouts.

In addition to providing a stopover spot for activist travelers, the LGLF also temporarily housed those needing a safe shelter at Venus. Members recalled two local adolescents who reached out using the in-house gay help line. They stayed a night or two, and members suspected that they were fleeing an abusive situation at home as a result of being gay.[109] It was extremely important that the LGLF served in this role as a safety net for gay and lesbian community members. Considering the frightening and dangerous repercussions that could arise for those who were inadvertently discovered (including homelessness and suicide) and the lack of available resources in Lawrence and the region, the LGLF's visibility could literally be a lifesaver.

Creating a Presence: Engaging KU and the Community

While national recognition was both impressive and important, the group was concerned first and foremost with being known and seen closer to home, particularly as the first organization of its kind on the KU campus. Many of the students the organizers were trying to reach were longing for connection but were isolated and used to hiding in the shadows. One of the most effective ways of promoting an organization is through word of mouth, which some LGLF members mentioned as their introduction to the group. Most students who were new to campus, however, had not yet figured out how to locate others who were gay or lesbian, so finding varied ways to reach out to them was important. Since this was a taboo topic in high schools, students were surprised and excited by the group's visibility and presence, which helped the group in its recruiting efforts.

Every fall, KU offered an event to introduce students to campus activities and resources. Groups set up tables in the Kansas Union to pass out information and interact with interested students. In 1970, the LGLF had a table in a prime spot, just inside the front door with its name on a large banner. Such a public display was a big step for the LGLF. The responses that group members received ran the gamut. Stout recalled an old high school classmate who seemed uncomfortable being in "close proximity to the queer booth" and a couple of straight guys who "reacted with disgust when they read our sign. . . . One of them said something like, 'Oh, Jesus Christ, not here!!!' and just kept on walking."[110]

Yet others appeared ambivalent, curious, and even grateful for the group's presence. For some who attended, this was the first time they had ever encountered such openness. Stout, who had just come out at KU himself less than two years earlier, remembered a male student who nervously approached the table, cautiously picking up flyers and pamphlets. After he left, Stout commented to Elaine Riseman, with whom he was working the table, "I don't think he's out yet." His hunch was confirmed when the student returned a short while later. Stout quickly recognized him as he asked, "Could I talk to someone about this?" After some introductions, they went to another area in the Student Union to talk. Said Stout: "This was his first contact with anyone or anything gay."[111]

Bob Warren was that student. He had attended Pittsburg State College (then called Kansas State College of Pittsburg) for two years after high school and had just finished serving three years in the US Army.[112] His experience at Pittsburg State was lonely: "At Pittsburg, there was no gay life." He described what occurred when he "happened" across the table after he had completed enrolling and getting his books. After picking up a few pamphlets and greeting the two people that were there, he got ready to head back to his apartment. But before he left the Union, he glanced through the pamphlets he received. Reading through them was like turning on a light switch. He had been wondering where the gay people were on campus—now he had some answers. He returned to the table and chatted with Stout. Warren recalled:

> We spoke a little bit about gay life in many different factions. Some social, some political, some of the coming out, some of finding other people, some of the discovery of, "No, I'm not the only person, and other people are really out and open about this." It was like, "Oh my God!" . . . And from there, I went to some additional meetings and then started to actually meet other real gay people, not just the accidental gay weekend person.

Peter Felleman was another involved member of the group who was initially drawn into the LGLF through an information table interaction. He remembered seeing member John Steven Stillwell, whom he knew from his film studies class, at the table. "I want to say that was the start of the next phase of my life. . . . That was a day of change, because I knew John Steven and we started talking, and it all just happened. I sort of started becoming involved. . . . That was just really, really, really important to me."

The information table served as an entry point, connecting Warren, Felleman, and others with a gay person on campus who "knew the ropes," to help them find a community at KU. Being able to find these connections in activities that all new students attended reduced feelings of otherness and communicated that "there's a place for me here."

Printed flyers and materials about the LGLF were another effective way of capturing students' attention, particularly those who were uncertain or fearful. They made a visible statement about the group and what it stood for. This seemingly basic task took on new meaning when considering the risk one took to be visually identified as aligning with the group.

On September 23, 1970, Steven Weaver and other group members stood outside the Granada Theatre in downtown Lawrence at a showing of the newly released movie *The Boys in the Band*.[113] The movie was considered groundbreaking for its raw portrayal of gay life in the 1960s, but as Weaver pointed out, it was "full of stereotypes." LGLF members were handing out flyers protesting these stereotypic portrayals. Since the movie had not yet been released, members' critique had to be general, stating: "Homosexuals in our society are consistently and cruelly oppressed by the myth that they are in some ways less than their fellow men."[114]

Weaver talked about the experience of standing on a busy street in the heart of downtown in front of the theater passing out leaflets for a gay organization. He observed, "It would be obvious that I'm gay. I think most people would make that inference.... For me, it was like pretty bold. Well, and in Kansas! [Laughs.] There's no anonymity, right? ... And you can't really be sure who you're going to hand a leaflet to." He added: "But can you imagine—for me, here I had not come out of the closet up to this point."

Passing out flyers in such a public way was a risky thing to do. And gay activism and the LGLF were just beginning to take off, so the community had had little exposure to these issues being discussed out in the open. Weaver explained what it was like not knowing the possible repercussions, particularly since a majority of those who were gay hid their identity: "You're just really putting yourself out there on the line." He remembered this experience as a "pivotal moment.... You're really exposing yourself in a way that almost nobody did." He described it as a "big day."

Others agreed that handing out materials was a big deal—a "coming out" experience and an assertion of their identity. "The newsletter was my coming out to almost everybody because I was handing out the copies on campus, and some people who I kind of knew from high school were among the people I handed them out to," commented Jim Pettey, who oversaw the group's newsletter. He went on to explain that the biggest reaction he dealt with was his own. His fear of receiving negative reactions from friends was always looming and was far worse than the responses he actually received. The relief many felt in being up front about their identity was powerful and freeing. They were creating a presence not just for the LGLF but for themselves as well.

As students took the risky step of revealing their sexual orientation at a campus info table, on a street corner passing out LGLF literature, or speaking with a classmate, many felt empowered but also vulnerable, exposed, and fearful of possible repercussions. Unlearning years of homophobic, shaming messages took time.

A Place for You at KU: Peer Counseling

A unifying message throughout the LGLF's educational programs, activism, advocacy, and community engagement was "There is a safe, affirming place for you at KU." A sense of self-worth was considered a civil right: "LGLF News is dedicated to the concept that a gay person can pursue happiness, freedom and choice of lifestyle as guaranteed by the Constitution. Enough said."[115] Gay and lesbian students had a pressing need to explore their feelings about being gay and find support, and now they had a place to turn.

Identity development is a critical task for college students. The ways in which they define themselves, interpret their internal experience, and make sense of the world colors all other aspects of their development, including cognitive, moral, and psychosocial domains.[116] This task is particularly challenging for LGBTQ students, who are faced with defining themselves within a heteronormative culture that labels them as deviant and maladaptive. D'Augelli argues that they must distance themselves from the "destructive mythology" to which they have been exposed and recognize its historical/political context in order to define themselves as nonheterosexual.[117] The rejection of the norm and the creation of a new identity, then, are central to developing one's identity as nonheterosexual. They not only have the task of defining themselves and determining how to express this definition but, in addition, must carefully consider the outcome of this expression.

This destructive mythology was deeply embedded in the culture in the 1970s. The American Psychiatric Association's definitions of mental health during this time were based on a medical model in which deviations from the norm were viewed as a failure to adapt to one's environment and an indication of mental illness. This view was facing scrutiny by civil rights and activist groups, as foundational assumptions about normality and social constructions of deviance, particularly related to homosexuality, were being challenged.[118] In 1970, however, when the LGLF began, homosexuality was still classified as a mental illness, and homosexual acts were a violation of state law. Mental health services that were affirming and sensitive to the needs of those who were not hetero-sexual were hard to come by.

Since the group began, LGLF members provided informal support and peer counseling to campus and community members.[119] They had an established, identified hotline that was widely publicized in the *UDK* and around town, and was routinely given out as a referral by the KU Infor-mation Center. Their aim: "We want to help you be you."[120] The hotline rang into Venus (and later, Bride of Venus), where many members lived. In addition, LGLF members who were comfortable in this role provided in-person support at Venus and in places that allowed for confidential conversations.[121] An LGLF newsletter stated, "If you have a problem, question, or concern, and would like to rap with a gay person or be coun-seled regularly on an informal, confidential basis, call [number listed]." They also provided local and regional gay-friendly referrals, including those for medical and legal services.[122] It was popular, utilized by stu-dents and other members of the campus community as well as those in local and regional areas and even across the country.[123]

There was a great need for this kind of assistance and support. By and large, the calls they received were from those legitimately needing help, although they did also receive some crank calls. Linker recalled, "We would get calls from nasty people, but they were actually a minority, and some of the calls were guys thinking they were being cute calling and us-ing vulgar terms for sex acts and could we accommodate them with that sex act, if you know what I mean. But most of the calls were legitimately people who were closeted and didn't have any outlet and wanted to talk to somebody."

Steven Weaver remembered a troubling situation that arose, demon-strating this need. "We got a call from somebody who read the article [Weaver's "Gay Is Good," which ran in *Vortex*] and was very upset, and he was somebody who was in the closet. And a couple of us—I think it was me and Richard Linker—we went over to his house and talked to him. It was kind of an emergency intervention because the guy was really crying and upset." Weaver put this situation in context, remembering how hidden gay people were at the time, "when so many people were in the closet and so few were not." He commented, "So this gave us an avenue to start to talk about it and start to think about it and start to act on it. And I'm very proud of that. Very proud of being in that place at that moment." For many, the opportunity to speak openly and have the "destructive mythology" exposed and challenged was the first step toward empowerment for many.

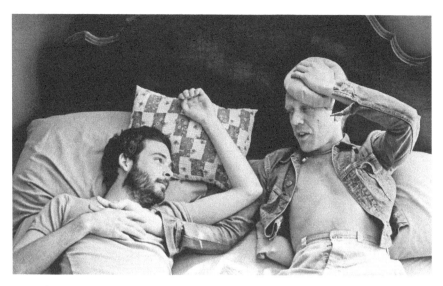

Overt harassment aimed at gay men was not often reported; however, it certainly occurred. Here, Michael Stubbs and John Bolin recover after being attacked by teenagers in Buena Vista Park (San Francisco) while sunbathing. Bolin was hit in the head with a tree limb. Stubbs was hit by a rock but escaped serious injury. Courtesy of John Bolin from his personal collection.

The house in which many LGLF members lived was originally named the Body Shop but was renamed Venus in 1970 to better reflect the sensibilities of the members. It was located in what was referred to as "Hippie Haven," where many radical, countercultural students lived. Houses were generally in poor condition. Photo by Michael Stubbs. Courtesy of John Bolin from his personal collection.

A Vietnam antiwar protest takes place near the Kansas Memorial Stadium on November 8, 1970. Courtesy of the University Archives, Kenneth Spencer Research Library, University of Kansas Libraries.

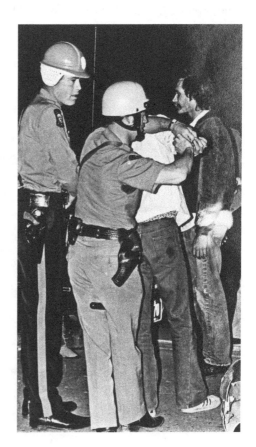

Police officers handcuff a student during the Days of Rage in the summer of 1970. Courtesy of the University Archives, Kenneth Spencer Research Library, University of Kansas Libraries.

Protesters block traffic during the Days of Rage in the summer of 1970. Photo by Steve Hix. Courtesy of the University Archives, Kenneth Spencer Research Library, University of Kansas Libraries.

A funeral procession takes place in downtown Lawrence on July 23, 1970, in remembrance of Rick "Tiger" Dowdell, fatally shot on July 16, 1970. Courtesy of the University Archives, Kenneth Spencer Research Library, University of Kansas Libraries.

LGLF members join students and community members on February 28, 1971, to celebrate International Women's Day and protest mistreatment of women on Jayhawk Boulevard in front of Watson Library on the KU campus. It was the first time this event had taken place at KU. Michael Stubbs (*left*) and John Bolin (*right*) walk with a banner, and Rick Moody is in the left foreground. Courtesy of the University Archives, Kenneth Spencer Research Library, University of Kansas Libraries.

LGLF founder David Stout during his time at KU. Stout led the first meeting to organize the group in his room in the Body Shop. Photo by Jamie Dibbins, June 1973, at Stout's residence on Ohio Street. Courtesy of David Stout from his personal collection.

John Bolin was one of the early activists who was important in getting the group started (in front of the Douglas County Water Treatment Plant, Lawrence). Photo by Michael Stubbs. Courtesy of John Bolin from his personal collection.

John Steven Stillwell was among the early activists who helped organize the group. During his time in Lawrence, he lived at both Venus and Pooh Corner (where he is pictured with a friend's dog). Photo by Michael Stubbs. Courtesy of John Bolin from his personal collection.

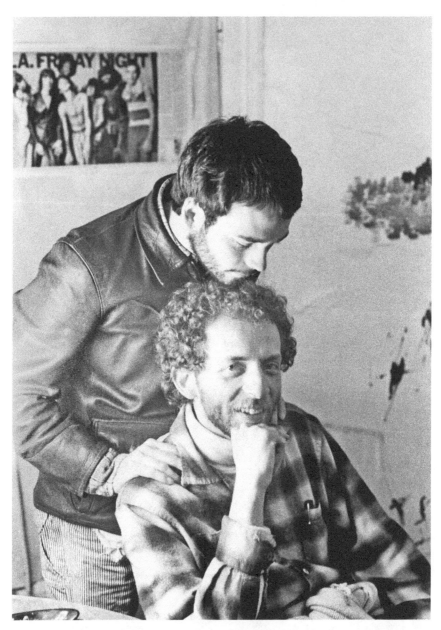

Michael Stubbs and Richard Linker (*seated*) in Linker's room in Pooh Corner. Stubbs, who had left Lawrence in 1972, had returned for a visit. Linker lived in both Venus and Pooh Corner. Stubbs and Linker were among the early activists who started the group. Photo by John Bolin. Courtesy of John Bolin from his personal collection.

LGLF member Reginald Brown (Reggie) on campus in the 1970s. Courtesy of Joe Prados from his personal collection.

Reginald Brown and LGLF member Joe Prados (*middle*) on campus with two unnamed friends in the 1970s. Courtesy of Joe Prados from his personal collection.

LGLF member Steven Weaver sits in the window of his room at Pooh Corner, a house in "Hippie Haven" where many group members lived. The poor condition and peeling paint is characteristic of the general disrepair of a majority of houses in the neighborhood. Photo by Michael Stubbs. Courtesy of John Bolin from his personal collection.

Gay Liberation Leader Stresses Point at Sunday Forum

... members of Minnesota group discuss goals with KU Front

Members of the New York, Boston, and Philadelphia Gay Liberation Fronts visit Venus after the 1971 national gay liberation conference in Austin. *Top left to right:* name unknown; John Bolin, Lawrence; David Elbaz, Boston; name unknown. *Bottom left to right:* Richard Linker, Lawrence; Peter Felleman, Lawrence; "Tall Victor," NYC; Earl Galvin, NYC; Kiyoshi Kuromiya, Philadelphia. Photo by Michael Stubbs. Courtesy of Michael Stubbs from his personal collection.

Opposite:
The LGLF holds its first official meeting in the Kansas Union on August 30, 1970. Organizers from the University of Minnesota FREE, Jim Chesebro (*left*), Michael McConnell (*middle*), and Jack Baker (*right*), lead the discussion. Courtesy of the *University Daily Kansan,* August 31, 1970, and the University Archives, Kenneth Spencer Research Library, University of Kansas Libraries.

DRESSED IN BEADS and lace, members of the Lawrence Gay Liberation Front rest after finishing a four-block cleanup on Saturday in the alley between Ohio and Tennessee streets. Equipped with brooms, rakes and large plastic bags, they scoured the alley between 10th and 14th streets and carried off sack after sack of litter. About 20 members of the front participated.

LGLF members participate in the Lawrence "Keep the Scene Clean" event, sponsored by the Women's Division, Lawrence Chamber of Commerce. Joined by their GLF guests from New York, Boston, and Philadelphia, they cleaned up alleys in the Oread neighborhood. *Left to right:* name unknown, Peter Felleman, David Elbaz, John Bolin, Kiyoshi Kuromiya, John Steven Stillwell, Earl Galvin. Photo by Tom Clark. Courtesy of the *University Daily Kansan*, April 5, 1971, and the University Archives, Kenneth Spencer Research Library, University of Kansas Libraries.

The Women's Coalition (WC) sponsored a dance on October 1, 1971, to help raise money for LGLF's lawsuit against the university. Controversy ensued when questions arose about who actually sponsored the event, the WC or the LGLF. The poster was created by LGLF member John Bolin. Courtesy of the University Archives, Kenneth Spencer Research Library, University of Kansas Libraries.

William Kunstler, LGLF's attorney, fields questions from KU students regarding the LGLF lawsuit against KU at a presentation in the Kansas Union on November 1, 1971. Courtesy of the *Lawrence (Kan.) Journal-World*, November 3, 1971, and the University Archives, Kenneth Spencer Research Library, University of Kansas Libraries.

THE UNIVERSITY DAILY
KANSAN

Bill Would End 'Duplication' In State Schools
See Page 3

82nd Year, No. 73 — The University of Kansas—Lawrence Kansas — Friday, January 28, 1972

Judge Cites Lack of 'Proper Respect'

Kunstler Rejected As Gays' Attorney

By MARTI STEWART
Kansan Staff Writer

A federal district court judge denied Thursday the Lawrence Gay Liberation Front's motion for a temporary injunction against the University of Kansas in a Topeka hearing that saw Front co-counsel William Kunstler denied recognition of the court.

George Templar the judge, told Kunstler that "in light of your notoriety" he would not recognize him and would not allow him to argue the case for the Front.

Templar said that, although the court may permit a lawyer from another district to practice in the courtroom, he was denying the privilege to Kunstler. He said that Kunstler did not have proper respect for the courts and that he found Kunstler's public statements abrasive.

Kunstler, in answer to Templar's statement, said, "I think what your honor has said violates fundamentally the Constitution of the United States. You are making a finding against me without a shred of evidence. I have never said I do not respect the law."

KUNSTLER ARGUED that in 25 years of legal practice he had never had disbarment proceedings brought against him, that he was now in good standing with several state bars and that he had had only one conviction for contempt.

"How can you possibly make a decision on what you've heard or read?" Kunstler asked the judge.

He asked Templar to give him a chance to argue the case and to judge his behavior. When his request was denied, Kunstler said the judge's statement was "unconstitutional and unconscionable."

"It is the first time in any year of my practice that I've had a judge say that," he said.

Templar reminded Kunstler that he had told Front co-counsel, Jack Klinknett, several days ago that if Kunstler appeared, he would not be allowed before the court.

KUNSTLER TOOK a chair in the courtroom and, although he did not argue the case, remained close enough to give advice to Klinknett, who took his place.

During a five-minute recess, Charles H. Oldfather, University attorney and professor of law, asked that Templar reconsider his decision.

Oldfather said, "I guess there are some times in one's life when one must stand and speak, and this is one of them."

He urged Templar to call a 15 minute recess so that he could discuss his decision with Kunstler in the judge's chambers.

Templar refused, saying, "I'm persuaded that his appearance will not help me make a decision."

Kunstler, during a later recess, crossed the court and embraced Oldfather.

Oldfather explained later that he had acted, "not as university attorney, but as a lawyer."

"I strongly disagreed with the judge's not admitting Mr. Kunstler," he said. "I guess I felt the occasion was one in which I should speak since I was present."

Kunstler arrived in Kansas on Wednesday and left Thursday before the hearing ended. He said he had to return to New York where he had a murder case being deliberated by a jury.

Klinknett, arguing for the Front's recognition as a University organization, said the members of the Front had been denied their constitutional rights under the First Amendment. He sought a temporary injunction against the University that would prevent KU from denying recognition until the case could be completed.

JOHN R. MARTIN, first assistant attorney general of the state, argued on behalf of the University that the Front had not been deprived of any rights and that it had all privileges granted to other organizations except for funding from the Student Senate.

Klinknett argued that the Front's rights were being abridged because lack of funding made it more difficult for the group to organize and to be heard by University students and the public.

Templar said that, as far as the evidence indicated, he did not see that the members of the Front had been discriminated against.

"THE COURT is not persuaded at this point," he said, "as far as granting an injunction, that the absence of official recognition of a student group constitutes irreparable damage to the group.

"The court does not see fit at this time to grant a temporary injunction."

Templar gave both attorneys 10 days to prepare their findings of fact and conclusions of law in the case. He will make a decision on the case at that time.

Kunstler Calls Judge's Statement 'Unconstitutional'
. . . Oldfather asks judge to reconsider . . .

Nixon Switches Stans To Campaign Position

WASHINGTON (AP)—Secretary of Commerce Maurice Stans stepped down from the Nixon cabinet Thursday, with the President's personal send-off, to become chief fund-raiser for Nixon's 1972 re-election campaign.

The President simultaneously announced a reshuffling of two top White House economic advisors to fill the gap. They were:

—Peter G. Peterson, 45, of Chicago, a former president of the Bell & Howell Photographic Equipment Co. He was picked as Stans' successor. Nixon said Peterson would carry on ideas he had been working on in his present post as executive director of the President's Council on International Economic Policy.

—Peter M. Flanigan, 48, a presidential assistant and a former campaigner for Nixon, who has specialized in economic and financial areas in the White House. He was moved into Peterson's spot.

Nixon appeared with all three in the White House press room to make the announcements.

He did not specify Stans' new Republican role, noting that he had promised not to discuss partisan political matters until after the convention.

Search Committee Stands

By RON WOMBLE
Kansan Staff Writer

Chancellor E. Laurence Chalmers Jr. said Thursday that there would be no change in the number of students picked to serve on the Search Committee.

The committee was appointed by Chalmers to make recommendations on the appointment of two new vice-chancellors for KU. The positions to be filled are the vice-chancellor for academic affairs and the Vice-chancellor for research and graduate studies.

The Student Senate voted Wednesday night to have David G. Miller, Eudora senior and student body president, ask Chalmers why only three of the 16 committee members were students.

Chalmers said Thursday, "I have received the same expression (that they were under-represented on the committee) from virtually every other group, which leads me to believe I have struck a point of balance."

Peter George, chairman of the Unorganized Housing Committee, pointed out Wednesday night that the Search Committee that recommended Chalmers had 50 per cent student representation.

"My responsibilities relate to more student areas than those of the Vice-Chancellor for Academic Affairs," Chalmers explained.

Chalmers said that if the committee had been appointed to select a Vice-Chancellor for Student Affairs, the student representation would have been much higher.

"In all probability any one (of the people on the committee) is capable of being far more representative than the special interest group he or she comes from."

Molly Laflin, Lawrence senior and vice-president of the student body, said she objected to the composition of the committee because of the positions of the committee members in the University structure. She said that students needed someone in the office of Vice-Chancellor for Academic Affairs who would "push for change for students."

"I think that the Vice-Chancellor for Academic Affairs should not only be able to work well with the various academic jurisdictions in the University, Laflin said, "but also strive to revitalize the educational program at KU."

"I can't help but believe that a committee composed of 12 members of the faculty and administration and only three students would consider the ability to work well with the Council of Deans, the College and the professional schools," she said, "a stronger qualification for the position than any interest or competence in the area of academic reform."

$2.5 Billion In Aid Could Go to North Viets

WASHINGTON (AP)—The United States told Hanoi envoys in last year's secret talks that Washington would be willing to undertake a $7.5 billion postwar reconstruction aid program for Indochina of which up to $2.5 billion could go to North Vietnam.

In reporting this Thursday night, administration officials said this "illustrative" figure was given for a five-year U.S. economic assistance program for South Vietnam, North Vietnam, Cambodia and Laos, once a peace settlement stops the fighting.

The aid concept was said to have been put forward by presidential adviser Henry A. Kissinger last summer after North Vietnamese negotiators presented a nine-point war-settlement plan, one point of which called for reparations to North Vietnam.

Kissinger, who met secretly in Paris with Hanoi envoys, told a news conference Wednesday that the United States felt it could not in honor agree to a peace settlement which includes reparations.

North Vietnam and the Viet Cong unleashed a barrage of criticism earlier Thursday against every major point of President Nixon's peace plan but stopped short of outright rejection.

The U.S. delegate told the Vietnamese Communists the United States will not complete a total withdrawal from South Vietnam until a final agreement is signed based "on all aspects" of Nixon's plan.

Janet Sears Speaks at Human Sexuality Seminar
Single parenthood, young marriage, abortion and adoption were alternatives discussed at a human sexuality seminar held Thursday night by the KU Commission on the Status of Women. (See story on page 2.)

South Viet Troops Engage Enemy In Central Highland

SAIGON (AP)—South Vietnamese troops stumbled on to a base camp occupied by a company of enemy soldiers in the central highlands, touching off on Thursday one of the sharpest battles since a North Vietnamese buildup began there two months ago.

South Vietnamese headquarters said 25 North Vietnamese were killed, 26 of them by air strikes, in the ensuing battle. The base camp was found 13 miles southeast of Tan Canh in the general area of the Ben Het border base.

The number of South Vietnamese casualties was not disclosed, but Saigon headquarters reported five government troops were killed and nine wounded in scattered battles across South Vietnam, in which it claimed 197 enemy soldiers died.

The Saigon command admitted it erred in reporting that four North Vietnamese tanks were destroyed in the central highlands, saying the vehicles actually were Soviet-built trucks.

But a field report later said one tank was in fact knocked out along with three trucks Wednesday.

THE ENEMY buildup in the central highlands has officials predicting a North Vietnamese offensive there, probably next month.

The U.S. Command reported an American district adviser was killed in the Mekong Delta when a motorboat was ambushed by Viet Cong troopers hiding along the bank of a canal. The South Vietnamese district chief was also killed in the ambush.

Command spokesmen also announced the withdrawal of the U.S. Navy's only remaining helicopter attack squadron after five years in Vietnam.

Bleachers Won't be Deserted Saturday
This student may think he has finally found a place of solitude for study, but the scene will be different Saturday night when the Jayhawks take on the Nebraska Cornhuskers in Allen Field House. If the Hawks win, they could tie the Cornhuskers for first in the conference. (See story page 3.)

William Kunstler speaks to reporters outside Strong Hall on the KU campus regarding Judge Templar's decision to not permit him to argue the LGLF's case in the courtroom. Photo by Greg Sorber. Courtesy of the *University Daily Kansan*, January 28, 1972, and the University Archives, Kenneth Spencer Research Library, University of Kansas Libraries.

"Hot to Trot," on January 28, 1973, was one of many LGLF dances that attracted hundreds of visitors from across the Midwest. Poster created by LGLF member John Bolin. Courtesy of the University Archives, Kenneth Spencer Research Library, University of Kansas Libraries.

Gay Services of Kansas Presents   [June 22, 1978]

Too Hot To Stop

First Annual Summer Fling

FRIDAY JUNE 22

Kansas Union Ballroom
Lawrence, Kansas

8pm - 1am
$2.00

Disc Jockey
WizarD
Playing Disco, Reggae
and Women's Music

Beer Served Until 12:00

Graphics by Sam Goldberg   Posters Compliments of **the lambda club** Topeka, Kansas

The poster for "Too Hot to Stop," held five years after "Hot to Trot" on June 22, 1978, provides a sense of the growth and popularity of these dances. By this time, they had hired a professional DJ, and dances were now being offered in the summer. Courtesy of the University Archives, Kenneth Spencer Research Library, University of Kansas Libraries.

GSOK members Todd Zwahl and Ruth Lichtwardt give a class presentation circa 1979 or 1980. *Jayhawker Yearbook*, 1980. Courtesy of the University Archives, Kenneth Spencer Research Library, University of Kansas Libraries.

Early LGLF members Leonard Grotta (*left*) and Reginald Brown (Reggie) (*right*) pose with the campus mascot, the Jayhawk, outside the Kansas Union at the "51 Years OUT" event, October 18–22, 2021. Photo by Matthew Petillo. Courtesy of the *University Daily Kansan*, October 28, 2021.

Gayla climax

A judge for the Mary Hartman, Mary Hartman look-alike contest congratulates Nancy Norris, Nevada, Mo., senior, for winning.

The contest was a highlight of the dance, sponsored by the Gay Services of Kansas, which was in the Kansas Union Ballroom Saturday night.

Staff photo by JAY KOELZER

LGLF hosted a Halloween dance at the Kansas Union Ballroom on October 23, 1976. The dance included a lookalike contest based on the popular TV show *Mary Hartman, Mary Hartman*, whose winner was Nancy Norris, KU senior. Close to fifteen hundred people from all over the region attended the dance. Courtesy of the *University Daily Kansan*, October 25, 1976, and the University Archives, Kenneth Spencer Research Library, University of Kansas Libraries.

Early LGLF members speak at a panel at the "51 Years OUT" event, October 20, 2021. *Left to right:* Lee Hubbell, Reginald Brown, Leonard Grotta, David Stout. Photo by Matthew Petillo. Courtesy of Matthew Petillo, *University Daily Kansan*.

Early women's community members speak at a panel at the "51 Years OUT" event, October 21, 2021. *Left to right:* Katherine Harris (KH), Stephanie K. Blackwood, Martha Boyd, Kathryn Clark, Deb Holmes. Photo by William Mockry. Courtesy of Wiliam Mockry from his personal collection.

The Women's Music Collective gathers for a reunion concert during the "51 Years OUT" event, October 23, 2021. *Left to right*: Kathryn Lorenzen, Susan Davis, Tamara Perkuhn, Holly R. Fischer, Julia Deisler, Deb Holmes, Mil Hood (sound). Courtesy of Deb Holmes from her personal collection.

Early LGLF friends reunite at the "51 Years OUT" event at the dance photobooth. *Back row, left to right*: David Stout, Leonard Grotta, Lee Hubbell, Joe Prados, Bob Friedland. *Front row, left to right*: Reginald Brown, Ruth Lichtwardt. Courtesy of Ailecia Ruscin, Oh Snap! Photography.

The Lawrence Women's Music Collective performs at a concert. Members include (*left to right*): Julia Deisler, Susan Davis, Holly R. Fischer, Deb Holmes, Kathryn Lorenzen, Sarah L. Photo by Kathryn Clark. Courtesy of Deb Holmes from her personal collection.

Kazoos were an important part of the Women's Music Collective repertoire and were frequently featured in concerts. *Left to right:* Julia Deisler, Holly R. Fischer, Susan Davis, Deb Holmes. Photo by Kathryn Clark. Courtesy of Deb Holmes from her personal collection.

The group Suffrage organically formed out of the larger Women's Music Collective. Suffrage was invited to perform at a variety of venues locally and regionally. *Back row, left to right*: Deb Holmes, Sarah L, Holly R. Fischer, Lynn Bretz. *Front row, left to right*: Kathryn Lorenzen, Tamara Perkuhn. Photo by Kathryn Clark. Courtesy of Deb Holmes from her personal collection, photo edited.

Kansan Photo by BOB GAYNOR

Dean Taylor Plays Coach

Ordinarily dean of women at KU, Emily Taylor donned a baseball cap Friday to coach a softball team comprised of members of the pom-pon squad. The game, against a team made up of faculty members, was one of the events at the T.G.I.F. sponsored by the Board of Class Officers at Lake Perry. Other features were bicycle races and, of course, beer drinking.

Dean Emily Taylor coaches a women's softball team for a Board of Class Officers event in 1972. She was a big supporter of the Holy Cow Creamers, providing financial assistance. Photo by Bob Gaynor. Courtesy of the *University Daily Kansan*, May 8, 1972, and the University Archives, Kenneth Spencer Research Library, University of Kansas Libraries.

Molly Laflin, a member of the Holy Cow Creamers softball team, makes a catch. Photo by Carl Davaz, a KU photojournalism student in the 1970s who became an award-winning photojournalist. Courtesy of Molly Laflin from her personal collection.

Holy Cow Creamers members wait and watch as their players go up to bat. *Left:* Marty Dunn; *middle:* name unknown; *right:* Kathy Hoggard. Photo by Carl Davaz. Courtesy of Molly Laflin from her personal collection.

Two members of the Women's Music Collective, Holly R. Fischer and Susan Davis, attend a social event. Davis opened her home to the feminist and lesbian communities, and it became a central gathering spot. Courtesy of Holly R. Fischer from her personal collection.

Janean Meigs, Susan Davis, and Toni Cramer sit on the front porch of Womanspace, a house that would serve as a community center for women. The three organizers had taken possession of the house at 643 Rhode Island Street earlier that day. Photo by Paul Dagys. Courtesy of the *Lawrence (Kan.) Journal-World*, August 28, 1976, and the University Archives, Kenneth Spencer Research Library, University of Kansas Libraries.

A property referred to as South Farm was located in a rural area south of town by the old Wakarusa Valley Elementary School. Many identified it as a place where feminists and lesbians would gather. Photo by Kathryn Clark. Courtesy of Deb Holmes from her personal collection.

Martha Boyd was a leader in the women's community and a graduate student staff member in the KU Dean of Women's Office. Photo by Kathryn Clark. Courtesy of Kathryn Clark from her personal collection.

Kathryn Clark and C. Lathrop sometime in the 1970s. Photo by Jane Nichols. Courtesy of Kathryn Clark, from her personal collection.

Stephanie K. Blackwood was a graduate student staff member in the KU Dean of Women's Office and worked closely with sororities and the Athletics Department. She held many leadership roles on campus and was involved in the lesbian feminist community. Photo by Kathryn Clark. Courtesy of Kathryn Clark from her personal collection.

Lawsuits and Leadership
Gaining Traction and Influence (1971–1973)

As the new semester began in the spring of 1971, the LGLF was thriving and growing. Members had established a speakers' bureau; brought in new members through their outreach, flyers, and newspaper presence; attended regional and national conferences; compiled resource lists of gay-friendly services; organized social events; and started a peer support line. This was an impressive accomplishment by any standard but was even more so considering that the group had only been in existence for six months, and all this took place as members were trying to establish the group while also preparing to take action against the university. Knowing the administration's stance, members decided to keep the pressure on and resubmitted their request for recognition. Again, Chalmers struck it down, despite the continued support of the Student Senate Executive Committee.[1] LGLF members were undeterred. It was time to move forward with their plan to take legal action. They formed a committee, with law student Barry Albin as chair.[2]

Members of the committee reached out to the KU School of Law and continued their conversations with Floyd Horowitz from the ACLU.[3] He referred them to Jack Klinknett, a licensed attorney who had graduated from Washburn School of Law a year and a half prior. Klinknett took an interest in the case due to his commitment to human rights and agreed to consult with members. He had, in fact, been arrested in 1965 for his involvement in the protest organized by the KU Civil Rights Council regarding discrimination against African Americans on campus and in the community.[4] Klinknett's experience, however, was limited, especially for a case such as this with the potential to be difficult and precedent-setting. This concerned group members, who anticipated a battle with formidable opponents. As Albin recalled, "we decided, as a group, that we wanted a 'name,' so I wrote this letter to William Kunstler, and asked him to come and help."

William Kunstler was most certainly a "name." A civil rights attorney with a national reputation for taking on high-profile cases, he had represented the Freedom Riders (1961) and the Chicago Seven (1969). In addition, he was director of the American Civil Liberties Union (1964–1972) and cofounder of the Center for Constitutional Rights (1966). He worked with Martin Luther King Jr. in the 1960s, assisting in legal battles that arose as a result of civil rights activism. He was known for his fearless, confrontational, "guerrilla theater" style in the courtroom as well as his penchant for representing left-leaning causes.[5]

Kunstler Takes the Case

Kunstler's visit to KU that spring to participate in a panel titled "Law and Dissent" was well-timed for the group. On March 23, 1971, on the heels of his defense of the Chicago Seven, he debated Robert Martin, president of the American Bar Association, on civil disobedience. Group members got the opportunity at the panel to speak to him in person about their case. Those in attendance included Chuck Ortleb, Michael Stubbs, Barry Albin, Reginald Brown, and Steven Weaver. Ortleb approached Kunstler after the presentation, bringing him up to date on the situation and asking him to represent the group.[6] They were committed to moving forward after Chalmers had rejected their proposal for a second time earlier that month.

Meanwhile, the case was drawing attention locally and nationally. Two weeks after the March panel and a week after Kunstler agreed to take on the case, Walter Cronkite reported it on the CBS Evening News.[7] That same month, a group of LGLF members attended the national Gay Conference in Austin, Texas, and returned fired up and reenergized.[8] In addition, they decided to continue utilizing all avenues available to challenge Chancellor Chalmers's decision. On March 29, LGLF members filed a campus grievance with the Judiciary Committee of the University Senate, charging the university with violating their constitutional and civil rights.[9] After much debate, the case was dismissed by the university on

June 29 when it was determined that it could not be resolved within the system.[10]

Group members were poised and ready to move forward the following month when Kunstler agreed to represent them in their lawsuit. Kunstler took this on as a civil rights issue, as he stated in his letter to Barry Albin, LGLF legal counsel: "I am happy to indicate to you that I would gladly represent you in your efforts to force the University to accede to your legitimate demands to be recognized as a legitimate group."[11] Ortleb commented on members' reaction: "To get a hero of the anti-war movement to take our cause was very exciting."[12] The ACLU was also officially on board and had agreed to represent the group a few days prior to Kunstler's letter of agreement. Jack Klinknett, who had been informally assisting the group, was the ACLU attorney assigned to the case, and he agreed to do backup work for Kunstler.[13]

Defying Dogma: Methodist Youth Camp

The group continued to receive a steady stream of requests from organizations and departments. In the summer of 1971, however, LGLF members received an unexpected invitation to speak at a Methodist youth camp. Religion was a difficult issue for many who were gay and lesbian. Kansas, on the periphery of the Bible Belt, had strong religious currents throughout the state. For many youth growing up in Kansas and the Midwest, religion was central in their upbringing and played an important role in their lives. As they became aware of their sexual orientation and the repressive attitudes regarding homosexuality that predominated in many denominations, many felt betrayed and conflicted. This workshop, then, was important on many levels, including the precedent it set and the effect it had on those attending.

The Baldwin United Methodist Youth Fellowship (UMYF) Institute was a weeklong event for high school students in the region and was held at Baker University in Baldwin City, Kansas. Keith Spare, who was a youth counselor at the Baldwin UMYF Institute, invited the group. "My twin brother Ken was on the Institute Board of Directors and participated on the planning committee for 1971. . . . Youth leaders were aware of the formation of gay liberation groups in Manhattan and Lawrence and argued this was a timely issue for Institute Youth as well."[14] Spare advocated for including gay awareness on the agenda and the Institute Board agreed.

They asked Spare, openly gay at K-State but not officially out to the entire United Methodist community, to find the participants. He explained: "I invited four friends who were openly gay men from Kansas University and members of the Lawrence Gay Liberation Front. [They] were radical long-haired fairies and wonderfully comfortable being openly gay. They were my closest friends at KU. I often stayed with them when attending the dances they held." Spare was looking for a meaningful exploration of the issues: "We agreed on the importance of being open and dialoging in a way that opened the eyes of all Institute participants."[15]

The four presenters—Peter Felleman, John Bolin, John Steven Stillwell, and Richard Linker—paired up, with Stillwell and Bolin taking on the first week, and Felleman and Linker taking on the other.[16] Linker recalled: "We used women's names, I think for a mild shock value and a nod to genderfuck, which if I haven't said so, was not the same thing as the discussions and debates over gender that are going on today."[17] Bolin was Crystal, Stillwell was Molly, Felleman was Pola, and Linker was Lydia. They donned dresses to go with their long hair, beards, and boots.

The four received an excellent reception from the youth, and their sessions were the best attended at the camp.[18] This disturbed the conservative church elders. Said Linker:

> I remember one time several of the elders sat in on a talk we were doing, and they often interjected a different, more biblical take on gay people. . . . That didn't go over very well with the kids. Especially this: One of our Lawrence friends came to that session with her two-year-old son. Somehow these men had found out that [she] was not married . . . and they started talking about how the baby represented our evil ways because he was a "bastard." Well, those kids were loving that baby and having fun playing with him, not to mention they just saw we lived more freely than they had been taught they could. So the words of the elders fell on deaf ears. By the way, that baby grew up to become a diplomat with the United Nations.[19]

The youth, demonstrating acceptance, care, and empathy, clearly got the message that the KU presenters were intending. Linker commented, "It was obvious we changed minds. So many of those kids were just so eager to hear what we had to say. Not just about being gay but about living your own life."

This presentation had a powerful impact on the audience. Deb Holmes, who had just graduated from high school, was in the audience for one of those presentations in 1971. She had been questioning her own sexuality. As she listened to the presentations and joined in conversations, it dawned on her: "They're describing my life." That was the turning point when she decided to begin identifying herself as a lesbian. A month later, when she stepped onto the KU campus as a first-year student, she looked up the LGLF and volunteered to help with the speakers' bureau.

The connections that Felleman, Bolin, Stillwell, and Linker formed with Institute participants were transformational, touching both participants and presenters on a deeply human level. Some of the participants, in fact, had begun to think about their identity in new ways. Felleman mentioned a gay camp participant who turned up on the doorstep of Venus, the house where many LGLF members lived, seeking guidance after the session was over.[20] Others confronted assumptions that constrained them. Bolin mentioned an encounter with a staff member who was struggling with his misogynistic stereotype of a stoic masculinity that limited his ability to connect with others. Bolin's own beliefs were also challenged, leading him to conclude that "my changes have not reached all my roots." He spoke as well with the minister's wife, who felt trapped and subjugated by her husband's possessiveness and control.[21] Her struggle reinforced his commitment to advocating for women and feminist ideals.

Their work with the youth led to many proud moments. Linker described a situation that occurred following a session he conducted among a group of African American youth. Their chaperone, a young African American man in his twenties, said to the boys, "I want you to look at how these men conduct themselves, and the pride and dignity with which they conduct themselves. You can learn from that. That's what I want to see you boys doing when you face the things you face as Black kids."[22] These conversations illustrated the synergistic, mutual learning that occurred in the LGLF's educational efforts.

Inverting Gender and Heteronormative Stereotypes

Following up on their experience with the Youth Camp, members began to more actively confront the restrictive norms related to gender expression in both their education efforts and their activism. Men and women had been engaging in nonconforming, gender-bending dress and behavior as an act of protest and empowerment for centuries. In the 1970s, however, it had taken on a new political significance that was both public and defiant. British human rights campaigner Peter Tachell explained that "the radical drag and gender-bender politics of GLF glorified male gentleness and gender role subversion. It was a conscious, if sometimes exaggerated, attempt to renounce the oppressiveness and privilege of orthodox masculinity and to undermine the way it functioned to buttress the subordination of women and gay men."[23]

Bolin recalled the evolution of male members' consciousness. Initially, Body Shop residents dressed in traditional male student clothing. Bolin was one of the first to begin pushing the envelope: "There was a small number—me included—that began to adopt feminine attire. . . . I took it the furthest." He continued: "Eventually drag was seen as a political statement. In a letter I wrote to Steven Weaver in 1972, I report on seven guests from NY that stayed at Bride [of Venus]. They excitedly shopped the jewelry sale at Woolworths [in Lawrence]. Confrontation, upending conventions were part of it. Also it was declaring queer identity, as far from the closet as possible."[24]

One of the ways male members accomplished this was by deliberately sending mixed messages about their sex through their attire, which some in the group referred to as "drag" and others as "genderfuck." Even though many used these terms interchangeably, they in fact were different. "Drag" referred to exclusively adopting women's dress, makeup, and other aspects of female appearance, often for performance but also as a statement of resistance.[25] "Genderfuck," which evolved out of the Gay Liberation Front–New York, involved men wearing both male and female clothing items.[26] Many would be attired in a dress and jewelry while wearing combat boots and jeans, sporting long hair and a beard as a defiant act.[27] While this was a deliberate action for Bolin and others in the group, it had a different meaning for other members. Stubbs commented, "We just did it because it was the fad among the Yippie politics of the time. We didn't think a lot about it." Fad or not, this became a high-profile issue for the group.

As the group continued, they challenged conventional attitudes about gender and sexual orientation, sometimes without saying a word. "We were very much into 'shock and awe,' to use a phrase," Hubbell elaborated.

"Like getting some of the guys who really liked to go out in drag . . . and then walking into Sambo's Restaurant [a popular Lawrence restaurant at the time], in drag, just to see how people reacted. [Laughs.]" Many stories were shared of male members wearing a dress or skirt to LGLF meetings, protests, and walks on campus.[28]

They also brought this presence to the community. A notable example was the LGLF's involvement in an annual Lawrence event, "Keep the Scene Clean," sponsored by the Women's Division of the Lawrence Chamber of Commerce.[29] This springtime community project involved cleaning up the alleys in the Oread neighborhood. The group participated in early April 1971.[30] Michael Stubbs signed up the group, thinking that it would draw attention to existing restrictive gender norms and elevate the LGLF's presence in the community. Peter Felleman remembered them picking up trash and cleaning the alleys with rakes, brooms, and shovels in their housedresses and aprons. Sharon Mayer added: "That was a big deal because Gay Liberation was very visibly represented . . . and it was a big hit."[31]

Challenging the status quo was a way of life for members. Richard Linker talked about going out on Friday nights to "liberate" the Bierstube or the Rock Chalk (local bars):

> The group of us would go up there, openly gay, and there might have been times when guys even wore a dress or two. . . . And we'd make our presence known. Not, like, confrontationally or anything. We'd just go up there and drink beer and laugh and talk to people and stuff and made no bones about . . . we were obviously gay. And I don't remember any unpleasantry in any of those situations.

Another way the LGLF challenged the status quo was to stage mass public displays of affection in residence hall lobbies. Donna Shavlik, who was assistant dean of women at the time, recalled several of these events occurring in the largest of the campus residence halls, McCollum Hall. They were not well received. This was clearly a political act, intended to disrupt conventional norms, get people's attention, and make a statement: "It was kind of an 'in your face' sort of thing." Shavlik explained that this evolved from a sense of frustration "with people's rights being trampled on in every way. It was important to them to be really public." She saw it as an assertion: "We're not going to go away, and we're going to be who we are in public." Later on in the 1990s, "kiss-ins" would become common forms of protest for the KU group and for other groups across the country.[32]

Presence and visibility were ongoing themes of the group. Hubbell went on to describe another example of a "shock and awe" challenge to the invisibility of gay culture at KU, when group members made a celebratory statement in Joe Prados's racy Camaro convertible as they drove on campus: "[We were] going down Jayhawk Boulevard yelling and screaming. . . . He had one of these Indianapolis pace cars that was really super. . . . Wherever it went, it stood out, and then to just be filled with a bunch of flaming queens, yelling and screaming, 'Yoo-hoo.' And just doing everything that was the stereotype." Inverting the stereotype in a very public way was a radical subversive act, challenging assumptions about gay identity and its presentation. Hubbell commented that after events such as these, people would sometimes comment, "I didn't know you were gay," implying that one could determine a person's sexual orientation by their appearance. Stating that he "apparently didn't fit the stereotype," Hubbell used the opportunity to expand people's restrictive notions of what it meant to be gay.

The range of the group's political acts as well as their boldness and creativity were instrumental in breaking down barriers and empowering those who were gay to connect with others. Kathy Hoggard, director of the KU Information Center in the early 1970s, credits the progressive campus and Lawrence culture for providing the support to move the group's efforts forward.[33] Hoggard, who was an activist and keenly aware of campus and community networks, observed: "If you were going to be progressive in any way, whether it was as a woman or as a gay person, or as a political animal, the KU campus was the icing on the cake, the place to be." She added that this progressive attitude was not commonly held throughout the state, with clear lines being drawn: "You would expect to find that here in that time but get twenty feet out of Lawrence or even off the campus and that crucible of progressivity [disappeared.]"

For some gay and lesbian students who grew up in communities that were on the other side of the political line prior to arriving in Lawrence, the progressive KU climate got them fired up and engaged. For others, their desire to change the world was not the driving force that led them to the group; it was the desire to overcome isolation, fear, and shame.

Leonard Grotta commented, "I think that as far as the motivation of most individuals, it was social and personal. You know, 'Oh, boy, I'm not the only one. I have a community out there and maybe I can meet someone.'" David Radavich agreed: "People were there to find support and solace and a space of comfort and welcome." This "space of comfort and welcome" that the LGLF provided for group members was itself political. Considering the feminist slogan coined in the late 1960s, "the personal is political," the personal feelings of isolation and loneliness that drew many members to the LGLF led them to explore the political underpinnings of these feelings, leading to an awakening of political consciousness and greater involvement.[34]

Meanwhile, word about the group had traveled. Hubbell recalled the many informal social gatherings and parties that had begun to spring up, commenting that "everybody then on campus knew LGLF." There was a growing sense of community. "As professors joined in, they would open their homes. . . . And that's where other people [said], 'Well, bring somebody new.' So it was indirectly because we existed, then other people started coming out of the closet."

In less than a year's time, the LGLF had done something few other groups across the country had achieved: it mobilized and catalyzed projects that already were having an impact on the campus climate. Members had not only laid the groundwork for their impending lawsuit but had also expanded their educational reach and activism. They were getting noticed and had begun forming a community.

The LGLF's Second Year: The Conflict Intensifies

The LGLF was beginning its second year on campus. Much had changed since the group began one year earlier: the voting age had been reduced from twenty-one to eighteen; the Apollo 14 moon mission had launched; and public opposition toward US involvement in the Vietnam War had grown. A quick glance at the *UDK* headlines in the first month of the semester indicated that KU enrollment had declined, students were not signing up for leadership positions as in years past, and the Greek system was being questioned.[35] One thing was apparent from these headlines: the climate was shifting and students' interest in civic engagement and activism was on the downturn. The LGLF, on the other hand, was seeing a different trend. There were no fewer than eight articles on the group in the *UDK* in this first month. The group had become a known entity.

At the first Student Senate meeting of the academic year, September 15, 1971, Senate members made a bold move and recognized the LGLF as a "legitimate student organization." This was close to a year after their first attempt. At the following meeting on September 29, Chancellor Chalmers rejected the request, the third time he had done so. He defended his decision, stating his belief that "colleges and universities needed to remove ourselves institutionally from involvement in the individual sexual proclivity of our students." This was referred to as "one of the most controversial issues at KU during the fall semester."[36]

Despite this snub, LGLF members were feeling emboldened and empowered by the support and affirmation they had received from Kunstler, the ACLU, and the Student Senate, in addition to the national news coverage of the impending lawsuit. Using as leverage the support they had garnered among Student Senate leaders and the growing discontent related to Chalmers's leadership, they decided to take a radical step, turn up the flame, and push back against Chalmers's decision. Members submitted a petition to the Student Senate to be reimbursed $600 for the group's anticipated court costs. Kunstler did not charge the group for his work; nonetheless, there were some fees for which it would be responsible. The Student Senate voted forty-five to twenty-three in favor of allocating the funding from a non–state-funded account over which they had authority.[37]

This should not be construed as a blanket endorsement of the LGLF by Student Senate members, however. While there was a great deal of support for the LGLF and gay rights in general by Student Senate members, there were also those who were in opposition.[38] With the increased focus on the group in the *UDK*, there was an influx of letters both pro and con, creating a heated dialogue. Some of the letters were even hostile. Writers argued sarcastically that if the Student Senate provided funding to the LGLF, they should also provide funding for the "Pretty Prostitutes of Potters," "Shaft Union—for anyone getting the shaft," and a number of other groups, including "the Heterosexual Liberation Front" and "the People's Popular Perverts for Liberty."[39] These mocking and derisive comments were an indication of growing resentment as the group had become more assertive in lobbying for equal treatment.

The passage of this resolution represented support and endorsement of the LGLF among some Student Senate circles. For others, however, their vote had a different intention: to assert their authority and snub the chancellor. An open forum was scheduled to reach a final decision.[40] In a letter to the editor in the *UDK* prior to this meeting, LGLF member Denis Brothers argued for the "student rights position" to appeal to a wider constituency. He asserted that approving the funding request was

> vital to secure the just rights of all students at this and other universities. . . . The controversiality of the group involved is immaterial. . . . Student Senate should thus reject the recommendations of the finance committee and show that it is really concerned with the rights of students and is not merely a pusilanimous [*sic*] assemblage unwilling to stand by the principles of justice in the face of controversy.[41]

The justice language and philosophy in this statement communicated group members' intention for this request to be a statement about reclaiming their rights. While the group had a pressing need for funding, it was not the primary motive for this request. It was a way to up the ante and further expose the university's discriminatory attitudes toward the gay and lesbian community. Student senator Mike McGowen stated in a *UDK* letter to the editor: "The issue should NOT be money but RECOGNITION." He chided Chalmers for his repeated rejections: "It comes down to the fact that a group of STUDENTS has formed a legal group, gone through the legal channels, gained unanimous Student Senate support for recognition three different times." He concluded: "This group has every right to be recognized and not be discriminated against."[42] During a heated discussion at a Student Senate meeting to resolve the issue, an individual identified as a Gay Lib[43] spokesperson said, "I see no reason why we can't have funds. Even without funds, the symbolic value [of recognition] is something to fight for. The administration can't run over students anymore, not even gay ones. The Student Senate should take a stand against ignorance. Are student rights a sham?"[44] The Student Senate voted to pass the funding request and resolution. The chancellor, however, was resolute in stating he would veto them. And he did.[45]

In solidarity and support, the Women's Coalition reserved space for a dance in the Kansas Union on October 1 to raise money for legal fees for the LGLF's lawsuit. They were approved to use the space, but during a Student Senate meeting that followed, Women's Coalition members stated that they had "acted on behalf of the Gay Lib group."[46] The appearance of deception, whether intentional or inadvertent, raised Chalmers's ire, and he put the dance on hold. Concerned that the Women's Coalition was serving as a "front" and the dance was really being sponsored by the LGLF, Chalmers charged that the LGLF had violated student organization funding regulations.[47]

Chalmers called a special meeting with the University Events Committee and the University Senate Executive Committee (SenEx) to review the request, which was termed "an unusual action." After the meeting got underway, the Women's Coalition was asked to send a member. Functioning as a collective, members argued that they would need to send a group. As they headed over to the chancellor's office, they picked up additional students on the way. A few met up with Chalmers, who was giving a presentation at the Kansas Union. They requested that he return to his office to discuss the dance. He agreed, "despite yesterday's exhausting experiences of insults around the gay issue . . . and the tragedy of Women's Coalition being duped by Gay Liberation." A reporter for the campus underground newspaper, the *Gay Oread Daily*, astutely observed, "It apparently didn't occur to him that many gay people are women—that the organizations overlap, and that, hence, 'duping' is rather an impossibility."[48]

SenEx Committee member George Laughead recalled the scene: "We were all in Chalmers's office. . . . It was filled up with the Gay Lib people because Larry Chalmers had stumbled a bit in his judgment and canceled the Gay Lib dance." Laughead noticed when he went out to encourage the group to disperse that "I didn't recognize a lot of the people. They weren't the same people that were hanging out at the Rock Chalk."[49] Laughead's observation that new people had joined in the confrontation was actually quite significant. The group had become visible and gained some political clout, expanding its reach to include those outside the activist circle, drawing in supporters, and engaging the community in the cause. Despite numerous questions about "petty details," a heated debate, and a confrontation with the chancellor, the SenEx Committee voted eight to four to approve the request.[50]

The *UDK* skirted around Chalmers's "duping" charge, stating: "Because of deceptive publicity the dance was misunderstood to be [a] function sponsored by the Gay Lib."[51] Whether deception occurred or not depended on which side of the argument one was on, but characterizing it as a misunderstanding provided an out for the decision-makers so they could move past the impasse and resolve the conflict. Approving the request was not the only positive outcome of this meeting. It also provided Women's Coalition members with an elevated platform, which was welcomed: "Just the fact that Women's Coalition/Gay Lib caused [s]o much upset is significant—we are being heard and making ourselves visible."[52] The dance was highly successful, drawing in a substantial crowd of approximately four hundred and raising nearly $185.[53] It also increased awareness and visibility of the group while launching what would become one of their most important signature programs.

Meanwhile, preparation for the impending lawsuit was progressing. Kunstler spent some time with group members figuring out a strategy. Richard Linker shared a story about an early meeting that "stunned and surprised" members: "[Kunstler] came to Bride of Venus. We all went up and sat down around the kitchen table, and what I remember is the first thing … after introductions … he pulled out the joint [from his pocket] and we smoked the joint with him." One might say that Kunstler "spoke their language." There were no reports of a repeat performance. On November 1, after meeting with key LGLF members earlier in the day, Kunstler met in the evening with approximately 120 students about the importance of the case. Kunstler stated that the case was "important for freedom of speech, freedom of association and for a 'well-rounded atmosphere' at KU." He anticipated that it would have a "vast effect."[54]

It is important to mention that in the fall of 1971, the Union Operating Committee reversed the ruling that unrecognized campus groups could not reserve rooms in the Kansas Union, and the LGLF was able to use this space for meetings.[55] It is not clear, however, what this entailed. There is some evidence that the group continued to be charged for renting the ballroom for dances and maintaining their office.[56] Some anticipated that this policy change would cause LGLF members to withdraw their suit, and dissuading the group from pursuing the lawsuit may have been the impetus for the Union policy change. LGLF legal chair Steven Weaver clarified, however, that this was no longer the primary issue in the complaint: "The University has violated not only the freedoms of speech and assembly but also those of student rights and responsibilities."[57]

There was further momentum the following year to change the organization registration system.[58] On February 20, 1972, the Student Executive Committee (StudEx) approved a proposal to delete the category
"recognized" from the policy, changing the two-tiered registration process to one. All groups who registered with the university could then
apply for funds if they could demonstrate that requests were for educational, recreational, or cultural purposes.[59] The LGLF battle was behind
the decision to pursue this change, as Balfour revealed in a letter to Vice
President of Student Affairs Robert Zumwinkle, University of Kentucky:
"We have been working on a formal statement about registration and recognition. As you could probably guess, Gay Lib essentially forced us into
this distinction (although we haven't told them that)."[60] The appearance
of a concern about fairness was in fact a veiled attempt to take care of the
"LGLF problem."

After the proposal was approved, however, there was controversy. The
LGLF and the administration both raised concerns. The LGLF opposed
the proposal on the grounds that it was "ineffective because the Chancellor and the Board of Regents still have the final word."[61] On the administrative side, Oldfather expressed concerns that the inclusive language
was too broad and the funding categories—cultural, educational, and recreational—were not clearly defined. Balfour emphasized that what had
been approved was a proposal only and still needed to be approved by
administration (a point not mentioned in earlier articles and interesting
to note considering his comments to Zumwinkle). He said he would not
approve the policy without changes.[62] There were no further articles on
the issue in the *UDK* through the following academic year, leading to the
conclusion that this proposal was not approved and died a quiet death.
The two-tiered process, in fact, was still in effect when David Ambler
assumed his post as vice chancellor for student affairs in 1977.[63]

Following this 1972 proposal, the LGLF was granted "registered" status.[64] While in concept this looked like a step forward, the additional
benefits it provided to the group were limited. Many continued to view
the group's activities as promoting sexual activity rather than providing
education, awareness, and advocacy. Falling back on the "sexual proclivities" clause, many Student Senate members used this to justify rejecting
the group's requests.

The media coverage of the group while the lawsuit was proceeding pointed to an important perceptual shift. An *LDJW* reporter covering Kunstler's impending visit to KU to discuss the lawsuit described the LGLF as "an organization moving toward legal equality for homosexuals."[65] While this description does not appear radical by conventional standards, it was a change in tone from the description a year earlier, "the organization for Homosexuals."[66] Instead of the group being solely defined by members' sexual orientation, the focus had shifted to its goals and purpose. The LGLF's lawsuit appeared to have raised the community's awareness of the group's broader civil rights focus, elevating the group's credibility.

The *UDK* likewise was broadening its scope. Just a few months after the LGLF publicly began discussing the lawsuit, a story on recognizing gay liberation groups on campuses in the Big 8 Conference appeared in the paper.[67] By raising the recognition issue as regional rather than just local, it gave more importance and significance to the LGLF's battle. In the same vein, during this time frame there was an increase in the number of articles on the LGLF in the *UDK* from eleven in 1970 to thirty-four in 1971. As gay rights issues were becoming more prominent and visible locally and nationally, it could be argued that the LGLF had a role in raising awareness and bringing these issues forward for local media.

The Lawsuit Heads to Court

As the new year was underway, the LGLF was moving forward. Members were ready to proceed with their lawsuit, particularly now that Chalmers had refused to grant the group official recognition three times. The lawsuit had been filed on December 15, 1971, with the US District Court in Kansas City, and a hearing had been scheduled for the beginning of the spring semester, on January 26, 1972.[68] There were two parts of the suit. The first was a request for a preliminary injunction to give recognition to the LGLF while the case was going on. Klinknett stated that this request was being made to stop "irreparable harm to the organization," arguing that the group needed access to student funds, a campus office, and listings in campus publications to function and meet its goals.[69] The second part of the lawsuit was a declaratory judgment regarding the constitutionality of the university denying recognition of the group. This would be heard at a separate date.

The suit named Laurence Chalmers, chancellor, and William Balfour, vice chancellor for student affairs, as defendants. Coplaintiffs in the suit included three students who were LGLF members: John Steven Stillwell, Steven Weaver, and Joseph Prados, and four additional students: Ronald W. W. Schorr, Chris Isaacs, Dennis Embry, and Ann Poppe.[70] In addition, six faculty members were coplaintiffs: David Willer, associate professor of sociology; John Wright, professor of psychology/human development; Michael Maher, associate professor of physiology and cell biology; Arthur Skidmore, assistant professor of philosophy; Donald Marquis, assistant professor of philosophy; and Kemp Houck, assistant professor of English. The faculty members' primary reasons for participating were to support freedom of speech and expression and to object to Chalmers's stand on the issue. Maher, the group's first advisor, also stated a desire to support sexual freedom and gay rights. Marquis explained: "A university is supposed to be an example of a society open to all views. Refusal of recognition is a denial of the policy of allowing all to be heard."[71]

The case got off to a rocky start. Scheduled to be heard on January 26, 1972, in the US District Court in Topeka, it had to be rescheduled to the following day since both plaintiffs' attorneys did not show up. Klinknett mistakenly went to the Kansas City courthouse rather than Topeka, and Kunstler's plane was delayed.[72] As the hearing began, Judge George Templar, who had warned that he might deny Kunstler entrance to the courtroom if he were to attend the hearing, followed through on his warning.[73] Templar addressed Kunstler before the proceedings began: "The court finds that your attitude toward the courts and judges is one of utter disdain. You have gone all over the country deriding the judiciary system. . . . I will not let you appear in this case."[74] According to Kansas law, an attorney who was not licensed in the state could not present a case in the Kansas court unless accompanied by an attorney with a current Kansas license. Since Kunstler was not licensed to practice in the state of Kansas, Templar used this to justify his decision to ban him from the courtroom, despite the fact that he was accompanied by Klinknett, who was licensed to practice in the state. Kunstler was prohibited from presenting arguments for the case or sitting with the LGLF legal counsel. Klinknett pointed out: "It was the only time in Kunstler's entire career where he was denied priory, the right to give effective representation of council to his client in any court, in any state."

Visibly upset, Kunstler reached out to Charles Oldfather, the university attorney who was representing the opposing side, for help. Oldfather, who was present in the courtroom, was representing the university but nonetheless recognized Templar's unfair decision. Oldfather, admitting his nervousness, stepped out of his role as KU attorney and appealed to Templar as a member of the American Bar Association to reconsider.[75] Oldfather, who demonstrated considerable courage and integrity in his decision to step forward, commented: "I may be fired tomorrow. I guess there are times a man must stand up and speak, and this is one of those times."[76] Tuttle commented on the powerful impact of the moment following Oldfather's statement when Kunstler, touched by his comments, reached out and embraced Oldfather in appreciation.[77]

Templar refused to change his decision. Klinknett, who had been working with Kunstler to prepare the case, had to take over. Remembering that day in court, Klinknett commented that as a law professor and seasoned attorney, Kunstler "knew his stuff. I didn't. I was still prepared to argue and represent my clients, and I did a horrible job of it." Nonetheless, Klinknett did not think that this mattered much, since "the arguments were already in front of the judge. . . . And so it wasn't that it was a critical issue how well I articulated . . . our case." He concluded, "It was a frightening moment to say, 'Well, you're the one that's going to have to saddle up and get on that horse and ride it toward that there cliff' [laughs]."

Klinknett viewed the administration's defense as politically motivated, emanating from the considerable pushback from alumni and community members who disapproved of the group, "so they took a position that I found almost absurdly thin and weak." Klinknett stated that the defendants' objections to the LGLF arose from concerns that official recognition would position members to use funds for morally inappropriate purposes; that "they cannot be trusted not to use these student-wide funds for prohibited purposes or for what we find distasteful in our imagination . . . That was their stand." Klinknett argued that the defendants had obstructed the group's First and Fourteenth Amendment rights, specifically freedom of speech and guaranteed rights, due process, and equal protection. He called for an injunction. In addition, Klinknett argued that KU had "violated the basic concept of a university as an institution dedicated to free inquiry and investigation and the expression of opinion free from restriction, such conditions being essential to the meaningful conduct of education and research."[78]

John R. Martin, the first assistant attorney general for the state who was representing the defendants, countered that the LGLF had been granted access to most of the benefits of recognition, including space for meetings. This statement, however, did not acknowledge the disadvantages that LGLF members faced without full access, including the inability to apply for funding or reserve space more than seven days before an event.[79] In addition, the LGLF was charged fees for space usage and was not listed with other campus organizations, limiting its visibility.[80] Most glaring, however, was the implication that the group was not worthy of equal treatment due to members' "sexual proclivities," a homophobic term that had been used exclusively for this group. Martin argued that Templar's decision was appropriate since sexual acts between members of the same sex were illegal, and the university was abiding by the law.

This "morality" defense, however, ignored that the group's primary focus was educational, and that the LGLF had no plans to offer events in which students would be engaging in sexual acts. The fact that similar groups addressing sexuality issues, such as the Women's Coalition, were granted recognition was also ignored. Both of these points were addressed in the document submitted to the court.[81] Templar denied the LGLF's request for an injunction, arguing that there was insufficient proof that the group would suffer irreparable harm if the injunction was not granted.[82] The court also rejected the writ of mandamus that was submitted to the Tenth Circuit Court of Appeals in Denver challenging Kunstler's exclusion from the trial's proceedings.[83] The case received national media attention, both decrying and applauding Templar's decision.[84] In his opinion page column in the *LDJW*, "Two Centuries Later," KU first-year student Paul Carttar argued that Templar "was afraid of embarrassment and loss of respect that Kunstler might cause him if allowed to argue," fearing he would become "another Julius Hoffman and Topeka another Chicago."[85]

The LGLF received another blow a few weeks later, on February 10, when Judge Templar ruled against the group's case. Claiming that no discrimination had taken place, Templar supported Chalmers's actions. The wording of his statement revealed the homophobic attitude that had played into his decision: "It is not difficult to understand the concern of

Chancellor Chalmers and his conclusion that school funds should not be made available for the purpose of opposing or supporting the discussion of bizarre sexual activities for which plaintiffs apparently seek formal and public approval."[86]

LGLF members were bitterly disappointed but regrouped and considered their next steps—should they put the lawsuit behind them or appeal the decision? Convinced that the university had violated their civil rights, they concluded that they wanted to appeal. They lost no time and met with Klinknett on February 16, less than one week after the decision, to discuss their strategy. First and foremost, they needed to secure funding to move forward. An ACLU decision helped them formulate a plan. Following Judge Templar's ruling, the Lawrence chapter of the ACLU adopted a resolution on March 5, 1972, condemning the denial of the LGLF's lawsuit against the university. Floyd Horowitz, ACLU chair, said Templar's decision was a "direct threat to the civil liberties guaranteed by the Constitution." This provided LGLF members with their next step. In honor of this resolution, the LGLF hosted a dance "In Celebration of the First Amendment" on March 10 in the Kansas Union Ballroom. This would help them generate funds for their appeal.[87]

LGLF Dances: "The Hip Place to Be"

While the primary motivation for sponsoring the March 10 dance was financial, members also felt it would be an excellent way to bring people in the community together. In addition, this dance and the ones that would follow served a subversive purpose, "challenging heterosexual norms of propriety, dress and behavior."[88] Proms and dances have had an interesting history, evolving from debutante balls of the nineteenth century, in which young women of means "came out" to society and potential suitors. These dances provided an outlet for young men and women to explore their sexuality in an environment that was considered socially acceptable. They also reinforced narrow margins of acceptability, promoting mainstream cultural values related to class, race, gender, and sexuality. As such, dances have served to not only enhance social standing among students in the dominant culture but also provide an opportunity for resistance by those outside of these margins. In fact, there was a student movement in the 1980s in high schools to hold alternative gay proms to protest the exclusion of gay, lesbian, and queer students from mainstream traditions and rites of passage.[89]

Following the lead of gay activists who engaged in the tactic of asserting their presence in heteronormative spaces, gay and lesbian students in the 1970s reclaimed dances to provide more positive social alternatives to shady pickup spots, mafia-owned bars, and public bathrooms.[90] And it is particularly relevant that the gay community co-opted the concept of "coming out," challenging the underpinnings of privilege, power, and traditional conceptualizations of gender and sexuality. But dances, in addition to being a political statement, were also about connection, celebration, and acceptance. All were welcome—gay and straight, campus and community members, in street clothes or in drag. This was one of the few environments in which all expressions of gender and sexuality were accepted. Dances were the most popular activity of campus gay groups across the country.[91]

Lee Hubbell spearheaded the event with the involvement of Joe Prados, among others. Hubbell, who had completed his bachelor's degree at KU in 1968 and then pursued graduate studies at Indiana University (IU), had just returned to KU as a graduate student to study the emerging field of computer science. After having coordinated dances for nongay organizations at IU, he thought this would be a good way to raise funds for the LGLF. Frank Burge, director of the Kansas Union, had generously made special arrangements to provide space to the group, but Hubbell commented that they needed to be able to pay at least twenty-five dollars a month.

Hubbell shared how this unfolded. "OK, now we're going to have a dance and so everybody at this dance are queers. And it's in the Union Ballroom. So everybody on campus can see it. [Laughs.] That's visible." The fear of hostility hovered over their heads. "Do we really have guts enough to do this? And we did. . . . I mean, we didn't know. We thought, 'We're probably going to get beaten up. . . . The frat boys are going to come here and beat us up.' Those are the kinds of things you thought about."

The dance, described as "astounding," drew in several hundred people and brought in $150.[92] Hubbell commented, "That's more money than . . . we would've ever gotten from the student organization [Student Senate]. . . . And I have to say that there were a number of guys from Kansas City that came over and they would give us a five-dollar bill or ten-dollar bill. It was open and we had a lot of support from nonstudents. . . . So it was really an icebreaker, that first dance."

The dances primarily evolved from a financial need, but they nonetheless were a radical action. "There were always some kind of political overtones," remembered Bob Warren. "But I can't imagine now, thinking back about it, how it could *not* have had a lot of political overtones. People were not open to gay people, period. It was just very groundbreaking, and just to be there, you didn't have to particular[ly] identify. You were just part of a movement." Weaver agreed: "It was gay people getting together and being out in public. And that, in itself, was quite radical. You can't imagine a gay dance there [KU] in 1967. And by 1977, nobody thought anything of it at all. It was another way of being groundbreaking." Michael Stubbs credited the visibility of the dances with their important, far-reaching impact:

> They were fantastic. I mean, just the visibility alone was fantastic. Everybody was so in the shadows before Stonewall. . . . The only reason gay marriage ever happened is because way back to that first gay liberation poster *Come Out*—when people came out to their family, by the time gay marriage happened, the public supported it because they all knew somebody who was gay. I really think that the Union dances were part of that evolution.

As Hubbell stated, to publicly declare one's identity in the face of possible ostracism, harassment, or violence took courage. Barry Albin discussed the reticence of some gay members in the community to attend due to a fear of being identified or labeled: "We at one point talked about the question of outlawing cameras because we were afraid that they would come in and take pictures of us." John Beisner, KU student body president from 1974 to 1975, also recalled this controversy, commenting that students, in fact, had expressed their concerns with him. He remembered that comments in the *UDK* about this generated discussion, which some attendees felt infringed on their sense of safety. The group decided not to ban cameras, however. Albin explained: "If you were going to come to the dance, you had to be brave enough to be who you were." He acknowledged that this was too big a step for some: "A lot of people . . . were not willing to be outed, and they didn't show up at the dances unless they went with someone. If they could go with somebody else that was straight, and they could build a plausible statement to anybody else—'I was there with my friends. We went to have a good time.'"

The popularity of the dances was remarkable, drawing in students and community members from all over the area. Early dances drew in four to five hundred people. As they became established, they had eight hundred to a thousand who attended from the four corners of the state as well as Oklahoma, Colorado, Nebraska, Illinois, and Texas.[93] Albin described the scene: "You can't . . . imagine what it was like. . . . This was a beacon of light for the entire five-state region. They came from everywhere and they were emboldened by what we were doing." Radavich, recalling that they were "crammed to the gills," commented that they were "fantastically successful. And a lot of nongay people went. . . . It was just astonishing. . . . And obviously there was still opposition in a lot of quarters, but still, this was the hip place to be. It was incredibly exciting."

The dances were known for their welcoming atmosphere. Bill Tuttle recounted, "They were just fabulous. They were the best dances at the university for several years, always just a hoot. People wore costumes and just carried on and just had a marvelous time." Lee Hubbell recalled a popular tradition: "the famous Can-Can Dance . . . a 'most scandalous' dance when done in the KU Union Ballroom by a very, very gay chorus line, including Drag Queens, one in a Bridal Gown."[94] They also were known for the diverse crowd of campus and community members they brought in. Their reach was notable, even bringing in families with children. Community member Christine Smith remembered: "They were, for many years, family dances. We took our kids and we all went to them, had a great time."

The dances could be described as "state of the art," which likely played a role in their popularity. Lee Hubbell, who was in charge of the music, served as DJ early on. He had a collection of 1950s and 1960s rock and roll music, an elaborate sound system, and a professional-level reel-to-reel tape deck that he would use to make mixes for the dance. Looking back, Grotta speculated that "it was almost [a] precursor of what came twenty years later with DJs and dance clubs."

The music, however, became a source of conflict as the dances continued.[95] As more people began to join, a rift grew between founders and some new members. Linker elaborated: "The new members thought we dominated the group. One of the bones of contention was that we were the ones who chose the music for the dances, and they wanted in on that."[96] The differences of opinion centered on continuity versus change. Founding members wanted a more classic rock lineup, while the newer members wanted disco. In addition, there were concerns, particularly from the women, about music choice. Linker remembered their contentious discussions about including Rolling Stones tracks due to their sexist lyrics. Despite this, the Rolling Stones won out and were included on the playlist. The conflict was eventually smoothed over by a shift in the way the group, as a collective, delegated projects. Linker explained: "My memory is that we felt we did all the work because no one else offered to, and so the role of leadership fell to us. So we turned the dances over to those people. I do not remember any of them taking part in the speakers' bureau or the court case against KU or indeed anything but the dances."[97]

The group went to great lengths to get the word out about the dances, contributing to the visibility of both the dances and the group as a whole. One of their particularly creative promotions was flying a banner over the KU stadium during a football game advertising their dance later that evening. Grotta observed that this helped get LGLF into the mainstream of campus life.[98]

KU professor emeritus Paul Lim had heard many positive comments about the dances but raised questions about their benefit for members of the gay community: "Whether they [thought] it was daring of them or whatever, or that maybe the gay dances had better music, better DJs—but it was fashionable for a lot of straight people to go. Of course, I think back then it was [that] people were still fairly closeted and so maybe precisely because so many straight kids were coming to these parties . . . a lot of gay people stayed away."

Lim's speculation that the "all are welcome" format of the dances was off-putting to some who were gay or lesbian had merit. For some, the enormity and diversity of the dances was overwhelming.[99] Others were looking for a gay-only environment. Said Michael Stubbs: "A lot of gay people, they wanted a gay scene. And the ballroom dances were not per se the old-fashioned gay scene where you go to pick somebody up and all that. Although, I suppose that happened. But there were children there and families. It wasn't the same as a gay bar, that's for sure."

For many who were gay, lesbian, queer, or questioning, however, these dances provided a safe environment to connect where they could be unabashedly themselves. David Jacobsen, a graduate student group member in the mid-1970s, stated, "This is the most many gays will do, is show themselves at this dance. The ones that won't come out on the streets will come out here because the dance is a safe place and the people don't feel that safety outside."[100]

Susan Davis, who lived in Kansas City, experienced this sense of safety and celebration when, at the invitation of friends, she attended one of these dances. Seeing women openly display affection toward each other may have given Davis the courage she needed that evening to acknowledge that she was a lesbian. Shortly after this experience, she moved to Lawrence and bought a house, which she began offering as a lesbian and feminist gathering spot. Commenting on the impact of this dance and subsequent ones to follow, she said: "Every once in a while, there is a spark and people can change direction or come to a new level of awareness." Dances were described as "liberating," "a dance where you can go in and cut loose," and "a wonderful, blow-out-your-ear dance." Others mentioned that the dances brought about feelings of belonging and connection. Many commented on the "very nice energy" that resulted from the inclusion of "a whole spectrum of all kinds of people."[101]

For others, the gay-straight mix allowed people to connect quietly. Kathryn Clark, who was married but in the early stages of identifying herself as a lesbian, stated:

> The gay dances were really important. . . . For me, I remember them as being so great because it was the first opportunity that I had to publicly be with this woman that I'd gotten involved with. She was also in a heterosexual relationship, and although both men knew we had begun to be involved, we were trying to balance conflicting commitments. So that was a place where both couples could go to the dance, but she and I could be together.

For some who were deeply closeted and conflicted, watching from the periphery provided some anonymity and protection as they were figuring things out. Trip Haenisch, who was one of these students when he attended KU in the 1970s, talked about going up to the sixth-floor balcony of the Union to watch the dance in the ballroom below. He was usually joined by his friend, who was also gay and in a different fraternity.

Haenisch mentioned that "we were constantly searching for other people that were also gay." On one occasion, he left the relative security of the balcony to attend the dance but admitted that details were a bit hazy. He stated, "I don't really remember it very well because I had to get drunk to even have the nerve to do it." He took great care to keep his identity hidden, commenting, "That would've been devastating to be called out on that."

The LGLF dances brought together people throughout the gay community. As mentioned earlier, many cliques and factions existed within the broader gay community at KU, leading to splintering and lack of connection. Joe Lordi, who had an early role in the group, commented on the ability of dances to break down barriers: "The dances were kind of how everybody got together. . . . And I think that was one of the themes of the Gay Lib were these dances, because they were kind of the unifying principle. . . . So yes, definitely dances were very, very important because it brought all kinds of gay people together." He recalled that "there were a lot of us. . . . For the most part, we were courteous to one another, although there were times when we weren't, but that's why those dances were important." The meaning and significance of the dances were widely understood throughout campus and beyond.[102] Said Albin, "It became a statement of your solidarity with us, to show up at those dances. . . . You felt great about yourself that people were out there dancing and you didn't know who they were, but they were all there supporting you. It was wonderful."

The dances were the chief means of funding the group's education and counseling programs and were said to be "the most successful money-raising events of any events sponsored by student groups at the time."[103] They were important not only for the group but also for the community, providing an entry point for those who were gay and lesbian to interact and connect in a safe space. The dances also welcomed and engaged members of the straight community to become allies. Straight attendees were challenged to look past a perceived sense of "otherness," fostering understanding and acceptance. In addition, the phenomenal success of the dances strengthened the visibility and voice of those who were gay and lesbian, contributing to strengthening the gay community.

Robbery at the Dance: A Call for Policy Changes

Although the dances had broad support across campus and beyond, they also were a very public target for those who were looking to undermine the group and communicate their opposition. On April 26, 1972, early in the evening of an LGLF dance, a group of twelve to fifteen men, believed to be members of the Black Student Union (BSU), forced their way in without paying.[104] They had been participating in Student Senate budget hearings directly upstairs from the dance, lobbying for additional funds. Tempers flared as they were told during the three-hour hearing that they were slated for a significant budget cut rather than the increase they had requested to create a counseling center for addressing drug abuse and draft concerns.[105]

The conflict began early on when spectators were seen on the balcony, jeering at dance participants. Later that evening, at around 10:30 p.m., a male student stole admission payments of seventy-five dollars from the cashbox.[106] A scuffle ensued, and the member overseeing the cashbox, Jim Pettey, was punched and got a cut on his face while attempting to stop them. Pettey recounted the experience as BSU members approached the table: "They were angry as they were coming out of the meeting. I remember that Chuck Ortleb, being innocent, wanted to ask them to join our dance. He said that since both BSU and LGLF were angry at the university, we should come together. Chuck said, 'Oh, let's invite them in!' and Reggie Brown said, 'Noooo! Don't do that!'" Brown was remembering BSU's conflict with Brown specifically and LGLF more broadly.[107]

Pettey went on to explain, "I wasn't actually taking the money, but I was standing next to the door. All I remember is one guy grabbed the money box, and I, like an idiot, went running after him as he went back up the stairs. The stairs were lined with guys coming out of that meeting." As he ran after the perpetrator, who was way ahead of him, he described what happened next: "People coming down [the stairs] just saw a white guy running after a Black guy, so they beat me up. . . . As I ran up the stairs, I was being slugged every few feet until I decided that, well, I wasn't going to catch him. I realized that I was being hit when my glasses broke. . . . I finally basically was pushed back down the stairs."

The incident was significant enough that David Dillon, student body president at the time, recalled more than forty years after the incident that he saw those involved running through a Student Senate meeting.[108] Ortleb, who ran through that meeting to try to retrieve the stolen cash, grabbed the microphone, announced the robbery, and took advantage of the opportunity to denounce the decision to not recognize the LGLF.[109] In a gesture of support, Frank Burge, Union director, canceled the room rental cost when he heard of the robbery.

The following morning, ten members of the LGLF and the gay caucus of the Women's Coalition, angered by the incident, went to Balfour's office with their concerns, taking Pettey and his broken glasses with them. Pettey, who also had a black eye under his broken glasses, commented that "in that meeting I felt like I was presented as exhibit 1A—evidence that queers aren't sissies."[110] They presented Balfour with a position paper, stating that the robbery was a "microcosm of the whole world of oppression suffered by Gay People on this campus."[111] Frustrated, they asked: "Why should we alone have to push the case for Gay Students? Why have you (the administration) never said anything about us. No other minority groups get official silence from your office. When you speak of minority groups why is it that the second largest minority in America—the minority of gay people—is never mentioned."[112] They reported that many members of the two groups had been harassed by other students, and they expressed their concern that the injured person could not claim his legal rights because he was gay, likely referring to the lack of remedies available at KU to those in the gay community who experienced discrimination and harassment. Members blamed the administration for the robbery, arguing that having to fight for student organization recognition deflected their energies away from educating to change attitudes such as those evident the night of the dance. To keep students on campus engaged in the fight, members widely distributed their position paper on campus.[113]

Group members then presented Balfour with seven suggestions (the term they used in the document) that they wanted to bring to the chancellor's attention for a response. These included directly engaging higher-level administrators to raise awareness about climate issues for gay men and lesbians, arranging for a dialogue with the chancellor, and calling for senior administrators to speak out about discrimination against those who were gay and lesbian. They also asked students and administrators to read recommended books on gay liberation to confront the homophobia on campus. A majority of the "suggestions," however, focused on campus policies and response. They included calling for the campus to investigate discrimination against those in the gay and lesbian communities, investigating campus hiring/firing practices and harassment in campus housing, and establishing protections. In addition, they called for creating a gay studies program and hiring full-time staff to address problems facing gay and lesbian community members.[114]

After the statement was read, Balfour spoke with group members to respond to their suggestions and concerns. The issue of group recognition was a central driver in the discussion. Still indignant and disappointed about losing their lawsuit, one of the first issues that the students brought up was having to pay rent to use Union facilities as an unrecognized student organization. Balfour assured the group that he would review the rights afforded both recognized and unrecognized groups "to see that everyone got fair treatment." A WC member then mentioned the hostile campus climate, informing Balfour that there had been harassment at an all-women's dance a week prior. Balfour responded by condemning the harassment as unacceptable but did not agree that there was a link between harassment incidents and LGLF recognition. Group members countered his response, stating that the way to begin addressing the problem was through education, but without adequate space and resources, they could not make headway on this goal.[115]

Recognizing at this point that the issues brought up by the group would not be solvable at his level, Balfour let the students know that their concerns would need to be brought forward to the chancellor. Balfour's decision to wait until this point of the conversation to refer group members to the chancellor may indicate that Balfour had hopes that he could pacify the group, protecting the chancellor from a confrontation.

Group members came to the meeting prepared with an action plan. They requested a series of "town hall" meetings to educate the chancellor about discrimination affecting gay and lesbian members of the campus community. Balfour did not respond to this request but agreed to publicly support the group and to set up a committee with the deans of men and women, Interfraternity Council, Panhellenic Council, Balfour's office, LGLF, and the gay caucus of the Women's Coalition to explore the issues raised about housing discrimination and harassment.[116]

Records indicate that Balfour took a step in responding to the group's concerns by assigning tasks to a student research assistant. These included organizing an information and referral-based training for residence hall staff on the "problems of gay students"; contacting other campuses to determine existing programs and practices; promoting the LGLF speakers' bureau; and attending campus decision-making meetings to advocate for gay students.[117] While the tasks listed were not detailed, they did tend to focus on individual rather than systemic solutions. It is not known what progress was made on these tasks. The LGLF did submit a "Position Paper on Library Material on Gay Liberation" to Balfour, suggesting that efforts were made to expand library resources on sexual orientation.[118] Members also submitted to Balfour a proposal to include sexual orientation in the affirmation action plan.[119] This suggests that the meeting brought about some forward movement, calling on the campus administration and the community at large to be accountable in addressing ongoing problems facing gay and lesbian students.[120]

LGLF Gay Counseling Services

In 1972, gay and lesbian students on campus were starting to speak out about their need to connect with others who had "been there" for reassurance, guidance, and support. Activism had been declining, and student support for civil rights issues had been waning.[121] A few months earlier, the LGLF and the Commission on the Status of Women sponsored a forum in which members of both groups discussed their personal experiences related to being gay. Panelists revealed the guilt and insecurity they wrestled with and opened up about the "gay hate scene" they experienced in which "straight people will consider you something to avoid and fear." They discussed the importance of receiving support from within the gay community to deal with these feelings.[122]

In late May 1972, Elaine Riseman saw the need to expand on the LGLF informal peer counseling service by providing trained counselors. She started a gay counseling service as her social work practicum project. She asked David Stout, who had returned to KU to finish his social work undergraduate degree, and David Radavich, who at this point was pursuing a master's in counseling psychology, to join her. Riseman had planned on partnering with the LGLF to incorporate this counseling service as one of the group's projects, so she, Radavich, and Stout met with the LGLF board. The board wanted in on the project. In June 1972, the three moved forward in establishing the Gay Counseling Service (GCS) and began seeing clients.[123]

Existing counseling options for those who were gay and lesbian were quite limited. Dennis Dailey, professor emeritus in the School of Social Welfare, observed, "My experience on the campus at that time—bless their hearts—was that the Student Counseling Service was not seen as a safe place to go, and I think the gay students figured that out. And they were right." Stout agreed. Based on his own observations and the feedback he received from others, he commented that the campus counseling/mental health services were woefully inadequate for gay and lesbian students, lacking in sensitivity, understanding, and expertise.[124]

Dailey and a few other therapists in the community who had specialized training in sexuality and sexual orientation provided counseling, but few clinics and services had specific training or knowledge to assist. Headquarters Counseling Center, a twenty-four-hour counseling crisis hotline in the community, was identified as gay-friendly.[125] Headquarters staff, in fact, took the initiative to reach out to the LGLF for training, expressing uncertainty as to how to best support gay clients.[126] Some religious-affiliated organizations, including the Wesley Foundation and Canterbury House, also provided informal counseling services.[127] The Gay Women's Caucus, a subgroup of the student organization Women's Coalition, was also listed as offering a counseling service to individuals questioning their sexuality beginning in the fall of 1972, which is when GCS began. The service offered by the Gay Women's Caucus was staffed by female and male counselors who were both gay and straight. This service was listed as being used primarily by women.[128]

Lynn Schornick, a KU undergraduate in the early 1970s, had an experience with a campus psychologist that describes firsthand the misguided and harmful advice that some therapists were dispensing to gay clients during that time.[129] As a "fifth-generation farmboy" from southeast Kansas, Lynn grew up not understanding his desires and felt totally alone with no one to talk to about his feelings. When he was in his senior year in 1972, the woman he had been dating for three years was getting impatient that he had not yet proposed marriage. He shared with her that he thought he might be gay or bisexual, and she asked if they could see a psychologist to discuss the issue.

When they met with the psychologist, Schornick discussed his attraction to men. The psychologist seemed to think this was a phase. Schornick shared his frustration: "How many times does a person have to tell their psychologist they have had sex with men, were fixated by men and thought of men when they were having sex with their girlfriend before that psychologist understood that the person is homosexual?" He contemplated the impact of the psychologist's advice: "What I received from the psychologist was uninformed and useless. In our final session, the psychologist told us that in times of uncertainty we often reverted to adolescent behaviors. I was graduating and was unsure of my future. All would be well, and there was no reason why we should not be married."

Schornick and his girlfriend were married in May 1972. He stated: "I struggled every day with my obligation and love for my wife and my desire to be with men. I sought counseling from a member of the recently formed Lawrence Gay Liberation Front [Gay Counseling Service]. I felt very comfortable discussing my ongoing conflict with the counselor [David Stout]. . . . He helped guide me to the self-realization of my homosexuality." He continued to see his GCS counselor, and in December he let his wife know that the marriage had been a mistake and he was requesting a divorce. They agreed to an amicable split.

Schornick and his wife delayed announcing their divorce until the end of the academic year because they were team teaching a class.

> When we filed, I went to our three major professors to let them know that we were getting a divorce and why. I didn't want her to face a barrage of questions. That is when my university employer became aware of my sexuality. He was concerned that he should fire me. His Executive Assistant stood up for me and I retained my job. That is the first time I felt discrimination in the workplace.[130]

Looking back on this experience, Schornick concluded that the support he received from GCS saved him from being "trapped in a heterosexual marriage. I am eternally grateful for the realization of my sexuality through the excellent skills of my LGLF counselor."[131]

As Riseman, Stout, and Radavich figured out the plan for moving forward, they created their own counseling approach for the GCS. Their new model was based on the paradigms they had learned in their classes, adapting them to reflect the needs of gay and lesbian clients. By viewing homosexuality as a "legitimate and acceptable alternative lifestyle that deserves societal acceptance," counseling was aimed at challenging social beliefs and structures that fostered feelings of inferiority and deviance and supporting "conscious and free decisions" regarding their lives. Stout described the approach as solutions-based and client-centered. Stout, Riseman, and Radavich met regularly to identify goals, formulate plans, and discuss techniques.[132]

Stout described meeting with small groups of three or four "to discuss their common issues related to coming out," and also paired up newcomers with more experienced group members for support and guidance.[133] Radavich recalled that for most clients, only a limited number of sessions were needed to address their presenting issues. When they understood that being gay was not the problem, "then all kinds of things clear[ed] up."[134] He also reported that Riseman took on the female clients while he and Stout worked with the male clients. Periodically Stout and Radavich met with clients together when a situation called for their combined strengths. They would meet with clients in private spaces on campus or in their homes since they did not have a designated office. No problems were mentioned as arising as a result of this.[135]

Riseman, Stout, and Radavich preferred to meet in person with those requesting assistance but set up a call-in phone line (which operated separately from the LGLF peer counseling and rap line) for those who were not able to come in or preferred anonymity. Leonard Grotta recalled the significance of this anonymity. Commenting that many people were afraid to attend LGLF functions and meetings for fear of being identified, the opportunity to speak with a counselor on the phone about the difficult, often shameful feelings allowed a struggling or apprehensive person the opportunity to "stick their toe in the water" and take a step toward empowerment. Radavich often would challenge clients' shame and mistaken belief that they needed to act more "normal" by telling them: "No, no, no—you can be who you want to be. There are ways to do this." He remembered that once the hotline got set up, "the phones were ringing off the hook." The GCS phone hotline had designated call-in hours. It was heavily utilized, and, like the informal hotline, calls came in from all over the country. While it was not the first service of its kind, it was certainly among the earliest.[136]

Despite the popularity of the service, the three realized that they would need a mechanism for promoting it and for monitoring calls. It was time to meet with Vice Chancellor Balfour. Continuing his role as a support to the group, Balfour authorized the campus switchboard to forward calls for the GCS on to them and to list their numbers as contacts.[137] Balfour also arranged for Riseman, Stout, and Radavich to form alliances and establish informal liaisons with professionals from related services such as the KU Guidance Bureau and KU Mental Health Clinic. Balfour was aware of problems with the services provided by the Mental Health Clinic psychiatrist and helped the three navigate this challenging relationship. The most effective means of getting the word out about this new service was word of mouth, or what Stout referred to as the "gay grapevine." They would provide counseling, assistance, and support to anyone with a need, including those who were questioning, coming out, or established in their identity as gay. In addition, they spoke with friends and family members of those who were gay or lesbian.[138] They also ran an ad in the *UDK* classified section on a regular basis (for instance, two times a week during the 1973–1974 academic year) to advertise the services.

Late in the fall of 1972, six months after the GCS began, Riseman, Stout, and Radavich had counseled approximately seventy clients. They each worked approximately twenty hours per week (sixty hours combined). By the spring of 1973, the number of clients had increased to approximately two hundred. Problems that had arisen included coming-out issues, difficulties, and concerns; relationship and marriage counseling; suicide ideation and attempts; finding a job; foster home placement for gay youth; deportation issues for international gay individuals; and sexual assault of gay and lesbian clients. The word of their skill and expertise had spread, and campus and local agencies were using them as a resource and referring clients to the service, including the School of Social Welfare, KU Medical Center, and some state agencies such as Kansas Vocational Rehabilitation. In addition, clinicians at the Menninger Clinic referred cases they could not handle to them.[139]

The GCS also received referrals from Kansas City and Ottawa University, a small, private Baptist institution. Stout recalled an invitation he received from a gay professor at Ottawa to provide counseling to a group of six to eight students "who were having problems reconciling their Christianity with being gay." This involvement was described as "under the radar." He commented: "Our relationship with Ottawa became nearly as intense as our relationship with Lawrence."[140]

The GCS was staffed during this time solely by the three students and operated without outside funding. Riseman, Stout, and Radavich needed additional help and resources. Overworked and exhausted by the demand, all three resigned as counselors in June 1973, after Riseman's practicum was completed. This left no one to take over the service. It almost collapsed. After a period of uncertainty and concern, a few people in the group stepped up to keep the GCS going.[141]

The national debate over the categorization of homosexuality as a mental illness brought this issue into the spotlight during this time. In 1970, activists began lobbying the American Psychiatric Association (APA) to reexamine the listing of homosexuality as a disorder in the *Diagnostic and Statistical Manual of Mental Disorders* (*DSM*) II, used to make mental health decisions.[142] The LGLF joined in these lobbying efforts. Radavich described a time when members took a stand and confronted Karl Menninger, head of the Menninger Foundation in Topeka, who has been considered a pioneer and leader in the field of psychiatry. During a presentation he gave on campus, LGLF members protested his clinic's treatment of gay and lesbian clients, including their practice of using electroshock therapy to "cure" those who were homosexual: "It was a little heated exchange back and forth about the first three minutes and we all left. But we made it known that we thought that he was a barbarian and should not be doing this. . . . The whole group got there early and sat in the front and gave him a bad time."[143]

In December 1973, the APA issued a Position Statement on Homosexuality and Civil Rights, condemning discrimination against those who were gay and lesbian. This resulted in the APA Board of Trustees voting to remove homosexuality as a disorder.[144] When asked about the impact this had on gay students at KU, many expressed that it had a liberating effect. Lee Hubbell stated, "It was like, 'Oh, thank God, at least we're no longer in the textbook.' . . . That was a step in the right direction because that was being used as a weapon against us."

A year after Riseman, Radavich, and Stout resigned, in the summer of 1974, the GCS was still struggling. The GCS was still being supported and funded by the group, now named the Lawrence Gay Liberation, Inc. (often referred to as LGL), but it did not have enough counselors to meet the need. Professor of psychology Michael Storms met with the students who were running the GCS to explore what could be done to build the service back up.[145] Storms, who was gay, taught classes and conducted nationally recognized research on sexuality, so he was well equipped to help the students with this challenge. Storms's willingness to assist the group helped the GCS get back on its feet.

As they headed into the fall semester of 1974, more counselors were brought in, and Riseman, Stout, and Radavich returned. The staff had tripled in size, with twelve on board. All staff identified as gay or lesbian.[146] Radavich, in an undated letter that was likely written in the summer of 1974, reestablished contact with community partners. He reported that the number of clients served since the GCS's creation was 350 to 400, a substantial client load. He also reaffirmed KU's commitment to the service, announcing Storms as the faculty advisor and group member Dick Perrin as the newly appointed executive director. Perrin took on the task of managing the administrative operations, freeing up counselors to focus on counseling. Radavich also mentioned avenues he planned on exploring to generate additional funding.[147]

Storms continued as the advisor for the GCS for many years, and Dennis Dailey also provided support to the service. The GCS was affiliated with the LGLF through the mid-1970s.[148] By 1977, the GCS either disbanded or was absorbed into another service. In a letter that year to Vice Chancellor Ambler, the group's co-coordinators, Jean Ireland and Todd VanLaningham, identified a counseling referral service for free counseling for gay and lesbian students, nongay friends, and family members provided by paraprofessional and professional counselors. GCS was not mentioned in this letter.[149]

Storms's and Dailey's expertise and guidance were critical in guiding and building this service. Given the repressive views regarding homosexuality and mental health that existed within the profession and the harmful therapeutic techniques that were often used (e.g., conversion and electroshock therapies), those providing counseling needed guidance in establishing gay-affirming models as they forged new territory. In addition to providing GCS counselors with the training they needed to assist clients, Storms's and Dailey's involvement also provided a sense of legitimacy and credibility that was important as GCS counselors trained campus and community organizations and agencies. This was a first step for many agencies, and not all had come around to this new approach.

The GCS played an important role in challenging the deviance and illness narratives about homosexuality that were common during the 1970s. The counselors did something radical by rejecting the common mythology and offering a new paradigm for conceptualizing the development and enactment of sexual identity. This paradigm was one of normality, affirmation, and self-acceptance. By providing validation, support, and resources to help those who were trying to figure out their sexuality and its effect on their daily life, the GCS offered connection to those who were isolated, clarity to those who were confused, and guidance and reassurance for those who needed direction. The GCS also had a role in reeducating service providers on campus and the surrounding community about ways of providing appropriate, growth-enhancing services.

Activist Initiatives: Pride Celebrations, Voters' Guide, and Discrimination Protests

The summer of 1972 was a busy one for the group. In addition to getting the GCS off the ground, planning their appeal to their defeated lawsuit against the university, and expanding their speakers' bureau programs, LGLF members continued their tactic of educating the campus by hosting large-scale events. They hosted the first-ever Christopher Street Day celebration (also dubbed Freedom Day) on June 24, joining other groups across the country.[150] This day was designated to recognize the Stonewall uprising, which had taken place on Christopher Street in New York. LGLF held its annual picnic at Lone Star Lake in the afternoon followed by a party in the evening. A report of the event earned a special column in the *UDK*, indicating that this event had, in fact, generated interest and attention to the group's efforts and gay liberation nationally.

This 1972 event began what was to become a long-standing tradition. The following spring, the group hosted Gay Pride Week. This very visible event was a mix of education and celebration and had a more radical focus than the Christopher Street Day event a year prior. A *UDK* article reported: "The L.G.L. has scheduled Gay Pride Week April 25–29.

[Reginald] Brown said, the week would feature a 'Guerrilla Theater' as a form of shock therapy to bring gayness to the attention of KU students. Brown said that there also would be outdoor activities such as a picnic and planned promenade by gays on campus."[151] This event would become an established and prominent feature of the group in the later 1970s and would continue to expand its radical and political impact in the 1980s and beyond.[152]

Just a few months later, the LGLF took on another political project—organizing, publishing, and distributing a voters' guide to inform members of the campus and community about the records of those running for office in the 1972 city and state elections on gay rights issues.[153] Members sent a questionnaire to candidates running for office asking for their views on a range of issues and listed their responses as well as those who did not reply. There is little information on the impact, reach, and longevity of this project; nevertheless, it reflects a shift in the group's focus, looking outside the campus boundaries to create a larger sphere of influence.

Another project the group took on that summer was protesting housing and employment discrimination. Two group members experienced housing discrimination in late June, prompting members to take action. Lee Hubbell, when asked about community issues affecting gay and lesbian students and residents, replied: "Discrimination in housing. Number one. Because if their landlord found out they were gay, they were evicted. And that was the most fundamental. Number two behind that was job discrimination."

This specific incident involved LGLF members and roommates Dick Perrin and Joe Prados, who were evicted from their Lawrence apartment, owned by Edmonds Real Estate, after six months. They reported being told that "their involvement in Gay Liberation, especially in the court case, made them undesirable as tenants."[154] Group members wrote a letter to the head of the company, Mark Edmonds, requesting his response. When this did not happen, the picketing began. The group was bolstered by the passage a few months earlier of amendments to the Kansas Act against Discrimination (44-1001), which prohibited housing discrimination based on sex. While this act did not specifically add protections related to sexual orientation, group members believed that increased options for investigating complaints could help leverage their complaint.

It was to go into effect July 1, 1972, and would be retroactive.[155] Leonard Grotta issued a public challenge to the agency, commenting in the press, "We'd like Edmonds to give a pledge in writing that he won't discriminate against gays. Otherwise we are prepared to take further action."[156]

Not hearing back, the group followed through on its word. On Monday, June 26, four to five group members walked the picket line all afternoon, carrying posters challenging Edmonds with messages including, "We want to rent houses, not closets." Passers-by supported the protesters. Edmonds did finally issue a statement while the group picketed, but he denied any wrongdoing: "This picketing is unjustified and based on erroneous and alleged facts. I have no further statements at this time."[157] Hubbell summed up the effect of the picketing: "It was very effective. The last thing in the world that a small town—Lawrence was a pretty small town then . . . but the small-town real estate firm and the rental agency didn't want a bunch of gay guys picketing with placards outside of their business. I mean, the shame of it . . . Some of the guys went in drag just intentionally."

Hubbell noted that LGLF also picketed against employment discrimination. He commented: "If we found out somebody was fired because they were gay, we would go down and picket." In addition, the group lobbied for legislative changes to national housing and employment protections. Members submitted a gay rights resolution for passage at all three Douglas County Democrats' local unit caucuses on April 8, 1972, calling for the obliteration of "all discrimination against homosexuals in the areas of housing and in all areas of employment, including education, insurance and the military" as well as in immigration.[158] This was quite an accomplishment when considering the opposition the resolution faced, referred to by County Chair W. J. Brink as, "that damned Gay Lib thing." State Democratic chair Norbert Dreiling was reported to have been asked if "the Democratic Party was the party of homosexuals." The reporter went on to say, "When he [Dreiling] stopped laughing, he said, 'We still believe in the perpetuation of the human race.'" Despite the blatant homophobic attitudes within the group, younger, vocal participants carried the vote, and the resolution was passed by all three caucuses. A statement about it ran in LGLF's newsletter: "Delegates are Pledged to take the resolution all the way to the Miami Convention in July."[159]

Refusing to Give Up: Appealing the Lawsuit Decision

In addition to pushing forward their political agenda, LGLF had also filed their lawsuit appeal in February of the spring 1972 semester, shortly after the February 10 denial. They were notified that the appeal would be heard on November 16, 1972.[160] The LGLF had a strong team representing their case, including William Kunstler, Jack Klinknett, and former liberal KU law professor Lawrence Velvel. LGLF members and the defense team were optimistic due to a favorable ruling a few weeks prior for the gay student organization at the University of Oklahoma, which had similar issues as the LGLF gaining campus recognition. The University of Oklahoma Board of Regents voted to not appeal the court's decision in favor of the group, in which the justices ruled that the university could not deny recognition because they did not agree with the group's goals.[161]

The hearing started out with some surprises. Klinknett had planned to drive to Denver with Leonard Grotta and a few other LGLF group members. He borrowed a friend's Volkswagen Beetle for transportation, and they headed out. They started off for Denver with time to spare. They got as far as Junction City, Kansas, and it became evident that the car wasn't going to make it. "So I rushed back to town," recalled Klinknett. "We limped back to Lawrence, and I called up on my friend and VW mechanic, Charlie Gruber, who more or less literally climbed out of his pajamas, went down to the shop and spent—I had never seen an engine come out of a car that fast." Gruber completed the task in record time: "Within two or three hours, he had yanked the engine, given it deep surgery, put it back together, and sent us on our way."

Leonard Grotta remembered that they arrived, very tired, in Denver at about 5:00 a.m., for their appointment later that morning. Grotta commented: "Jack Klinknett got up and showed up, but he told us that it was probably going to take all of 10 minutes once he was called, and we should just sleep. So we did."[162] Grotta called their hearing "anticlimactic" but described the exhilaration he felt in being actively involved and, for the first time, open, out, and visible.

Despite members' determination, the rest of the day, unfortunately, was not as successful as the Volkswagen repair. Kunstler presented on behalf of the team, approaching the case as a violation of equal rights.

Stating that "the lives of homosexuals had been made 'a living hell' because of general ignorance," he argued that the LGLF should be recognized
to educate the public about gay issues.[163] Kunstler further contended that
as an organization that was primarily educational, group members were
denied their rights of free speech and assembly by the university. Despite
a strong argument, LGLF members were notified that their appeal had
been denied in March 1973.

The group refused to give up. One more avenue existed: to take the
case to the US Supreme Court. In the summer of 1973, the LGLF requested a writ of certiorari to hear the case in hopes of overturning the
lower court decision. A ruling that was used as a guide in drafting their
argument, *Healy v. James*, had been issued one year prior in 1972. This
ruling determined that a campus organization could not be denied recognition because it advocates for the legalization of conduct that is ruled as
illegal, since advocating for changing the law is not the same as breaking
the law. Despite this landmark decision, the justices declined to hear the
case.[164]

LGLF members had come to the realization that the courts were not
going to resolve the problem. Disappointed but philosophical, they began
to make other plans. They published a statement in their newsletter, *Up
Front*:

> Despite the fact that the LGLF has now reached the end of its series of
> court battles, this will not deter the gay people of Kansas University
> from working for the ideals of human liberation which are obviously
> necessary. This will be done in many ways, not only through the pro-
> gram of Lawrence Gay Liberation Inc. and the Gay Caucas [*sic*] of
> Women's Coalition, but also in everyday interactions on an individual
> basis. Think about that the next time you say 'Hi' to a friend![165]

In the spring of 1973, the group was granted corporation status and
officially changed its name to Lawrence Gay Liberation, Inc. At the time,
there were between ten and fifteen incorporated gay groups nationally.[166]
The reason given for this move was to protect member lists and provide
tax exemptions. A more primary reason, however, was to gain visibility
and legitimacy.[167] Group members determined that this strategic move
was worth the risk, despite the caution they received from Jack Baker
that incorporation put them in a position to be sued more easily by the

university in federal court as a state entity and that the move might be "more of a headache than its [*sic*] worth."[168] Said Barry Albin, who by this time was a licensed attorney and led the initiative, "I think we got what we wanted. We wanted to make the state recognize us. And we did that by getting incorporated. By allowing us to be incorporated, the state said, 'This is within the public policy, with the public interest.' And they couldn't, therefore, say that we were immoral. . . . We were trying to become proud of being who we are."

Being designated as legitimate by the state gave the group some protection, bolstered members' confidence, and opened the door for the group to take on a greater role in political activism challenging restrictive state laws and policies.[169] Their incorporation status was only official for one year, effective March 2, 1973, and forfeited in 1974 when the required annual report was not submitted.[170] This, however, did not seem to have an effect on the group, since the intended benefit, pushing back against the university and courts by gaining recognition and establishing its legitimacy, had been achieved.

This led the group to consider reapplying for recognition yet again. Lee Hubbell, acknowledging that the group's focus on education had become less of a priority than it had been earlier, said this aspect of the group's mission had recently been strengthened. Nevertheless, the group decided to wait to reapply until a "water-tight argument" could be made.[171]

Throughout their three-year battle, the group tenaciously refused to be overpowered. Members had not abandoned their revolutionary orientation. They had, however, tempered their approach and become more adept at working within the institutional system while simultaneously pushing from the perimeter, challenging the inequities and homophobia that existed.

In 1973, after the LGLF case had concluded, John R. Martin, Kansas assistant attorney general, spoke with the press about the case. His comments made it clear that the LGLF's lawsuit had been a battle over morals and the state's refusal to include those who were gay and lesbian in the definition of human rights. Martin, who represented the university in the original case in 1972, argued at that time that KU's refusal to recognize the LGLF was appropriate based on state law. In an interview in 1973, however, he stated that the university could recognize the group and would only be in violation of the state law if the group openly promoted sodomy.[172] This was in direct opposition to his argument in the 1972 court case in which he claimed that the group violated state law in all respects. Martin's 1972 argument claiming that the LGLF had been granted all the rights it sought ignored the restrictions that the group still faced by not being officially recognized.

Despite Kunstler's acclaim in representing difficult cases, some questioned if Kunstler's involvement, despite the tremendous visibility it drew in, might have actually hurt the LGLF's case. Kunstler's style had been described as "theatrics over substance," and his reputation at times overrode the issues at hand in a case.[173] John Beisner, KU student body president from 1974 to 1975, commented: "It was labeled as the Kunstler lawsuit, and I think that his presence caused this to be an issue about him as opposed to . . . the organization." This being said, however, it is unlikely that LGLF members would have had a successful outcome to their case under any condition since one could speculate that the outcome had already been determined. Steven Weaver concluded: "It's kind of funny because even in the end, we won. [Laughs.] . . . I think if the court had held properly, it would have held against the university, because it was discrimination, just pure and simple. But in the scheme of things, the way history was moving, this was just sort of a little blip." Bob Warren agreed: "Those of us in the organization were so proud that we had gotten to slap this suit on the table and say, 'Lookit. We're here, like it or not, and we're here to stay, and we're real. This is not just [a] passing social thing. This is something different, and you've got to deal with it.'" He concluded that, despite the loss, "we all felt vindicated and a high degree of success in pulling it together. . . . It wasn't just the KU gay lib that we were pushing, fighting for. It was the gay lib for every organization with a similar pursuit in the nation."

Group members had not given up on their goal of gaining recognition. But having received validation in other ways, they decided it was time to shift their focus. They put their energies into their activities and services, which, in fact, was a defiant act.

Concluding Thoughts: LGLF Members' Early Activist Efforts

In summary, the LGLF's five tactics in the early 1970s—educational programs, activism, community engagement, dances, and peer support/the

Gay Counseling Service—laid the foundation for connecting and empowering those who were gay and lesbian on campus and in the community at large. The group's comprehensive approach challenged homophobic attitudes, practices, and policies, while facilitating change in the cultural and political climate. By calling for acceptance and inclusion, the group encouraged others to join in the cause, which had an important role in bringing people together and establishing the gay community in an intentional, organized way. The LGLF's ongoing presence and visibility gave other students on campus the courage to embrace their identity and proudly come out of the shadows to connect with others. In addition, these tactics promoted important discussions throughout the state about homosexuality, lessening the stigma and encouraging members of the gay community to come together and advocate for change.

"There Are a Lot More Homosexuals at the University Than We Thought"

Challenging Attitudes and Anchoring the Foundation (1975–1979)

As the 1975 academic year began, the Lawrence Gay Liberation Front, now named Lawrence Gay Liberation, Inc. (LGL), had evolved from its beginnings five years prior. The lawsuit that group members filed against the university in 1971 for failing to recognize the LGLF as a legitimate student organization was, for the time being, behind them. As new members came on board to this now-established group, they continued the group's earlier efforts, which included education, advocacy, medical and legal referrals, social interaction, and counseling. Their focus and approach, however, had shifted. This chapter examines the evolution of the group in the second half of the decade and highlights significant member initiatives from this time period that had a lasting impact.

To understand this shift, it is important to consider changes that had taken place nationally and at KU. The climate on college campuses across the country had changed substantially since the group's beginnings. Arthur Levine, in his book *When Dreams and Heroes Died* (1980), characterized it as a time of pessimism and disillusionment. Students during this era witnessed a war that they perceived as senseless and observed the political corruption inherent in the Watergate scandal, souring them on a belief in the existing institutions and systems in place. And as Levine's title highlights, many of their heroes had indeed died, including John F. Kennedy, Martin Luther King Jr., and Malcolm X. Students of this era elevated their predecessors of the 1960s to near-mythical status, leaving them with a feeling that in the existing climate they had nothing to fight for.[1]

Scholar Helen Horowitz characterized this as a time of shifting focus in which students "dropped earlier concerns for relevance and societal well-being and concentrated on enhancing their competitive advantage for professional schools." A sense of idealism and view of college as a laboratory for social change was replaced with what Horowitz described as "a quest for grades." Students from middle-class and privileged back-grounds, fearing downward social mobility, focused on individualistic goals rather than civil rights activism as they looked for ways to maxi-mize the selling power of their degree, fostering a climate of competition.[2] The Gay Liberation Movement had just begun to gain momentum at a time when students' interest in political and cultural change was waning. By the midpoint of the decade, this individualistic focus had influenced gay rights organizing as well.[3]

This change in climate was also apparent on the KU campus. Chancel-lor Archie Dykes commented in an *LDJW* article about "a greater concern about academic performance than in the past." Mike Harper, chair of the Student Senate Executive Committee (and student body president the following year), agreed, expressing concern that students were spending so much time studying that they were not paying attention to campus issues, leading to students "losing what power they gained during the ac-tivist 1960s."[4] A *UDK* article about the KU School of Business mirrored these observations, noting that due to a 40 percent increase in enrollment over a five-year period, the school was facing "growing pains."[5] It is likely that these growing pains were the result of students signing up for a de-gree they perceived as having greater buying power.

Tedde Tasheff, KU student body president from 1976 to 1977, recalled the climate on campus during this time in which KU's public image was at a low ebb. Chancellor Dykes, who arrived at KU in 1973, was selected for the job, in part due to his public relations skills. One of his primary tasks was mending fences with regents, state lawmakers, and commu-nity members who had soured on the institution during Chalmers's ten-ure.[6] His less student-centered approach was not embraced by all.[7] "We were at the end of ... the activism that I associate with KU in the late sixties, early seventies. There just wasn't a lot of visible activity in that regard. . . . I just don't think the undergrad population was that involved. The Vietnam War was over, Archie Dykes was chancellor—it's a different time," Tasheff explained. "If somebody other than Archie Dykes had been chancellor then . . . I think the mid-seventies would have likely been a time where more progress would've been made and the spirit of activism would have been more widespread and enjoyed."

Attitudes about sexuality in 1975 had evolved, but one thing that had not significantly changed was an understanding of the gay and lesbian experience. One can look to a community program sponsored by the Department of Religion as an example of subtle ways in which the message of deviance continued to be communicated. This four-part series, "Community Morality," included homosexuality as one of the topics of discussion. The goal of the program was to "make the Lawrence community aware of and involved in determining public morality," implying that homosexuality was in fact a moral issue.[8] Many gay and lesbian campus and community members commented on the impact of these negative messages, sharing that they lived in the closet "to avoid persecution and harassment from members of the straight or heterosexual majority."[9] The discrimination against gay men and lesbians during this period was described as covert and insidious.

While homosexuality was more intentionally included in general discussions about sexuality in the mid-1970s than at earlier times, it was often misrepresented. An article in the *UDK* reported on a 1974 national survey on college students' attitudes about sex in which 61 percent of college student respondents favored sexual freedom as compared to 43 percent in 1969. This attitudinal shift did not necessarily extend to sexual orientation, however. Bill Robinson, assistant dean of men in the mid-1970s, was not convinced that people had become more accepting, stating that he feared that despite the appearance of increased openness, attitudes related to homosexuality were becoming more polarized. Lee Hubbell agreed, stating, "It is more of a tolerance—but considering that we've gone from outright persecution to tolerance in a relatively short time, it is a pretty big step." Hubbell went on to clarify that the issue had broader cultural implications: "It is more an awareness for individual freedom that we're concerned about, not necessarily sexual freedom."[10]

Catching More Flies with Honey:
A More Nuanced Approach

The Lawrence Gay Liberation Front evolved in the mid-1970s, modifying its name and approach, reflecting this change in climate. The group was now focusing less on overt political activism and more on education and social connections as the early radical founders were graduating and moving on and younger members were taking over.[11]

Just a year earlier, in 1974, the group had been in serious trouble. Membership had significantly declined, and meetings had ceased to be productive. Dick Perrin, who was keeping the group going, had begun dating Bob Friedland, and they both were concerned. Friedland stated: "I'm not a marketing person. But I had ideas about what it was going to take because Lawrence Gay Liberation Front was dying."[12] Mentioning that there typically were about four people at a meeting, Friedland observed that "the meetings would go on and on with all kinds of political bullshit.... They needed to do something to clean that up.... I just had this idea to create visibility. Make it seem larger than it was." They made posters and put them up all over campus. Friedland used humor to catch students' attention with such slogans as "I'd rather be a fruit than a vegetable." The group also set up two helplines that rang into Friedland's apartment. One was for counseling, and one was for information about socializing.

Perrin and his roommate, Reginald Brown, joined Friedland in the efforts to draw people back in. They made a list of all the gay people they collectively knew in Lawrence, which Friedland estimated was about one hundred. He called all of those on the list that he could reach, letting them know they were going to resume holding Lawrence Gay Liberation meetings. He told them that meetings would be structured differently than in the past, steering away from highly charged political discussions. There would be a short business update, and a majority of the time would focus on socializing. "I figured that was one way to catch more flies with honey than with vinegar. And I remember the meetings went from like four people to close to forty people," Friedland explained.[13] Commenting that there was no other place on campus for gay students to congregate, this emphasis on socializing was the draw that they needed. He stated that "even though there weren't a huge number of gay people there, I just had this vision of creating a presence." They accomplished this through the gay dances, broad advertising of the phone lines, the new meeting format, and better utilization of their office space in the Kansas Union. The shift away from politics was intentional. Friedland commented on the discontent that had been brewing in earlier meetings: "If it's going to be two hours of in-fighting, it's not going to serve anybody. How are people going to socialize? It was not as much of an anti-politics for me, but it's more about how are you going to attract people?"

The group's ability to survive and rebuild was a testament to its importance. Student groups often face difficulties in maintaining momentum and moving forward on long-term initiatives and goals with the constant change that naturally occurs.[14] While the way in which LGL communicated its goals and philosophy had changed, its revolutionary message had not. Members continued to push for comprehensive changes in the way homosexuality was conceptualized, stating: "The focus must shift from conflict with the straight world to creating a place for ourselves. . . . Our task is to direct energy into creating what has never really existed before—the gay community." They continued to challenge oppressive attitudes and practices but adopted a more nuanced approach rather than the militant response of the early gay activists. As they stated, "For ourselves, we have found the best way for a homosexual to live his/her life is to not define oneself against a heterosexual norm. . . . Obstreperous rebellion and self hatred can be seen as two sides of the same obsession with what straight people think."[15]

In 1975, as the new leaders and members came on board, the group they inherited was on firm ground. In a *UDK* article reporting on the group's "new" focus, LGL co-coordinators Dick Perrin and John Steven Stillwell commented that the group "now spends its time and resources on expanded programs and services for the local gay community." Perrin stated that money from dances and private donations made it one of the wealthiest student organizations on campus. He estimated that about thirty people attended meetings, maintaining its growth from the previous year.[16] The listing of programs was comprehensive in scope: the speakers' bureau, weekly discussions on topics related to sexual orientation, a newsletter, a quarterly journal, a readers' theater group, counseling, referrals, dances, and social events. Some of these programs and services suffered during the period of low membership but were rekindled and strengthened as membership revived.

Expanding Programs, Services, and Initiatives

A few new initiatives introduced in the spring of 1975 included a KU Free University course, "Gay Sexual Awareness," and *Wheat Dreams*, a new journal of fiction, graphics, poetry, and essays contributed by gay KU students and people in the community. This journal was an attempt to get group members reengaged in political discourse and action. Richard Linker, one of the early politically engaged members and education coordinator of the group, stated that the increased energy directed to social activities was to the "detriment of our political development." John Steven Stillwell, also an early politically engaged member and co-coordinator of the group, stated that the general decline in political activism among students was not specific to those who were gay: "It's unfashionable now."[17]

The group in the mid-1970s had evolved to being primarily male, even though the LGLF had originally been conceptualized as a group for both men and women.[18] In fact, many of the early active members were women. The leadership model created when the group began called for both a male and female coordinator to colead the group.[19] In addition, documents, statements, and position papers issued on behalf of the group were gender inclusive in their language. From the beginning, however, there were more male than female members. Nonetheless, women's presence and involvement in the early 1970s contributed to the growth of the group.

In the mid-1970s, women migrated from the group to a separate space following national trends.[20] Beth Bailey pointed out that sex in the gay liberation and women's liberation movements had very different meanings—what was liberation for men was oppression for women. Bailey observed, "Gender inequity motivated them [women], not sexual liberation."[21] Lesbians, caught between their intersecting identities, often did not fit comfortably in either movement. Yet they often found that their needs and interests were better met separately from men.

In the fall of 1976, group members took a big step. They again changed the name of the group from Lawrence Gay Liberation Front, Inc., to Gay Services of Kansas (GSOK). The first *UDK* article in which this new name was used was dated October 25, 1976.[22] Stout speculated that the departure of the last of the founding members in 1976 (both Stout and Riseman graduated that year) and the change in culture and group priorities provided a natural segue for this shift. "We moved on. So did the group."[23] It reflected the group's increased focus on education and services that had begun a year earlier. GSOK was described as an active part of student life during this time, collaborating with and cosponsoring activities with many activist and mainstream groups.[24] The four primary areas of focus that the group established early on were still going strong throughout the rest of the decade. The speakers' bureau continued receiving numerous requests with an increase in those from faculty. Dances had increased in popularity among those who were both gay and straight. Referred to as "the big thing" by member Ruth Lichtwardt and others, the dances in the mid- to late 1970s drew attendance numbers reported to be between 1,000 and 1,800 people.[25] The Gay Counseling Service continued to be sponsored by GSOK through 1975 and possibly longer, and counseling for gay and lesbian students continued to be available.[26]

Midwest Gay Conference

The group had not lost its activist edge and continued to get the attention of KU's administrators, the regents, and state legislators. In the fall of 1975, GSOK took steps to organize the first Midwest Gay Conference at KU.[27] Members began spreading the word to other regional gay groups about the conference, which was slated to be held the following year at KU. They unfortunately had not obtained the necessary approvals prior to taking this step, and when Chancellor Dykes got word of the event, the response was far from positive. The chancellor's executive secretary, Richard von Ende, issued a letter to Executive Vice Chancellor Shankel and Vice Chancellor Balfour in October 1975. Referring to GSOK'S unapproved announcement as a "preemptive strike," von Ende expressed his displeasure at being blindsided when the regents contacted him to state that they were "very concerned" about the complaints they had received about the event. Von Ende's characterization of the group's action as a call to battle clearly communicated the tension that existed and the animosity that the administration harbored toward the group. Von Ende let Balfour know in no uncertain terms that the event could not take place:

"I have personally assured the chairperson of the Board of Regents that the University will not serve as host for the conference."[28]

Von Ende reminded Balfour that an appropriations bill was slated to be presented to the Kansas legislature during that time and that the main item of discussion would be the demonstration that was being planned for the 1976 Republican Convention, to be held in Kansas City, with Bob Dole as the Republican vice presidential candidate. Von Ende stated, "I am seldom accused of prudishness or conservativism, but I can honestly say that I can hardly think of anything that could cause the University more difficulty than having a regional Gay Conference." This put administrators in a difficult political position: alienate the regents and larger community or anger liberal-thinking students if word got out about the chancellor's stand, neither of which were good options.[29]

This came on the heels of a complaint about three months earlier against GSOK to Chancellor Dykes, issued by a prominent Menninger Clinic psychiatrist, Dr. Harold Voth. Voth, described in an *LDJW* article as "a well-known opponent of homosexual rights," told Dykes that he had received letters from individuals who were concerned about the "perversion" of homosexuality on the KU campus.[30] Two of the letter writers commented that "there are a lot more homosexuals at the university than we thought" and expressed concern that "these dances sponsored by the 'Gay Libs'" were bringing gay people from all over the vicinity. They cautioned that this "forbodes ill for the University and its students." In particular, they were concerned because "young people . . . are often seduced by these people and led into practicing this form of deviant behavior."[31]

The other two letters described the dance scene. One stated, "There were men embracing men, caressing each other and women embracing women, doing the same. . . . It began to look really vulgar so I left." The other commented that "more than half the couples attending appeared gay" and mentioned that "many came in drag." The second author then stated, "I especially noticed the males, some of whom had gone to great lengths to alter their appearance toward the feminine."[32] These two complaints read more like written statements that the authors had been asked to submit rather than letters that had been organically generated. And while that might not have been the case, surreptitiously stacking the deck to build a case against radical, controversial groups was a tactic that was being used to undermine and discredit by some in the more conservative camps. Executive Chancellor Shankel informed Dykes that he had brought the matter to the attention of Balfour; the deans of men and women; and Michael Davis, campus general counsel; and they would meet to discuss it.[33] The dances were allowed to continue.

Balfour let von Ende know that he had communicated to GSOK members that they could not hold the conference on campus. This memo, curiously, was more publicly supportive of the group than had been the case previously. Balfour began by stating that he was "working with the group to minimize the anger" regarding the decision to not allow the conference. He then mentioned other campuses who had held similar conferences without incident, and he also defended GSOK's premature announcement to other groups as a common practice. Countering the complaints von Ende levied against the group, Balfour followed up by saying, "Luckily we are dealing with mature, stable individuals who understand, but they do not agree."[34]

Two years later, on September 10, 1977, GSOK tried again to sponsor a conference and this time succeeded. The Kansas Gay Political Conference was held on campus in the Kansas Union, which was off limits in the group's earlier attempt. The political climate had shifted following the 1976 Republican Convention, and this time this initiative was allowed to move forward. The conference featured gay rights leaders from across Kansas and included state representative Mike Glover. Former group member Barry Albin, who by this time was a licensed attorney, copresented with Glover. The conference focused on pressing statewide legislative concerns such as Wichita's gay rights ordinance, which was being aggressively challenged at that time by antigay advocate Anita Bryant. It also addressed strategies for bringing about sexual law reform in Kansas.[35]

During the conference, the attendees formed the Kansas Coalition for Human Rights, an organization created to advocate for gay and lesbian human rights on a statewide basis. The group planned on partnering with a lobbyist in the state legislature. GSOK president Todd VanLaningham, still a student, was selected to serve as the interim chair of the group's board of directors. He was also the codirector and a member of the lobbying techniques subcommittee.[36] This event, impressive by any standard, was even more so considering GSOK's status as a student organization. By publicly bringing forward issues related to equity and public policy, the group was influencing the culture and advocating on a level of statewide significance.

Campus Student Government Presence

Another important action the group took on was an involved but behind-the-scenes role in campus student government. John Beisner, KU student body president from 1974 to 1975, recalled his experience running for office with the group UniCampus. The group's vision was to identify a slate of candidates that reflected the demographics of the campus, including gender, ethnicity, and other historically excluded identity categories. As an advocate for diversity and an ally of the group, Beisner recalled that there were concerns about representing the gay and lesbian communities. UniCampus members did not want to explicitly label coalition members as gay or lesbian to protect their privacy, so they were careful to not specifically identify members of the gay community who were part of the coalition. Including LGL members was important to the coalition, and Beisner stated that those who were familiar with the group would recognize that it was represented. Members, however, were not distinctly called out. He reiterated: "I should be very clear that that was not a GLF decision. That was a decision by those who were on the slate."

UniCampus members' efforts to include not just the voice of the gay community but specifically the voice of LGL support the observation that the group held an important leadership role on campus that was widely recognized. Beisner's recollection that the decision to not explicitly identify gay slate members was on the part of the slate, not LGL, is important. While the group established a policy early on of not outing members, the attitude shared by members was one of pride in their gay identity.[37] With this in mind, it would be unlikely that they would be reticent to be identified as gay on the slate.

LGL's influence in student government was largely behind the scenes, but at times members took a more visible role. Steven Weaver criticized student body president candidates Dave Shapiro and Tedde Tasheff in a 1976 *UDK* letter to the editor for not taking a more supportive stance on recognizing the group, at this point called GSOK. Shapiro opposed recognizing the group while Tasheff took a more noncommittal stand, agreeing to support GSOK recognition if the administration supported it. Said Weaver, "Tasheff and Shapiro seem to suffer from a myopia that badly affects the student populace—the belief that since gay people here don't wear labels, armbands, buttons or signs—i.e., since they are invisible—they don't exist." Weaver went on to express concern that the Senate's earlier support had been replaced by indifference.[38]

Wear Blue Jeans If You're Gay Day

Members stayed on top of campus and national issues affecting the gay community, and they put into action some important initiatives during this time to bring about systemic change. This was particularly notable since, in general, activism had lost ground as a priority for students.

Raising awareness through everyday actions can be one of the most effective means of getting people's attention and shaking up the status quo. As students jumped out of bed, anxiously eyeing the alarm clock to try to make it to class on time, the last thing they needed was one more thing to think about. GSOK and the Lawrence Lesbian Alliance (LLA) had other ideas, however. They took the standard student uniform—blue jeans—and turned it into a political statement. On October 14, 1977, the two groups sponsored "Wear Blue Jeans If You're Gay" Day.[39] This event originated at Rutgers University in April 1974 and was being sponsored on other campuses across the country as well. Gay and lesbian members of the campus community were encouraged to wear blue jeans on the designated day to challenge heteronormative attitudes and to normalize the gay experience.[40] GSOK members, adopting Rutgers's approach, commented that the event was "designed to educate and maybe embarrass a few heterosexual students."[41] GSOK and LLA engaged in a large-scale advertising campaign to gain campus attention, and "everyone knew about it."[42] Many were offended, taking out ads in the campus paper to protest and denounce the day, calling for students to "wear a shirt if you're not gay," and to "not be afraid of 'them.'"[43]

In a *UDK* editorial, student Rick Thaemert described the group's tactics as irritating and the event as a publicity stunt. Responding to comments by GSOK members that the event was meant to get people's attention and show that "gays have a sense of humor," Thaemert claimed that "gays have the power of intimidation that other minority groups don't." Not explaining this perceived power, he countered that "people will find no humor in being intimidated by a minority." Despite his irritation, the group's tactics appear to have worked, since Thaemert conceded that "no one should denounce their scheme as being ineffective." He stated that the event had the potential to increase empathy and awareness through understanding another's experience, appearing to support the outcome.[44]

Former KU student Chris Caldwell brought an interesting perspective to the event. Caldwell, who in 1977 was Student Senate treasurer and a fraternity member, had not yet identified himself as gay. He stated that he had very little awareness of what was happening on campus related to gay issues. When asked if he had any awareness of GSOK, however, he pinpointed this event as one of the things he remembered: "It . . . put everyone in a complete bind about 'what do I do?' . . . Because everybody wore jeans ninety-nine percent of the time then. It really was brilliant because did you say, 'Okay, I'm going to wear jeans that day because I'm going to pretend this doesn't exist. Or if I acknowledge it exists, then I can't wear jeans.' It . . . really was a terrific idea, a terrific way to force people to think about and talk about the issue."

Steven Hill, in a letter to the *UDK*, agreed, stating, "It is exactly that that will gauge the success of the campaign. How many actually had to give it a second thought, not how many wore jeans, is the key."[45] John Beisner also remembered students' concerns about figuring out the day's clothing choice. He recalled: "I don't think campus-wide there was an enormous amount of recognition of the gay community on campus or of that entire realm of issues. And I do remember that event causing very substantial discussion among students on campus. 'Well, I'm not gay. What do I do?'" Todd VanLaningham, GSOK director, summed up the message that was intended: "We want people to stop and think, 'What if people thought I was gay?' Every day of their lives gay people and lesbians have to conform to heterosexual society. Let's have one day when they [heterosexuals] have to do what we want."[46] Members' ongoing effort to demand equal treatment and respect required that people pay attention to the assumption of heterosexual privilege. Many were not ready to think about it.

The event was also held the following year on November 2, 1978. It was promoted as the major feature of a weeklong GSOK fall festival from October 30 to November 3. Unlike the year before, however, it did not receive the same widespread attention. In a *UDK* letter to the editor, graduate students Louis Camino and Kathy Petrowaky raised the questions: "Why is this? Could it be that people are now more secure about their self-concepts and less threatened by how others interpret such superficialities as dress? Or could it be that everyone wearing jeans that Thursday was gay? Maybe no one reads the Kansan anymore and so didn't even know it happened? Or are people just getting bored?"[47] The lack of interest was particularly surprising given the ongoing conversation in the *UDK* a few weeks earlier about an article in the ultraconservative campus magazine, *Today's Student*, which had been included in the *UDK* as an insert.[48] GSOK publicity director Julie Freeman denounced the magazine as a "marvelous display of sexist hypocrisy" and debunked writers' assertions that same-sex relationships are unfulfilling and lack respect: "How much longer must we be labeled, degraded, and rejected by a homophobic society because of whom we choose to love?"[49] The low interest might have resulted from reduced publicity efforts compared to the year prior. It is also possible that nongay students were done talking about this issue for the time being.

Despite the lackluster response in 1978, Wear Blue Jeans if You're Gay Day nonetheless played an important role in changing the campus culture. Beisner summed it up: "To my recollection, [it was] one of the first really broad discussions of what gayness was." He called it a "watershed event" because many who had ignored the issue were forced to think about it. "And it generated this great awareness of that in a way that frankly the GLF recognition issue several years earlier did not. Because it was not viewed [as] . . . a couple of people who are challenging the university administration on an issue that we don't care about. It was much more a front-and-center subject of discussion."

Wear Blue Jeans If You're Gay Day opened the door for other large-scale events, most notably Gay Awareness Week. The LGLF coordinated Gay Pride Week in 1973, but it did not become an established feature of the group until 1978 when GSOK organized the Fall Festival. In 1978 it was primarily a social event, featuring a potluck, dance, and the more subdued Jeans Day event. Former GSOK president Todd VanLaningham also spoke.[50] The festival was important in setting the stage for the creation of the larger event the following year.

In the fall of 1979 GSOK collaborated with the Commission on the

Status of Women, the Women's Coalition, and the service group KU-Y (YMCA and YWCA) to create Gay Awareness Week. The focus this time was primarily educational. The final program was an open panel in the residence halls enlisting members of the speakers' bureau to coordinate a question-and-answer session. Copresidents Todd Zwahl and Kim Gilbert stated that the purpose was to raise awareness of the "substantial gay population in Lawrence and to educate the public about the special problems and discrimination faced by gay people in Lawrence today."[51] Gilbert spoke from personal experience. On one occasion in the late 1970s when she and another group member were preparing to give a talk in Kansas City, "we had to enter through a picket line of sign-waving evangelical bigots." On another occasion, she and her friends were ordered to leave a popular Lawrence disco when they danced with same-sex partners. Other patrons also "had walked out in solidarity, called for a boycott, and planned a protest in front of the club that evening—which of course we attended. It was nice to know that at least some of the community had our backs."[52] Gay Awareness Week continued to expand in size and importance through the decades and has become a campus tradition.

Fighting for Inclusion: KU Affirmative Action Policies

In 1977 many campuses across the country were looking more closely at their affirmative action policies. That year, a case had been brought before the Supreme Court, *Bakke vs. Regents of the University of California*, in which a white male student sued the University of California system, claiming he had been the target of reverse discrimination.[53] While a case of reverse discrimination in admissions was new territory for college campuses, concern about affirmative action was not. Many campuses had begun establishing policies and plans early in the 1970s following the passage of the 1964 Civil Rights Act. This legislation prohibited discrimination against racial minorities and women in education, employment, and public accommodation.[54] KU, slow in moving forward, received a push in November 1970 when women in the campus organizations Group W and Women's Equity Action Coalition sent a letter to Chancellor Chalmers urging him to take immediate action to establish an affirmative action program.[55]

Seeing no progress, a second more definitive push came in 1972 with an action on February 4 by a group of KU women who organized after hearing noted poet and feminist Robin Morgan speak on campus two days earlier. Frustrated by the administration's lack of response to long-standing concerns regarding women's rights at KU, the women, who called themselves the February Sisters, protested against the inequitable practices and the lack of services for women on campus. To get the administration's attention, they took over the East Asian Studies building and presented Chancellor Chalmers with a list of six demands they identified as nonnegotiable. One of their demands was the creation of an affirmative action program.[56] The Sisters left the building the following morning with assurances from Chancellor Chalmers that their demands would be met.[57]

Although Chalmers stated that efforts had been underway to create a program prior to the February Sisters' action, it wasn't until six days after their protest, on February 10, 1972, that the first Affirmative Action Office was finally created. Chalmers also appointed an affirmative action board and named a woman as chair.[58] Two offices were established: one for issues affecting women and the other for issues affecting minorities. These two offices were later combined. Shirley Gilham, who had administrative experience at the KU Law School and played a key role in establishing and directing the KU Information Center, was hired to oversee it.[59] She was the top choice of the search committee. A year after the office was created, in March 1973, the first KU affirmative action plan was adopted.[60]

Initial efforts focused primarily on recruiting a more diverse faculty, with a goal of increasing the numbers of women and nonwhite individuals hired.[61] Those who were gay and lesbian were not included either in terms of promoting equal opportunity or providing protections, as was the case across the country.[62] This exclusion did not receive campus or local media attention, but the LGLF noticed and took action. They had crafted a comprehensive document, "Affirmative Action Board Proposal: Provisional Affirmative Action Plan, Modifications Proposed by the Lawrence Gay Liberation Front," dated November 8, 1972.[63] Stating that it had come to the LGLF's attention that no specific reference had been made to gay people in the final draft of the Provisional Affirmative Action Plan, they lobbied for inclusion. Members stated that discrimination was a serious issue at KU for "those with sexual orientations other than conventional heterosexuality." As a result, they stated that gay men and lesbians in academic and administrative positions resorted to "the adoption of roles and behaviors counter to their own personalities," which affected their well-being and effectiveness.

The proposal outlined three requests:

(1) Include specific language prohibiting discrimination in employment, education, and public accommodation based on sexual orientation. Sexual orientation should in no way be considered as a criterion in a range of decisions including employment, financial support, and organization recognition.
(2) Explicitly include sexual orientation as a protected group when mentioning protected minority groups.
(3) Identify an office that would handle affirmative action-related concerns for the gay community.

Balfour had a copy of this document, but there is no information about the document's inclusion in discussions regarding the final draft. These issues were not addressed in the final document.

In 1977, the initial campus policy and plan were revised. This updated document, reported to be two years in the making, was submitted to Chancellor Dykes for review.[64] This time, however, the exclusion of the gay and lesbian community as a protected class received notice on campus and in the media. The primary motivation for the overhaul was the passage in 1973 of Sections 501 and 504 of the Rehabilitation Act, which included those with disabilities as a protected class in equal opportunity and nondiscrimination policies.[65] Individuals with disabilities were not specifically included in the original KU policy and plan. A threat of an affirmative action–related lawsuit by two KU students regarding campus hiring processes may also have contributed to the effort.[66]

It is useful to clarify that there were two different documents being reviewed. The first document was the affirmative action plan, which provided guidelines for recruiting and selecting employees to promote and maintain an equitable workforce. The second document was the grievance procedures, which were a part of equal opportunity provisions to protect against discrimination. The Affirmative Action Review Board had recommended a year and a half earlier to add sexual orientation to the equal opportunity section of the plan, the campus grievance procedures.

This would allow nonheterosexual campus members who experienced discrimination to seek redress and action through the campus.[67]

The draft was reviewed by many stakeholders on campus, including deans, the Human Relations Committee, and campus organizations and groups. All agreed that sexual orientation would remain in the final draft submitted to the chancellor. Dykes, however, removed it from the final document, which was planned to go into effect August 1, 1977, prior to the beginning of the semester. In an article dated August 11, 1977, Dykes stated that sexual orientation would not be included in either the grievance procedures or the affirmative action plan.[68]

When asked why he had not approved this change, Dykes replied, "We have felt that we ought not go beyond the federal guidelines because there's a two-edged sword—the more you protect, the more you open yourself up to charges of reverse discrimination."[69] Dykes's language suggests that his decision may have been influenced by *Bakke vs. Regents of the University of California*, a case still in the courts at the time. Dykes's argument, however, lacked merit. His concern about not going beyond the federal guidelines contradicted an earlier decision that was made by KU administrators and Affirmative Action Advisory Board members about implementing federal guidelines related to affirmative action hiring practices. University counsel Michael Davis had stated that the campus plan was "patterned after federal guidelines" but did not strictly replicate federal regulations: "There are parts of the university's affirmative action plan which are part and parcel of the federal plan. But there are parts that aren't in the federal plan. There are requirements and there are requirements."[70] It appeared that on this issue, Dykes was not willing to add protections beyond the minimum requirements, despite the legal and ethical benefits of doing so.

GSOK director Todd VanLaningham spoke openly about his concerns, bringing it forward for public debate as a human rights issue. He expressed his surprise at the turn of events, stating that Executive Vice Chancellor Shankel had reassured him that sexual orientation would be included in the grievance procedure and affirmative action plan.[71] In a letter to VanLaningham in February 1977, Shankel wrote, "Our affirmative action guidelines should incorporate sexual preference in all of those provisions which deal with discrimination. Discrimination on the basis of sexual preference would be forbidden under the guidelines."[72]

The Affirmative Action Office staff and Balfour, who had assumed a new role as the university ombudsman, agreed to informally assist those who were gay and lesbian who experienced harassment, even though they could not provide formal avenues for redress.[73] VanLaningham said GSOK had been advised to "keep a low profile" on the decision. GSOK had no intention of doing so. VanLaningham, in protest, called for the community to send letters supporting sexual orientation inclusion in the plan to the chancellor. He also scheduled a meeting with the chancellor to discuss his concerns.[74]

Following this meeting, VanLaningham received a letter from Dykes, dated September 20, 1977: "This is to tell you that I have given further thought and careful consideration to your recent letter about our proposed Affirmative Action plan. I believe I am now in agreement with the points raised in your letter. Consequently, I expect we will retain in the Affirmative Action plan the provision which prohibits discrimination based on 'sexual orientations.'"[75] The problem, however, had not been solved. The revised affirmative action grievance procedures were approved by Chancellor Dykes on December 12, 1977.[76] However, sexual orientation was not fully included in key aspects of the policy as Dykes had stated to VanLaningham.

Shirley Gilham Domer, who had taken on the position of assistant to the chancellor, stated that the new plan "included more groups in its provisions and also clarified certain provisions of the old plan" as well as contained a "more complete prohibition against discrimination."[77] VanLaningham was frustrated and strongly disagreed with Domer's statement. Sexual orientation had been added to the Affirmative Action Handbook, the campus document that included the policy and plan, definitions, and details. It was also included in the definition of discrimination in the handbook glossary, listing it in a protected category with race, religion, color, sex, disability, national origin, and ancestry. Yet sexual orientation was not identified in the initial statement as being a protected category, as Dykes had stated in his letter to VanLaningham, nor had a complaint process been added.[78] VanLaningham commented, "The University wasn't serious about banning discrimination based on sexual preference when they drew up the Affirmative Action Plan. If they were, they would have provided an avenue to file complaints in the affirmative action grievance procedure." He added: "As far as I'm concerned, we aren't covered fully and we won't be satisfied until we see a statement from the University Counsel (Mike Davis) guaranteeing that the plan covers discrimination of sexual preference fully."[79]

The discussion was not over. As the following academic year got underway, questions regarding this exclusion were again raised. VanLaningham, who speculated that Dykes had "single-handedly" removed the clause, reasoned: "The Office of Affirmative Action wanted the clause in, Dr. Shankel wanted it and the Affirmative Action Board wanted it."[80] Dykes responded that he did not remember who had removed it, even though less than a year had passed since he had signed the document. In addition, he appeared to have forgotten his comments in an earlier *UDK* article in which he stated that he would not support the inclusion of sexual orientation as a protected category due to his concerns about going beyond the federal affirmative action and nondiscrimination mandates.[81] Dykes was described by those who worked closely with him as "meticulous" with details and thorough in his review of every policy that came across his desk.[82] This, then, suggests that Dykes had not forgotten but was unwilling to claim the decision he made, having some awareness of the hostile climate this omission created. University general counsel Michael Davis speculated that it would probably take a lawsuit challenging this exclusion for the situation to change.[83]

GSOK's important leadership role increased awareness about the need to include sexual orientation in campus nondiscrimination policies and put the campus on notice. Sexual orientation was finally added to the KU nondiscrimination policy in 2002 following the 1998 amendment to the US Equal Employment Opportunity Commission Affirmative Action Guidelines that included sexual orientation as a protected class.[84]

Student Organization Registration Process

GSOK members had many important objectives on their agenda to address in 1977, from ongoing programs and services to large-scale events, as well as campus affirmative action policies. In addition, a key issue they were planning to address that was central in the group's challenge to the university was the denial of their numerous requests to be recognized as a legitimate campus organization. While the Student Senate had voted in favor of granting campus recognition to the group in the early 1970s, support was less certain in the late 1970s. Political advocacy was not the priority it had been earlier, and more people were vocally opposed to the gay community and the group. GSOK members knew that a battle would likely be ahead of them.

In 1977, the Student Senate was under scrutiny. Senate members were questioning the overall functioning of the Senate organization. Concerns had been raised the previous spring related to committee functioning, the legislation process, and the leadership of the organization. There had been significant conflict in the Senate that previous year regarding the decision to substantially reduce funding for Recreation Services and to defund women's intercollegiate athletics. This brought about a reexamination of internal Senate structures, including the way in which student organizations were recognized and funded.[85]

In the fall of 1977, GSOK decided that despite uncertainty about the Student Senate response, they would again move forward to request that the group be recognized. About five years earlier, GSOK had been granted access to office space as well as space in the Kansas Union. Members considered this a step forward. They objected, though, to the university's unwillingness to recognize the group, an issue on which they would not back down. John Beisner commented that it "continued to be a bone of contention that the university administration was not recognizing the group."

That September, student body president Steve Leben spearheaded a proposal that would turn this inequitable situation around, changing the way in which student organizations were officially recognized. This would qualify GSOK for student fee funding. Leben proposed streamlining the process by eliminating the approval of the vice chancellor for student affairs for recognition, thereby restricting the administration's authority and control over the process.[86] "My view was every student organization should have that same ability," he commented. "The student government should provide you the basic organizational funds to keep you going. I felt that the student body, not the chancellor's office, should decide whether we were funding a group like Gay Services [sic] of Kansas." This, in fact, was LGLF members' objection to the SenEx proposal to change the two-tiered registration process in 1972.[87] Leben's primary motivation for introducing this major change was his belief that the existing process was discriminatory, especially related to those who were gay and lesbian: "When I ran for student body president, I talked with people there . . . about the idea that they [GSOK] should be in the game just like every other student group able to come to Student Senate and ask for money."

The first introduction of the bill in late September was not successful, losing by a mere six votes.[88] Students chided Senate members for letting worry about potential controversy override the opportunity to increase control over Senate funds: "What all this has meant is that groups like . . . Gay Services [GSOK] are eliminated from the funding process without student opinion on whether they should be allowed. . . . The Student Senate should not hide under the shelter of the administration's recognition regulations just to avoid tough questions about controversial groups."[89]

The GSOK kept the heat on, reminding administrators that they were not, as Leben stated, "in the game." GSOK director Todd VanLaningham voiced his concern to David Ambler, who came to KU in the fall semester of 1977 as the new vice chancellor for student affairs. Ambler, who had previously served as vice president for student affairs at Kent State University and had a key role in responding to the 1970 shooting on that campus, was familiar with controversy. In a letter to Ambler dated October 28, 1977, the tension between GSOK and the administration was evident. VanLaningham admonished the administration for not including GSOK in the student directory, stating that the omission "hinders visibility and accessibility. We would like to believe that the omission is inadvertent but past history would lead us to believe that this is another act of blatant discrimination against gay people and our group."[90]

Later that month, the Student Senate developed an interim plan and appointed three students to serve as advisors to Ambler on the student organization recognition process. They were charged with providing recommendations to Ambler regarding organizations who had applied for recognition, but they had no voting power, and Ambler made the final decisions. This did not sit well with some, who felt that the Senate had dropped the ball by failing to establish a process that substantially increased student voice in the process and solved the recognition problem.[91] Unbeknownst to many in this debate, Ambler was in the challenging position of managing the administration's discomfort related to GSOK while also trying to respond to student concerns.[92] He was walking a difficult political tightrope.

Leben resubmitted his proposal, citing that a full quorum was not present for the initial vote. He reminded Senate members that even if the proposal passed, there was no guarantee that it would be approved by the administration.[93] Leben described the meeting as "a very heated debate that included my vice president stepping down from the chair to oppose me on the issue." Others joined in, siding against Leben. Leben intentionally presented it as a student rights rather than a gay rights issue and did not directly enlist the GSOK to support his proposal. He explained his reasoning: "It would not have helped them or the cause for the Student Senate to make it a large gay rights issue. That was definitely not the way to pitch that argument at that point in time. . . . The pushback that I was getting was coming from people who were not aligned with the culture . . . definitely hostile." Leben mentioned that in the late 1970s, there was more openness about being gay, but there still was a great deal of opposition, which was at the center of the controversy. A *UDK* article, in fact, mentioned that there had been allegations that Leben "was using the proposed policy as a smokescreen for trying to advance the cause of gay rights."[94]

Chris Caldwell, Student Senate treasurer during Leben's tenure who came out as gay after he graduated, commented on the hostile climate that existed as well as Leben's courage in pushing through this proposal: "Steve did not have a girlfriend in college. And I remember there was a lot of . . . ugly, murmured, basically fag bashing of Steve." He mentioned that Leben was not a part of the "white frat boy" culture, which he said dominated the Student Senate ranks. Caldwell described an incident generated by the fraternity contingent in the Student Senate, exposing the negative sentiments some members held toward the gay community. Leben received a letter from this contingent "that was in very ugly terms describing, accusing him of being gay which was considered an accusation. And Steve, both being upset about it but also being the type of person who wasn't going to change his course," did not let this deter him. The second time the proposal went forward for a vote, it was passed by a close margin of forty to thirty-four, with students voting to officially support the change. Given the contentiousness that arose, this can be considered a notable accomplishment. Administrators still had to weigh in, however, for any change to actually take place.[95]

The following semester, spring of 1978, university general counsel Mike Davis issued a statement that the administration could not support the Student Senate proposal.[96] Davis justified the decision, referring to the 1973 court ruling in which KU was granted the right to deny the LGLF's recognition request. The previous semester, Ambler had taken a cautious stand on the passage of Leben's proposal, citing that a change in policy should be a "joint venture" between students and the administration.[97]

This decision caused indignation and frustration, prompting the entire editorial staff of the *UDK* to print an unsigned editorial (which indicated unanimous group endorsement).[98] They challenged the decision and argued for reconsideration, reproaching the university for "cowering behind the policy" to avoid controversy. This editorial was important for two reasons. First, it was a bold move on the part of students to take the administration to task for their decision. Of greater significance, however, was the willingness of a mainstream organization to show support and advocate on behalf of GSOK and the gay community. This editorial conveyed a far different tone than earlier articles, supporting the group and its right to be recognized.

This show of support may have emboldened GSOK members to engage in what was referred to as a "brilliant" move—asking Student Senate presidential candidates prior to the February election to sign a letter endorsing Leben's recognition plan.[99] Four of the five candidates signed the letter, and the fifth candidate supported the plan but could not sign the letter because he was in class (ironically, he was running with the Apathy Coalition). The letter argued that the existing process ignored Senate funding guidelines, looking not at the activity to be funded but instead at the organization when approving funding requests. Further, the letter stated that the purpose of the group should not factor into the funding decision if the activities for which funding was requested met the delineated criteria. An editorial in the *UDK* endorsed GSOK members' action, calling it "an important step toward redefining and equalizing the Student Senate's primary function—the allocation of funds to student organizations."[100]

The funding issue at the center of the discussion was in itself important. The more basic issue driving the debate, however, was voiced by

GSOK member Michael Johnson, echoing concerns raised by early LGLF founders: "First of all, we need to get them to know we exist."[101] The quest for recognition and equal treatment had, in fact, always been at the heart of the funding debate for the group. By getting the buy-in of incoming Senate leaders, GSOK members had positioned themselves to build their ally base and hold student leaders accountable.

This strategy appeared to be effective. All three of the presidential candidates were vocal in their support of GSOK and spoke explicitly to the issue of respect that the group had been working so hard to garner. Candidates Clair Keizer and Bob Tomlinson acknowledged its importance and value, commenting on the need to increase the voice of minority groups. Margaret Berlin, the candidate who would be elected president, went a step further: "I will press to have the recognition policy dropped. This will leave the administration out of it."[102] Berlin would have the opportunity during her tenure to work on this policy.

In September 1979, GSOK codirectors Todd Zwahl and Kim Gilbert brought the issue to the fore again, submitting an application for organization recognition.[103] Careful to fill out the application to meet all the criteria listed, including articulating that the group was not political and was open to all regardless of sexual orientation, the request nonetheless was denied. The reason stated in the letter the group received from the Student Organizations and Activities Office was that "your organization is substantially oriented toward support for particular personal and customarily private activities, habits, or proclivities." The thorny word "proclivities" was back in the spotlight. The letter, in addition, questioned the group's statement on the application that membership was open to all.[104]

GSOK members appealed the decision, citing two main arguments. First, they challenged the characterization of the group as oriented toward "customarily private activities," stating that all events and activities were public and open to anyone who wanted to attend. Next, they included what they titled "Current Trend of Decision in the Federal Courts," listing and detailing cases that had been ruled in favor of gay and lesbian student organizations across the country who had challenged their universities related to their First Amendment right of freedom of association.[105] This got administrators' attention. They were concerned that the group was planning on filing another lawsuit to challenge administrators' decision to not recognize the group.[106]

Students' push to change this policy required careful thought within the administration to determine an appropriate response and solution. Ambler worked carefully out front and behind the scenes to facilitate this change, facing obstacles in his efforts. Ambler recalled his introduction to the administration's stand on addressing gay and lesbian issues on campus:

> The day I arrived, Don Alderson, who was dean of men, had been the interim vice chancellor for a year and a half, and he had left a stack of papers on the desk for me. On the top of that pile was a ripped-out section of the *Daily Kansan,* and it was a story about how . . . the organization [GSOK] was preparing to take the university to court again over their denial of being eligible to receive funding from the Student Senate. The article was circled in red pen. And the note on top of it said, "Dave, we need to talk about this—Archie." Archie being Archie Dykes. And I remember picking it up and reading it and thinking, "Well, that's a hell of a way to welcome me to the university" [laughs]. But anyway, it signaled to me that this was an issue that the university administration had strong feelings about.

Chancellor Dykes did not want to draw attention to GSOK or increase the visibility of gay and lesbian issues on campus since this had the potential of raising the ire of the regents, the legislature, and the public. This had been demonstrated four years earlier when GSOK's plans to host a Midwest gay rights conference created disapproval, prompting Dykes to veto the event. Any support the administration showed for GSOK, then, had the potential to affect funding and support of the university, leading Steve Leben to comment: "I would . . . perceive that this would be the type of thing that he [Dykes] would certainly not have wanted to be out front on." Ambler's "welcome" from Dykes was indicative of the attitudes that would prevail in his attempts to change the policy and the culture. As Ambler picked up the baton from Alderson, whom early LGLF group members called out as being hostile to gay and lesbian students, he was taking on an issue that had been primed to be unsuccessful. Therefore, as the Student Senate lobbied Ambler and the administration to change the student organization funding process in 1977, Ambler also reached out to administrators behind the scenes for a solution, keeping in mind the historical lack of support.

Ambler acknowledged the difficulty of his role in supporting students and principles of free speech and civil rights while serving as an administrator. He understood the administration's concerns about being perceived as gay-friendly while, on the flip side, dealing with another high-profile lawsuit, both of which had the potential to damage KU's public image. He stated that "it could frequently put a student affairs officer at loggerheads." His ability to be seen by both camps as supportive was advantageous. Chris Caldwell, who recalled Ambler being supportive of students, astutely observed Ambler's influence with the administration: "If he'd slammed the door in their face, it wouldn't have gone anywhere."

Ambler, understanding the dynamics of cultivating change within an academic environment, commented on his strategy: "I tried to share research and information about other lawsuits that were going on across the country that clearly said there's no basis on which to deny this group. . . . I kept presenting information that clearly showed that another case would probably find our policy in violation." Ambler reorganized the Student Affairs Office in 1978 following his first year in the position, creating the Student Activities Office to oversee and support student organizations. He commented, "That process of registering got turned over to Ann [Eversole, the first director]. And I remember saying, 'Ann, clean it up. [Laughs.] . . . If we're going to do it, let's make it meaningful.'"

As Eversole took on the existing system, some issues surfaced. Ambler became aware of the lack of consistency and equity in applying regulations when some students brought this to his attention: "I remember sometime during my first year, a group of students came in and filled out a form and got registered and then came in to tell me that it was purely a trumped-up group. There was no such purpose. . . . They were trying to demonstrate how easy it was to become registered and recognized unless you were one of these high-profile organizations [referring to GSOK]." Eversole worked to make the existing system more consistent and uniform while Ambler continued to explore a more comprehensive way of fixing an inequitable process. He worked behind the scenes speaking with administrators, faculty, and students, hearing what he described as "mixed views."

Ambler characterized KU as more informal and student-centered than many universities at the time, likely reflecting the state's populist tradition. He was impressed with the degree of involvement students had in campus policy and funding decisions. In addition, he commented on faculty members' activism and involvement in civil rights issues, including issues related to gay rights. Overall, his assessment was that the climate at KU for gay and lesbian students was more favorable than at many universities across the country, "in spite of the battles we had." He was surprised that faculty governance had not been more actively involved in opposing the discriminatory group recognition policy, but he credited a "partially underground, accepted" gay and lesbian faculty organization on campus as having an important role in quietly influencing the climate.

Ambler's commitment to and plan for creating a more equitable process was central in pushing forward a new, redesigned policy. The primary motivation for this to move forward, though, really emanated from GSOK members and their well-crafted appeal to the administrators' decision to again deny recognition. Dean of Students Caryl Smith had not yet responded to GSOK's appeal submitted in early fall 1979. In a memo dated April 3, 1980, from Ambler to Chancellor Dykes, Ambler stated, "We need to come to some decision regarding the appeal Caryl Smith is sitting on from the Gay Services organization."[107] He continued, outlining three options: (1) maintain the policy and deny recognition; (2) maintain the policy and grant recognition; or (3) change the policy, eliminating the "recognized" category.

Stating that the first two options would bring the university unfavorable publicity, Ambler recommended the third option, a change to the system. He suggested that they delay a response to the appeal until Student Senate funding allocations for the year were determined, and then respond to the group, neither approving nor rejecting their request but explaining that the category of "registered student organization" would be eliminated in the following academic year. He stated that this strategy would be the most likely to keep the issue from "blowing up in our faces and giving them the kind of publicity they desire." He reasoned that "our position will be very defensible in that we have neither said yes nor no to the Gay Services group. We have simply recognized their right to exist on campus like other campus groups."[108]

On the face of it, Ambler's language could suggest that he was concerned primarily with placating GSOK and putting a lid on the controversy rather than responding to students' serious concerns and addressing the problem. However, his earlier comments about the campus climate, his statement in the letter regarding the group's right to exist, and his consistent support for civil rights and equity, make it far more likely that he was trying to communicate his allegiance to the administration and speak to Dykes's concerns while navigating a difficult political landscape in order to move the change through.

Ambler, strategizing to gain the chancellor's endorsement, worked with Executive Vice Chancellor Shankel to draft a memo to the chancellor. He explained his approach: "What I wanted ... was simply a registration process that complied with the rights of people to assemble and so forth, and that the decision on whether or not somebody was eligible for funding should be left with the Student Senate who we had delegated the ability to allocate that student activity fee. I sent that memo in and waited for what kind of reaction we'd get." In the spring of 1980 Ambler received the chancellor's reply. He commented that many times, Dykes's response "came back with just your memo with some notes. . . . And this said, 'Dave, OK.' I was a little shocked that he had decided to accept." It is interesting to note that the week following this interchange, Dykes announced his resignation.

Following Dykes's approval, the two-pronged system was eliminated and all organizations who applied would be registered. This entitled them to the opportunity to request funding and access campus resources without the earlier restrictions. Ambler described the process: "With the exception of groups that are religious or political in nature, the Student Senate could consider funding any registered student group for any activity that is a legal act and does not violate University regulations."[109] Ann Eversole commented on the egalitarian principles that guided the process: "Everybody ought to have an opportunity to apply. . . . It was just fair." Ambler expressed disappointment that this could not have been accomplished more quickly. He acknowledged, however, that the issue of timing was critical in getting to the end goal: "So the timing worked out on it, but on the other hand, people's civil rights are pretty important and it's hard to justify delays in achieving those. . . . I don't know how much was—what the university did—as to the winds of society changing, but I felt good that we had, over a period of time, made giant steps forward in achieving rights of this organization."

Ambler's comments on the role of timing in the passage of this policy are important from another perspective. While the term "sexual proclivities" was removed from the policy, the term that was added, "legal act," could have continued GSOK'S battle. An argument could be made, as had been done in the past, that homosexual acts were illegal, the group condoned these acts, and therefore the group should not be approved. But campus administrators, following Ambler's lead, chose to not pursue that path.

In 1980, close to ten years after the first challenge took place, GSOK had finally achieved what the founders of the LGLF began—they had been seen, heard, and included. The group could now be registered the same way as other campus organizations and considered on merit rather than identity. Their fight for justice had a major role in making the campus more equitable for all.

Concluding Thoughts: LGLF Members' Later Activist Efforts

At the end of the decade, GSOK had rebuilt itself after coming close to dying and had evolved into a powerful, established voice for the gay community. The mechanisms that were originally created to generate comprehensive change, including the speakers' bureau, activism, dances, and the Gay Counseling Service, were still going strong during the second half of the decade. Two name changes—from Lawrence Gay Liberation Front to Lawrence Gay Liberation, Inc., to Gay Services of Kansas—reflected a shift in the group's focus to be more educationally based. This did not, however, indicate that activism was no longer important. Instead, it demonstrated a shifting of approach and emphasis. In the second half of the decade, GSOK members relied more on working within existing frameworks, such as following the Student Senate's process and collaborating with mainstream organizations to achieve their goals.

The group brought forward initiatives that had a lasting impact on the campus: the campus-wide awareness campaign Wear Blue Jeans if You're Gay Day, the campus affirmative action policy, and the student organization recognition process. GSOK members' efforts generated new, necessary conversations. And by challenging inequitable policies and bringing allies around the table, gay rights issues had been identified as important to the overall goals of the campus.

In addition, GSOK's efforts to expand visibility and awareness through the creation of Gay Awareness Week and the challenge to antigay

legislation through education and letter-writing campaigns were important contributions. And the importance of the social aspect of the group,
mentioned by many, cannot be underestimated. It provided a positive,
safe, affirming way of connecting with others to reduce feelings of isolation, shame, and deviance. The group had in the latter half of the 1970s
maintained its momentum, impact, and relevance, having a central role in
the evolution of the KU and Lawrence gay community. They had moved
forward and anchored the foundation.

This story has focused on the years from 1970 to 1979 due to their
importance in the history of the group. The decade that began with a
lawsuit had ended with a victory: full recognition. Ending the chapter
here, however, does not indicate that the group's story had come to a
close. This early era laid the foundation for what was to come in the fight
for gay rights.

6

"We Are Here and We're Not Going Away"
The 1980s and Beyond

By 1980, the Gay Services of Kansas (GSOK) was well known and had established a presence. However, despite many gains, the group's work was far from over. Members continued through the twenty-first century to provide support and a much-needed safe space as they pushed for gay and lesbian rights. This chapter will provide some important highlights of the group's evolution as a legitimate organization from 1980 to the current times. It is not intended to be a comprehensive review, but rather centers on the ways that group members continued to carry out the foundational vision and mission set by the early organizers. It focuses on key ways the group continued to build a gay community in their fight for "equality under the law, equality of opportunity, and equality in the society," as stated in the first LGLF constitution.[1]

In the early 1980s, with the elimination of the bifurcated recognition system, the group finally gained recognition. The access to funding that recognition afforded, although helpful, was not the primary motivation for group members' push for this change. The group was insisting on its right to equal treatment. In fact, in 1982, two years after the policy change, group members convened to decide if they wanted to request Student Senate funds. The answer was a resounding no. They received considerable revenue from the dances, which were still going strong. Members had concerns that there would be strings attached to Senate funding, which would place controls and restrictions on group activities, to be "used as a club to keep us in line."[2]

A year later, in 1983, the group had a change of heart. Their resounding no turned to yes as they decided that the time had come to request Student Senate funding, because they "deserved the same support as other student organizations."[3] In addition, a new campus policy in 1980 prohibited the sale of 3.2 beer in the Kansas Memorial Union where dances were held. This change was made in anticipation of a forthcoming state alcohol policy that would have a negative impact on the campus if violated. This dampened students' and community members' interest in attending dances, the group's primary source of funding.[4] Subsequently, group members saw dance attendance drop to about two hundred, greatly reducing their revenue.[5]

GSOK's request for funding exposed the underlying homophobia that was still brewing. Many opposed the request, resulting in letters to the *UDK* and heated Student Senate meetings, which foreshadowed the challenges the group would face with the Student Senate in the future. Yet the group's funding request was approved "without a hitch." They were approved for far less than they requested: of the $1,146.44 they requested, $493 was approved for office rent and phone charges. This reduction was "somewhat standard" for a small organization during a budget crunch.[6] In order to allow the sale of alcohol and reduce costs, members decided to take the dances off campus. They established a deal with a community venue, Hole in the Wall Hall (later renamed the Bottleneck), but dances were still held occasionally at the Kansas Union for Halloween and Valentine's Day. The dances continued through the 1990s and remained popular.[7]

The recognition and increased visibility that the group had garnered brought about stability, but it came at a price. During the 1980s, the group experienced increased confrontation, hostility, and harassment.[8] It is no coincidence that this evolved as word began to spread in 1981 about the AIDS epidemic. Advances in acceptance that had been achieved in the earlier era were now threatened both locally and nationally. Fear and misinformation created panic, fueling hostility toward those who were gay, dramatically changing the climate in the gay community.[9] Lee Hubbell recalled: "You're talking about before AIDS and after AIDS. . . . There's a clear line there. That changed everything." Paul Lim recalled that many who had bravely come out of the closet in the 1970s went quietly back in. He talked about the effect the "gay disease," as it was called, had on the campus community: "There was such a stigma. There were certain faculty members who died of AIDS and suddenly if you were once friendly with them, once they had AIDS, a lot of people began to shun them, unfortunately."

Jim Scally, who was administrative assistant to Chancellor Dykes in 1976, died of AIDS in 1996. During his tenure on campus up until the time of his death, he took an active role in the gay community. He was an involved member of Gay and Lesbian Services of Kansas, helped organize Gay Pride Week activities, was involved in efforts to pass the Simply Equal Amendment, and was a member of the Gay and Lesbian Academic and Staff Association.[10] He had the courage to contribute to the cause and was well known throughout campus. But this also led to Scally's concerns about KU administration and Kansas legislature members finding out he was gay for fear of repercussions. Lim remembered the AIDS fear that carried through to the 1990s: "[Scally] died of AIDS. But . . . what he died of was hushed up. It was never mentioned. They didn't talk about it, and his grave at Pioneer Cemetery went unmarked for a long time. Then I think people got together and paid for a tombstone, for a marker."

The epidemic affected the group directly as some members contracted AIDS and died during the 1980s. Many more died of the disease in the following decades. As was the case in many corners, the initial response early on was one of denial. Joe Lordi remembered: "There was an article in this Gay News about this gay cancer, and we all kind of looked at it and thought, 'What the hell are they talking about?' Little did we know then. Little did we know."[11] LGLF member Chuck Ortleb, however, did take notice. After graduating from KU, he went to New York and established two influential gay publications, *Christopher Street* and *New York Native*, the latter of which was the first to report on AIDS in May 1981.[12] While many challenged his views, which some considered controversial, Ortleb's publications had a major role in raising the visibility of AIDS nationally.

Throughout the 1980s, the campus saw a surge of homophobic harassment and intimidation unlike anything seen in the prior decade. This was mirrored nationally as the New Right became more prominent. As the group (now named Gay and Lesbian Services of Kansas—GLSOK) had more involvement with the Student Senate, new battles ensued. In 1983, a conservative Student Senate coalition emerged that had previously voiced disapproval over funding for the group. Ironically it called itself the Freedom Coalition.[13] One of the Coalition's main platform issues was to "terminate funding of specific groups and projects that are viewed as morally unsupportable by a substantial segment of the student body."[14] This was aimed specifically at GLSOK. No other groups had been identified or included in the discussion. The Freedom Coalition lost its bid for Student Senate leadership, yet it did not lose its influence. Four Freedom Coalition members still served on the forty-five-member Finance Committee. This seemingly small number was actually significant when considering that only thirteen to sixteen members usually attended.[15] The vitriolic conversations that took place about funding the GLSOK required a more confrontational style on the part of group members. They also brought in many straight mainstream student, faculty, and administrative allies. Student Body President Carla Vogel and Vice President Boog Highberger advocated for the group, with Vogel vowing to defeat any appropriations bills that did not include funding for the GLSOK.[16]

Those opposed to the GLSOK pushed back and circulated a petition to block the group from receiving Student Senate funding, which the Senate called "discriminatory." Hostility and harassment directed at the GLSOK increased, including highly offensive T-shirts that were distributed throughout campus. Many wore them as a statement of their disapproval of the group. In the style of the Ghostbusters image that was popular during this time, the shirt had an image of a limp-wristed, wavy ghost with a line diagonally through the image and the word "Fagbusters." Its origins were unknown until a determined *UDK* reporter, John Hanna, uncovered the creator: Steve Imber, a leader in the Freedom Coalition and a Student Senate member.[17] The distribution and sale of the T-shirts brought about a flood of letters and editorials in the *UDK* condemning both the shirts and their originator. Even those who considered homosexuality to be "wrong" opposed Imber's tactics, as reflected in an editorial written by *UDK* staff columnist Bruce F. Honomichl. Commenting that he personally did not support homosexuality, he asserted that the GLSOK was the "apparent victim of a nasty little game of political double-talk." He denounced Imber's actions: "The promotion of these attitudes is contrary to the purpose of any university." One letter writer, in fact, suggested wryly that GLSOK should sell "Steve Imber t-shirts with the logo 'Bigotbusters.'" Following this exposure and negative sentiment, Steve Imber lost credibility and support. His petition to revoke GLSOK funds was defeated.[18] However, the controversy continued, and a second petition was circulated to ban the GLSOK from being on state property. Following these events, the Student Senate Executive Committee issued a statement condemning these actions that had created "an atmosphere of persecution and threats of violence" aimed at gay and lesbian students on campus.[19]

The Fagbusters T-shirt, petitions, and hostile letters in the *UDK* were just some of many acts of hostility that were occurring. Additional acts included verbal harassment and threats, a Student Senate Finance Committee request for the organization to submit a listing of members, and incidents in which gay students and faculty allies had their car tires slashed and lug nuts loosened. Another incident arose when an instructor, Felix Mose, had students conduct surveillance on people as a class assignment. GLSOK president Ruth Lichtwardt was selected as a "subject" by some students in the class. They scrutinized her, followed her around, and intimidated her.[20]

Lichtwardt commented on this increased hostility in an interview by *Rolling Stone* for the article "AIDS on Campus": "AIDS has given people an excuse to hate gay people. . . . People who used to argue against [GLSOK] on other grounds are now completely forgetting those grounds and using AIDS."[21] The group adopted additional measures to protect members' confidentiality and safety. As an example, a 1980s GLSOK office manual stated, "The most important thing is—DO NOT GIVE OUT NAMES, ADDRESSES or PHONE NUMBERS—over the phone or to people who walk in."[22]

The harassment and violence aimed at the gay community had become such a problem that faculty circulated a petition initiated by Professor Bill Tuttle requesting that the administration address it. Tuttle, who had just returned to KU in the fall of 1984 following a sabbatical at Stanford University, was so alarmed that he engaged professors Beatrice Wright (psychology), Bob Shelton (religion), and Norm Forer (social welfare) to join him in drafting this petition. Tuttle described it as a "statement to respect human rights."[23] It was widely circulated throughout campus.

Two weeks later, senior administrators finally took action. Vice Chancellor David Ambler joined Executive Vice Chancellor Robert Cobb in issuing a letter supporting free expression of ideas and condemning coercion, harassment, and threatening behavior. Also widely circulated was an excerpt from Chancellor Gene Budig's 1983 convocation speech denouncing "bigotry, intolerance, racial or sexual discrimination, anti-semitism, or the like. These are the product of a closed mind."[24] Tuttle commented that the administration's responses "were very, very helpful. And it definitely turned the tide." Additionally, Ruth Lichtwardt and Steve Imber, the student senator who had opposed the group, were requested to draft and publish a joint statement in the *UDK* asking "for everyone on both sides of the issue to cool it." This helped diffuse the situation.[25]

This increased hostility in the 1980s required a shift in approach and response for the group. The strategic political maneuvering within the system that was a hallmark of the 1970s evolved into a more aggressive, confrontational approach to counter the overt harassment that had emerged. The hostility on campus reflected the change in the national climate, which had become more conservative, not only due to the AIDS epidemic but also to the rise of the religious Right.[26] The group addressed this head-on by taking on a visible role in campus politics and increasing their public statements about inequity.[27]

Specific tactics included marches, protests, parades, promenades, and Gay and Lesbian Awareness (GALA) Week. GALA Week was reintroduced to the campus by member and dance DJ Joe Baldwin, who drew in members and made it highly visible. The group changed its style but not its comprehensive focus and commitment to civil rights. The peer counseling program continued to be well utilized, and peer education programs were still frequently requested. The group prepared instructions and guidelines for peer educators that suggested a concern for minimizing hostility in presentations in addition to providing coordinated training and oversight.[28]

In addition, women took on a more involved role in the group during this time frame under the leadership of Ruth Lichtwardt, who became director in spring 1983.[29] An indication of this trend was the 1981 addition of the "L" to the name, Gay and Lesbian Services of Kansas (GLSOK). Intentionally identifying lesbians in the organization's name communicated inclusion and a return to the group's original intention and plan when it was created in 1970.

As the group moved into the 1990s, the issue of gay rights gained political momentum nationally, refocusing from the private to the public sphere. Gay and lesbian activists demanded that policies be restructured to protect their interests and their civil rights, including same-sex marriage, domestic partner and adoption benefits, antidiscrimination measures, employment protections, nonheterosexual individuals in the military, and gay and lesbian representation in decision-making bodies.[30] College campuses across the country saw a resurgence in activism as the population had become increasingly diverse. This resulted in students challenging campuses to be more inclusive and responsive. Robert Rhoads described it as such: "Thus for many students, the dream of freedom and justice for all has been recharged and the Civil Rights Movement has been resuscitated in the form of the Multicultural Student Movement of the 1990s."[31]

Group members recognized in the early 1990s that their name again needed to be updated to be inclusive of bisexual students. They expanded their name to Lesbian, Bisexual and Gay Students of Kansas, or LesBiGay OK. It is also important to note the change of order in this title. Men in the group made the decision to challenge the prevailing male dominance in these organizations, opting for a less prominent place in the title in the name of equity. Their name would change again in 1997 to Queers and Allies: LesBiGayTrans Services of Kansas, or Queers and Allies for short. One of the group members involved in the change explained: "So why the word queer? Because 'lesbian, bisexual, transgender, and gay' is a big mouthful and 'queer' is one all-inclusive syllable. Because it is a little edgy, and it does push the envelope a little. Because 'queer' is a word gaining wider and wider acceptance in political and academic circles, and we consider ourselves to be part of the forefront of this movement."[32]

Changes in the group's name during this time reflected the change in the group's evolving goals and orientation. The group continued the range of programs and services that had been central throughout the life of the group, but members had shifted their approach to more publicly challenging the heteronormative culture and discriminatory policies. This included protests against the ROTC, which actively recruited at KU yet barred those who were not heterosexual from enlisting or receiving ROTC-related scholarships.[33] GSOK expanded their ranks by reaching out to other multicultural organizations to participate in the protests. Dilley noted that they were successful in garnering support and getting the attention of the campus, challenging Department of Defense discriminatory practices and the KU administration, who allowed the organization on campus. It was also reminiscent of anti-ROTC demonstrations in the late 1960s and early 1970s at KU in which numerous campus groups joined together in protest.[34] Other acts of public protest included kiss-ins; AIDS candlelight vigils; GALA Week queer promenades involving same-sex couples holding hands walking down Jayhawk Boulevard; and public demonstrations against antigay, hate-mongering Baptist minister Fred Phelps, who began coming to campus in the early 1990s to protest the LGBTQ community.[35]

In the 1990s, the group collaborated with the Lawrence community to support and lobby for an important initiative, the Simply Equal Amendment. This amendment was created to add the term "sexual orientation" to the City Human Relations Ordinance to provide protections for gay, lesbian, and bisexual Lawrence residents in employment, housing, and public accommodations. The GLSOK formed a group with members of the community called the Freedom Coalition, which supported rather than undermined gay rights, as the earlier Student Senate group with the same name did a decade earlier. The GLSOK had a substantial role in these efforts, with members serving on the steering committee. As a result of combined campus and community efforts, the ordinance was adopted in May 1995 despite considerable opposition from conservative and religious leaders in the community. Lawrence was the first city in the state to accomplish this.[36]

Dilley identified members' approach in the 1990s as shifting toward a "queer" framework that built on the group's political and confrontational approach of the 1970s. A central tenet of the LGLF from its beginnings was to challenge existing systems to bring about change. But first the group needed to be recognized and seen, establishing its existence. Dilley explained this evolution: "Queer students utilized many of the same tactics as those of gays in the 1970s, but instead of simply promoting non-heterosexual visibility, queer acts were crafted to invert public and private space and to highlight the power differentials embedded within the norm of heterosexuality."[37]

During the fifty years following the birth of the group, members had established an identity and a presence. Members over the years relentlessly challenged inequity with force, determination, courage, and creativity. This challenge has been central in breaking down deeply established taboos and changing the cultural discourse about sexuality to redefine power. The group therefore was successful in facilitating institutional change and asserting its power by making the discrimination visible and rewriting the heteronormative discourse.[38] "We are here and we're not going away"—the group's revolutionary mantra—changed the conversation and the culture, paving the way for greater acceptance and inclusion.

Now, in the current era, one can look to the way in which sexual minority issues are integrated into institutional policies and the KU campus culture. A few of these developments include educational and awareness programs such as SafeZone training, monthlong "Outober" and "Gaypril" events, and the Kansas Drag Showcase; Lavender Graduation; peer support groups; speakers and events on current issues; integration and inclusion of LGBTQ issues in many academic departments, including Women, Gender and Sexuality Studies; the establishment of the Sexuality and Gender Diversity Faculty Staff Council; policy initiatives such as all-gender restrooms, name and gender marker changes on KU records, and gender-inclusive campus housing; scholarships for LGBTQ students; and the creation of discipline-specific LGBTQ student organizations.[39]

One of the most notable advances has been the establishment in 2014 of an office to provide services to the KU LGBTQ community and the hiring of the first full-time director. Finally, the 1970s founders' dream of an established office to advocate and advance LGBTQ rights on campus had become a reality. While there had been a part-time graduate student position charged with addressing LGBTQ concerns since the 1990s, individuals in that role did not have the resources, campus connections, or leverage to deal with difficult, embedded problems. The creation of the center, named the KU Center for Sexuality and Gender Diversity (SGD) in 2015, has provided the vision, oversight, people power, and administrative support needed to make headway since its founding in 2014. In addition to providing essential services and support, SGD coordinates with academic programs, administrative departments, and student services and organizations to integrate those who are LGBTQ into all aspects of the university. In spring 2021, the SGD moved into its new home in the Kansas Union.

This brought about changes to the organization as well. In 2014, Queers and Allies changed its name to SpectrumKU to more intentionally communicate the group's inclusive philosophy to "celebrate the wide spectrum of gender and sexuality diversity across KU campus and their various intersectionalities."[40] During the 2018–2019 academic year,

SpectrumKU disbanded due to low interest and involvement, as well as tensions that had escalated related to the future direction of the organization. During the 2019–2020 academic year, SGD reestablished a group that was reminiscent of the LGLF to "create a welcoming environment for LGBTQ students at the University of Kansas and strengthen all aspects of our identities in a safe space" by "explor[ing] what our identities mean to us through social events, activism, and community discussion."[41] The challenges of the COVID-19 pandemic that began in the spring of 2020 hampered the group's community building goals as most campus classes and activities were held remotely, restricting in-person gatherings. The SGD has since established a wide array of student groups as the disruption of the pandemic has eased. These groups provide diverse opportunities to get involved, connect, and find one's community, including ones for trans students, students of color, and graduate students.[42]

While the conceptualization and understanding of sexual orientation and gender identity have evolved since the creation of the LGLF in 1970, the needs that gave rise to its creation have continued. Ron Gans, an early member of the group, captured the role the LGLF has played in addressing these needs and creating a community: "[The group] formed almost like a force field around our lives."[43] The group has been a safe place, empowering members through the years to form strong connections, fight difficult battles, and celebrate advances. In a 1995 article in the *UDK*, Joe Cuevas, who then was codirector of LesBiGay OK, commented about the lasting impact of the group: "The early struggles have helped people of my generation so much. Without them [the founders], we wouldn't be where we are now." Lee Hubbell summed up the LGLF's role in creating the foundation for fifty years of LGBTQ advocacy at KU and in the community: "We opened the window."[44]

Conclusion

It was a clear fall afternoon in October 2021. Fifty-one years had passed since David Stout founded the Lawrence Gay Liberation Front. The university had changed greatly in that time, and so had Stout. His long brown (sometimes blond) hippie hair was now short and white. He had retired after a long, successful career as a social worker. He had moved to Taiwan and met his husband, Ozzie, who had flown halfway around the world with him to see where it all began. Stout now stood in front of the brick edifice of the Kansas Union, the very same building where half a century earlier, he had handed out leaflets for the fledgling group and attended the fabulous LGLF dances. And when he walked inside with Ozzie, he saw something on the main level he could only have dreamed of in 1970: an official LGBTQ center—sponsored by the University of Kansas.

Stout wasn't the only one who had returned. Dressed in a colorful dashiki with one gold earring hanging from their ear was Reginald Brown. With tears in their eyes, they choked up while describing first seeing that center: "That is so nice . . . This is what we wanted."[1] Many of those original gay rights pioneers had returned to the nest: Michael Stubbs, a historian and retired film location manager; Leonard Grotta, who had illustrious careers in journalism and real estate and had flown in from California; and Joe Prados, Lee Hubbell, Bob Friedland, Sharon Mayer, Bob Warren, Ruth Lichtwardt, and dozens of others. People had traveled from all corners of the globe to reunite in Lawrence for a weeklong celebration titled "51 Years OUT!: Celebrating Gay Liberation History of KU and Lawrence" (it would have been a fifty-year anniversary but was delayed due to the coronavirus pandemic of 2020). This celebration offered a week of events including panel discussions featuring original LGLF and women's community members; lectures by current scholars on LGBTQ issues; a carillon concert at the bell tower; social gatherings; and even a dance in the ballroom. But this time around, all these events were done with the official blessing of the University of Kansas.

The *Lawrence Journal-World* featured this event on the front page, and Kansas Public Radio featured it on their program *KPR Presents*. There were an unprecedented number of campus and community cosponsors— eighteen—which also demonstrated a change in attitude since the 1970s. This included the KU William Allen White School of Journalism and Mass Communications, whose students produced a powerful documentary.[2] Over five hundred campus and community members attended the events throughout the week. The women's community had organized a reunion of their 1970s music group, the Lawrence Women's Music Collective, in tandem with the larger event, and women likewise came from coast to coast to attend.

Excitement filled the air as old friends—many who hadn't seen each other since the 1970s—laughed, exchanged hugs, and reunited as if no time had gone by. Most of these early activists were now retirees looking back on distinguished, diverse careers, everything from college professor and architect to nonprofit organizer. And now they were going to share their stories with the current generation of college students.

Kicking off the Friday night dance, D. A. Graham, the interim vice provost for diversity, equity, inclusion and belonging, commented on the LGLF's importance: "I understand that throughout history in our KU and Lawrence communities, leaders were not always supportive and, in fact, were complicit in causing harm to queer and trans people. Fortunately, we have come a long way in the last several decades, due in large part to the Lawrence Gay Liberation Front and other community organizers. I commend and thank you all for your dedication and work." Affirming KU's commitment to maintaining these hard-fought rights and praising current campus efforts, he invited everyone to "celebrate the last five decades of activism and resilience of LGBTQIA+ people in Lawrence and at KU."[3] A ballroom full of LGLF alumni and current KU students and community members joined in enthusiastic applause.

This weeklong reunion was important for many reasons. First, it was a chance for LGLF members to be welcomed back with open arms by the very university that had refused to recognize them. Next, it was a chance for the younger generation of college students to learn about this movement in history. Finally, it was also a chance for group members and the community to reflect on the lasting impact the group had made. A lot had changed in fifty years, and this milestone year was a perfect time for the community to honor these early activists.

Lessons Learned from Early Activists

The progress that has been made in advancing LGBTQ rights since 1970 has been transformational. People who identify as LGBTQ have won several victories, including the rights to marry, adopt children, and openly serve in the military, and protection against employment and housing discrimination. In addition, openly LGBTQ individuals hold many leadership positions in politics and public service across the country. These advances were considered unattainable in 1970.

When the Lawrence Gay Liberation Front started in 1970, members did not know that they were making history.[4] Their efforts to connect with other gay and lesbian people and their demand to be treated equally and with respect emanated from a very personal place. Their actions, however, transcended the personal and impacted the larger public sphere. This led Steven Weaver to call their actions revolutionary:

> We very much thought of ourselves as radicals and revolutionaries, and people who were headlong going to overthrow the way things were. . . . The irony of that for gay people is that we actually did. It didn't necessarily happen the way we thought it would. But by doing the simplest of things, which was saying, "You've got to come out of the closet," and by coming out of the closet, and then helping somebody else come out of the closet, it was a revolution that took place in one person at a time over the thirty, forty years to get to the point where we are today.

The "51 Years OUT!" event was an important reminder of the long-term significance of the group's actions. Determining the impact of an organization on the culture of a community is a challenging task. Change is difficult to quantify and often cannot be seen directly. Nonetheless, reflecting on these early actions through a contemporary lens provides the context to better understand the ways in which these earlier experiences contributed to the cultural shifts and progress that have occurred. With this in mind, this next section will discuss some key ways the early activists' actions changed the climate and the culture. Their successes can provide important lessons to guide the next generation forward.

Creating a Presence

When LGLF began in 1970, members understood that the group first and foremost had to create a presence and get the attention of the campus. At their panel during the "51 Years OUT!" event, LGLF members recalled that it was key in all the actions that the group pursued. Lee Hubbell explained: "First we had to be visible—then we could work on tolerance."[5] John Beisner, student body president in the mid-1970s, commented that the group's visibility was an important step in creating public awareness that there were, in fact, many gay and lesbian students on campus, despite thoughts to the contrary. LGLF members were described as, in the words of Ann Eversole, "not anonymous," "put[ting] themselves out there," and "put[ting] the campus on notice." This visibility also provided members with a platform for legitimizing their identity and confronting their own internalized homophobia. Their presence was far-reaching, encompassing both mainstream and radical communities.[6]

For those who were closeted, this visibility could be threatening and uncomfortable. Former student Trip Haenisch, who described the group as "radical," "crazy," "scary," and "dangerous," talked about his resistance and discomfort: "To me, they were scary because if . . . you're closeted, those people are in a position to out you. So those were the people you least wanted to be around if you're closeted." He described the conflict he experienced, feeling simultaneously pulled toward and pushed away from the group: "I would say anybody that was a closeted gay would actually run in the opposite direction. I was really curious, but I certainly didn't want anybody else to know that I was curious." Leonard Grotta recalled seeing students wandering past the group's meeting room in the Student Union every week, pausing and looking in but not entering. "They weren't quite brave enough to go. . . . They wanted to but they were afraid to."

This did not mean, though, that the group's presence escaped the attention of gay students who were not out. Chad Leat observed: "I think it is fascinating that they [LGLF members] created awareness to allow the rest of us to ride on the coattails." Trip Haenisch added: "Now I have immense respect for people that have the courage to stand up and be who they are, fight for the right to be who they are. But then my feeling was totally different. It was kind of self-serving, and my response was all based on my own fears." Professor emeritus Dennis Dailey observed from his experiences in speaking with students: "I don't think that the activities of the GLF went unnoticed by any gay person on this campus. . . . And I think they responded all across the spectrum from 'Holy shit, these guys are going to get me into trouble' on one end to 'Thank God somebody's finally doing something about this.'"

This presence also had broader implications. Bob Warren commented that it reminded the community that "gay lib was not something that [only] happened in New York on Christopher Street . . . in West Hollywood . . . or even San Francisco. This was in your backyard or your front yard. And we are here, and we are everywhere." This led him to conclude, "I thought that was very important to bring it home." Steven Weaver added that it provided a visible challenge to people's preconceptions about what it meant to be gay: "When I would go out and I would be openly gay . . . there were people looking and watching. And those people had never seen a gay person before, so it was eye-opening for them. . . . All of a sudden, people started to look at things differently, think about things differently, question certain assumptions that they'd had."

Lesbians, on the other hand, asserted their presence primarily as feminists, rather than focusing on sexual orientation. Sexism was rampant in many aspects of college life and the world at large and was a common experience for many lesbians. Feminists had a strong presence on campus, organizing and protesting to make their voices heard. LGLF members supported their efforts and often joined them. They were also visible as campus leaders. Kala Stroup explained that this was challenging, since many organizations were primarily male-dominated and hostile to women's presence. Many lesbians, both quiet and outspoken, were among the feminists who stepped up to the challenge.

LGLF members and early activists created a presence that made them hard to ignore. They made inequity and injustice visible and did not back down. Their success came from challenging homophobic stereotypes through their actions and presence while welcoming people "into the circle" with positivity and openness. The greater LGBTQ openness and presence in current times compared to fifty years ago reflects the culture shift that has evolved from this early activism. It is important, however, to also recognize current attempts to increase visibility that play on outmoded campy, stereotypical images that reduce LGBTQ people to a caricature rather than viewing them as complex and dimensional, thereby reinforcing myths and pigeonholing. Early activists' educational framework can provide a template for how to be "out there" in today's society and articulate issues in ways that promote pride, respect, and progress.

Hybrid Leadership—Challenging the Establishment while Navigating the System

LGLF members accomplished something that was uncommon among gay rights groups in the 1970s: they worked both within and outside of institutional structures to change attitudes and systems. Keeping in mind that the group evolved from radical activist organizing as well as from within the university organizational structure, members recognized that they would need to engage with both in order to be successful long term.

David Ambler concluded, as an administrator on the inside track, that the LGLF was able to move forward "because there was a university culture to support it in spite of opposition even among some in the administration." Much of this support was behind the scenes. "The administration itself could have taken a much harder line in so many instances," acknowledged Kathryn Clark, "but in general they erred on the side of allowing discourse and supporting students of all kinds."

Many KU faculty and administrators in leadership roles who were concerned about civil rights understood the polarized environment that tied the hands of decision-makers. They also recognized their ability to shake up the inertia it created. Ambler identified the importance of allies in pushing for accountability: "[They were] people who didn't have to worry about their own personal safety or how they were perceived . . . who would take the university to task on anything they thought was discriminatory." This provided a base of support for members when the going got tough.

In addition to the group's ability to create an ally base was their ability to utilize both radical and mainstream approaches as they strategically addressed campus issues affecting gay and lesbian students. LGLF founders, while influenced by the radical New Left agenda, were also influenced by their personal experience and academic disciplines emphasizing a relational, environmental systems approach.[7] Therefore, by shaking up and challenging existing systems while also working within those systems to change them, LGLF members created a hybrid paradigm.

Research indicates that LGBTQ leaders who are effective in bringing about change do not adopt a specific philosophical or political approach but instead are able to adjust their style to meet the needs of their stakeholders and the external climate in which they operate.[8] It is not the leaders' or group's level of radicalism per se that is important, but rather the group's ability to translate its vision to meaningful priorities that are mindful of the climate in which it operates, determining how far it can go in pushing against institutional norms and culture to accomplish its mission. LGLF members walked this difficult tightrope as they made decisions that challenged administrative authority. When LGLF members' request for official university recognition was denied, they had no precedents or examples to guide them but relied on their vision and instincts. Their persistence, as well as their refusal to accept a resolution short of full inclusion, resulted in a victory for the group in 1980 and a significant change in the campus culture. Steve Leben summarized the importance of this action for the group: "Mak[ing] themselves equivalent to many other student organizations to me was an important legacy."

Although the LGLF was not successful in winning the lawsuit, its challenge to the university got administrators' attention and resulted in a change to the larger system. Group members' actions affected not only this policy but also the way in which student organizations were conceptualized and funded from an equity perspective. The LGLF's lawsuit also generated discussion about student involvement and voice in institutional decision-making processes. Therefore, the LGLF's quest for recognition had a secondary outcome of challenging institutional authority structures related to student governance.[9]

Group members periodically struggled with these difficult leadership decisions. After losing the lawsuit, Stout expressed frustration for trying to work within the system. This approach had splintered the LGLF and left him feeling defeated. He wondered if a more forceful, radical approach going "outside of the system" would have been more successful. But in reconsidering the group's actions, he analyzed the issue from another angle. "The Lawrence Gay Liberation Front has done more than confront the system. It has joined the system to also give it shape from within." He recognized the enormity of the task and the difficulty in one organization taking on this task single-handedly:

> There is only so much that a given number of people can do, but Gay Liberation of Lawrence in the past two years . . . has been discovering more and more the infinite variety of ways to skin that cat. . . . They have discovered that the more you entrench yourself into the body of the system, the more aware that system becomes of your presence, [and] the more it must accommodate that presence.

Stout posed the question, "Should Lawrence Gay Liberation, Inc., resort to radical means and try to force the issue?" but concluded that "if radical means are too radical, we . . . know that there will be adverse reactions."[10]

The decision on the part of group leaders and members throughout the era to not only engage in confrontational approaches but also apply more inclusive, nuanced mechanisms to address ongoing problems was controversial. They ran the risk of alienating their base of support and losing momentum and credibility among more radical group members as well as members of the campus and community, who might view their efforts as too mainstream. Fortunately, the risk paid off, and the group's success indicated that this approach had been effective.

The lesson to be learned from this is that leaders who embrace approaches that broaden their operating base are most likely to succeed. The group's efforts to bring about change through a civil rights lens, using education, inclusion, and humor to create a bridge rather than a divide was unique, notable, and courageous. Members were fearless in challenging those in positions of authority while also working within the system to generate conversations in classrooms, hallways, and places where people lived and congregated. As KU professor and author Jeffrey Moran stated, "Only when the language of opposition had become commonplace, unremarkable coming from the mouth even of a Kansas farmboy, could the

changes in attitude and morality be called revolutionary."[11] This charac-
terizes the climate that the group fostered, earning them this "revolutionary" label.

Leading the Way by Example—Becoming Role Models and Mentors

Professor emeritus Dennis Dailey observed that many students he spoke
with in the 1970s who were gay or lesbian felt all alone since there were so
few role models and mentors to guide them. Publicly identifying as gay
or affiliating with the gay community was simply too risky for a majority
of those who could fulfill this role. Bob Warren commented, "Well, we
didn't have any [mentors or role models]. You're absolutely correct in
that. There were no known public officials that were openly gay. There
probably were some, but we didn't know who they were, and they weren't
about to tell us either." Susan Davis observed that for lesbians, different
generations did not frequently mix, and "the younger crowd were the
ones reaching out to form a community." Younger women's visibility was
uncomfortable for older women, who were more likely to be secretive
about their identity, limiting intergenerational connections.[12]

Without this public acknowledgment, many students denied their
identity or remained closeted. Said Chris Caldwell, "I actually hadn't pro-
cessed being gay myself yet. Like I say, I was deeply closeted, both from
the world and from myself. Another part about it is, which of course is
not that unusual looking back, although it seems strange now—I didn't
know gay people."[13] Not knowing others who were gay or lesbian was a
common experience, fostering feelings of deviance and isolation, particularly for those who had not connected with a community.

For many LGLF members, their first role models and mentors were
others in the group. "I think it was built into what the organization
was," Bob Warren recalled. Members learned many lessons from each
other. Many commented that David Stout's support helped them feel
understood, supported, and empowered. His journey from hiding and
self-recrimination to a place of positive self-acceptance provided an encouraging, hopeful example.[14] Michael Stubbs's and John Bolin's passion
and political savvy also motivated others to become involved in campus and community LGBTQ activism. LGLF member Chuck Ortleb,
who became the publisher and editor-in-chief of the early national gay

publications *Christopher Street* and *New York Native*, inspired many with his openness and boldness in being out and outspoken. Caldwell recalled that the self-acceptance he witnessed in group members left a strong impression.[15] Lesbian feminists also looked to each other for guidance and inspiration, forming tight-knit communities that were spaces of safety and support. Positive portrayals such as these upended negative gay and lesbian stereotypes, providing a new roadmap for those trying to figure out how to build a life for themselves.

Many members who benefited from the mentoring and support were then able to pay it forward. Joe Lordi, who was a mentor to many in the group and on campus, commented: "I told people to be themselves, never apologize, and you don't have to be loud and mouthy. Just be who you are ... And a lot of people have thanked me through the years for being me. Because it gave them the courage to be who they are." Reginald Brown commented on the importance of this role: "I have to represent, not only for myself, but for ... the gay person who is afraid and needs to see somebody like me."

There were those in the LGLF as well as in the larger movement, however, who did not see mentors as important or necessary to their efforts to build a gay community. Steven Weaver explained this perspective: "We didn't need mentors particularly because we considered ourselves to be overthrowing the establishment. Overthrowing the way that things were." But while some LGLF members were looking to overthrow the establishment, others were just beginning to discover the politics inherent in being gay. Many group members, in fact, commented on finding their own activist voice while in the group.[16]

Members recognized the power of mentoring in their lives. Bob Friedland credits a new sense of empowerment from the mentoring he received: "I would have never imagined that I'd someday be going in drag in a maternity dress in early December onto the campus ... that I'd be someday wearing a pin that said, 'How dare you presume I'm heterosexual.' ... I went from this new self-discovery to my own version of radicalism." And Bob Warren remembers the relationships that have enriched his life:

I made friends there that I still am in touch with, and I have fifty years later great admiration and respect and warm feelings for them for both being brave and being who they were, going on and finding their successes and dealing with all of the struggles that we have somewhat unfairly, in my mind, had to deal with. . . . So out of my experiences in meeting these people at KU, I think I helped clarify in my own mind what some of my personal lifetime objectives would be, and some of the paths that would help me get there and how to stay away from some of the paths that I thought would not help get me there. And I look back on that as being very, very fortunate.

Half a century later, in part due to the work of the LGLF and early activists, there are many gay and lesbian role models and mentors who are committed to openly sharing their knowledge and support. Students recognize the value of these relationships, relying on their wisdom and guidance to navigate difficult terrain. Niya McAdoo, KU student body president in 2021–2022, commented that it was helpful and reassuring to hear during the "51 Years OUT!" events that early activists faced similar challenges related to acceptance, support, roadblocks, representation, and resources: "It was good to hear that we aren't alone in that." She added: "We have those stories . . . here's what worked, here's what didn't work, and then we're able to use those conversations and use those experiences to lead what we're continuing to try to do on campus."

Redefining Sexuality and Gender

LGLF members intentionally engaged in actions that challenged conventions related to sexuality, gender, and gender expression. Some members attended meetings, social events, and public places in drag to get people's attention. Michael Stubbs explained: "It was all about shocking people and jolting their perceptions." They also organized events such as Wear Blue Jeans If You're Gay Day and the dances, defying the narrow way in which gender was defined. In addition, these issues were addressed in their speakers' bureau presentations, consciousness-raising and rap sessions, and counseling services. As they interacted with others—whether in bars, with classmates, or at planned events—they brought up topics related to conformity, social acceptance, and normalcy to help others expand their thinking about these issues.

A particularly harmful stereotype they confronted was characterizing gay men as effeminate, regardless of the way they expressed their gender identity. Leat described the effect: "'Queer'—it was just a feminine man, period, full stock [*sic*]. There wasn't any variability beyond that." This raised a contradiction—wanting to challenge existing definitions while appearing "normal" at the same time. Haenisch shared, "I don't remember anybody that was just kind of like a normal guy who said, 'I'm also gay.' It was only people that were very obvious were the ones that people knew."[17]

Within the group, there were differences in members' comfort and/ or agreement with unspoken codes regarding the ways in which people expressed their gay identity. For some, adopting a mainstream or nonconforming style was a personal choice. For others, it was a political statement. Group member Dick Perrin stated in a *UDK* interview that "much of the 'camp' behavior of gays was an imitation of the stereotyped behavior they used as a device to scorn heterosexuals."[18] Not all agreed with this tactic, however, and felt that this undermined the group's efforts to be taken seriously.

For more mainstream group members, the flamboyant, radical gender presentation was contrary to their gender expression and sense of self. Lee Hubbell commented that people who operated in the extremes made him uncomfortable and "pushed his buttons." In an interesting twist, he spoke about another group member, Leonard Grotta, whom he described with admiration as "bolder than I was [laughs]. . . . He would do anything." Yet in talking with Grotta, there is a different side to the story. "Sometimes I think you went overboard trying to fit in to the community because you were so happy to have one. Like a 'camp' sensibility—'oh, girl' this, 'oh, girl' that. I think maybe some people got just a little bit too carried away because they were just so happy to have a group to belong to that they were going to belong to it 110 percent." This put Grotta in an uncomfortable spot: "I can see it as humorous but that was a little bit difficult for me." Group members like Grotta therefore may have been spurred on to adopt a code in which they were not entirely comfortable in order to belong, which communicated to others a level of acceptance to which they did not ascribe internally.

Jim Pettey added another perspective about the labeling that occurred not only on the part of straight outsiders but also among themselves: "You know, I was kind of in the middle. . . . I was a long-haired hippie, but I wasn't effeminate." He explained, "I was at one [LGLF] meeting, and they were all talking about something. . . . It was the radical femmes, and I said, 'I don't understand what you're saying.' And they turned to me and said, 'Well, you wouldn't know that. You're very masculine. You're a very manly man. You wouldn't understand this gay femme stuff.'" Assumptions held by those within the gay community could also lead to pigeonholing and stereotypes. From time to time, cliques arose within the group along gender presentation lines, underscoring the importance of education for not only the broader community but also group members themselves.

Despite these differing perspectives within the group, members prioritized making the group a safe and accepting place for all expressions of gender identity while respecting individuals' differing comfort levels. The group's intentional actions pushed up against stereotypes and unspoken codes, challenging the notions of binary gender and a singular gay identity. Their efforts facilitated a shift in considering gender and sexual orientation as socially constructed, existing on a continuum.[19]

It is important to note that women did not face the same level of scrutiny or censure regarding gender expression. As the women's movement gained traction, many feminists rejected traditional sex stereotypes, adopting behavior often labeled as "masculine" out of defiance. "We were very casual about our beings," Susan Davis said. Regardless of their sexual orientation, these women were often labeled as lesbians. In general, however, there was greater latitude for women who strayed from the conventional norm than for men, and these deviations commonly did not evoke the same hostility. Nonetheless, this does not minimize the negativity, exclusion, and covert discrimination that nonconforming women sometimes experienced.

Normalizing Gay, Lesbian, and Nonconforming Identities

LGLF's programs and presence played an important role in normalizing the gay experience at KU and beyond. "The dynamism and the positive-ness of it. . . . I mean, you didn't have to sit at home and hate yourself. And you didn't have to be alone," David Radavich explained. This was an experience shared by many. After years of feeling lonely and alone, Ron Gans also experienced a normalizing effect: "Suddenly, I had this social life. I mean, like a normal social life. I had friends." After years of therapy to deal with feelings of isolation, he no longer felt the need and quit. What he had been seeking all along was connection and recognition. For gay men and lesbians working toward self-acceptance, telling their stories was often a starting point in challenging the heteronormative mythology they had internalized.[20] The counseling services overseen by the group as well as those through the Women's Coalition and Womanspace provided a mechanism to talk about what had been hidden and shameful, normalizing individuals' experience. For many who used these services, they were for the first time not only affirmed but understood.

The group itself served as a safe haven. "People were there to find support and solace and a space of comfort and welcome," Radavich observed. Leonard Grotta elaborated: "You're the only one in the whole world and suddenly you find you're not the only one ... and it makes a very big difference psychologically on an individual level. . . . It was very uplifting for everyone involved and just to find out that you're part of a community you didn't know was there was wonderful." Steven Weaver had a similar reaction: "It was so exciting to meet people like myself. To just walk in, and here's a bunch of people who have the same kind of politics I had, and the same kind of educational perspective I had, AND they are gay. Up to that point, I hardly knew any gay people at all." This acceptance was transformational for many. Said Bob Friedland, who described himself as presuicidal prior to joining the LGLF: "[It] was so important to me because it was a refuge of people that I didn't have to explain myself to. . . . They're the ones who guided me through."

Dennis Dailey described some of the issues that gay and lesbian students shared with him: "Some of those kids who were struggling—struggling with a roommate, struggling with feeling alienated from their mom and dad, struggling from a loving, dear sister who found out they were gay and hasn't talked to them since—all of that stuff ended up in my office, very quietly, very tearfully, very frightened, wanting to know what to do." He commented that LGLF "truly was for many of them a safe harbor." Noting that LGLF did not have a large number of female members, he commented that lesbians created safe harbors through their affiliations and close-knit communities. Many lesbians referred to these communities as their "logical family," which differed from the biological family that they were born into. These chosen families truly foster[ed] and nurture[d] and support[ed] you."[21]

Bob Warren thought of this support as a safety net, allowing students to establish a home base: "Gay lib was a tool. I always felt it was a social environment and a tool where you could stick your finger in all these different puddles and know that you were never going to get burnt. . . . If you didn't care for their style of what they were pushing for within the organization, you still had camaraderie and enough openness about finding a path."

Surrounded by a safety network, members were able to be authentic. For many, this was a new experience. Brown recalled walking down Jayhawk Boulevard holding John Bolin's hand in public, feeling a sense of freedom: "He was the first man I remember walking hand in hand with. In public. And that just stood out to me as if it happened yesterday. That was just such a feeling." Dailey concluded that the validation the group provided was of paramount importance:

> I think what it was about was something profoundly deeply human. And it was, I think, the accumulated lifelong search by this minority group, almost any minority group, to legitimize itself . . . to be who they were. . . . And the political arguments and all that were interesting and rhetorical, and they were of the time and all of that. But when I sat with individuals and we were just talking, when we were down at the end of the street down at Twelfth and Oread having a beer, it was very, very personal. It was about being less frightened, feeling better about themselves.

Group members confronted misperceptions by outsiders that they were "different" by reaching outside of their circle, welcoming in allies. This approach was unique within the gay liberation movement in which many groups mirrored the militancy and confrontational approach of the Gay Liberation Front of New York. Kathy Hoggard commented on the sense of joy and exuberance at the group's dances, which formed a bridge between the gay and straight communities and drew people in:

> I can't think of another organization that really wanted to make a significant change in the rest of us who presented themselves in such a warm and friendly and open way as they did with these dances. It was either brilliant or lucky, or both. So they said, "We love you. You don't love us, maybe, but we love you and we want you to come and get to

know us better, and we're going to put on a dance." Who else ever did that? And it was so inclusive—and so much on campus is exclusive. You are excluded from a sorority if you don't make it, or a fraternity, or excluded from the basketball team. You are excluded from going on to get your master's if you don't make it. And so much about college is winnowing people out. And here is something that says, "We're going to change the world, but we're going to invite all of you to be a part of it."[22]

This atmosphere of welcome, joy, and connection drove the women's community. Their wine and cheese gatherings, softball teams, Lawrence Women's Music Collective, lesbian houses, and gatherings at Susan Davis's home provided safe havens in which all—lesbian and straight— were accepted. Martha Boyd explained: "All these little circles . . . they all kinda intersected." As the many little circles extended outward, the feminists' sense of celebration drew people in, diminishing a sense of otherness. The ability of LGLF and women's community members to push up against stereotypes and deliver difficult, controversial messages while extending the invitation for others to join in a welcoming, positive way was unique and important in changing attitudes and normalizing the gay experience.

Keep On Keeping On: The Power of Persistence

Group members' perseverance in the face of adversity is what kept the LGLF afloat—especially during times the group almost dissolved. Their tenacity is what allowed the group to survive on the KU campus for close to fifty years, an achievement very few student groups have ever attained.

Jack Klinknett, the attorney who assisted with the group's lawsuit, witnessed members' persistence firsthand when the lawsuit was defeated: "The case itself, whether it had been won or lost, I don't think mattered that much. I think it was just one more event that was occurring in an ongoing process of hanging in there and bringing about change." He recalled a quotation by George Bernard Shaw stating that change is brought about by "unreasonable men and women" who refuse to conform to the status quo, and he concluded, when thinking about LGLF members' persistence: "You either say, 'Well, I'll live with this,' or 'I won't live with this.' . . . I will hang in there for a day, a week, a month, a year, the rest of my life, and keep pushing for what I think is an important set of changes." Looking back, Trip Haenisch considered the challenges of maintaining this resolve in the face of opposition:

> It takes those people that just won't say no and that are brave and are willing to fight to change things. It really takes a strong person to do that. It's a risk. You risk a lot. . . . Sometimes you have to have those people that are willing to look a little bit crazy and be a little bit demanding to actually change things. And so I give those people so much credit as I look back. They had integrity.

Without a road map, group members relied on the mantra "The personal is political" and followed their instincts and convictions. This engaged others to join the fight. Klinknett captured the significance of their persistence: "They were pioneers. They were coming out, and they had no way to know how this would affect them, positively or negatively, to just come out. That was [the] courageous part. Like any other work that you may need to do on yourself or you may need to try and do on your culture, that's the hard part, is just to admit that it's there to do." The path had not been an easy one. Early on when the LGLF began and later in the mid-1970s, the group came dangerously close to disbanding. But dedicated members were willing to pick up the torch and do the work to keep the group moving forward.

C. J. Janovy, who wrote about LGBT activism in Kansas, stated that one of the lessons learned about bringing about change is "Prepare to lose. In many of these stories, people lose twice or three times before they get a win. But with each loss, you win new friends and allies."[23] Group members knew about loss. With all the setbacks the group faced, whether that was the denial of recognition from the administration or the loss of their lawsuit, they never let these short-term losses impede their long-term vision.

Group members, now with fifty years of hindsight and experience, also know that lasting change requires reaching across generations to stand side by side in keeping the message and momentum going. During the "51 Years OUT!" event in 2021, antigay protesters from the Westboro Baptist Church (WBC) showed up on two separate days outside the Kansas Union shouting vitriolic messages. Their homophobic, hateful

gay-bashing at KU had been going on since 1992.[24] Students quickly organized a counterprotest across the street, and LGLF alumni and campus
community members joined together forming a group that was more than
double the size of the WBC group.

David Stout, feeling the need to fight fire with fire, got up on the bench
directly behind the group and made some sexually explicit, in-your-face
comments and gestures to ridicule the protesters. A student protesting
the WBC joined Stout, keeping the taunts going. Together they engaged
the crowd and riled up the WBC protesters. Stout reported that "very
shortly, the protesters called for their car, loaded up, and took off." Reginald Brown, recalling the many protests in which they participated in the
1970s, commented, "Same shit, different half century."[25]

Looking Forward

Reaching across generations to protest, organize, and preserve history
is critical in engaging current generations to continue the progress. "51
Years OUT!" event participants reflected on the meaning of this early
history and its impact.[26] One participant commented after the event on
"how much we have accomplished since 1970," while another stated "our
history/herstory is ever present. Though it's great to have these remind-
ers, many of these folks are still here, every day, just doing what we do
which can, and will have an impact on future generations. It shows what
a few like-minded people with some perseverance can accomplish." Being
reminded of this history, one participant shared, "I felt very renewed in
my feelings. It filled me with pride."

It also enlightened current students about the meaning of this history. Niya McAdoo shared her thoughts on the impact of hearing these
early stories at the event, tweeting: "The 51yrs out Gay Liberation Front
panel was amazing tonight—felt so good hearing about queer history at
KU and being in the room with so many elders." She reflected: "We're
able to use those conversations and . . . experiences to lead what we're
continuing to try to do on campus," concluding that "it was good to hear
that we aren't alone in that [and] we haven't been alone."[27] In a feedback
form KU student Rachel Lane shared:

I was incredibly overwhelmed with the happiness of getting to experience and learn the history of a community I am so proud to be a part of. It's so important to have these stories told so that queer people in future generations are able to learn and understand more about themselves. I have never gotten to experience this level of queer community especially involving people from older generations. I am so grateful for these events."

Leonard Grotta and Reginald Brown spoke to *UDK* reporter Matthew Petillo about the importance of making this history visible. Brown observed: "I think that within the gay community, there is a lot of history that is lost because it's not passed on. We lost an entire generation due to the AIDS epidemic, so it's up to us who are here to pass it on . . . to those who follow." Grotta commented on the importance of knowing one's roots, to develop "a sense of heritage, [because] they are not alone, [and] there are people who came before them and people will come after them."[28]

Gay and lesbian activists of the 1970s ventured bravely into uncharted territory, challenging stereotypes, pushing for equity, and creating affirming communities. Reginald Brown spoke of the importance of preserving and building on this legacy: "I trust our own legacy. The point is if we don't keep our own legacy alive, if we aren't visible, we don't exist. Be proud of who you are and never allow yourself to be othered."[29]

Celebration is an important aspect of this legacy. LGLF's dances were known far and wide for their "blow out your ear," "fantastic," no-holds-barred approach. LGLF members recognized the value of integrating joy and celebration into their events. It was fitting, then, that the "51 Years OUT!" culminating event was a dance, "STILL Too Hot to Trot," named after its 1973 predecessor. It drew in a large, diverse crowd of all ages, ethnicities, genders, and sexual orientations. As people danced to music from the 1970s and beyond, including the highly popular "YMCA" and disco hits of Donna Summer and the Bee Gees, the excitement and joy were palpable. Members of LGLF and the women's community laughed and had fun reminiscing as they tried to keep up with the students. At one end of the room, there was a couple with an impressive dance routine, and at the other end was a couple whirling around the dance floor as a woman guided her partner in a wheelchair to the rhythm of the music. Later in the evening, a large group of South Asian students, who were there for an earlier event and were outfitted in traditional garb, glanced into the room with curiosity. After being welcomed in, they ran en masse onto the dance floor, enthusiastically joining in the festivities. As they waved their arms gracefully in the air and moved with the music with the others, they raised (battery-operated) candles that magically lit up the room, capturing the mood.

One participant commented, "The dance at the end of the week was a real culmination and celebration. What an honor to dance with the LGLF founders in the ballroom where so much history was made!" David Stout, remembering early dances, observed that "the high energy level was about the same as 50 years ago. Not as many people in attendance as 50 years ago. No wallflowers like there were 50 years ago. People showed no apprehension about being there like a few did 50 years ago."[30] The reduction in numbers certainly was a by-product of the pandemic, but the change in attitudes that Stout described indicates that a significant change has taken place. The stigma and fear that were present for LGBTQ people in the 1970s have evolved into an environment that is more accepting and affirming. Times have changed, but one thing has remained the same since the first LGLF dance: the desire to connect with others and belong to a community.

As Stout addressed the crowd at the "51 Years OUT!" dance, he emphasized the need to pass the torch to future generations. Commenting on the importance of learning from the past to make gains in the future, he stated: "It is my hope . . . that fifty-one years from now, there will be five or six of you, like the five or six of us, that will be here. And you will tell the next generation, 'Fifty-one years ago I was in this room, and I saw and met the original people who started all of this one hundred years ago.'" Reginald Brown followed up on Stout's comments, reminding them: "You are our voice. You will stand on our shoulders and do things that we never thought of."[31]

Michael Stubbs commented on the importance of passing the torch and standing on shoulders to continue the LGLF founders' efforts to advocate for respect and equal treatment:

We have made astonishing progress in the last fifty years, but at the same time a conservative backlash has been brewing that threatens the democratic foundation of our country. . . . I believe the current

LGBTQ movement and those who are fighting for justice and equality for all Americans will need to embrace the unity that was a hallmark of the early days of GLF in order to fight the antidemocratic forces descending on the world today. . . . The call today is to put our differences aside, respect each other, and save democracy.[32]

History can teach us critical lessons about the importance of valuing and embracing all expressions of human experience and ways in which we have missed the mark. It also can guide us as we look for current solutions to address long-standing injustices. Gay and lesbian activists have fought long, hard battles that cannot and should not be forgotten. The stories included here, at times painful and at others exuberant, need to be understood to continue making progress for full inclusion for those who are LGBTQ. And like the early LGLF activists, we should settle for nothing less in order to create a better world for future generations.

Key Individuals Who Appear in This Book

Many people who were involved with and had an influence on the gay rights movement in the 1970s are listed in this book. All had a role to play; however, the sheer numbers make it impossible to list all of them. The following are some of those who are mentioned.

KU Lawrence Gay Liberation Front Members

Barry Albin
John Bolin
Jon Blevins
Denis J. Brothers
Reginald Thomas Brown (Reggie)
Robin Burgess
Patrick Dilley (1990s)
Peter Felleman
Ron Flowers
Julie Freeman
Bob Friedland
Ron Gans
Kim (Kay) Gilbert
Leonard Grotta
Lee Hubbell
Michael Johnson
Gary Kanter

Ruth Lichtwardt (1980s)
Richard Linker
Joe Lordi
Sharon Mayer
Chuck Ortleb
Dick Perrin
Jim Pettey
Joe Prados
David Radavich
Elaine Riseman
Mark Sramek
Laurie Stetzler
John Steven Stillwell
David H. Stout
Michael Stubbs
Todd VanLaningham
Bob Warren
Steven Weaver
Todd Zwahl

KU Faculty, Staff, and Administrators (positions held in the 1970s, unless otherwise noted)

Donald Alderson, dean of men
David Ambler, vice chancellor of student affairs (beginning 1977)
William Balfour, vice chancellor of student affairs
Gene Budig, chancellor (1981–1994)
Frank Burge, director of the Kansas Union
E. Laurence Chalmers, chancellor (1969–1972)
Dennis Dailey, faculty, Department of Social Welfare
Shirley Gilham Domer, assistant to the chancellor
Archie Dykes, chancellor (1973–1980)
Ann Eversole, director, Student Activities Office
Kathy Hoggard, director, KU Information Center
Floyd Horowitz, faculty, Departments of English and Computer Science;
    ACLU president, Lawrence chapter
Paul Lim, faculty, Departments of Theater and Dance

Timothy Miller, faculty, Department of Religion
Charles Oldfather, university attorney
Del Shankel, executive vice chancellor
Donna Shavlik, assistant dean of women
Frank Shavlik, assistant dean of men
Caryl Smith, dean of students
Kala Stroup, dean of women
William (Bill) Tuttle, faculty, Department of American Studies (courtesy appointment in Department of History)
W. Clarke Wescoe, chancellor (1960–1969)

KU Students/ Student Leaders

David Awbrey, student body president, 1969–1970
John Beisner, student body president, 1974–1975
Margaret Berlin, student body president, 1979–1980
Mert Buckley, student body president, 1973–1974
Chris Caldwell, Student Senate treasurer, 1977–1978
David Dillon, student body president, 1972–1973
Bill Ebert, student body president, 1970–1971
Trip Haenisch, fraternity member, 1974–1978
Michael Harper, student body president, 1978–1979
Boog Highberger, student body vice president, 1983–1984
Steve Imber, Student Senate member and leader in the Freedom Coalition, ca. 1984
George Laughead, Student Senate Executive Committee (SenEx) member, 1970–1971
Chad Leat, fraternity member, 1974–1978
Steve Leben, student body president, 1977–1978
Rusty Leffel, founder, Students Concerned about Higher Education in Kansas, 1966–1973
Niya McAdoo, student body president, 2021–2022
John Spearman, president, Black Student Union, from 1970 (end date unknown)
Tedde Tasheff, student body president, 1976–1977
Carla Vogel, student body president, 1983–1984

Women's Community (includes straight and lesbian feminists)

Jolene Babyak
Stephanie K. Blackwood
Martha Boyd
Lynn Bretz
Judy Browder
Kathryn Clark
Susan Davis
Julia Deisler (Julie)
Casey Eike
Holly R. Fischer
Constance Fleming
Pat Henry
Deborah S. Holmes (Deb)
Marilyn Kent
Molly Laflin
C. Lathrop
Kathryn Lorenzen (Kathy Buehler/KB)
Jane Nichols
Tamara Perkuhn (Tammy)
Polly Pettit
Tonda Rush
Kathy Schick
Christine Leonard Smith

KU/Lawrence Community Members

C. J. Brune, community activist
Charles Gruber, realtor
Jack Klinknett, attorney, ACLU Lawrence chapter
Daniel Ling, property owner

Key Individuals from Outside of Lawrence
(administrators, faculty, community members)

Jack Baker, community activist, University of Minnesota

Gary Gardenhire, Bruce McKinney, and Gina Barnett, cofounders, first Wichita State University gay student group

Brandon Haddock, director of the LGBT Center, Kansas State University, 2010 to present

Roger Heineken, Student Affairs administrator and historian, Emporia State University

William Kunstler, civil rights attorney

John R. Martin, Kansas assistant attorney general

Michael McConnell, community activist, Lawrence, Kansas City, and Minnesota

James Rhatigan, vice president of student affairs, Wichita State University

Keith Spare, founder, first gay student group at Kansas State University

George Templar, Kansas federal district judge

Harold Voth, psychiatrist, Menninger Clinic

The Power of Connections: Lawrence Lesbian Communities in the 1970s

In the summer of 1971, eighteen-year-old Deb Holmes couldn't wait to start her first year at the University of Kansas.[1] Holmes was no stranger to political activism. During her high school years in Topeka, she had attended racial equality and antiwar demonstrations, where she and her friends joined in protests and carried signs. Holmes was looking forward to continuing to find her voice and predicted that her college experience would be transformative. But she couldn't have predicted how transformative the summer beforehand would be.

Growing up, Holmes had been very involved in her Methodist youth group. Its progressive attitudes about social justice resonated with her and provided her with a sense of community. After graduation, she signed up to attend the Senior High Institute, an annual weeklong event held over the summer. That year, the theme was "Alternative Lifestyles." As she engaged in discussions and listened to the two presenters, who were members of the LGLF, talk about being gay in a straight society, sparks went off for her as she heard their stories. It was at that point that she decided to live openly as a lesbian.

In September, when the semester began, Holmes found herself on the doorstep of Venus, a commune where many LGLF members lived.[2] Reaching out to them was a priority when she got to KU. She wanted to let them know that their presentation over the summer had had a big impact and she was excited to sign up to join their speakers' bureau. Her first presentation was to a large sorority, which she described as "memorable," because she knew she was reaching others as she herself had been reached.

Holmes continued her involvement in the speakers' bureau but did not feel drawn to become an active member of the LGLF. "I led first with being a feminist more so than being a lesbian," she said. Many lesbians shared Holmes's sentiments. The broad feminist issues brought forward by the women's movement—economic and workplace disparities, restrictive cultural stereotypes limiting women's access and opportunity, the Equal Rights Amendment (ERA), and the prevalence of sexual violence, to name a few— were critical to many lesbians but not top priorities on the gay activism agenda. When looking for an ideological home, they found it in the women's community. LGLF cofounder Laurie Stetzler reflected: "While I was a part of the initial organization of the GLF, I swiftly turned my activism to the Feminist uprising."[3]

Martha Boyd remembers this well. She grew up in Manhattan, Kansas, and, like Holmes, got involved in civil rights activism in high school. While at KU, Boyd continued her activism efforts and worked as a graduate student for the Dean of Women's Office. She had a "front-row seat" in discussions going on related to gender equity. "I can remember distinctly, and it got echoed nationally, that men are on the steps with the megaphones and the women are in the basement with the Gestetners [duplicating machines]," Boyd recalled. "And it's like—no. No. We're not going to do that anymore. We're not second hand, we're not the gofers. We're not the 'and also participated.' *That* line was pretty clear insomuch that it then carried over to other groups in terms of the LGBT community." Women, and women who were lesbians, were tired of being subordinated.

Just like Holmes and Boyd, many lesbians on campus and in the community gravitated toward the women's movement as their "ideological home" rather than the LGLF, and they formed communities separate from gay men. Their story nevertheless is essential in understanding the LGLF, on whom this book is focused, as well as the climate that existed at the time for those who were gay and lesbian, leading to the development of a gay community at KU and Lawrence. This appendix will explore gender differences within the local gay community, including lesbians' unique contributions, their rich history, and the ways in which they found connection.

Lesbians had an important role in creating the Lawrence Gay Liberation Front in 1970. When the group began, the founders, two lesbians and five gay men, intended for the group to be a gender-inclusive organization.[4] Many in the group were involved in the women's movement and incorporated feminist philosophies in its creation. Two male members, John Bolin and Michael Stubbs, were also members of the campus feminist organization, the Women's Coalition.[5] As one of the only men in the Women's Coalition, Stubbs acknowledged the importance of respecting women's space and priorities, commenting: "I guess we had special status as gay men. We never spoke, just listened."[6] In addition, the LGLF was structured to ensure that women had an equal voice in the leadership. The co-coordinators were David Stout and Elaine Riseman.[7] Despite these efforts, women were in the minority, representing only about 20 to 40 percent of the membership in the early 1970s. And despite David Radavich's observation that "[women] were certainly a central presence in an ongoing way," some women did not feel fully included.[8]

LGLF member Sharon Mayer recalled the pull that some women experienced. She observed that a small number came to LGLF meetings but wanted to put their energies into issues that focused on women rather than the group as a whole.[9] Male member Lee Hubbell and other men in the group noticed this gender imbalance and reached out to a small group of lesbians on campus who were not in the LGLF and were trying to organize. They invited the women to join the group, but they declined. Hubbell recalled their response: "We have our own issues, and our own issues are different than the men's," referring in part to the double discrimination they faced as women and lesbians. Hubbell empathized: "We weren't feeling the discrimination because we were men. . . . And that was one thing they articulated and why they didn't really want to get involved with us. They weren't against us, [but] they weren't receptive to the way we wanted to support them." In addition, different communication styles created friction between the men and women. Many lesbians, tired of getting the runaround, communicated in a direct, blunt style that some men in the group considered confrontational and aggressive, generating discomfort.[10] Nonetheless, a small group of women continued to be involved in the LGLF.

Kathryn Clark, who came to KU from Idaho, encountered some of the differences that gay men and lesbians experienced that influenced perceptions and choices early on in her KU career.[11] Clark was raised in a fundamentalist Christian family. She initially attended a religious college but transferred to the state university in Idaho because "it was clear there wasn't going to be any freedom of discussion that might challenge or question our faith." There she met her husband. They were active in progressive politics and were searching for a more politically engaged community. On finding out that her husband's brother was planning on going to KU, they decided to follow him and got involved with the Lawrence hippie/radical community.

Shortly after arriving at KU, Clark discovered that she was a lesbian. As she began figuring out this new life, she noticed that lesbians were more likely than gay men to have been in a committed heterosexual relationship prior to coming out, resulting in issues related to marriage, divorce, and children. "There were women who were leaving their marriages and needed a place to live or were afraid they were going to lose their kids, and it was not always because their marriages were violent or even bad, just that their hearts took them down another path. But in order to go down that path, you had to totally rip apart this other thing that you've been dedicated to." This often resulted in difficult choices and decisions. Lesbians also wrestled with decisions when thinking about having children, and "sometimes arranged sperm donations, or the father was a part of their whole family structure, but their primary heart relationship was with a woman." These sometimes-complicated relationships factored into issues that were top priority on their agenda.

The LGLF "gender problem" showed up not only in the issues on the agenda but also in how women's voices were included in the organization. Initially when the group began, LGLF leadership consisted of a male/female team. When the male coleader, David Stout, left the group, the female co-leader, Elaine Riseman, took over, ensuring that women's perspectives were given equal airtime. After the first year, the shared-gender leadership model had been forgotten and men were exclusively selected for the top leadership roles, up to the late 1970s when women again assumed some of these roles. As a result, women felt like secondary members with limited power and authority. Holmes reflected: "I think sexism was/is rampant, and I don't think that we were conscious of ways to bridge that divide. I don't know that the men were conscious of that either." Clark added, "The nature of belonging to groups at the time tended to have men dominate the conversation and decisions—to a degree, women were finding their own voice and it was easier to do that in an all-women's group."[12] There were reports of women's voices not being heard in the LGLF. Former KU student Richard Crank observed a confrontation when he attended a meeting in 1971: "I remember very clearly that at one point a woman stood up and said, 'We're tired of all your patriarchal approaches to these meetings. The women are leaving. See ya. [Laughs.] We're going to have our own group.'"[13]

"Competing oppressions" came up as an issue in gay groups across the country, significantly affecting lesbians. Feminists had been portrayed in national mainstream media as "man-haters" intent on controlling and castrating men. Lesbians were particularly suspect. Consequently, feminist organizations such as the National Organization for Women tried to distance themselves from lesbians to avoid addressing and confronting this stereotype as well as the heterosexism within their ranks.[14] The New Left movement was known for its homophobic and sexist attitudes and negative treatment of women. This in turn influenced the early gay liberation efforts, which adopted a very masculine rhetoric that created a hostile environment for women.[15] As a result, lesbians, who were impacted by both sexism and homophobia, were marginalized and excluded. Lesbians of color were additionally impacted by pervasive racism, which was a serious issue in all of these groups. The need for a safe space where their voices were respected and heard was of paramount importance if they were to make headway.

This created a "chicken-and-egg" situation. As gay groups were not welcoming of lesbians, women did not attend, which in turn allowed groups to continue without being challenged for this misogynistic treatment. Sharon Mayer did not personally observe sexism among early male members, but she was aware of the perception that the LGLF was not welcoming to women. She understood their perspective but was concerned that their avoidance of the group would just perpetuate the problem. "There weren't a lot of women in Gay Liberation anyway, and then after a certain point, there basically weren't any, and so then there was like: Well, here you are, you don't have any women—well then, come to the meetings. But they didn't." LGLF group member Steven Weaver had some thoughts about this: "They wouldn't necessarily be at meetings because they didn't necessarily want to be in a room full of men. . . . But they were very involved in things like the dances."

Lesbians' inclusion in feminist circles was mixed, as was common at universities and communities across the country.[16] The KU Dean of Women's Office was a place that lesbians could count on for support, affirmation, and advocacy. Emily Taylor, who served as dean of women from 1956 to 1975, considered homosexuality to be a normal aspect of sexuality. Taylor did not share the view of the dean of men, Don Alderson, that gay and lesbian students were a threat to the campus community, and she did not seek opportunities to discipline or expel students who were discovered to be lesbian or gay.[17] The office was known widely as a safe place for gay and lesbian students. In 1975, Taylor left her position at KU to assume the role of director of the

Office of Women in Higher Education of the American Council on Education in Washington, DC. Kala Stroup, who had a long history of higher education leadership and advocacy for women, took over as KU dean of women. She continued the tradition of support for gay and lesbian students. Martha Boyd, who worked with Stroup, confirmed this, pointing out that all three graduate students who worked for her were lesbians.[18]

Stephanie K. Blackwood, a graduate assistant in the Dean of Women's Office who was assigned to work with sororities, experienced this support firsthand. Sorority women began to suspect that Blackwood was a lesbian, and rumors had begun to circulate. Blackwood consulted with Stroup about the best way to handle the situation to minimize possible negative fallout on the office. Stroup advised her to openly address the rumors: "Kala wanted me to 'own it,' and I knew she had my back." Blackwood commented that Stroup "was the first person who ever invited me to come out at work and to speak publicly" about her sexual orientation. Blackwood met with office staff to share what was going on and recalled feeling empowered and bolstered. She reflected, "We had a rock star group of people. There was no question. . . . It was a great, great group." Stroup elaborated on her intentional inclusion of lesbians: "I always made sure that we had lesbians on staff—residence halls, scholarship halls, sororities—we wanted to make sure they were represented. Word of mouth, a sympathetic ear, is what was so necessary for all of them— for coming out, for friendships, for checking on things, all that . . . We were a feminist office—opening opportunities for women—we really were feminists and we labeled ourselves that way."[19]

There were two feminist student organizations on campus at the time— the Commission on the Status of Women (CSW), which was connected with the Dean of Women's Office, and the Women's Coalition (WC), which evolved from the counterculture, activist community. While both groups had similar goals, the coalition was the more radical of the two and had a strong lesbian presence.[20] The CSW had a more mainstream focus, reflecting Taylor's approach of working within systems to bring about change. It began in 1958 as a committee of the long-standing Associated Women Students (AWS), which had a role in overseeing the student living organizations and was advised by Taylor. In 1969, the AWS decided to name the entire organization Commission on the Status of Women to reflect its shift from housing-related concerns to broader issues related to women's equity on campus and nationally.[21] The WC, on the other hand, was formed in the spring of 1970, just a few months prior to the LGLF. The CSW and the Women's Coalition often partnered on projects.[22] The WC office was in the Wesley Building across from the Student Union, where it eventually moved, and was a central hangout for women students. It served as a makeshift women's center after the Student Senate rejected the funding request from Patti Spencer, one of the WC's founders, to establish a women's center on campus in July 1970.[23] The WC provided an influential voice on campus and was a central organizer in the 1972 February Sisters protest in collaboration with others. The women's community as a whole organized and led the February Sisters protest, but many lesbians were part of this group.[24]

It is important to mention that these were white spaces; few, if any, people of color participated. Putting this in context, KU was a predominantly white institution in the 1970s—95 percent of the students enrolled in the fall of 1977 were identified as white.[25] Holmes, who has been a leader in diversity education throughout her career, identified this as an issue the community "failed at." "As we sought to make these connections and to change structures, and to do things differently . . . the systems that we were building in the communities . . . did not cross racial barriers." She further commented on the need for cross-race conversations: "Many white lesbians were/are still discovering our whiteness, the privileges that come with it, and the superiority we have absorbed through our socialization."[26]

While the WC was a home of sorts for lesbians, there were gaps in the support they received from the group. A 1971 issue of the WC newsletter featured an article about members' decision to not join the LGLF lawsuit as plaintiffs on behalf of the WC.[27] Spencer explained that there was concern about alienating current and potential coalition members who were uncomfortable with and did not support the lawsuit. Casey Eike, who served as a staff liaison to the WC, clarified: "The controversy was that 'we [WC] don't want to dilute our cause by bringing in any other causes and especially much more radical or not as accepted.' Not that any of it was really accepted at the time. It was all pretty new, but there was always that fear of we won't get our point across because people will focus just on this and dismiss this other viewpoint." The problem of "competing oppressions" presented a quandary for the group: risk losing traction in advocating for feminist issues if they were perceived to be in alignment with gay liberation or risk alienating the lesbians in the group by not supporting the gay community.

In 1972, more conflict arose, and the February Sisters' takeover of the East

Asian Studies building split the group. Many older members left, and February Sisters leaders stepped in to take on the leadership of the group. Ann Francke, one of the WC's leaders, attributed some members' fear of lesbians and their "refusing to confront their bigotries" to the weakening of the group. Following the split, the WC shifted its focus, becoming more political while more visibly addressing lesbian issues.[28]

Building Connections, Building Community

It was during this time that the small group of lesbians who had been involved with the LGLF reached out to the WC to form a subgroup, the Gay Women's Caucus. They cited a need for their own space to discuss the double oppression they experienced. A spokesperson for the group stated, "I think we have things in common with the Gay Liberation Front, but we decided it was really time to get the women together." The Gay Women's Caucus worked together with the LGLF on many programs and initiatives, including the dances and a meeting with Balfour in 1972 to improve campus climate for those who were gay and lesbian.[29]

Organizing was happening in the Lawrence community as well. The Lawrence Lesbian Alliance, described as a community spin-off of the WC, started up in 1974. Other groups arose, including First Fridays, a once-a-month lesbian potluck, which had a diverse, loyal following and continued for many years as an important lesbian connection. In addition, the Sister Kettle Café, run by a women's collective, was a welcoming environment for lesbians and the alternative community, serving as a "crossover to the non-lesbian/gay community."[30] The complexity and interconnectedness of the community intersections were described as "a variety of Venn diagrams," in which there was some level of connectedness but also "multiple circles of gay women that did not necessarily overlap or interact too much with each other." The interactions among lesbian subgroups were depicted as "accommodating and friendly."[31] These lesbian-identified spaces put Lawrence on the map as a lesbian-friendly town and had an important role in building the community.

As lesbians became more visible and outspoken in the mid-1970s, the cultural climate started to shift. Articles in the *UDK* that focused specifically on lesbian issues began appearing, suggesting that lesbians were developing a greater presence independent of gay men. In addition, in February 1973 a new campus newsletter for lesbians, the *Lavender Luminary*, was first published.

Writers for the newsletter described it as "a forum for a feminist Lesbian energy," stating: "We feel that the Lesbian Community needs an avenue of expression for our politics, skills, and creativity."[32] This lesbian feminist energy was in full swing in 1974 when activist Jill Johnson came to speak at KU.[33] Johnson, who had written *Lesbian Nation* and spearheaded the lesbian separatist movement Radicalesbians, spoke to an overflow crowd of mostly women in the Kansas Union. Johnson's talk was so popular that in addition to all seats being full, students were lined up down the hallway to hear her speak.[34]

The separatist movement evolved across the country in 1970 in response to lesbians' feeling of exclusion from both the women's and gay liberation movements and their desire to create an alternative women-only environment in which they would not be sidelined.[35] Men and women who associated with men or mainstream society were excluded. Separatists reasoned that because patriarchy fueled inequality and oppression of women, these issues could not be tackled with men and those who supported men in the room.[36] Some lesbians, however, disagreed with this approach as being restrictive in moving the agenda forward. "If you're a feminist who happens to be a lesbian, you have a broad agenda that includes all sorts of issues that affect all women, and they go across a wide spectrum," observed Kathryn Clark. On campus and in the Lawrence community, the lesbian separatist philosophy was embraced by some, while others opted for a more inclusive approach.

There were women in the movement who embraced lesbianism primarily as a political statement and an act of rebellion.[37] It was the political ideology rather than romantic attractions to other women that motivated their involvement. For young women in college who were beginning to explore their identity and their sexuality, this could create confusion as they were drawn to the heady energy of the movement and its ideals but not the desire for a female partner. Some, in fact, have commented that this led to them entering into lesbian relationships that they later realized were not congruent with their feelings. For some, this generated feelings of duplicity and internal conflict.[38]

A few years later, in 1976, the campus experienced the "intense energy" of African American feminist Flo Kennedy, a dynamic figure in the women's movement. Kennedy, an early member of the National Organization for Women, founded the Feminist Party, which nominated Shirley Chisholm for president. She was a popular, outspoken activist for feminism and civil rights from an intersectional perspective. Born in Kansas City, Missouri,

Kennedy challenged the exploitation of women. It is interesting to note that she worked on occasion with William Kunstler, who just a few years prior to her presentation had been representing the KU LGLF. Kennedy's presentation was sponsored by the Student Union Activities, the Women's Coalition, and the LGLF.[39]

Tonda Rush was influenced by Flo Kennedy's message. Rush transferred to KU from Emporia State College as a junior and entered directly into the School of Journalism. Initially, Rush felt "a little at sea" as an outsider in a department that was not entirely welcoming to women. She was looking to find a community. When she joined the *UDK* staff, Rush found some like-minded colleagues and friends. But it wasn't until she roomed with women associated with the Dean of Women's Office and the women's community that she found the feminist connection she was seeking. This growing feminist consciousness led her to attend Kennedy's presentation. It "really threw a spark into the tinder box of the women's movement," recalled Rush. "That layer of activity around Flo Kennedy was huge. . . . She gave everyone marching orders: Go out and change the world. So women did. . . . She found a willing community and a set of ears, and it seemed to me that during that time, lots of things began to happen."

Things were indeed happening. Women were finding their own ways of connecting. Martha Boyd observed that the "confluence" of social and political forces was the "perfect storm" for women to assert their "women-centric" approach and come into their own. "I think just in life, men don't connect the same way women do," stated Susan Davis. Women, in comparison to men, were characterized as social initiators, creating community through their affiliations.[40] Key ways that KU and Lawrence women connected to build their community included lesbian wine and cheese gatherings, the Women's Music Collective, softball teams, Womanspace, and lesbian communes.

Lesbian Wine and Cheese Gatherings: "You Could Hardly Get in the Door"

Informal social gatherings that brought women together from all over Lawrence were a hallmark of the lesbian community. Kathryn Clark hosted one of the first gatherings in the early 1970s shortly after she had moved out on her own into a small studio apartment in town. She recalled how these got started: "I think that was probably because all we could afford was some wine and a bit of cheese and it was easy for people to contribute something. You could hardly get in the door."

As everyone squeezed into the small space, Clark turned to the woman sitting next to her. After introductions, Clark asked, "'Where do you live?' . . . She named one of the sororities. And I just looked at her, and I said, 'Well, what are you doing here?' [Laughs.] And she replied, 'Well, what are *you* doing here?' And I answered, 'Well, it's my house.' [Laughs.] And she said, 'Well, I thought this was for gay women,' and I said, 'It is! What are *you* doing here?'" Looking back, Clark concluded: "It was early enough in my identity as a lesbian that I couldn't believe anybody who was in a sorority would actually be gay, but in fact, there were a lot of sorority women who were gay."

These gatherings continued "at least once a month . . . at different people's houses." The word got out informally: "It was absolutely word of mouth." Clark shared that these gatherings "evolved into all-women dance parties, and although it was predominantly gay women, there were often straight or bi women who would attend. It was one of the ways in which the women's community really formed." By drawing in lesbians from the many groups on campus and in town, there was "cross-fertilization," bringing about a sense of unity and a broad base of support that diversified and strengthened the community.

Lawrence Women's Music: "A New Way to Come Together"

Most people growing up in the 1960s and 1970s can remember the hours spent in music stores, leafing through record bins, looking for the "must-have" LPs of the day. Music had an important role, particularly for women as they were trying to figure out who they were, rejecting outmoded norms, and calling for equality in their lives, work, and relationships. Just mentioning the names Aretha Franklin, Helen Reddy, Sweet Honey in the Rock, Bonnie Raitt, Meg Christian, and Cris Williamson (to name a few) reminds women who grew up during that era of the powerful messages of agency, rebellion, and emancipation in the lyrics.

In the mid-1970s, some Lawrence women gathered on Susan Davis's porch to make music together. As they strummed, sang, and harmonized, they decided to pull together a band they called the Lawrence Women's Music Collective (sometimes called "the Collective" for short).[41] Fueled by feminist ideology and a love of music, this all-women band had a diverse playlist, including progressive folk rock, blues, and country, with a little swing and reggae thrown in. Members told *LDJW* reporter David Chartrand that "their hope [was] to make a statement for women."[42] Lawrence's reputation as a vibrant arts community, supporting and promoting grassroots artists and musicians, got the group off to a good start.

Their concerts were a community connector, bringing together people from throughout the region. Not only was the Collective well known in the Lawrence community, but it also had linked up with the influential Foolkiller folk music community in Kansas City. Many have likened Collective concerts to LGLF dances in terms of their draw and visibility. The concerts were an opportunity to celebrate the gay community in an atmosphere of positivity and unity. Clark remembered: "It was really important. And when they played, everybody came out."[43] She noted that men and women, straight and gay, attended.

Kathryn Lorenzen (known also as Kathy Buehler and KB in the 1970s), who was a member of the Collective and now is a recognized musician and songwriter in the Kansas City area, observed: "We were important to the gay and lesbian community, but those weren't the only people that came to see us. . . . A lot of the threads of it were as much social as they were musical . . . because we were all mindful that we were giving the lesbian community and the women's community a new way to come together." On their opening night at Off the Wall Hall, they "not only filled the house but nearly brought it down. . . . People were standing out of their seats, stomping their feet and singing the finale louder than the band."[44] Off the Wall Hall, a large, converted warehouse, was a downtown Lawrence fixture.[45]

While an all-women's group is not unusual in current times, the fact that it was considered so in the 1970s is a reminder of the boldness of these women's actions. The group's uniqueness was mentioned by Chartrand, who stated: "The collective is conspicuous for two reasons: It is talented and it's totally female. Not that the two are mutually exclusive. It's just that the combination is as rare as it is fresh." Chartrand's observation, intended as a compliment, drew attention to the fact that women were not taken seriously in many realms in the 1970s, including music.[46] There were nine members of the Collective, including Kathryn Lorenzen, Lynn Bretz, Deb Holmes, Marilyn Kent, Julia Deisler, Susan Davis, Holly Fischer, Tamara Perkuhn, and Sarah L.[47] Many, but not all, of the members were lesbian.

An important guest contributor was Beth Scalet. Scalet lived in Lawrence and supported the Collective. Active in the music community, she went on to establish herself as an important presence. Lorenzen pointed out that Scalet blazed the trail in the Lawrence community in many ways: "Beth was a touchstone for the gay community because she had been this very, very visible musician, and then she came out." Lorenzen described Scalet as "a source of identity pride" and "a role model." She had received numerous awards for her songwriting and was inducted into the Kansas Music Hall of Fame in 2008. Known for her contemporary folk style and lyrics addressing difficult topics, including domestic abuse, she often performed with Collective member Lorenzen.[48]

A smaller group called Suffrage organically emerged from the Women's Music Collective and was made up of Collective members. A poster for the group had this description: "SUFFRAGE is a group of 5 women with occasional guest performers. Individual backgrounds range from classical to rock, enabling the group to do a wide variety of material. Using both acoustical and electric instruments, SUFFRAGE performs country, folk, blues, and rock music. Recent material focuses on original music and work by other women artists." Members included Kathryn Lorenzen, Deb Holmes, Lynn Bretz, Tamara Perkuhn, Holly Fischer, and Sarah L.[49]

Both groups had a busy performing schedule and were quite popular. In addition to concerts, they were also called on to perform at special events, including a women's music festival in Stillwater, Oklahoma. Some members also performed at the first National Women's Studies Association Conference, which was held on the KU campus. They sang a newly composed song for the opening session, which drew approximately nine hundred attendees.[50] A strong bond formed among members, and for decades they have gathered for reunions, which speaks to the lasting connection among members.

While the Women's Music Collective was taking off in Lawrence, women's music was getting attention across the country. Feminist and lesbian women were wanting music that reflected their experience and perspectives. Bonnie Morris, historian for Olivia Records, the first feminist and lesbian record company, described the movement's evolution. Although powerful protest music arose in the 1960s, Morris commented that "viewpoints from the feminist journey were still nowhere to be found in the mainstream beyond the tokenism of Helen Reddy's 'I Am Woman.'" Olivia Records was founded in 1972 by a group of lesbians in California who oversaw all aspects of the business. Their new sound included "songs that didn't candy-coat female friendships but actually acknowledged racism as well as homophobia."[51]

This music also enlightened women who were beginning to learn about the politics of their sexual identity. After graduating, Stephanie Blackwood lived for a year on the Eastern Shore of Maryland and spent a significant amount of time in Baltimore with a group of lesbian feminist activists and students at Johns Hopkins University. She recalled going to Mitch's, "one of the first dyke bars on the East Coast." Olivia Records artists, including Margie Adam and Cris Williamson, would come to Mitch's to perform. Blackwood commented that while she listened, "I began to get it. My education in the political side ... of this life."[52] Holmes commented that the Collective used much of this music in their performances, and it had another role as well. In addition to the "profound impact" the music had on "keeping the community connected," it also actually became a shorthand. "You meet somebody, you don't know if they're lesbian, you say, 'By the way, have you ever heard of this particular artist?' It was kind of like code language because you were still concerned about safety or concerned about outing yourself, outing somebody else."

The lesbian artists represented by Olivia Records were tremendously popular with Lawrence women. "The Unitarian Church in Kansas City used to host Holly Near and Cris Williamson, and there would be big parades of cars going out of Lawrence to Kansas City to those concerts," Rush described. "And I can remember some of the men in the gay community saying, 'I don't know why we can't have musicians like that.' [Laughs.]"

Softball: A League of Their Own

Making music and hosting wine and cheese parties were not the only ways that lesbians connected with each other. America's greatest pastime was very popular among students in the 1970s. Many residence halls and Greek houses created baseball and softball teams, and KU offered many intramural teams as well.

In 1974, a group of Lawrence feminists formed their own softball team. Kathy Hoggard, who was on the team, recalled: "A lesbian friend told me she wanted to form a women's softball team for the City of Lawrence League.

She speculated that if the team included dean of women's staff people, then Emily Taylor might write the check for our team fee." Hoggard and her friend, who were eager to play, identified candidates. When they all signed on, Hoggard went to Taylor and made the ask. Before Hoggard finished her pitch, Taylor agreed to pay the team fee for one year but stipulated that Hoggard "would have to show some imagination and broaden the group to include other women active on campus who were lesbian or otherwise marginalized. Of course, I told her that was a fabulous idea and that she should consider it done. Emily wrote a check for the fee, [and] we played our first of many seasons."[53]

With their team fee paid, they now needed a sponsor. One of the team members, Jane Nichols, had a connection to the Holy Cow Creamery, an ice cream shop in Odessa, Missouri.[54] This sponsorship lasted two years, during which time the group went by the name the Holy Cow Creamers. Unofficially among fans and within the confines of the group, however, members had dubbed the team "Archie's Dykes," referring to Chancellor Archie Dykes. Team member Jolene Babyak commented that it was "an idea proposed by [a] straight woman, and laughed about, but nixed by the gay women." When asked if the name was meant to be a friendly joke or a jab, team members gave mixed responses. Tedde Tasheff, who was KU student body president from 1976 to 1977 and worked with Dykes, described it as "humorous poking," a "great contrast" to the "button-down Archie Dykes thing." Team member Polly Pettit agreed: "I just felt like it was an inside joke, that it was just the last thing that he would have appreciated, having a feminist softball team named after him with that double meaning." Clark added, "We were perfectly clear that it was not a reference he would have liked, so it was tongue in cheek, and pushing the envelope that the chancellor might have a bunch of very accomplished women known as his 'dykes.'"[55] LGLF member Leonard Grotta mentioned that feminists and women in the LGLF were not pleased with Dykes's selection as chancellor in 1973, particularly as Dykes was reported to be unsupportive of the gay community.[56] "They had little buttons pressed, printed up to wear that said, 'I like Dykes,'" which were meant to sarcastically communicate their displeasure.[57]

The Creamers practiced once a week, which was challenging since there were so many City League teams competing for space.[58] They had no manager or coach and carried feminist principles into the management of the team. Some of the rules they followed included: those who attended practices got to play in the next game; players got to play an equal amount of time in each game; and for half of their time, they got to play their favorite position, regardless of their ability in that position. While good for morale, this created some problems.

The team, who was first in the league and undefeated, was bumped up to a more advanced league a year or two later when they went to register. Clark, Babyak, and Hoggard noted that the disparity between the two leagues was "huge." Babyak recalled: "They had uniforms, and they had two coaches, male coaches with clipboards, and some of the women wore cleats! [Laughs.]" Playing by the same rules they followed previously, she reported that they "lost horribly." "If we had somebody who couldn't catch or throw," Clark added, "these teams would just pound every ball to that person. [Laughs.]"[59]

The team included Casey Eike, Kathy Hoggard, Martha Boyd, Kathryn Clark, Deb Holmes, Molly Laflin, Polly Pettit, Lynn Bretz, Jane Nichols, Kathy Schick, and Marilyn Kent. Clark recalled the camaraderie that developed among the diverse group of women, whom she referred to as "radically active feminists": "In the beginning, we were kind of a motley crew. But because a number of the women had been tomboys and played sports, we were just a bit better than the regular Level One of the city teams. And so for a while, we won every game pretty soundly." Their love of the game, shared commitment to the feminist movement, and success on the field built strong friendships among the group. Stephanie Blackwood remarked that "they were tight" and that the team was "legendary, if not for its playing, then for its notoriety in the women's community."[60]

The Creamers' impact extended beyond the game. In 1975, team member Kathy Hoggard called on her teammates to assist with a community-based Women's International Year celebration that she had been asked to organize. She recruited Deb Holmes to spearhead the project and Casey Eike and Martha Boyd to assist in the planning. The event featured presentations on a wide range of issues, including lobbying for women's issues; the influence of Title IX on athletics; women's health; the ERA; and socialist feminism. Some issues arose when an anti-ERA group lobbied to be included as presenters, demonstrating the tension between feminist and more conservative women in town. Over two hundred attended, and many applauded the organizers' efforts.[61] Hoggard shared with Holmes that their feminist values and commitment to each other went beyond the game. She concluded: "We had the right resources there—the people."[62] The Creamers were legendary both on and off the field for their leadership.

Word got out about the Creamers, and other women were excited to get involved. Blackwood credited a "new energy in Strong Hall" (where the Dean of Women's Office and high-level administrative offices were housed) as the impetus that got a second team started. She recalled that lesbians working in Strong Hall began to connect, deciding to create a new, all-lesbian team, the Apple Valley Chickens. The Creamers, on the other hand, had both lesbians and straight women as players.[63] Joe and Kala Stroup sponsored the Chickens from the team's beginnings in 1976 during the time that they owned Apple Valley Farm in the small community of Perry, not far from Lawrence. "The lesbians all knew that that was their softball team," Stroup elaborated. "Joe and I underwrote it, financed it—it was a small amount, and our daughter was the bat girl." The softball teams were "tremendous fun" and provided an opportunity for camaraderie and connection. Many who did not play showed up in the stands as "fan girls," loudly cheering for the team. Blackwood summed it up: "We had a great time. And that was like the magnet for all these other lesbians."[64]

The games were never without their surprises and unexpected moments. Boyd shared a story of Constance Fleming, who had a major role in feminist circles. She had taken a stand against a city ordinance that had been passed a short time earlier prohibiting indecent exposure, including women baring their breasts in public. In opposition, she frequently sat shirtless outside the library.[65] The police department knew her well. She decided to attend one of the games to cheer on the team—with something missing. Team members were warming up on the field, and their supporters had begun to take their seats behind the bench. Boyd recalled: "I pitched, and Steph [Blackwood] was shortstop, and she said, 'Don't look now, Boyd, but Constance is here.' And I said, 'Oh?' and I looked over there, and here she comes walking in—this is July—in shorts and her shirt draped over her shoulder." Boyd looked at Blackwood and said, "'You suppose she's going to sit behind our bench?' Which she of course did. Yeah—those were interesting times."[66] Fleming's attire drew much attention, both positive and negative, and always made a statement.

Softball went strong for several more seasons, and the lasting impact was felt for decades. These teams provided a chance for lesbians in Lawrence to connect over a love of the game, as well as to form a community.

Womanspace: A Gathering Place for Women

KU women who were looking for guidance and support could call on campus entities, including the Dean of Women's Office, the Commission on the Status of Women, and the Women's Coalition. For women in the community, however, it was a different story. KU services would quietly provide the help that they were able, but they were limited by time, resources, and their mission to serve the campus. There had been talk in Lawrence feminist circles for some time about the need for a place for community women to meet and get information and resources—a community women's center. Two particular issues that moved these conversations forward were activist Robin Morgan's speech in February 1970 calling women to action, bringing about the February Sisters' protest, and discussions a few years later about the need for transitional services for women who had been abused by their husbands.[67]

Susan Davis entered into these conversations when she moved to Lawrence in 1975 with her two young daughters. She relocated from Kansas City to get involved in the Lawrence feminist community after attending an LGLF dance at KU with friends. It was there that she realized that she herself was a lesbian. She started out in a small, cramped studio apartment and then moved in with a friend in a small house. Soon thereafter, she purchased a three-story fixer-upper and rented out rooms to some of her new Lawrence friends. She began hosting informal drop-in get-togethers, and her house quickly became a feminist gathering place as she developed connections with women all across town.

In the spring of 1976, a group of women wanted to move forward to create a transitional care center for abused women but were unable to secure the funding for a space. Acting on the advice of Constance Fleming, the "shirtless" feminist with considerable influence in the community, Davis stepped forward.[68] Davis's commitment to the community has been a driving force in her life: "I love the community. I love contributing . . . I like being a part of moving forward or changing for the positive."

Davis purchased a ten-room house at 643 Rhode Island Street with the plan to turn the deed over to a corporation that was dedicated to running it. The house was purchased outside of the student-populated Oread neighborhood to make it more accessible to the entire community. That spring, approximately sixty women gathered to organize a collective to take on this responsibility and make plans for the space. More joined as the planning continued, identifying a long list of goals, including serving as a gathering spot for women of diverse ethnicities and backgrounds; providing space for transitional care services trainings and workshops; serving as a way station for abused women; creating offices for a therapist and an attorney with specific expertise related to women and sexual abuse; providing a practice and performing space for the Lawrence Women's Music Collective; and creating a women's bookstore and a place for classes on a variety of topics. Kathryn Clark, who was involved in the organizing, commented, "It was intended to meet what was really an unmet need at that point in time. And it did become a gathering place." On September 1, 1976, Womanspace opened its doors to the community.[69]

The house was busy. Groups who used the space paid a token rent of twenty-five cents per use or approximately five dollars for an entire class. This provided a majority of the income to cover Davis's $250 monthly house payment for a short period of time.[70] Activities on the standing calendar included potluck dinners, dances, coffeehouses, and a counseling clinic. Former student activist Pat Henry, by this time a licensed therapist, provided counseling on a range of issues.

Some of the visions for the space, however, did not materialize. There were disagreements about the scope of services that would be provided to abused women. In addition, the groups planning on using the space—the transitional services group and Lawrence Women's Music Collective—found other venues that worked better for accommodating their needs, resulting in the space not being utilized as fully as had been expected. Davis wondered if the house's location away from downtown was a deterrent. And sadly, they did not provide legal services due to the tragic death of the attorney slated to take on this role. This underutilization made it difficult to make monthly payments, which contributed to its closing.

Another contributing issue was a philosophical split that arose among lesbian members. Those who identified with the more radical "women-only" separatist philosophy did not want males of any age in the space. This was in opposition to the more inclusive stance of moderate lesbians and was a serious problem for women who had male children. This friction continued, affecting the house's role as a refuge for all women. Another issue that arose was the inability to reach women in the community who had the greatest need for services. "We thought somehow that if we came down from Oread Hill, whether we were affiliated with the university or not, and established a house for women, that the women of Lawrence from the working-class communities were going to find us and flock over to be helped," Clark recalled. "It was a little bit of a fairy tale. As far as I know, we had no connections or way to establish connections with that community. And if we had just wanted to help the more loosely established, peripheral edge of the university community, then it probably would have been better to locate the house up closer to the Hill."[71]

Womanspace had a short life of a few years but nonetheless was an important contribution to the community.[72] It served as a springboard to the development of essential domestic violence services and raised awareness of the need for women-centered services that promoted independence and self-sufficiency.

Lesbian Communes: "When We Were All Together, We Were Pretty Fearless"

In college, group living experiences are important in building a sense of connectedness and community. Many gay and lesbian students found a connection in residence halls, scholarship halls, Greek houses, and other campus-affiliated living organizations. Some, however, sought out a less-traditional living experience that allowed them to be authentic, out, and among others with whom they could relate. Commune houses were a popular choice. In the 1970s, these houses were primarily in the Oread neighborhood adjacent to campus ("Hippie Haven") but were also in other parts of the city and the more rural outskirts.[73]

A farm outside of Lawrence has been mentioned by many as a place that was a gathering spot for feminists and lesbians. In the summer of 1973, when Martha Boyd returned from a trip to Europe, looking for somewhere to live before the semester began, she connected with a high school classmate who was transferring to KU.[74] Her friend had rented a house on a farm south of Lawrence and was looking for a roommate. Boyd, wanting to be up front, shared with her friend prior to moving in that she was a lesbian. Her friend, in turn, surprised her by revealing that she had already heard this through the grapevine, and it was not an issue.

Within a year, more roommates joined. It quickly became a spot where feminists and lesbians would gather, and many who lived there referred to it as South Farm. Together, the women managed all aspects of the farm while also being students. There were, among other things, a barn, a large plot of land, a quarter-acre garden, a chicken coop, and horses. The farm was known to many throughout the area for the wildly popular parties, get-togethers, and even "naked volleyball tournaments."[75] Their parties drew large crowds, with partygoers' cars lining the entire quarter-mile gravel road leading to the farm.

The dynamism, political energy, and social consciousness among those who gathered there sparked many important conversations. "We sat around and drank coffee or beer, whatever it was, at the kitchen table in that farmhouse and discussed *everything*. It was like an Algonquin group," Boyd remembered. "A lot of things came out of that. People would say, 'Well, I think we need to do this.' And I'd say, 'Okay, then who do we need to talk to?' And off they'd go to talk with somebody." The projects that began springing up cultivated connections among women throughout the community, described as "little circles that intersected." They empowered women to take action and included awareness programs, informal gatherings, and the creation of services to address sexual abuse. This led Boyd to comment that "South Farm was just a very unique place at a unique time."[76]

A conversation that Boyd had with a friend brought to light some of the challenges that lesbians encountered within the women's movement at the time. The friend told Boyd: "This place just reeks of feminism and intellectualism." When Boyd asked her to explain, she quipped, "Well, you *do* know what that is?" When Boyd admitted that she did not, her friend responded in a tone that suggested that "that" was not a good thing: "That's *lesbianism*."[77] The assumption that lesbianism and feminism are inextricably linked was common in the 1970s, leading to some problematic outcomes. Both groups were maligned, but lesbians were by far the group that generated the most discomfort, as the example above illustrates. This exposed some of the homophobic, stereotyped attitudes that circulated among both straight women and lesbians, contributing to conflict and, on occasion, hostility. "At times," Clark remembered, "it was said that the lesbian community was too 'much'— too loud, too demanding, too in your face. Historically, a favorite mode of attempting to silence or modify the behavior of women was [to] call them a lesbian."[78]

Many other feminist and lesbian living communities existed in town. Some began by happenstance as a few friends roomed together and then invited others to join. Some of these were properties in the Oread neighborhood owned by Daniel Ling.[79] Ling was known for his lack of involvement in and attention to his properties, which were generally in a state of disrepair and neglect. Ling's lack of attention, however, did have its advantages. Renters were able to bring in new residents without being noticed, making it easier to start up a feminist or lesbian house without any scrutiny. They often were named by street number and had their own identities. "And so you knew people by 'Oh, do you live in 1603, 1124, 917?'" said Clark. "So you kind of immediately knew the community of women that was there."[80]

Susan Davis's house on Mississippi Street (not to be confused with Womanspace, which did not house people) drew in feminists throughout the town and exemplifies the impact of these communities. "Susan's house had been a way station for generations of lesbians," reflected Stephanie Blackwood. "There was a huge amount of power in our gatherings. When we were all together, we were pretty fearless, and we had collective action that created change on campus and in the community." Collective member Kathryn Lorenzen commented on Susan's influence: "Susan was the sun that we revolved around."[81]

Another important community to mention briefly is sororities. Lesbians in sororities had a challenging balance to maintain in the 1970s. Homosexuality was not openly endorsed in the Greek system.[82] Codes of behavior that reinforced heteronormative expectations about gender roles were defined and communicated. Those who violated the norms could be ostracized or disciplined, or both. On the other hand, there were many lesbians in sororities who benefited from and thrived in the rich women-focused environment that provided friendships and relationships. Word often traveled fast, and many sorority members looked the other way or quietly supported their lesbian sisters without turning them in. Stephanie Blackwood knew this dynamic all too well.

Blackwood hailed from Hoisington, Kansas. Her 4.0 GPA and nearly perfect score on the ACT could have been her ticket to just about any college she chose. But an offer of a full ride scholarship brought her to KU in 1970. She enjoyed her time at KU as a straight-passing sorority member. She lived in her sorority for three years, only discovering that she was a lesbian in her last year. "It was my senior year, and what happened was I fell in love. It was that simple. It never occurred to me up to that point. I was living in a sorority house—I was a Kappa Kappa Gamma. Very happy in my life. I was connected to a lot of really wonderful women in my house, coincidentally some of whom later came out as well. Surprise! It was like dominoes falling." As she thought about her sisters who followed her, she concluded, "Things started changing rapidly in the spring of 1974, not because I came out but probably because of the cumulative effect of the many movements for rights that were underway in the 1970s."[83]

At the end of the academic year, Blackwood experienced firsthand the culture of "unspoken knowing" that existed. She and her sorority sisters were sitting on the lawn the week of graduation, listening to music and reminiscing. She sat with one of her pledge sisters, Kathy DeYoung, "and some sappy Carpenters song came on the stereo that was propped in the window. I started sniffling and she leaned over and put her arm around me and said, 'Are you thinking about Sarah [Blackwood's girlfriend] or are you going to miss *me*?' And I thought—Wow—I've never talked with DeYoung about Sarah. I said, 'How do you know about Sarah?' And she said, 'Everybody knows about Sarah!'" Keeping secrets in a sorority is a difficult undertaking, to say the least. But in this case, not having to keep this secret among her sisters was a welcome relief. Blackwood expressed her surprise after discovering they had known for the entire year: "I loved that they didn't care! They just didn't care! In fact, they liked her a lot!"[84] The Dean of Women's Office, charged with overseeing women's living organizations, kept lines of communication open while encouraging members to navigate the system with respect and propriety.

Gay men and lesbians at KU were noted for having different approaches when it came to political action. While the LGLF got much attention in the early 1970s for its political involvement, this focus became less central for the group following the end of the lawsuit in 1973. Some speculated that the LGLF was "no longer political," but in actuality it was in the process of redefining its activism as it focused on rebuilding its member base and determining its future directions.[85] LGL coordinator Ron Flowers and social activities coordinator Mark Sramek commented in a 1975 *UDK* article that men were more focused on social activities while women were more interested in a political, feminist agenda. "The more action-oriented people were the lesbians and not the gay men," echoed Kathy Hoggard.[86] While this might seem like a flip in roles from men's and women's earlier efforts, it in fact was consistent with earlier behavior. Men tended to rely on the more formal structure of the group for organizing, while women relied more on their organic community connections. Kala Stroup observed that there were many lesbians who took on leadership roles on campus. And having experienced the pervasive sexism within many male-dominated organizations and student government, they were impatient to make their voices and ideas heard. "So they were lesbians, but they were also feminist lesbians and leaders."[87]

Women's Transitional Care Services and Rape Victim Support Service

Many significant initiatives evolved from the conversations that took place around the kitchen table at South Farm, in Susan Davis's living room, in meeting rooms at Womanspace, and many other places around town. It is particularly important to briefly mention the evolution of two of these initiatives that continue to be vital to the Lawrence community: Women's Transitional Care Services (WTCS) and Rape Victim Support Service (RVSS).

Prior to Womanspace, Women's Transitional Care Services existed as an informal network of support, referral, and occasional homestay services for abused women and their children. Women in both the feminist and lesbian communities whose views ranged from radical to mainstream were part of this network. When Womanspace opened its doors in September 1976, WTCS was able to move some of its existing services, particularly workshops and counseling, to this new space. In addition, organizers used the space for planning meetings and trainings.

During this time, five women began the work to create a full-fledged service. Three of the women, Sandy Eiges, Beth Black, and Judy Browder, were students in the KU School of Social Welfare. For their practicum, they had submitted a proposal to create this service. Three faculty supervisors signed on to the project. In addition, two Women's Coalition leaders, Toni Cramer (who was involved in Womanspace) and Marilyn Hayes, joined the effort.[88] There was a split among Womanspace organizers: some wanted the house to also serve as an overnight shelter, but those creating the full-fledged service insisted that this should not occur. Judy Browder explained that going this route "brought up all kinds of issues around security and safety" for the house, the staff, and the women being served. Despite the push to do otherwise and the friction that this generated, Womanspace did not become a shelter.[89]

In 1977, a year after these early efforts, WTCS was officially founded as a community nonprofit agency. Described as a "majority lesbian, radical organization," it was the first women's shelter in Kansas and one of the first in the country.[90] The first shelter house was purchased in August 1978 and was located at 1317 Kentucky Street in the Oread neighborhood. It functioned as a collective, and founding members included Valerie Kelly, Pamela Johnston, Judy Dutton, Diana Bankston, Mary Lisa Pike, Judy Browder, and Maura Piekalkiewicz. Their purpose was straightforward: "to provide services, by women, for women relating to both economic and psychological needs as women confront personal crisis." The movement to address domestic violence in Lawrence had its roots in progressive social change movements, including women's liberation, civil rights activism, the New Left movement, the national battered women's movement, and radical feminism. This was the framework under which WTCS was created. "The women who founded and ran WTCS were making a 'radical' departure from the way that battered women had previously been treated in the community," stated Elizabeth Miller, who conducted research on WTCS history. "They were making the issue of abused women public, while privately providing a safe space for victims of domestic abuse to escape their abuser, and the services and support needed to empower battered women to lead an independent life."[91]

Throughout the years, the service has grown and evolved. In 2010, the name was changed from WTCS to the Willow Domestic Violence Center to reflect its broader mission and focus. A second shelter was added in 2020. The Willow currently provides services to survivors of domestic violence and human trafficking of all genders in Douglas, Jefferson, and Franklin Counties on issues including court navigation and support, youth services, emotional support, housing and emergency funding assistance, education, and more.[92] It serves as a leader throughout the region providing training and consultation.

Another issue of great concern to women in Lawrence was rape and sexual assault.[93] It became a rallying cry within the women's movement, and efforts were ramping up across the country, particularly on college campuses where women were assaulted at an alarming rate. This topic was discussed frequently among the various women's communities, but it took an assault for action to occur. Pat Henry, a student at KU, had been assaulted in the spring of 1972, and the support she had received had been woefully inadequate. "She just wasn't going to put up with that," asserted Kathy Hoggard. "So she put the call out for women to come together and form an organization."[94]

Henry named the organization the Rape Victim Support Service (RVSS) and reached out to Emily Taylor for assistance and support. Taylor had established sexual assault prevention presentations and self-defense workshops in the late 1960s and agreed to support Henry's efforts. Taylor also included Kathy Hoggard, director of the KU Information Center, in the project and appointed Assistant to the Dean of Women Casey Eike to join Hoggard in assisting Henry.[95] Polly Pettit and Molly Laflin, student staff on campus, were also involved, and they were joined at a later point by community organizers Jo Bryant and Nan Harper.

Hoggard commented on the behind-the-scenes support provided by campus administrators that was critical to moving the service forward: "The three of us were empowered by our bosses. For me, it was Dr. Balfour. For Casey [Eike], it was Dean Taylor. For Polly [Pettit], it was Shirley [Gilham] Domer [head of the Affirmative Action Office for Women]."[96] Henry, who was a student and had a job that did not compensate her for these efforts, was restricted in her ability to assume the leadership role in the organization she had created. Eike, Hoggard, and Pettit worked with Henry to take on these responsibilities, understanding the inherent conflict and friction this had created. "Eventually Pat Henry came to work with me at the Information Center, and that sort of solved the problem right there," Hoggard commented.

Another student who had an important role in the inception of RVSS was Vicki Larason Landman. Kathy Hoggard described her as a feminist leader on campus: "She helped to start the Women's Political Caucus chapter on campus. And everything having to do with women that I can remember happening then, Vicki had a very big hand in it." Landman worked in the Office of Affirmative Action for Women with Shirley Gilham and Polly Pettit. In the summer of 1973, she was tragically killed in a boating accident. Polly Pettit was one of those deeply affected by the tragedy: "When she died . . . I felt like I needed to do something to honor her commitment, and so I decided to then volunteer with what became RVSS."[97] Vicki Landman's work inspired others to follow in her footsteps.

As RVSS got off the ground, Eike and Hoggard brought in and trained volunteers in the feminist and lesbian communities to assist survivors and provide workshops and trainings throughout the community. Many of these early volunteers were involved in the interconnected feminist circles together, including softball, the Women's Music Collective, and South Farm. It was the first rape crisis center in Kansas and one of the first three centers established in the country.[98]

Casey Eike and Polly Pettit, the first codirectors, received two grants from the Law Enforcement Assistance Administration (LEAA) to build the program. The first grant was designated for the creation of educational materials, including the film *No Pat Answer*.[99] The second LEAA grant funded a statewide conference held in Lawrence, planned and organized by Pettit and Eike, to help establish programs around the state. Communities, desperate for these services, reached out to Pettit and Eike, who traveled throughout the state to provide consultation and assistance. They also received a grant from the Kansas Humanities Council to create a film focused on the sexual abuse of children and facilitate discussions. RVSS was ready to take this on since "RVSS was starting to get more of those cases," and materials on this topic were nonexistent.[100] Hoggard commented on Eike's and Pettit's influence and impact in the state and nationwide as they helped organizations start similar services, since "there weren't experts to call upon."[101] In fact, Hoggard, Eike, Pettit, and others working with the service had become the experts.

RVSS was established as a community agency in 1978. The agency has taken the lead throughout the years to tailor services to the expanded needs of the communities it serves (Douglas, Franklin, and Jefferson Counties) and is a leader in the state. Current services include therapy and support groups; 24/7 advocacy and response; training to community drinking establishment managers and staff; and prevention and education.[102] It is now named Sexual Trauma and Abuse Care Center to clearly communicate the agency's overriding commitment to survivors as well as its expanded focus since its inception.

It is important to note that both WTCS and RVSS were the first centers in the state to provide specific services for those who were lesbian, gay, and transgender. Both agencies continue to provide comprehensive, trauma-informed, needs-based support for those who identify as LGBTQ, and both are leaders throughout the region.

Double Discrimination: Sexism and Homophobia in Lesbians' Lives

Women across the country in the 1970s were demanding an end to the discriminatory treatment that affected their livelihood and lives. Lesbians were doubly challenged. Already encountering discrimination as women, they also had to deal with homophobia (which in many cases was based on people's assumptions rather than actual knowledge of an individual's sexual orientation). This became even more difficult when factoring in an individual's other identities, such as race, ethnicity, and disability. Lesbian activists during this time had to learn to make very conscious decisions about how out to be as well as what opinions to express and when to express them.

This hit close to home for KU students. Deb Holmes knew the risk she was taking by pursuing a degree in education. Gay and lesbian educators routinely had their careers cut short if they were found out, so they were vigilant and watched their step. "Because I went into education, I was very aware that my identity as a lesbian would be, could be problematic relative to just popular school of thought about sexuality rubbing off on children, folks recruiting young people," explained Holmes. "There was just all this mythology going on. And it was also a threat to the women's movement."[103]

After graduating, Holmes began teaching in the Lawrence public schools. She described her team teacher as "very homophobic." Working in this stressful environment took its toll, and she was "very careful about my identity." She remembered the impact: "I went to work, and I had to exist in this environment that scared me. And then I would come home, and I would nest in my niche and surround myself with folks that I could feel comfortable around. And I lived that way for quite a while—I mean like decades. I worked hard and I played hard." Safe spaces were of paramount importance for many. Deb Holmes captured the sentiment: "It offered the propping up that was needed to survive some of what was out there."[104]

It was not uncommon for lesbians to encounter "rescuers"—men with heterosexist notions who believed that lesbians had just not met the right man, and they were the ones who could set them "straight." This could be particularly difficult when it surfaced in the work environment. "There's a lot of 'Me Too' stuff that crossed those lines . . . related to lesbian experience even though one might not expect that," Holmes stated. Lesbians were in an untenable position. "And then how do you fight them off, and what do you say? And then the ones that would hold it over your head—blackmail you—'I'm going to tell if—yadda, yadda.' That stuff was real. And I think from a political point of view, it certainly silenced me for a long time related to my identity as a lesbian."[105]

Women in male-dominated disciplines also had a challenging environment with which to contend. Tonda Rush described the sexism she encountered as a journalism student:

> There were people on the faculty that were just not sure women should be in the newsroom still. . . . There were certainly people in the faculty who were not happy to have women so prominent in the school . . . and there were some that actively tried to weed out people they considered feminist or somehow not part of what they wanted to see in the mainstream. . . . It was not a very welcoming place in a lot of ways.

Rush was fortunate to find a faculty ally who helped her navigate within the department: "He wasn't sure he wanted the women in the newsroom, but if they were going to be in there, by God, they'd better be talented and tough in there." He nurtured and guided her and helped her take on projects that showcased her talents. "I remember that fondly," she recalled.[106] This mentoring likely played a part in her becoming the leader of the National Newspaper Association.

Not all lesbians found that support. When Stephanie Blackwood was completing her thesis on *Sports Illustrated*'s treatment of women athletes in the 1970s as a journalism graduate student, her all-male faculty committee asked her to tone down her conclusions—"to be less forceful and be less focused on the misogyny." She had not mentioned to any of her committee members nor others within the department that she was a lesbian, yet during her thesis defense, one member threw her a curveball. The first question he posed involved two out lesbian sports legends: "So Stephanie, do you think Martina Navratilova and Billie Jean King would feel welcome when you go to the Wheel [a local bar and student hangout] after your softball games?" The reference to her involvement in the lesbian softball team was calculated to out her and throw her off guard. Blackwood's face turned "fire-engine red" from embarrassment and anger: "I can feel the heat just crawling up my neck. And I thought, 'These fuckers want to make me believe that they are on to me. They think that everything that I have written [in the thesis] has been affected by, has been biased by my work in Women's Athletics and my sexual orientation.'" She countered this underhanded jab with her own: "Billie Jean and Martina would certainly be welcome at the Wheel any time, but I'm not really sure what that has to do with *Sports Illustrated*." A committee member asked a follow-up question "trying to make light of it" and minimize the inappropriate, homophobic question that Blackwood never forgot. She now sees it as just one more example of the pervasive sexism and homophobia that coursed through academic institutions at that time.[107]

In addition to the sexism that women encountered in academics, sexism in athletics was also receiving a great deal of attention. These both had given rise to the drafting of Title IX of the Education Amendments of 1972. This amendment prohibited discrimination on the basis of sex in education programs receiving federal financial assistance, including athletics.[108] KU, like other institutions across the country, was reevaluating its policies and programs. The progress taking place for women in athletics was celebrated in many circles, but some felt that men's sports were being cheated since some men's funding had to be shifted to fulfill the mandate.

This increased focus created tensions for women in athletics in general but was particularly difficult for lesbians, who felt that they had to keep their sexual orientation hidden to avoid additional scrutiny and sidelining. Lesbians of color faced three levels of discrimination: racism, sexism, and homophobia. Racial discrimination, pervasive and entrenched, was a serious problem at KU and other campuses across the country. Adding gender and sexual orientation to the mix required lesbians to make difficult decisions about where they directed their focus and energies. Although many women of color were represented within various sports, they often received fewer institutional opportunities and less funding and support than their white counterparts.[109] The profound impact of racism became a primary focus, overshadowing the sexism and homophobia that they might experience.

This was the environment that Stephanie Blackwood encountered when she was recruited by Marian Washington as an undergraduate to play on the KU women's basketball team. Washington became the team coach one year after the passage of Title IX. An accomplished athlete, she received numerous awards and honors for her basketball skills and also paved the way for women of color in athletics.[110]

Blackwood had never been coached but had some of the skills Washington was looking for. She described it as "one the most formative and memorable experiences I've ever had." She explained: "I was surrounded by lesbians who were not going to ever admit it. It seemed to me that they didn't like that I was out. Throughout collegiate women's athletics there was a 'code of silence' about sexual orientation among athletes, coaches, and administrators. It took Billie Jean and Martina to really break through so that lesbians in sports could be themselves on and off the courts and playing fields."

Blackwood commented that staying on the team until the end of the season was the hardest thing she ever did.[111]

Washington later hired Blackwood as KU's first sports information director for women's athletics. She discovered that it was not just the students who were closeted: "I was surrounded by coaches who were lesbians, who socialized with each other but were not public and were not much involved with the women's community. So I toned it down a lot." Washington's willingness to hire Blackwood as the first full-time women's sports information director spoke volumes about her commitment to inclusion. While Blackwood did not broadcast her sexual orientation, especially in her academic department, she was an out member of the dean of women's staff. In addition, she had been involved in many organizations on campus and in the community as an out lesbian, which most likely did not escape Washington's attention. Adding a lesbian to her department in a misogynistic, homophobic environment was courageous. Blackwood said, "Marian was willing to take chances and put herself on the line to do the best for the KU women's athletic program, always with the goal of creating opportunities for talented women athletes."[112]

A year later, Blackwood was recruited and hired by Ohio State University as sports information director, and she discovered that this reticence to be "out and proud" was not specific to KU. She had to take great care in her interactions with lesbian coaches and lesbians working in athletics at other Big Ten universities: "The internalized homophobia in women's athletics was pervasive. But with good reason. Women coaches suspected of being lesbians were fearful of rumors that might have a negative impact on their ability to recruit student athletes." There was zero tolerance for publicly identifying oneself as lesbian, and "as far as we knew, there were no gay male coaches." When she revealed to the Ohio State women's athletic director that she was a lesbian and was "really unhappy" about having to keep her identity hidden, "I was invited to get another job. So, there were no protections."[113]

Concluding Thoughts: Lesbian Communities

The 1970s were a time of connection and growth for lesbians across the country as well as in the KU and the Lawrence communities as a separate lesbian consciousness was just beginning to emerge. "There's the old joke—every lesbian in the world thought they were the only one in the world. 'Oh, there's someone else like me?'" quipped Boyd.[114] "And that was pervasive. Because if you are a minority anyway in terms of being female with second status, and then if you're lesbian, you're so compromised with that that your sexuality isn't nearly as much of a threat to the status quo as a gay man." These larger conversations were providing opportunities for lesbians to begin finding each other and discover that they were not "the only one." At KU and in the Lawrence community, lesbians found many ways to connect, including the wine and cheese gatherings, the Women's Music Collective, softball, Womanspace, and women's communes. Described as "women with a list," they engaged in political organizing through their social connections, often over a cup of coffee or on the softball field.[115] The lesbian community, or communities to be more accurate, were interconnected pockets throughout the town, including both students and townies.

While there certainly were lesbians who struggled with the pervasive messages of shame and deviance, the general message communicated by members of the lesbian community was one of pride, empowerment, and celebration. The LGLF as a group was also known for its celebratory, assertive presence, but individually, members described greater struggles with shame and hiding than the women. This comment from LGLF member Barry Albin describes this struggle: "I read what it meant to be homosexual, and I said, 'Oh, my God, I'm one of those. What am I going to do?'" Women, on the other hand, tended to stand steadfast in their positive self-regard, as Susan Davis shared: "We didn't think there was anything wrong with us. At all. I don't think that had anything to do with who said what in the American Psychiatry Association or the government could have told us elsewise. We were pretty sure we were good to go."

KU student Laurie Stetzler shared a similar sentiment in an article she wrote for the underground newspaper, *Vortex*:

The revolution will not truly be here until revolutionaries smile at two lesbians walking hand [in] hand. What is it that makes this love something to be pointed at? I am tired of living in a closet. I am sick of not being allowed to kiss my love in public. I am indignant at the stares we attract when I hold my love's hand.

I have never really considered the differences between myself and heterosexual people. I have not thought it important. Nor has the difference

been apparent. But my awareness has been changing. I have started no-
ticing the ruts, the total lack of comprehension, the inability to confront
themselves in some of my "liberated" friends.

When I confronted myself on my homosexuality, when I could look
my friends in the eye and say, "I'm gay, ain't it fine!" I discovered a whole
new sense of freedom inside me. It opened up a new pathway in the search
to make myself whole. I learned a new way of finding joy and relevance.[116]

The important work carried out by lesbians in the 1970s brought about a
thriving community that would grow in the next decades, making Lawrence
a welcoming, supportive home for lesbians and feminists. The many events
they launched were vehicles through which they expanded connections and
brought others into the circle.[117] Hoggard summed up the impact of these
communities: "Women, lesbian and straight, working together on issues
common to all women—women learning to respect differences and find common ground."[118]

Gay Activism on Other Campuses across the State in the 1970s

KU was not the only university in the state that was trying to figure out how to negotiate the "gay issue." Public universities throughout the state wrestled with the challenge of maintaining positive relationships with the regents, lawmakers, and the public they served on an issue that was contentious for many. Kansas was not known for its liberal leanings on this issue, but Beth Bailey provided some perspective: "It's not that Kansans were particularly conservative on this issue; the vast majority of Americans opposed homosexuality, let alone gay liberation."[1] The LGLF's very visible actions were being watched closely at KU and beyond. This appendix will briefly explore how gay activism unfolded at Kansas public four-year institutions in the 1970s to provide some context related to the role the LGLF played in shaping and influencing the movement across the state.

KU's more conservative neighbors, Kansas State University to the west and Wichita State University to the southwest, are the next largest institutions in the state. These two campuses have different environments compared to KU, based on their missions and roles within the state, the communities in which they exist, and the student populations they serve. Their unique cultures have resulted in different approaches to getting the gay activism ball rolling on their campuses in the 1970s.

Kansas State University: Quietly Establishing a Presence

Kansas State University (K-State), located in the town of Manhattan, was created as the state's land grant institution to provide education on agriculture, science, military science, and engineering.[2] Described as a "small city ag school" that embraced its rural identity, it drew in many students from small farming towns in the western part of the state.[3] Many gay and lesbian students attending K-State grew up in these communities and were used to people turning a blind eye as long as their sexual orientation was kept under wraps and not mentioned.[4] Former KU student Jim Pettey shared a commonly used nickname that communicated the campus's reputation: "K-Straight."

Keith Spare, who spearheaded efforts to create a gay community at K-State, understood this all too well.[5] He grew up in Padonia, Kansas, a small farming community in the northern part of the state. Early on, he learned the necessity of building relationships with people with whom he did not necessarily see eye to eye to get things done. This helped him when he got to K-State to strategically navigate the conservative political environment to get a gay liberation group started.

Spare entered K-State in 1968. His involvement the previous year in a self-guided Kansas City Urban Plunge experience had a profound impact, leading to a growing awareness of his gay identity and his call to advocate for change. During this experience, he met Kansas City gay activist Scoop Phillips, whom he would later call on as he was getting the K-State gay liberation group started. As Spare developed a strong friendship with Phillips and learned of the gay activism happening in the Kansas City area, he became involved with the Phoenix Society for Individual Freedom in Kansas City. This organization was Kansas City's first homophile organization, committed to "improving the legal, social, and economic status of the homosexual in society."[6] Kansas City was known throughout the country as one of the leaders in gay activism prior to the Stonewall uprising. Due to Kansas City's important role in the movement as well as its central location, it was selected as the site for a critical national meeting in 1965. This resulted in the creation of the North American Conference of Homophile Organizations, or NACHO.[7]

Spare's skills in building relationships were evident when he got to K-State. He continued his long-standing involvement in the United Methodist Youth Movement in Manhattan and also took on a leadership role in the United Methodist (UM) campus group. This led Spare to reach out to KU's LGLF, inviting four members of the group to participate in the UM summer youth camp.[8] And early on in 1970, Spare also joined the Manhattan community organization, the University for Man Community Center, that would become important in establishing the K-State group. The Center (UFM) had just opened in 1968 and provided free classes to all in the K-State and Manhattan communities.[9] It evolved from the Free University movement, which began at the University of California, Berkeley in the 1960s to provide underground education on activism, organizing, and political action.[10]

Spare taught classes for the UFM, including "alternative lifestyles" and "draft help." His involvement in antiwar activism and his commitment to help young draft-aged men utilize all their options and resources inspired Spare to create the K-State University Selective Service Information and Counseling Program, an accomplishment not often achieved by a part-time student employee. When he staffed tables to promote draft counseling, he also saved room at the table to get the word out about the gay activism that was gaining momentum. This provided an inconspicuous, safe spot for LGBTQ students and faculty to get information and stay connected.

Spare continued to work within his circles to create opportunities for gay men and lesbians in the community to connect. Momentum to create a gay community had begun. Since the UFM was not overseen by K-State, it was uniquely situated to offer programs that might have received opposition from campus administration. In the summer of 1969, the UFM offered a discussion group that included the topic of homosexuality, called Taboo Topics. It was sponsored and facilitated by Robert Sinnett, founder of the K-State mental health center and cofounder of UFM.[11] Spare's efforts were getting attention, spurring interest in creating a conference that was hosted on the K-State campus in December 1970. During the conference, Spare presented a session on gay issues, joined by his friend Scoop Phillips. During the talk, Phillips proclaimed that Manhattan needed a gay community. Spare and others there agreed. Following the conference, Spare received what he referred to as "you mean I am not the only one" calls from attendees. This prompted him to quickly organize. A small group began meeting regularly with Spare that fall, and the group officially began in January 1971.[12]

Brandon Haddock (they/them), director of the K-State LGBT Center since its opening in 2010, recalled conversations they have had with LGBTQ alumni from the 1970s. Generally speaking, alumni who were out and comfortable with their identity remember their time at K-State fondly and did not report negative experiences while they were students. Yet others have described their experience to Haddock as "horrific" and have felt alienated from their alma mater due to their negative memories. Haddock remembered encounters with several alumni who came back to visit K-State and broke down crying because they were so thankful that this center now exists. One alumnus commented that he never imagined a center could exist for LGBTQ students at K-State and grieved for the person he was at K-State because of all the pain he went through.

As the group continued to meet, they decided to call it the Manhattan Gay Liberation Front and listed it in the UFM catalog. As they grew, they needed a larger space, so they approached the Baptist Campus Ministry Center, which was off-campus where Spare's office was located. This was a short-lived solution, however. Only a month after they began using this as a meeting spot, some complaints surfaced, and the group was asked to leave. Undeterred, they found an alternate space and continued to promote the group in the UFM catalog. Spare commented that the prevailing homophobic attitudes on campus and in the community were particularly toxic with the overlay of religion factored in. He noted that K-State students were fearful of being discovered. "Being a homosexual at K-State is still a hidden role which requires persons to travel to Kansas City or Topeka if they want to connect with other homosexuals."[13]

As the group became established and more visible, members continued to hold discussion groups and provide presentations on gay issues to the community. In addition, members created a Gay Hot Line, working with a successful campus peer-led phone call-in support service. Spare had a major role in creating this established service and also trained its volunteers, so he had a blueprint to follow as he and others got the Gay Hot Line started.

When Spare graduated from K-State in May 1971, he remained on campus in his draft counselor role, which allowed him to help the group continue to grow. In March 1972, UFM hosted a second conference, and this time the group was listed as a cosponsor. The group now went by the name the Manhattan Gay Consciousness Group, reflecting its focus on personal exploration rather than political action.

By 1973, the group had been in existence informally for more than two years, with no apparent public concerns or conflict being voiced. In contrast, the KU LGLF had been embroiled in numerous conflicts with administrators, the regents, and alumni across the state and had filed a lawsuit against the university. Dan Biles, a writer for the campus newspaper, the *K-State Collegian*, noticed this disparity. He attributed this to the two groups' different approaches in addressing systemic campus, local, and national gay and lesbian political issues and discrimination: "At K-State, the Gay Conscious-ness group is fighting no political or legal battles. The goal in Manhattan is awareness; the methods are quiet and subdued." Spare made it clear that this was intentional: "This is the reason why there has been no overt political ac-tivities," he said. "In the past, group members have been more concerned with dealing with themselves rather than openly confronting the community."[14]

Another important difference was the two groups' sponsoring organiza-tions. The K-State group evolved from a class offered through the community organization, UFM, and was not overseen by the campus. As a result, it was not constrained by the rules, regulations, and political challenges that faced the KU group.[15] The strategy of keeping a low profile and avoiding political con-troversies gave the group the flexibility to focus on members and build a strong foundation.

When K-State group members went forward to the KSU Activities Board in 1974 to request official recognition by the campus under the name "Chil-dren of Sappho," no objections were raised. The obscure name likely con-tributed, but, in addition, the lack of controversy that the group engendered kept them out of the spotlight, minimizing concerns. Spare commented that the LGLF's initiative influenced K-State's efforts to get their group off the ground. The LGLF led the way in asserting the right to exist, encouraging other campuses to follow suit.

K-State and KU group members occasionally interacted and supported each other's efforts, despite their limited association. LGLF members men-tioned presentations that they gave in Manhattan with the K-State group as well as their efforts to back the group in their bid for official recognition in 1974.[16] LGLF members often attended K-State dances and vice versa in solidar-ity. Joe Lordi recalled attending the first K-State dance on November 16, 1974, and other LGLF members mentioned attending these dances.[17] In addition, there were reports that K-State and KU members frequently dated each other.[18]

Throughout the years, the K-State group continued to serve as a "home" for gay and lesbian students. The administration took a major step forward in advancing gay rights in August 2010 when the K-State LGBT Resource Center opened its doors. This was the first center of its kind to be estab-lished in the state. This was a notable accomplishment for a campus that had been perceived as provincial in its attitudes related to diversity and LGBTQ inclusion.

Wichita State University: Pushing through Student Opposition

Wichita State University, which started out as a private, religiously affiliated college, became the Municipal University of Wichita after successfully lobbying the city for financial support in 1926. Seeing the benefits of affiliating with the state higher education network, it joined the other Kansas state institutions on July 1, 1964, and changed its name to Wichita State University.

Unlike KU and K-State, which are located in small towns in which the university is one of its most central features, Wichita State University (WSU) is located in the heart of a large, metropolitan city. Many Kansans considering college, particularly those from small towns in the western part of the state, were drawn to Wichita's big-city ambiance. The WSU website boasts: "As Kansas' largest city . . . Wichita is the commercial, financial, medical, cultural and entertainment hub for the state."[19] For students who were beginning to question or come to terms with their sexuality, Wichita offered a sense of anonymity. It also had a thriving gay community, with some established hangouts and community organizations that catered to those who were gay and lesbian.[20] That could not be said, however, for the WSU campus.

The first WSU group came about through student initiative. When Gary Gardenhire arrived at WSU in 1976 to pursue graduate studies following his graduation from Antioch College in Ohio, he wanted to connect with other gay and lesbian students.[21] Remembering what worked at Antioch, he thought the best way to accomplish this was to hold a gay dance. He was disappointed to discover that, unlike Antioch, there was no gay student organization at WSU. He met Bruce McKinney, a transfer student at WSU from Coffeyville, Kansas, who had been involved with the Wichita Gay Community Association, and a third student, Gina Barnett. They decided to create a group at WSU. The three applied for official recognition, and their request was approved by the Student Government Association (SGA) in September 1976. The Student Homophile Association (SHA), the first recognized gay student organization at WSU, was born.

This recognition was not without opposition. Many on campus did not approve of the group or believe there was a need for it. It took some quiet support to move past the opposition and gain approval. James Rhatigan, WSU vice president of student affairs during this time, commented that "our student government was in on this recognition," with some behind-the-scenes work taking place in order to bring this about. McKinney credited Rhatigan for his advocacy, "suggest[ing] that the only reason student counsel [*sic*] even recognized the group and gave them funding its first year" was due to his intervention.[22]

The opposition that Gardenhire, McKinney, and Barnett experienced in seeking group recognition was unlike the KU group's experience in 1970. While KU's primary pushback was from the chancellor and the regents, WSU's was from student government members. When asked his thoughts about why the chancellor did not express concern, Rhatigan commented:

> Well, they didn't know about it. I mean, it would surprise me if they did. We never told anybody we'd recognized any gay group. We just did. So you'd have to be an energetic regent to even know it. Well, I just told our president what we were going to do, but I was not seeking his permission. I just didn't want him to be sandbagged. I said, "We're going to recognize. Now, you don't need to know anything about it. . . . If we have a problem, then we'll bring you in, but 'til then, this just is an issue between students and student government." [The chancellor said,] "Fine with me!" [Laughs.]

The voice and presence of senior leadership in the process appeared to have made all the difference.

SHA was able to gain recognition as a student organization but had to maintain a low profile. Rhatigan explained: "We recognized them under the covers like that because that's how they could get money. You can't really exist on our campus as an organization unless you have some money. . . . Nobody was aware of their meetings. Their meetings were all just for themselves. It gave them the right to reserve rooms and so forth. And that's how they existed for years." Rhatigan also mentioned that during the group's tenure, he knew of two or three student body presidents who themselves were gay, unbeknownst to the campus, which likely lent some support to the group by student government leadership.

The climate for gay men and lesbians at WSU and the community at large during that time was described as the "Dark Ages," and people were referred to as "vicious." Teutsch recalled that students were "pretty condemning," calling SHA members names, and worse, scratching their cars and tearing down or defacing their posters.[23] Rhatigan described gay and lesbian students on campus as "really fearful," which led group members to be cautious in addressing highly charged, political issues.

The response to SHA in the campus and local newspapers was negative. Parents and donors expressed concern and disapproval. Shortly after this publicity, McKinney's advisor told him that he would not be getting his teacher's license. McKinney left school but stayed involved with the group. Gardenhire, McKinney, and Barnett refused to give up despite these setbacks, but they were worried about bringing in enough funding to cover costs for the dance. They nonetheless continued to move forward and held the dance on March 22, 1975, charging a two-dollar entrance fee. To their relief, they were able to cover their costs and more. Due to their successful outreach, an estimated three hundred attended, generating a substantial sum for a student organization. Members of the KU LGLF were there with bells on to provide their support. Gardenhire recalled: "The first admitted [to the dance] was a carful of boys who [came] down from Kansas University's homosexual alliance."[24]

SHA dissolved in the late 1970s following the graduation and departure of key organizers. New groups arose to fill the gap and keep the momentum going. These groups developed many important programs for WSU and Wichita, including Wear Blue Jeans If You're Gay Day, dances, and Pride Week.[25] It is possible that KU's introduction of these programs in the early and mid-1970s inspired WSU's groups to follow in their footsteps.

KU, K-State, and WSU: Different Strategic Tactics

Openly endorsing gay and lesbian campus student organizations was a risky proposition for college administrators in the 1970s. Gay student groups were created at three Kansas institutions during this time: KU, K-State, and WSU. This was an impressive accomplishment given the culture of the times, particularly for a conservative state in the Midwest. One might credit luck or happenstance to this outcome. It was nothing of the sort. It took intentional efforts by student organizers and allies to navigate through the obstacles to make this happen. Student organizers had a personal investment in their group and its aims, which fueled their dedication and persistence. They also strategically employed tactics to engage others in the fight.

KU, the first Kansas campus to form a gay rights student organization, began this process in the summer of 1970. They received significant resistance, fighting a ten-year battle for official recognition. KU students' key tactics included forming broad connections and engaging allies, challenging homophobic stereotypes and assumptions, operating from a civil rights/activist focus, and working within and outside the system to challenge inequity. They also were steadfast in their commitment to their mission and refused to back down. They took on programs and initiatives that focused on bringing about change, whether at the individual, organizational, or systemic levels. KU had many gay and straight faculty who went to bat for the group, working behind the scenes by contributing funding, quietly advocating for institutional changes and support, and promoting events. Additionally, they had the support of a few highly placed administrators who used their influence to advocate for the group. KU also reached out to student and campus organizations to increase buy-in and broaden their base of support. And by emphasizing their civil rights focus, members communicated a sense of legitimacy and importance regarding the group's purpose. This positioned group members to address and agitate against inequitable policies and practices with the advantage of being in a liberal-leaning community that fostered activism.

K-State and WSU took a different approach than KU, recognizing that a political, activist approach would not have been effective on their campuses. By avoiding political topics and keeping a low profile, organizers were able to navigate the more conservative political environment in which both campuses operated.

K-State focused on individual awareness and support. It was hard to argue with their goal of providing support and growth opportunities to students. This reduced administrators' concern of controversy that a more political agenda might produce. The group, as a result, was viewed as relatively non-threatening and escaped scrutiny. K-State students skillfully used their connections to get things done, skirting around campus processes that could hinder their progress. They informally begin meeting in late fall 1970 with off-campus sponsors who could provide them with "open door" oversight, so they could introduce presentations and discussions that had the potential to be rejected through campus channels. When the group did approach the campus in 1974 to be recognized, it had been in existence for more than three years, all but invisible to straight members of the community. They introduced the group under the name Children of Sappho in their request for official recognition, a name that obscured the true purpose of the group from those who were not knowledgeable or involved with gay culture (a move reminiscent of the Mattachine Society). This approach was successful, and the group was granted recognition with no apparent opposition.

WSU's group first evolved to fill a specific social need, to host a gay dance, steering clear of politics. Like K-State's group, they also kept a low profile. The WSU group began organizing four years after the KU and K-State groups. The national climate had changed to some extent, and the idea of a gay group on a college campus was not quite as taboo but was still not accepted. Nonetheless, there was still opposition, primarily from students. WSU was in the unique position of having senior administrator James Rhatigan, WSU vice president of student affairs, on their side. His belief in the group's right to exist led him to engage in active, behind-the-scenes advocacy. It was his intervention rather than the involvement and support of other communities that convinced student government members to grant official recognition.

It is curious that state regents and legislators took such a strong stand against the creation of a gay student organization at KU in 1970 yet had no reaction when K-State's group received official campus recognition in 1974 and WSU's group in 1976. It is unlikely that politicians' attitudes had softened dramatically in that short span of time, and no legal or legislative changes had occurred that could explain this change of heart. The removal of homosexuality from the *Diagnostic and Statistical Manual of Mental Disorders* (*DSM*) in 1973 was certainly significant but was not mentioned as having a dramatic impact on decision-makers. KU, the flagship campus, was held to a higher standard and was expected to set an example for the other state institutions. It could be argued that the aim in 1970 was to exert control during a time of great unrest and send a message that deviance and disruption would not be tolerated. By making an example of the KU LGLF, administrators may have been attempting to rein in the radical, counterculture contingent across the state. It could also reflect the regents' and legislators' concern regarding their public support base, and donors in particular. They may have decided to take a hard line on an issue that was a thorn in the side of many who viewed the group and the issue as immoral. KU alumni, parents, and community members had written letters of disapproval to local newspapers as well as Chancellor Chalmers censuring the group. KU's image was slipping. Regents, lawmakers, and administrators were concerned.

Emporia State University: "Kansas Society Was Not Ready for Gay Teachers"

In the 1970s, there was some limited gay organizing at Emporia State University, but efforts were informal and sporadic. The campus, then known as the

Kansas State Teachers College (KSTC), had a narrower focus than it does currently, preparing students who were pursuing careers in education.[26] Education was a challenging profession for those who were gay and lesbian. They knew that they must keep their sexual orientation hidden due to the public's paranoia that gay and lesbian teachers would corrupt and endanger children. There was rampant discrimination against gay and lesbian teachers across the country, since protections did not exist, either in the workplace or in education. Many were indiscriminately fired when their identity was discovered. And some who were straight were fired because of innuendo and rumor. In academic programs, students were under the watchful eye of advisors and could be summarily censured by being denied the recommendations they needed for their teaching license. In addition, their certification or license could be denied or revoked if their sexual identity became known to administrators in the program (as occurred to WSU student Bruce McKinney).[27]

Roger Heineken, a well-known Emporia historian and storyteller who retired from a long career in the Student Affairs Division on campus, remembered KSTC in the 1970s as a student. He commented on the way in which national trends affected the state. "Kansas society was not ready for gay teachers, though they were in every district in the state. As a state school back then, I think administrators had to walk a thin wire. Personally, I think most faculty were empathetic toward all students. But there was a limit in how they could mentor and educate in a largely conservative state."[28]

Gay and lesbian students attending KSTC in the early 1970s, many of whom felt isolated and vulnerable, were likely to have been aware of the risks involved in being out on campus.[29] Issues related to sexual orientation were not discussed—it was an unspoken taboo. Students, faculty, and staff alike did not want to suggest this as a subject of discussion for fear that their motives would be questioned and suspicions would be raised, regardless of their sexual orientation. The exception was in a small number of classes, including sociology and psychology, where the topic was discussed cautiously from an academic perspective. Heineken described the climate: "The awareness of any 1970s LGBTQ activity was non-existent, in my opinion. So much else in the early 1970s was going on with the women's movement, Vietnam issues, racial equity, and even with these, [KSTC] was not an activist/radical campus compared to KU and other larger institutions."[30]

Despite this invisibility, there was quiet monitoring. There was speculation that during this time the dean of men kept a log of students he suspected were gay. Dismissing students for this offense, though, would have caused enrollment numbers to dip further, which the university could not afford. Those who had the most to be concerned about, however, were faculty and staff, who were censured if they were identified. Heineken mentioned that there had been talk of gay and lesbian staff and faculty who had been fired or harassed, and those who had died by suicide during that time period that were not spoken about but were known by some in the related divisions or administrative units.[31]

In 1972, an informal gay group began in the community and involved both students and community members. The group of about twenty were in their twenties and included mostly men, but some women attended as well. Some of the leaders of this informal group were connected to gay and lesbian students on other campuses, including KU, which motivated them to get the group started. Their vision was "to produce positive, healthy outcomes (issues-based) supporting the members."[32] They met biweekly, alternating between a social meeting and a meeting focusing on current topics. Factions arose, splitting between those who wanted the group to be strictly social and a smaller number of those who pushed for a more task-oriented focus. This was a common problem for gay groups during that time period, including KU. The Emporia group could not get through this conflict and fell apart in 1973.

In 1980, KU Executive Vice Chancellor Del Shankel sent a memo to Chancellor Archie Dykes regarding a survey that was conducted on gay student groups on state regents' campuses in the 1970s. Shankel stated that Emporia had a gay group on campus that was recognized during this time period but did not receive funding. He further commented that the group had not reregistered since 1978, suggesting that they had registered for a continuous period of time previous to this memo, dated May 27, 1980.[33] A document housed in the Emporia archives lists a group, Gay People of Emporia, as active in 1974–1975 and 1976–1977. No other information about this group was found, however.[34]

Gay and lesbian students connected primarily at underground parties and college bars, some open and some closeted, influenced by Kansas alcohol laws.[35] Heineken elaborated, "In the very late 1970s a new bar/tavern opened close to campus called Barlogas. It became popular with lesbian students in particular. They were eventually asked to not be there as it was giving the bar a 'reputation.'"[36] Another popular meeting spot was a park right across the street from the campus. Joe Lordi, who received his undergraduate degree from KU and attended Emporia from 1974 to 1975 for graduate studies (which by then was called Emporia Kansas State College), agreed that interactions were informal. He recalled: "The place where gay people met there was in Hammond Park. . . . I met enough people to know that it was going on. But nothing official. No dances, no publications. I mean, it was a different kind of town than Lawrence. I mean, it was a different kind of school, frankly." Gay and lesbian students at Emporia had some connections with KU group members and attended many KU dances.

Heineken shared his thoughts about three key changes that provided the momentum for gay and lesbian communities to develop at Emporia State University (ESU) starting in the 1980s.[37] First was the American Psychiatric Association's decision in 1973 to remove homosexuality from the DSM, depathologizing and normalizing homosexuality. While this did not appear to influence some Kansas lawmakers and decision-makers, it did have an impact on the Emporia campus. A second change was the HIV/AIDS epidemic. The confusing, contradictory information that circulated and the escalation in discrimination against gay men that occurred caused many in the gay community to band together and organize. This brought about a visible, involved student organization at ESU in the mid-1980s. A third change was the retirement of old-guard administrators and faculty, who were likely to endorse the harmful mythology and stigma related to homosexuality, coloring their views and subsequent actions. Heineken summed up the effect of some of the discrimination that occurred at their hands: "Deep closets produced this kind of injustice while keeping established faculty and staff in their place and safe."[38]

Pittsburg State University: "There Was No Gay Life"

Pittsburg State University first began as a teachers' college to address the teacher shortage throughout the state. It was originally a branch of the Kansas State Teachers' College in Emporia, along with Fort Hays State University.[39] Bob Warren, who attended Pittsburg State from 1965 to 1967 prior to transferring to KU, described the environment for those who were gay and lesbian: "At Pittsburg, there was no gay life. . . . I don't remember ever hearing the word 'gay' or any organizational movement or any political—nothing. . . . It just wasn't there." He had heard after he had left that there was one bar in town that a few gay people frequented. He described the gay presence as invisible. "There was a certain amount of stuff about the Vietnam War, yes. Things about Black Power. And Abbie Hoffman was known to people on campus. There was a radical element, but there wasn't any gay component of that, or I would have remembered it and attached on to it to some degree."

A search through Pittsburg State Archives records, including student handbooks of that time, led Steven Cox, professor and curator, Special Collections and University Archives, Pittsburg State University, to conclude that no official groups existed in the 1970s. This was reinforced by library dean Randy Roberts, who was a Pittsburg State student in the mid-1970s. It was also confirmed in a 1980 KU memo reporting on gay campus organizations throughout the state during the 1970s. Cox speculated that any gay activity and organizing that took place happened underground.[40]

Very little information is available about interactions between gay and lesbian students at Pittsburg State and KU. There are records and newspaper articles indicating that Pittsburg State is one of the campuses for which the KU LGLF provided presentations.[41]

Fort Hays State University: "A Less than Welcoming Environment"

Fort Hays State University (FHSU), similar to Pittsburg State University, first began as a teachers' college, serving as another branch of the Kansas State Teachers' College in Emporia.[42] Similar to its other western neighbors, Wichita State and Pittsburg State, homosexuality was not a topic that was openly discussed, and those who were gay and lesbian knew to keep a low profile. Brian Gribben, coordinator, Government Documents and Special Collections, Forsyth Library, reported that no information surfaced about gay and lesbian students or student organizations in the 1970s when he conducted a comprehensive search through the campus archives. Gribben offered this possible explanation: "As you might suspect, our LGBTQ students during this period were navigating a less than welcoming environment that may have precluded public activities." Gribben suspected, based on what he had heard through the grapevine, that the university may have actively discouraged organizations serving LGBTQ students. In addition, the university archives may not have collected LGBT information and "may have been negligent in curating relevant collections." He mentioned that "in the *University Leader* [the FHSU student newspaper], we did discover allusions to a pretty invasive application originating in the Registrar's Office. Apparently, the application for out-of-state and graduate students was designed with intended bias against LGBTQ students."[43]

Henry Schwaller, a KU student in the early 1980s, grew up in Hays. Based

on his extensive FHSU network, he confirmed that there were no gay liberation groups at FHSU during the 1970s. This was also confirmed in the 1980
memo from KU Executive Vice Chancellor Del Shankel to Chancellor Archie
Dykes mentioned earlier in this appendix.[44] It wasn't until later that a student organization would get started. Said Schwaller, "There was a student
organization, I believe it was organized by Craig Rumpel [a close friend], in
the late 1980s or early 1990s, and it successfully fought to have sexual orientation added to the University's non-discrimination policy."[45]

Concluding Thoughts: The LGLF's Influence on Campuses across the State

The actions of the Lawrence Gay Liberation Front influenced campuses
throughout the state with its visibility, intentional outreach, and celebratory,
inclusive dances. The LGLF gained local, state, and even national media attention in the 1970s. Many LGLF members, in fact, decided to come out to
their families out of concern that they would read it first in their hometown
newspapers.[46] The group's visibility and unapologetic, proud presence captured the attention of gay and lesbian students on other campuses, and this
boldness encouraged them to take steps to mobilize "at home."

In addition to the LGLF's media presence, the group also influenced other
campuses through their intentional efforts to connect. LGLF members were
reported to have made presentations at other campuses throughout the state
in addition to informally connecting and attending gay-related events on
other campuses. Many campuses reached out to the LGLF for assistance in
dealing with campus gay-related issues, including Ottawa University and the
KU Medical Center.

Later in 1977, the KU group, whose name had changed to the Gay Services of Kansas (GSOK), brought together gay activists across the state for
their regional Kansas Gay Political Conference. Many GSOK/LGLF members had a pivotal role at this and other local and national conferences, pushing for change and taking the risk of being visible. With the LGLF being
by far the most political of the gay organizations in the state during that
time, its members served as role models and leaders, challenging inequitable LGBTQ-related policies and practices. In 1977, WSU followed suit and
challenged the powerful, nationally organized opposition to Wichita's progressive nondiscrimination policy that had been steadily growing. This

nondiscrimination policy was not able to withstand the opposition and was repealed, but progress was made through the demonstration of community support for its gay and lesbian members.

A third important influence was the LGLF dances. They have been described as a regional unifier, connecting gay and lesbian people from all over the state. People remembered them as popular events that students at the other state institutions knew about, talked about, and attended. Joe Lordi described them as "the thing that drew everybody together." The need to connect was critical and a driving force for gay and lesbian students across the state. One of the most common themes arising from interviews conducted for this book was the sense of isolation that gay and lesbian people felt, pointing to the need to establish a sense of belonging and community. Dance attendees spoke of the freedom of being able to express their gender in whatever way they chose without fear of censure, which they described as "incredibly affirming" and "liberating."[47]

KU has often been thought of as leading the way in establishing new directions for state higher education institutions, but other institutions have also shared in this distinction. While KU has an impressive history of students and allies advancing gay rights, K-State has recently been recognized as outpacing KU's efforts. K-State established its LGBT Center in 2010, four years before KU established its Center for Sexuality and Gender Diversity. In recent years, K-State has been recognized as an LGBTQ-friendly campus, receiving five out of five stars on the Pride Index, "the premier LGBTQ national benchmarking tool for colleges and universities to create safer, more inclusive campus communities."[48]

This high ranking resulted in K-State being selected as one of the 2023 Best of the Best LGBTQ Campuses by the Pride Index, the only Kansas institution to be included on this list.[49] This is the second year that K-State has received this ranking, pointing to the institution's commitment to creating a welcoming, supportive climate and addressing the needs of LGBTQ members in their community. Emporia State and WSU also received high marks on the Pride Index, with Emporia receiving 4 out of 5 stars and WSU 4.5 out of 5. KU, the only other Kansas institution rated, received 4 stars.

It is important to mention that KU's score increased by one star from the previous year. These ratings indicate that KU has made significant strides in expanding and strengthening institutional response and services, thereby creating an environment that is more responsive to LGBTQ needs. Currently there are some initiatives in place, particularly related to campus policies and student and academic life. Improvements are needed, however, in the areas of infrastructure support, recruitment, alumni connections and involvement opportunities, and safety measures to support LGBTQ students more effectively. KU has been actively addressing these issues, yet this ranking is a powerful reminder to campus administrators that LGBTQ inclusion is essential in institutional planning and implementation efforts throughout the university and cannot be relegated to a single individual or unit. The vision needs to be shared and efforts need to be adequately staffed and funded to be successful.

Notes

Preface

1. David H. Stout, "Emergence (see?)," vol. 2 (unpublished manuscript, 6 vols., November 25, 2011), University Archives.

2. Christa Hillstrom, "The Power of Oral History: Personal Narratives Take Us Deep into the Human Rights Stories Hidden behind the Headlines," *Yes! Magazine*, June 7, 2014, http://www.yesmagazine.org/peace-justice/invisible-hands-voi ces-from-the-global-economy-1/the-power-of-oral-history.

3. Martha Howell and Walter Prevenier, *From Reliable Sources: An Introduction to Historical Methods* (Ithaca, NY: Cornell University Press, 2001), 112–118.

4. The event took place in 2021 rather than 2020, the actual fifty-year anniversary, due to the COVID pandemic.

5. Beth Bailey, *Sex in the Heartland* (Cambridge, MA: Harvard University Press, 1999).

About the Identity Terms Used in This Book

1. Lillian Faderman, *The Gay Revolution: The Story of the Struggle* (New York: Simon & Schuster, 2016); "Erasure of Bisexuality," GLAAD, https://www.glaad .org/bisexual/bierasure.

2. Stephen Whittle, "A Brief History of Transgender Issues," *Guardian*, June 2, 2010, https://www.theguardian.com/lifeandstyle/2010/jun/02/brief-history-trans gender-issues.

3. See Genny Beemyn and Susan Rankin, *The Lives of Transgender People* (New York: Columbia University Press, 2011), 159.

4. Noel Gutierrez-Morfin, "GLAAD Officially Adds the 'Q' to LGBTQ," October 26, 2016, NBC News, https://www.nbcnews.com/feature/nbc-out/glaad -officially-adds-q-lgbtq-n673196.

Introduction

1. The information and quotations in this section are from Leonard Grotta, interview by author, March 13, 2013. All interviews conducted by the author are

digital audio recordings and are in the author's possession unless otherwise noted. Also, unless otherwise noted, it is assumed throughout the book that quotations from individuals interviewed by the author are from their interviews.

2. D'Emilio quoted in Sam Danley, "How KC Played a Role in LGBT History," *UNews*, October 25, 2016.

3. Brett Beemyn documented that 175 college organizations had been established by 1971 in the article "The Silence Is Broken: A History of the First Lesbian, Gay, and Bisexual Student Groups," *Journal of the History of Sexuality* 12, no. 2 (April 2003): 222. Patrick Dilley also cited this in his book *Queer Man on Campus: A History of Non-Heterosexual College Men, 1945–2000* (New York: RoutledgeFalmer, 2002), 168.

4. Quotation from David Radavich, interview by author, March 15, 2013.

5. Sharon Sievers, "Gay and Lesbian Research in the 1980s: History and Theory," *Radical History Review* 50 (May 1, 1991): 204–212.

6. Robbie Lieberman, *Prairie Power: Voices of 1960s Midwestern Student Protest* (Columbia: University of Missouri Press, 2004).

7. C. J. Janovy, *No Place Like Home: Lessons in Activism from LGBT Kansas* (Lawrence: University Press of Kansas, 2018).

8. Mary L. Gray, Brian J. Gilley, and Colin R. Johnson, *Queering the Countryside: New Frontiers in Rural Queer Studies* (New York: New York University Press, 2017); Colin R. Johnson, *Just Queer Folks: Gender and Sexuality in Rural America* (Philadelphia: Temple University Press, 2013); Will Fellows, *Farmboys: Lives of Gay Men from the Rural Midwest* (Madison: University of Wisconsin Press, 2001); Samantha Allen, *Real Queer America: LGBT Stories from Red States* (Boston: Little, Brown, 2019).

9. Beemyn, "Silence Is Broken," 206.

10. Dilley, *Queer Man on Campus*; Patrick Dilley, *Gay Liberation to Campus Assimilation: Early Non-Heterosexual Student Organizations at Midwestern Universities* (New York: Palgrave Macmillan, 2019).

11. Beth Bailey, *Sex in the Heartland* (Cambridge, MA: Harvard University Press, 1999), 4.

12. KU ScholarWorks, KU Libraries, https://kuscholarworks.ku.edu/handle/1808/5330.

13. Albin has conducted seventy-five interviews for this project. Currently, twenty-six are available through KU ScholarWorks, and the remaining interviews will be added at a later date. Email from Tami Albin, January 23, 2023.

1. "The Times They Are A-Changin'"

1. Helen L. Horowitz, "The 1960s and the Transformation of Campus Cultures," *History of Education Quarterly* 26, no. 1 (1986): 11–15, 24–33; Robert A.

Rhoads, *Freedom's Web: Student Activism in an Age of Cultural Diversity* (Baltimore: Johns Hopkins University Press, 1998), 2–4, 35–39; John D. Skrentny, *The Minority Rights Revolution* (Cambridge, MA: Belknap Press of Harvard University Press, 2002), 50–55.

2. Skrentny, *Minority Rights Revolution*, 2.

3. Horowitz, "1960s," 16–33; Rhoads, *Freedom's Web*, 2–4; Skrentny, *Minority Rights Revolution*, 2–7; William M. Tuttle Jr., "KU's Tumultuous Years: Thirty Years of Student Activism, 1965–1995," in *Transforming the University of Kansas: A History, 1965–2015*, ed. John L. Rury and Kim Cary Warren (Lawrence: University Press of Kansas, 2015), 227–228.

4. John D'Emilio and Estelle B. Freedman, *Intimate Matters: A History of Sexuality in America*, 2nd ed. (Chicago: University of Chicago Press, 1988), 319–322; Rhoads, *Freedom's Web*, 59.

5. "Homosexuality in America," *Life*, June 26, 1964.

6. John Bolin, email to author, September 26, 2020.

7. All remaining quotations in this paragraph are from "Homosexuality in America."

8. James W. Button, Barbara A. Rienzo, and Kenneth D. Wald, *Private Lives, Public Conflicts: Battles over Gay Rights in American Communities* (Washington, DC: Congressional Quarterly, 1997), 2, 203; Will Kohler, "Gay History—June 26, 1964: LIFE Magazine Covers the 'Sordid World of Homosexuality in America,'" *Back2Stonewall* (blog), June 26, 2020.

9. D'Emilio and Freedman, *Intimate Matters*, 319.

10. John Bolin emails, September 26, 2020, October 25, 2020, July 21, 2021.

11. Tom Burke, "The New Homosexuality," *Esquire*, December 1, 1969.

12. Richard Linker, document sent via email, June 3, 2020.

13. John D'Emilio, *Sexual Politics, Sexual Communities: The Making of a Homosexual Minority in the United States, 1940–1970*, 2nd ed. (Chicago: University of Chicago Press, 1983), 198; D'Emilio and Freedman, *Intimate Matters*, 293–295; Anthony R. D'Augelli, "Lesbians and Gay Men on Campus: Visibility, Empowerment and Educational Leadership," *Peabody Journal of Education* 66, no. 3 (1989): 129–131; Button et al., *Private Lives*, 2–3, 23–26, 59–63; Beth Bailey, *Sex in the Heartland* (Cambridge, MA: Harvard University Press, 1999), 188–189.

14. Anthony R. D'Augelli, "Identity Development and Sexual Orientation: Toward a Model of Lesbian, Gay, and Bisexual Development," in *ASHE Reader on College Student Development Theory*, ed. Maureen E. Wilson and Lisa E. Wolf-Wendel (Boston: Pearson, 2005), 393–403.

15. Ruth E. Fassinger, "Lesbian, Gay, and Bisexual Identity and Student Development Theory," in Wilson and Wolf-Wendel, *ASHE Reader*, 405–411.

16. D'Augelli, "Lesbians and Gay Men on Campus," 124–127; Susan R. McCarn and Ruth Fassinger, "Revisioning Sexual Minority Identity Formation: A New

Model of Lesbian Identity and Its Implications for Counseling and Research," *Counseling Psychologist* 24 (1996): 508–534.

17. David Radavich, interview by author, March 15, 2013; Ann Eversole, interview by author, April 26, 2013; John Beisner, interview by author, June 13, 2013; Paul Lim, interview by author, June 24, 2013; Stephanie Blackwood, interview by author, October 16, 2019.

18. David Awbrey, interview by author, June 10, 2013; Trip Haenisch, interview by author, October 25, 2013; Chad Leat, interview by author, October 2, 2013.

19. D'Augelli, "Identity Development," 393–403; McCarn and Fassinger, "Revisioning," 508–534.

20. D'Augelli, "Identity Development," 401.

21. Martha Boyd, interview by author, September 16, 2019.

22. David H. Stout, "Emergence (see?)," vol. 2 (unpublished manuscript, 6 vols., November 25, 2011), University Archives; Lee Hubbell, interview by author, March 8, 2013.

23. John Bolin, interview by author, March 13, 2021; John Bolin email, July 21, 2021.

24. Stout, "Emergence (see?)," vols. 1 and 2.

25. Richard Linker, interview by author, June 5, 2020; Linker document.

26. Hubbell interview.

27. Sarah Evans, *Personal Politics: The Roots of Women's Liberation in the Civil Rights Movement and the New Left* (New York: Knopf, 1979), 16–23, 212–215; D'Emilio and Freedman, *Intimate Matters*, 308–318, 321.

28. D'Emilio, *Sexual Politics*, 226–228; Terence Kissack, "Freaking Fag Revolutionaries: New York's Gay Liberation Front," *Radical History Review* 62 (1995): 112; Bailey, *Sex in the Heartland*, 188, 193–195.

29. Bolin email, October 25, 2020.

30. Fassinger, "Lesbian, Gay, and Bisexual Identity," 405–411.

31. Button et al., *Private Lives*, 23–24; Skrentny, *Minority Rights Revolution*, 315–317.

32. D'Emilio, *Sexual Politics*, 108–109; Kissack, "Freaking Fag," 106–111.

33. Brett G. Beemyn, ed., *Creating a Place for Ourselves: Lesbian, Gay and Bisexual Community Histories* (New York: Routledge, 1997), 4; Elizabeth A. Armstrong and Suzanna M. Crage, "Moments and Memory: The Making of the Stonewall Myth," *American Sociological Review* 71 (October 2006): 724–751, quotation on 724; Greggor Mattson, "The Stonewall Riots Didn't Start the Gay Rights Movement," *JStor Daily*, June 12, 2019, https://daily.jstor.org/the-stonewall-riots-didnt-start-the-gay-rights-movement/.

34. Michael McConnell with Jack Baker, *The Wedding Heard 'Round the World* (Minneapolis: University of Minnesota Press, 2016), 55–61; Bruce Johansen, "Out of

Silence: FREE, Minnesota's First Gay Rights Organization," *Minnesota History* 66, no. 5 (2019): 186–201, quotation on 197; Ken Bronson, *A Quest for Full Equality*, n.d., 11–12, https://www.lib.umn.edu/sites/www.lib.umn.edu/files/2021-11/quest-copy .pdf.

35. Bailey, *Sex in the Heartland*, 4–6, 175; Rusty L. Monhollon, *This Is America? The Sixties in Lawrence, Kansas* (New York: Palgrave Macmillan, 2004), 13, 21.

36. Monhollon, *This Is America?*, 1–8, 43–61; Robbie Lieberman, *Prairie Power: Voices of 1960s Midwestern Student Protest* (Columbia: University of Missouri Press, 2004), 108, 147–148, 217–220.

37. Monhollon, *This Is America?*, 12.

38. Monhollon, *This Is America?*, 142–182; Hubbell interview; Michael McConnell, interview by author, April 15, 2021.

39. Mike Shearer, "Student Tells of His 'Gay' Life," *UDK*, October 25, 1968; Joe Prados, interview by author, April 2, 2013; Lim interview.

40. David H. Stout, "Radical Means: Their Implications to Social Workers Striving to Change the System" (unpublished manuscript, November 1, 1972), Queers and Allies Files; Bailey, *Sex in the Heartland*, 175; Stacey Reding, "Paving Gayhawk Lane: The Lawrence Gay Liberation Front and Chancellor Chalmers' Veto" (unpublished research paper, December 13, 2001), Queers and Allies Files; David Stout email, July 8, 2018; Michael Stubbs email, May 13, 2020.

41. Stubbs emails, May 13, 2020, and May 9, 2021.

42. Lieberman, *Prairie Power*, 96, 108–117; Christine Smith, interview by author, June 17, 2013; Michael Stubbs, interview by author, May 6, 2020.

43. This included the Civil Rights Council, the Student Peace Union (SPU), Congress of Racial Equality, the League for the Practice of Democracy, Students for a Democratic Society (SDS), Student Nonviolent Coordinating Committee (SNCC), and the Student Mobilization Committee. See Lieberman, *Prairie Power*, 108; Monhollon, *This is America?*, 64–69; Smith interview.

44. Sharon Mayer, interview by author, August 28, 2019.

45. Bolin interview; Alice Echols, "'We Gotta Get Out of This Place': Notes toward a Remapping of the Sixties," *Socialist Review* 22, no. 2 (1992): 24. In her article, Echols referred to this as "slumming." Bolin commented that many did not own cameras and identified this as a reason there are few photos of this time.

46. Quoted in Sam Ross-Brown, "An Unfinished Revolution," *Utne Reader*, February 14, 2014.

47. Robert Pardun, *Prairie Radical: A Journey through the 60s* (Los Gatos, CA: Shire, 2001), 2.

48. Megan Heacock, "A Look at KU's Changing Face of Activism," *UDK*, December 4, 2009; Ross Brown, "Unfinished Revolution"; Lieberman, *Prairie Power*, 146.

49. Todd Gitlin gives a good description of the climate in *The Sixties: Years of Hope, Days of Rage* (New York: Bantam, 1987), 61–274. For other good local descriptions see Tuttle, "KU's Tumultuous Years," 235–247; Lieberman, *Prairie Power,* 217–220, 247–257.

50. Lieberman, *Prairie Power,* 212, 250; Smith interview; Stubbs email, May 13, 2020.

51. Information and Bolin's quotations in the following paragraphs come from his emails (September 26, October 25, and December 1, 2020) and interview.

52. Stubbs interview.

53. Bolin and Stubbs email exchange with author, October 25, 2020; Bolin email, May 14, 2021.

54. Bob Dole was giving a speech at Kansas State University, May 18, 1970. Details about this event were from Bolin's and Stubbs's emails to author, October 25, 2020, and May 14, 2021, as well as information from the Dole Institute regarding Dole's appointments in 1970.

55. Bolin email, October 25, 2020.

56. Bolin email, December 1, 2020.

57. Information and quotations in this section are from the Stubbs interview.

58. G. Joseph Pierron, "Henry Agnew Bubb," Kansapedia, Kansas Historical Society, last modified September 2016, https://www.kshs.org/kansapedia/henry -agnew-bubb/18156. Bubb's disapproval of homosexuality was communicated in a note he sent in 1972 to Chancellor Raymond Nichols with an ad for a 1972 LGLF dance attached, asking, "Do you approve of this use of the Student Union?" Henry Bubb to Chancellor Raymond Nichols, n.d., Balfour/Alderson Files.

59. Stubbs email, April 29, 2020.

60. Sandra Levinson and Carol Brightman, *Venceremos Brigade: Young Americans Sharing the Life and Work of Revolutionary Cuba* (New York: Simon & Schuster, 1971), 15; Jean Bowdish, "The Venceremos Brigade: 50 Years of Solidarity with Cuba," *Workers World,* October 31, 2019, https://www.workers.org/2019/10/44220/.

61. Allen Ginsberg, "Gay Sunshine Interview," *College English* 36, no. 3 (1974): 392–400.

62. Stubbs emails, May 13 and 29, 2020.

63. John Dart, "City Commune's Goal: Helping Revolutions," *Los Angeles Times,* July 20, 1970; Rev. Jim Conn, "James Donaldson: An Organizer's Long Legacy," *Capital and Main,* February 1, 2017. The Urban Plunge evolved from a program developed by Chicago clergy and was expanded by the New Adult Community, a communal village in Los Angeles that aimed to address societal oppression through self-reflection and interaction with historically excluded communities.

64. EROS Urban Plunge handout, April 25–27, 1969; courtesy of Larry Fry, Wesley KU.

65. EROS Urban Plunge handout; Monhollon, *This Is America?*, 65. The KU University Christian Movement was a coordinated group of Protestant and Catholic ministries on the KU campus.

66. Bolin email, November 30, 2020.

67. Bolin email, November 30, 2020.

68. Bolin email (November 30, 2020) and interview.

69. John Bolin in email from Michael Stubbs, May 9, 2020.

70. Stubbs email, May 9, 2020.

71. Barbara Taylor, "Urban Trip . . ." *Reconstruction*, March 3, 1969, 7.

72. Bolin email, October 6, 2020.

73. Stubbs interview; Stubbs email, May 9, 2020; Bolin email, May 11, 2021.

74. Stubbs interview.

75. Monhollon, *This Is America?*, 140; Ross-Brown, "Unfinished Revolution."

76. Boyd (September 16, 2019) and Clark interviews.

77. Dick Larimore, "Landlord Denies Huge Profits on Housing," *UDK*, April 30, 1971.

78. Kathryn Clark email, February 18, 2020.

79. Boyd (September 16, 2019) and Stubbs interviews.

80. "Emergence (see?)," vol. 2.

81. Reding, "Paving Gayhawk Lane"; Stout, "Emergence (see?)," vol. 2; Albin interview; Chuck Ortleb, personal communication, December 5, 2014.

82. Stout, "Emergence (see?)," vol. 2.

83. This included Michael Stubbs, John Bolin, Peter Felleman, John Stephen Stillwell, Richard Linker, and Phil Thornton (a friend of the LGLF but not a member).

84. Linker email.

85. Felleman interview; Linker email.

86. Stubbs email.

87. Ortleb, personal communication, December 5, 2014.

88. Bolin email, October 12, 2020; Stubbs interview.

89. Linker email.

90. Bolin email, June 26, 2020.

91. Felleman interview.

92. Mayer (August 28, 2019), Stubbs, Bolin interviews.

93. Steven Weaver, interview by author, May 18, 2020. See chapter 6.

94. There were also some straight residents, but they were in the minority (Felleman interview).

95. Stubbs interview.

96. Mayer (August 28, 2019), Stubbs, Felleman interviews; Linker email; Bolin email, September 14, 2020.

97. Felleman email, May 24, 2021.

98. Members began moving out in February 1972 (Bolin email, May 11, 2021).

99. Bolin email, May 11, 2021; Felleman email, May 24, 2021; Mayer interview, August 28, 2019.

100. Weaver and Bolin interviews; Bolin email, May 11, 2021.

101. Lordi interview; Bolin email, March 13, 2021.

102. Discussed in more detail in appendix B.

103. Lieberman, *Prairie Power*, 255.

104. Fowler was editor and publisher of the Beat magazine *Grist*, which frequently included articles by gay and lesbian writers. Jim McCrary shared this in an email to John Bolin, November 8, 2020 (provided to author with permission).

105. Shearer, "Gay Life"; "Emergence (see?)," vol. 2; Albin and McConnell interviews.

106. Prados and Lim interviews.

107. Stout, "Emergence (see?)," vol. 3.

108. Albin, Linker, Leat interviews; Chris Caldwell, interview by author, October 23, 2013.

109. The "code" is discussed in Jonathan N. Katz, *Gay American History: Lesbians and Gay Men in the U.S.A.*, rev. ed. (New York: Penguin, 1992) and George Chauncey, *Gay New York: Gender, Urban Culture, and the Making of the Gay Male World, 1890–1940* (New York: Basic Books, 1994).

110. Grier quoted in Jason Gordon, "Back to the Front: The Lawrence Gay Liberation Front and the Struggle for Recognition" (unpublished research paper for Dr. Bill Tuttle's class, December 13, 1996, University of Kansas, used with permission from Dr. Bill Tuttle).

111. "Gay Scene K.C.," Making History: Kansas City and the Rise of Gay Rights, University of Missouri, Kansas City, https://info.umkc.edu/makinghistory/gay-scene-k-c/.

112. Keith Spare, "Prairie Fairie" (unpublished manuscript, August 1, 2020), used with permission of author.

113. Spare email, July 13, 2021; Ortleb, personal communication, December 5, 2014.

114. Hubbell, Prados, Lordi, Albin interviews; Bolin email, May 13, 2021. The Jewel Box has an important place in Kansas City gay history. See "Gay Scene K.C."

115. In the 1970s, Kansas law stipulated that public establishments serving alcohol had to function as private clubs, and any patrons entering had to sign up as members. This caused problems for gay and lesbian patrons who did not

want their identities to be known. As Boyd stated, many proprietors made arrangements with police, so they did not have to release this information. Also see D'Emilio and Freedman, *Intimate Matters*, 294.

116. Reding, "Paving Gayhawk Lane"; Stout, "Emergence (see?)," vol. 2.

117. Stout's quotations in this section are from "Emergence (see?)," vol. 2.

118. KU Analytics, Institutional Research, and Effectiveness, KU Fact Book, Enrollment Data, https://air.ku.edu/interactive_factbook/historical-trend. Undergraduate enrollment: 78.9 percent in 1966; 77.3 percent in 1972. Male enrollment: 62 percent in 1966; 60 percent in 1972.

119. According to the US Census, the population of Lawrence in 1970 was 45,498.

120. Quoted in Sid Moody, "K.U.'s Class of 73 Matured in Troubled Years, New Attitude," *Kansas City Star*, May 13, 1973.

121. John H. McCool, "Cause for Concern," (November 18, 1971), K.U. History website, https://kuhistory.ku.edu/articles/cause-concern.

122. See Monhollon, *This Is America?*; Tuttle, "KU's Tumultuous Years"; "150 Sit-In-Stand-Out by Wescoe's Office," *UDK*, March 9, 1965; "Arrests No Curb on Demonstrations," *UDK*, March 9, 1965; "Chancellor's Statement," *UDK*, March 9, 1965; Bill Mayer, "Rights 'Sit-In' Continues at KU," *LDJW*, March 9, 1965; "Sit-In at Wescoe's Office," *LDJW*, March 8, 1965; "Timetable of a Sit-In," *KU Today*, April 10, 1965.

123. Monhollon, *This Is America?*, 63-75.

124. Susan B. Twombly, "'Lift the Chorus Ever Onward': Leading the University," in Rury and Warren, *Transforming the University of Kansas*, 48-53.

125. Lieberman, *Prairie Power*, 114; Hub Meyer, "Wescoe Seeks Action," *LDJW*, May 10, 1969.

126. Rick Pendergrass, "Governor's Reaction: 'Peace' Demonstration," *UDK*, May 12, 1969.

127. Pendergrass, "Governor's Reaction"; "Unrest Nothing New," *UDK*, October 2, 1969.

128. Bill Tuttle interview by author, March 21, 2013; "Wescoe Asks for Support in Handling Current Crisis," *LDJW*, May 12, 1969.

129. "KU Unit Ousts 33 of 71," *LDJW*, June 2, 1969.

130. Lieberman, *Prairie Power*, 114; Tuttle, "KU's Tumultuous Years," 239.

131. "A Look at KU's Changing Face," *UDK*, December 4, 2009.

132. Monhollon, *This Is America?*, 142-143, 178-181; Lieberman, *Prairie Power*, 110.

133. "Blacks Urged to Take Arms," *LDJW*, April 10, 1970.

134. Jerry Schwartz, "Arson Suspected in $1 Million Union Loss," *LDJW*, April 21, 1970.

135. Smith interview.

136. Monhollon, *This Is America?*, 164–165.

137. "One Oread Shot Not Policeman's?," *LDJW*, July 22, 1970; Jerry Schwartz, "Youth Is Killed in Gun Battle," *LDJW*, July 17, 1970; Jerry Schwartz, "Seven Arrested in Local Unrest," *LDJW*, July 20, 1970.

138. Schwartz, "Seven Arrested."

139. "One Oread Shot."

140. Jerry Schwartz, "Leawood Youth Killed in Monday Flareup," *LDJW*, July 21, 1970; Jerry Schwartz, "Quiet but Tense Climate in City," *LDJW*, July 22, 1970.

141. Oldfather quoted in Jamie Tilma, "The Lawrence Gay Liberation Front 1970–1973" (unpublished research paper for Dr. Bill Tuttle's class, December 18, 1993, University of Kansas, used with permission from Dr. Bill Tuttle).

2. "Out of the Johns and Into the Streets!"

1. Michael Stubbs email, February 12, 2022.

2. David Stout's writings were relied on substantially as they are the most comprehensive firsthand recounting of the beginnings of the group. He used original LGLF documents from the group's office files that he reviewed in the 1970s (which were unfortunately not kept). Also included is information from former LGLF members John Bolin and Joe Lordi, who had kept written logs (Bolin's are quite extensive), and recollections of many others who were involved in the beginnings of the group. Written information from the media and archival documents were also utilized.

3. "Population of Cities in Kansas, 1900–2020," Institute for Policy and Social Research, University of Kansas, https://ipsr.ku.edu/ksdata/ksah/population/. The population of Rolla in 1970 was 400, while the population of Lawrence at that time was 45,698. Many students from small, rural communities were intimidated by the size of KU and Lawrence.

4. The quotations and accounts in this section come from David H. Stout, "Emergence (see?)," vols. 1 and 2 (unpublished manuscript, 6 vols., November 25, 2011), University Archives.

5. Mike Shearer, "Student Tells of His 'Gay' Life," *UDK*, October 25, 1968.

6. Stout, "Emergence (see?)," vol. 2; Lee Hubbell, interview by author, March 8, 2013; Chad Leat, interview by author, October 2, 2013.

7. Beth Bailey, *Sex in the Heartland* (Cambridge, MA: Harvard University Press, 1999), 62; Bill Tuttle, interview by author, March 21, 2013.

8. Tami Albin, interviews with David Stout (1–8), interview #1, digital video recording (November 1, 2010, in author's possession); Stout, "Emergence (see?)," vol. 2.

9. Stout, "Emergence (see?)," vol. 2; David Stout email, May 21, 2020; Richard Linker, interview by author, June 5, 2020; Linker document sent via email, June 3, 2020; Bolin email, December 1, 2020; Weaver email, April 4, 2021. Stillwell was one of the first group members to die of AIDS in the 1980s.

10. Weaver email.

11. Tuttle interview; Stout, "Emergence (see?)," vol. 2.

12. Reginald Brown, interview by author, May 27, 2020.

13. Tonda Rush, interview by author, November 19, 2019; Sharon Mayer, interview by author, August 28, 2019; Susan Davis, interview by author, November 18, 2019.

14. Kathy Hoggard, interview by author, July 12, 2013; Mayer interview, August 28, 2019.

15. Most existing documents list the year in which the group started as 1970, a fact supported by recollections of original founding members. A few early documents, however, refer to the founding year as 1969. This includes a statement issued by the KU News Bureau and a *UDK* article ("Approval Denied to Gay Liberation Front"), both issued in September 1970. They stated that the LGLF first applied for official recognition as an organization "a year ago," which would have been September 1969. Dilley, in his book *Queer Man on Campus: A History of Non-Heterosexual College Men, 1945-2000* (New York: RoutledgeFalmer, 2002), also commented on this confusion. He pointed out that KU historical records citing the founding dates listed both 1969 and 1970 (169). This confusion may have been perpetuated by contradictory dates in promotional materials for significant events. For instance, printed material for KU Gay and Lesbian Awareness Week (GALA) in 1989 listed that year as the twentieth anniversary of the founding of the LGLF, making the founding year 1969. "GALA History," *Vanguard* 20, no. 1 (April 7, 1989), Queers and Allies Files. Yet materials for 1995 GALA events celebrated the twenty-fifth anniversary of the group, making 1970 the founding date.

Historical records provide no explanation for the 1969 listing, and no early student organization registration records were found in the files. There are two possible explanations for this. David Awbrey, student body president from 1969 to 1970, recalled a student who in 1969 was forming a KU chapter of the Mattachine Society that did not materialize (as discussed in chapter 1). It is possible that the Mattachine Society's fleeting efforts to organize became linked to the LGLF the following year. Therefore, it could be a case of mistaken identity in which people thought of the two separate groups as the same organization. It could also be attributed to human error. Whoever prepared the 1970 KU News Bureau statement may have made an unintentional error that was picked up by *UDK* reporters and others and was perpetuated as fact. Those who were there, however, have unanimously agreed that the group was established in June 1970. Most written accounts, in addition, list June 1970 as the correct date.

16. Tami Albin interview #1, 2010; David H. Stout, "Radical Means: Their Implications to Social Workers Striving to Change the System" (unpublished manuscript, November 1, 1972), Queers and Allies Files.

17. "Lawrence Gay Liberation" (Preservation of Individual Rights), n.d., Queers and Allies Files.

18. Leonard Grotta email, September 2, 2020.

19. Queer Nation NY, http://queernationny.org/history.

20. John D'Emilio, *Sexual Politics, Sexual Communities: The Making of a Homosexual Minority in the United States, 1940–1970*, 2nd ed. (Chicago: University of Chicago Press, 1983), 233–235; Robert A. Rhoads, *Freedom's Web: Student Activism in an Age of Cultural Diversity* (Baltimore: Johns Hopkins University Press, 1998), 17–25; Stout, "Radical Means."

21. Stout, "Emergence (see?)," vol. 2.

22. Stout, "Emergence (see?)," vol. 2.

23. "Lawrence Gay Liberation Front," n.d., Queers and Allies Files.

24. "Liberation Front"; Linker document; Chuck Ortleb, personal communication, December 5, 2014; Stout, "Emergence (see?)," vol. 2.

25. "Protest!!!!!!!!," n.d., Queers and Allies Files.

26. "Four Hundred Miles Away," *Gay Oread Daily*, October 29, 1971; *Gay Liberation News*, April 26, 1972, both in Queers and Allies Files.

27. Jackson helped purchase ammunition from a Topeka gun store and had transported it to Lawrence the day after the fatal shooting of Rick Dowdell. Those who protested his firing, including the LGLF, claimed that KU did not have the right to fire Jackson without due process. In the LGLF's Solidarity Statement, they stated that Jackson's firing was "like the Regents' refusal to recognize Gay Liberation in which they are different tools of the same elite which divides the people." From "Solidarity Statement," 1970, Queers and Allies Files; "Vote to Fire Chalmers Fails," *Summer Session Kansan*, July 28, 1970.

28. Linker document.

29. "Liberation Front"; Joe Prados, letter to the editor ["LGLF Constitution"], *UDK*, October 14, 1971.

30. Bolin email, December 1, 2020.

31. Sherry Mallory, "Lesbian, Gay, Bisexual, and Transgender Student Organizations: An Overview," in *Working with Lesbian, Gay, Bisexual, and Transgender College Students: A Handbook for Faculty and Administrators*, ed. Ronni L. Sanlo (Westport, CT: Greenwood, 1998), 322–324.

32. Stout, "Emergence (see?)," vol. 2.

33. Stout, "Radical Means."

34. ECM staff Scott Gustafson email, September 19, 2020. The United

Ministries in Higher Education changed its name to Ecumenical Christian Ministries later in the 1970s.

35. "Lawrence Gay Liberation Front Emergency Position Paper," April 28, 1971, Queers and Allies Files; Stout, "Radical Means."

36. David Ambler, interview by author, May 24, 2013.

37. Terence Kissack, "Freaking Fag Revolutionaries: New York's Gay Liberation Front," *Radical History Review* 62 (1995): 107.

38. Stout, "Emergence (see?)," vol. 2.

39. Barry Albin, interview by author, June 28, 2013.

40. David Radavich, interview by author, March 15, 2013. David changed his last name from Radd to Radavich after he graduated from KU to return to his surname's historical origins (David Radavich, personal communication, March 15, 2013). He is referred to as Radavich except when identified as Radd by other members or in documents.

41. Radavich and Barry Albin interviews.

42. Hubbell interview.

43. Patrick Dilley, *Queer Man on Campus: A History of Non-Heterosexual College Men, 1945–2000* (New York: RoutledgeFalmer, 2002), 161–185; Patrick Dilley, email to author, May 27, 2021.

44. Kissack, "Freaking Fag," 108; Leonard Grotta, interview by author, March 13, 2013; Radavich interview.

45. "Lawrence Gay Liberation Front Statement," n.d. (published prior to the group's August 30, 1970 meeting), Queers and Allies Files.

46. Stout, "Emergence (see?)," vol. 2.

47. Steven Weaver, interview by author, May 18, 2020.

48. "National Register of Historic Places Registration Form" (submitted August 17, 2009, Sec. 8), 16, courtesy of Richard Crank.

49. Kissack, "Freaking Fag," 114–116; David A. Carter, *Stonewall: The Riots That Sparked the Gay Revolution* (New York: St. Martin's, 2004), 231; Stout, "Emergence (see?)," vol. 2.

50. Stout, "Emergence (see?)," vol. 2.

51. Weaver interview; Ortleb, personal communication, December 5, 2014; Grotta interview; Barry Albin interview.

52. Stout, "Emergence (see?)," vol. 2.

53. Ron Gans, interview by author, June 4, 2020; "Tommy the Traveler 6: The Raid at SuperDorm" (part 2), *The Herald*, Hobart and William Smith College, June 19, 2019, https://hwsherald.com/2019/06/19/tommy-the-traveler-6-the-raid-at-superdorm-part-2/; Alice Askins, "1960s Student Unrest in Geneva," *Historic Geneva* (blog), September 15, 2015, https://historicgeneva.org/organizations/student-unrest-in-geneva/.

54. Stout, "Emergence (see?)," vol. 2.

55. Barry Albin interview; Michael Stubbs, interview by author, May 6, 2020; Weaver interview; Peter Felleman, interview by author, June 3, 2020.

56. D'Emilio, *Sexual Politics*, 226; Alice Echols, "'We Gotta Get Out of This Place': Notes toward a Remapping of the Sixties," *Socialist Review* 22, no. 2 (1992): 14–16; Kissack, "Freaking Fag," 112.

57. Hubbell email, April 29, 2013; Grotta, Barry Albin, Weaver, Linker interviews.

58. D'Emilio, *Sexual Politics*, 235; Rhoads, *Freedom's Web*, 169–170, 177.

59. D'Emilio, *Sexual Politics*, 235; John D. Skrentny, *The Minority Rights Revolution* (Cambridge, MA: Belknap Press of Harvard University Press, 2002), 184; Elizabeth A. Armstrong, *Forging Gay Identities* (Chicago: University of Chicago Press, 2002), 56–80.

60. Skrentny, *Minority Rights Revolution*, 177.

61. David H. Stout, "The Lawrence Gay Counseling Service" (unpublished manuscript, April 25, 1975), Queers and Allies Files.

62. *Oread Daily*, September 28, 1970. Copies of the *Oread Daily* articles were provided by John Bolin.

63. *Oread Daily*, July 13 and 15, 1970; Marc Stein, "Guest Opinion: Recalling Purple Hands Protests of 1969," *Bay Area Reporter*, October 30, 1969. The "Purple Fist" likely refers to a demonstration that took place in San Francisco in October 1969 targeting the *San Francisco Examiner*, which ran a derisive article about the gay community. Radical gay protesters demonstrated and left handprints in purple paint throughout the building.

64. Michael Stubbs email, June 8, 2002; Frank Tankard, "The Reconstruction Will Not Be Televised," *LJW*, February 6, 2009. *Reconstruction* was first published in February 1969. It merged with the *Kansas City Screw* and became *Vortex* that September. It was named after Allen Ginsburg's poem, "Wichita Vortex Sutra." The final issue of *Vortex* was dated December 1971.

65. Stubbs email, May 13, 2020.

66. "Come Out," *Vortex*, September 2–14, 1970, Queers and Allies Files.

67. Ortleb, personal communication, December 5, 2014; Stubbs interview; Weaver interview (quotation).

68. Bolin quoted in Stacey Reding, "Paving Gayhawk Lane: The Lawrence Gay Liberation Front and Chancellor Chalmers' Veto" (unpublished research paper, December 13, 2001), Queers and Allies Files.

69. Stubbs email, May 27, 2021. See chapter 1 for further details on Stubbs's involvement in the Brigade.

70. Stubbs to Bolin letter, 1970, provided by Stubbs to the author.

71. Sharon Mayer, interview by author, October 9, 2019.

72. D'Emilio, *Sexual Politics*, 123; Kissack, "Freaking Fag," 107, 110, 112, 114–116;

Charles Outcalt, "The Lifecycle of Campus LGBT Organizations: Finding Ways to Sustain Involvement and Effectiveness," in Sanlo, *Working with Lesbian, Gay, Bisexual, and Transgender College Students*, 329–337; Kristen A. Renn, "LGBT Student Leaders and Queer Activists: Identities of Lesbian, Gay, Bisexual, Transgender and Queer Identified College Student Leaders and Activists," *Journal of College Student Development* 48, no. 3 (May 2007): 320, 326; Stout, "Emergence (see?)," vol. 2; Armstrong, *Forging Gay Identities*, 86–90; Stubbs interview.

73. Michael Stubbs email, February 12, 2022.

74. Kissack, "Freaking Fag," 115 (quotation); Carter, *Stonewall*, 215–221.

75. D'Emilio, *Sexual Politics*, 223–234 (quotation on 233); Kissack, "Freaking Fag," 115.

76. Carter, *Stonewall*, 218, 221, 233–236; "Gay Activist Alliance Firehouse: A 'School for Democracy,'" National Parks of New York Harbor, Stonewall National Monument, https://www.nps.gov/articles/gaa.htm.

77. Stout, "Emergence (see?)," vol. 2.

78. Ortleb, personal communication, December 5, 2014.

79. Stout, "Emergence (see?)," vol. 2.

80. Joe Lordi, interview by author, August 26, 2020.

81. Stout, "Emergence (see?)," vol. 2.

82. D'Emilio, *Sexual Politics*, 223–239; Outcault, "LGBT Organizations," 329–337.

83. Dilley, *Queer Man*, 15–36; Renn, "LGBT Student Leaders," 312, 315, 317–320, 327.

3. From Vision to Reality

1. David H. Stout, "Radical Means: Their Implications to Social Workers Striving to Change the System" (unpublished manuscript, November 1, 1972), Queers and Allies Files; Barry Albin, interview by author, June 28, 2013.

2. David H. Stout, "Emergence (see?)," vol. 2 (unpublished manuscript, 6 vols., November 25, 2011), University Archives; Steven Weaver, interview by author, May 18, 2020.

3. Stout, "Radical Means."

4. Stout, "Emergence (see?)," vol. 2; Weaver interview.

5. Michael Stubbs email, May 13, 2020.

6. "Biography of William Balfour," Personal Papers of William Balfour, University Archives.

7. Stout, "Emergence (see?)," vol. 2; Lee Hubbell, interview by author, March 8, 2013; Kala Stroup, interview by author, October 30, 2019.

8. Stout, "Emergence (see?)," vol. 2.

9. "KU Gay Liberation Front Entitled to Recognition," *LDJW*, August 28, 1970; Stout, "Emergence (see?)," vol. 2.

10. Stout, "Radical Means."

11. "Vote to Fire Chalmers Fails," *UDK*, July 28, 1970; Del Shankel, interview by author, March 14, 2013; Bill Tuttle, interview by author, March 21, 2013.

12. "Vote to Fire"; Phillip Brownlee, "Barred from Justice," *UDK*, October 30, 1995.

13. Tuttle interview; "Simons Family Selling Journal World to Ogden Newspapers, Inc.," *LJW*, June 17, 2016. Dolph Simons Jr. was publisher of the *LDJW/LJW* from 1962 to 2004. He had a great deal of political clout in the Lawrence community and frequently wrote about KU.

14. Beth Bailey, *Sex in the Heartland* (Cambridge, MA: Harvard University Press, 1999), 178–179; Stout, "Emergence (see?)," vol. 2.

15. John Crofoot to Vince Bilotta, August 18, 1971, box 1, State Correspondence Files, Chancellor's Papers, University Archives, Kenneth Spencer Research Library, University of Kansas, Lawrence.

16. Kansas Penal Code, Section 21-3505, July 1, 1969. On July 1, 1969, Kansas undertook a comprehensive revision of the state criminal code, passing a law to criminalize sodomy. It became the first state in the nation to pass a law to criminalize sexual acts between consenting adults of the same sex. This law went into effect on July 1, 1970.

17. Bailey, *Sex in the Heartland*, 178–180.

18. Jason Gordon, "Back to the Front: The Lawrence Gay Liberation Front and the Struggle for Recognition" (unpublished research paper for Bill Tuttle's class, December 13, 1996, University of Kansas, used with permission from Bill Tuttle).

19. Michael H. Hoeflich, "In Piam Memorial—Francis Heller," *Kansas Law Review* 61, no. 5 (June 1, 2013): 913–921.

20. Brownlee, "Barred from Justice."

21. Stout, "Emergence (see?)," vol. 2; Hubbell and Albin interviews.

22. "KU May Give Recognition to Gay Liberation Front," *LDJW*, June 22, 1970.

23. "KU Students Okay Senate Code Plan," *LDJW*, February 21, 1969.

24. Robbie Lieberman, *Prairie Power: Voices of 1960s Midwestern Student Protest* (Columbia: University of Missouri Press, 2004), 156.

25. "KU May Give Recognition"; "Senate Resolution Gives Support to Gay Front," *UDK*, September 14, 1970.

26. "Gays to Issue Reply about Recognition," *UDK*, September 10, 1970.

27. Cass Peterson, "Gay Lib Gets No Response on Request," *UDK*, August 31, 1970.

28. Stout, "Radical Means."

29. Stout, "Emergence (see?)," vol. 2.

30. Peterson, "Gay Lib"; Michael McConnell with Jack Baker, *The Wedding Heard 'Round the World: America's First Gay Marriage* (Minneapolis: University of Minnesota Press, 2016), 65–81.

31. Quotation from Jim Chesebro in Peterson, "Gay Lib"; Stout, "Emergence (see?)," vol. 2.

32. Joe Prados email, September 11, 2020.

33. Quotation from Jim Chesebro in Peterson, "Gay Lib"; Stout, "Emergence (see?)," vol. 2.

34. "K.U. News Bureau Official Recognition Statement," September 5, 1970, Queers and Allies Files.

35. "Lawrence Gay Liberation" (Preservation of Individual Rights), n.d., Queers and Allies Files.

36. Stout, "Emergence (see?)," vol. 2.

37. "KU Gay Liberation Front Entitled to Recognition."

38. Karl E. Johnson to William Balfour, September 1, 1970, box 1, Personal Papers of William Balfour, University Archives.

39. "KU Gay Liberation Front Entitled to Recognition."

40. Stout, "Radical Means."

41. Delbert Shankel to Chancellor Dykes (memo), May 27, 1980, Ambler Correspondence Files.

42. Stout email, May 13, 2021.

43. Stout, "Emergence (see?)," vol. 2.

44. Stout, "Radical Means."

45. "Gays to Issue Reply."

46. "KU Senate Hits Gay Snub," *LDJW*, September 10, 1970.

47. Donna Shavlik, interview by author, April 22, 2013; Casey Eike, interview by author, August 25, 2013; Kelly C. Sartorius, *Deans of Women and the Feminist Movement: Emily Taylor's Activism* (New York: Palgrave Macmillan, 2014), 104–106.

48. "Gays to Issue Reply."

49. Stout, "Radical Means."

50. Stout, "Emergence (see?)," vol. 2.

51. Stout, "Emergence (see?)," vol. 2.

52. "On Our Own," Statement by the women and men of the Lawrence Gay Liberation Front, *Vortex* 4, no. 2 (1971), University Archives.

53. Anthony R. D'Augelli, "Identity Development and Sexual Orientation: Toward a Model of Lesbian, Gay, and Bisexual Development," in *ASHE Reader on College Student Development Theory*, ed. Maureen E. Wilson and Lisa E. Wolf-Wendel (Boston: Pearson, 2005), 393–403.

54. Vivienne C. Cass, "Homosexual Identity Formation: Testing a Theoretical Model," *Journal of Sex Research* 20, no. 2 (1984): 143–167; Ruth E. Fassinger,

"Lesbian, Gay, and Bisexual Identity and Student Development Theory," in Wilson and Wolf-Wendel, *ASHE Reader*, 405–411; D'Augelli, "Identity Development," 393–403.

55. Sara M. Evans, *Personal Politics: The Roots of Women's Liberation in the Civil Rights Movement and the New Left* (New York: Knopf, 1979), 214–216; Terence Kissack, "Freaking Fag Revolutionaries: New York's Gay Liberation Front," *Radical History Review* 62 (1995): 121–124.

56. Martin Duberman, *Stonewall* (New York: Penguin, 1993), 221.

57. Nikos A. Diaman, "Consciousness-Raising," Gay Liberation Front, 1995, https://www.angelfire.com/on2/glf2000/past.html.

58. Kissack, "Freaking Fag," 121–124.

59. Joe Prados, interview by author, April 2, 2013; Richard Linker, interview by author, June 5, 2020; Weaver and Albin interviews; Stout, "Emergence (see?)," vol. 2.

60. Evans, *Personal Politics*, 214–216; Leonard Grotta, interview by author, March 13, 2013; David Radavich, interview by author, March 15; 2013; Prados, Albin interviews.

61. Albin, Prados, Weaver interviews; Stout, "Emergence (see?)," vol. 2.

62. David H. Stout, "The Lawrence Gay Counseling Service" (unpublished manuscript, April 25, 1975), Queers and Allies Files.

63. "Lesbian Group Seeks Community," *UDK*, October 19, 1973.

64. Given the hostile culture for gay men and lesbians at the time, many viewed any form of acceptance as progress. Some, however, felt that working for "tolerance" undermined their efforts, playing into a "homosexual" rather than "gay" paradigm, and subverted the goal to be fully accepted.

65. Stout, "Lawrence Gay Counseling."

66. "On Our Own."

67. "Gay Front Asks Regents to Reconsider Application," *UDK*, September 11, 1970.

68. Information was retrieved from David Stout, who reviewed all the records kept in the LGLF office in the 1970s. He included this compilation in his 1975 paper. In addition, information was obtained from other group members and newspaper articles.

69. Stout, "Lawrence Gay Counseling"; Mona Dunn, "Student Shouts Turned to Murmurs," *UDK*, April 21, 1972. Presentations in 1972 included Pittsburg State University and Missouri Western State University. Kansas State University was also included in the 1972 and 1973 listing and LGLF records, but Keith Spare, who founded the K-State gay group, does not recall these occurring.

70. Greg Kuplen, "Local Gay Lib Changes Name," *UDK*, April 11, 1973; Stout,

"Lawrence Gay Counseling." The other colleges included Washburn University, Emporia State University, and Butler Community College.

71. Jan Hyatt, "Area Gay Group No Longer Political," *UDK*, February 6, 1975. Interviews and *UDK* articles also indicated that presentations continued to be a key feature of the group. Additional information about the longevity of this program was obtained from Lesbian, Bisexual, and Gay Services of Kansas Awareness Week 1995 Program—McKinney Collection, box 31, folder 39, University Archives.

72. Stroup interview; Martha Boyd, interview by author, February 18, 2021.

73. Stroup interview; Kathryn Clark, interview by author, February 13, 2020. Some of the units and organizations that participated included the Dean of Women's Office; Professors Dennis Dailey and Michael Storms; campus ministers; and members of the LGLF and the Gay Caucus of the Women's Coalition.

74. Martha Boyd, interview by author, September 16, 2019; Clark and Stroup interviews.

75. Radavich interview; Stout, "Lawrence Gay Counseling."

76. Grotta interview. Brown used he/him pronouns and was referred to as Reggie in the 1970s but later shifted to using they/them pronouns and going by his full name, Reginald.

77. Reginald Brown, interview by author, May 27, 2020; "Sow and Grow Storytelling Show," VOCAL–NY, Generations Project, April 11, 2020, University Archives, https://www.facebook.com/160825401172543/videos/817151605477178/.

78. John D'Emilio, *Sexual Politics, Sexual Communities: The Making of a Homosexual Minority in the United States, 1940–1970*, 2nd ed. (Chicago: University of Chicago Press, 1983), 152–153.

79. Anthony R. D'Augelli, "Lesbians and Gay Men on Campus: Visibility, Empowerment and Educational Leadership," *Peabody Journal of Education* 66, no. 3 (1989): 126–127.

80. Huey P. Newton, "The Women's Liberation and Gay Liberation Movements," BlackPast, https://www.blackpast.org/african-american-history/speeches -african-american-history/huey-p-newton-women-s-liberation-and-gay-liber ation-movements/. On August 15, 1970, prior to this convention, Black Panther cofounder and leader Huey Newton delivered this speech that challenged members to confront their negative attitudes toward gay men and lesbians, calling for support and inclusion. Newton stated that "homosexuals are not given freedom and liberty by anyone in the society. Maybe they might be the most oppressed people in the society."

81. D'Emilio, *Sexual Politics*, 230; Elizabeth A. Armstrong, *Forging Gay Identities* (Chicago: University of Chicago Press, 2002), 63–66.

82. Todd Gitlin, *The Sixties: Years of Hope, Days of Rage* (New York: Bantam, 1987), 374, 394; Michael Stubbs, interview by author, May 6, 2020.

83. Marc Stein, "'Birthplace of the Nation': Imagining Lesbian and Gay Communities in Philadelphia, 1969–1970," in *Creating a Place for Ourselves: Lesbian, Gay and Bisexual Community Histories*, ed. Brett G. Beemyn (New York: Routledge, 1997), 266–275; Stubbs email, June 8, 2021. The convention was held November 27–29, 1970, in Washington, DC. Stubbs and Bolin had been given plane tickets to attend by Carl Miller, a member of NYC-GLF's Seventeenth Street Collective. Stubbs stayed there after his return from Cuba.

84. Duberman, *Stonewall*, 259–260; Stubbs interview; Bolin email, November 30, 2020.

85. Kissack, "Freaking Fag," 112–113.

86. Stubbs interview; Stout, "Lawrence Gay Counseling."

87. Gary Kanter email, August 3, 2020.

88. Stout, "Emergence (see?)," vol. 2; Stout, "Lawrence Gay Counseling"; Stout email, August 3, 2020; Bolin email, November 30, 2020.

89. Kanter email, August 3, 2020.

90. Bruce Johansen, "Out of Silence: FREE, Minnesota's First Gay Rights Organization," *Minnesota History* 66, no. 5 (2019): 186–201.

91. Lars Bjornson, "Experts Frozen Out at FREE Convention," *Advocate*, November 1, 1970, 1–24; Johansen, "Out of Silence," quotation on 197; Ken Bronson, *A Quest for Full Equality*, 11–12, https://www.lib.umn.edu/sites/www.lib.umn.edu/files/2021-11/quest-copy.pdf.

92. John Bolin, "Purple Gaze," *Vortex* 3, nos. 4–5 (1970): 9, 19, University Archives.

93. D. L. [Lars Bjornsen], "Around the Movement," New York Mattachine Times, November-December, 1970, quotation on page 19; see also Jim Chesebro, "The First National Gay Lib Convention: One View from Minneapolis," in Bronson, *A Quest for Full Equality*, 51–60; Bronson, *A Quest for Full Equality*, 11.

94. For more about gender inequality in the gay liberation movement, see Alice Echols, "'We Gotta Get Out of This Place': Notes toward a Remapping of the Sixties," *Socialist Review* 22, no. 2 (1992): 9–33; Terence Kissack, "Freaking Fag."

95. Quotation from Sue Born, a member of FREE's Coordinating Committee, as shared with Jim Chesebro, in Chesebro, "First National Gay Lib Convention," 52.

96. Bolin, "Purple Gaze," 9, 19.

97. Chesebro, "Gay Lib Convention," 51–60; Bolin, "Purple Gaze," 9, 19.

98. "Purple Gaze," 9, 19.

99. Johansen, "Out of Silence"; McConnell with Baker, *Wedding Heard*

'Round the World, 55–63; "Gay Liberation Leader to Speak at KU Forum," *UDK*, April 27, 1972; Bronson, *A Quest for Full Equality*, 29–30.

100. McConnell with Baker, *Wedding Heard 'Round the World*, ix; Erik Eckholm, "The Same Sex Couple Who Got a Marriage License in 1971," *New York Times*, May 16, 2015. Knowing that their request would not be approved using their given names, Baker used a gender-neutral first name on the application.

101. Stubbs interview; Jim Pettey, interview by author, September 4, 2020; Pettey email, May 26, 2021; Bolin email, December 1, 2020; Michael McConnell, interview by author, April 15, 2021.

102. McConnell with Baker, *Wedding Heard 'Round the World*, 37–45; "Gay Liberation Leader to Speak"; Stout, "Emergence (see?)," vol. 2.

103. Stout, "Emergence (see?)," vol. 3; Albin interview; Leroy Towns, "Capitol Comment: Gay Liberationists Shake Up Senators," *Hutchison News*, March 25, 1973.

104. State of Kansas Articles of Incorporation, Lawrence Gay Liberation Inc., April 2, 1973, Balfour/Alderson Files.

105. Stout, "Lawrence Gay Counseling"; Stout, "Emergence (see?)," vol. 3; Towns, "Capitol Comment."

106. Stout, "Lawrence Gay Counseling"; Grotta interview.

107. "Gay Sunshine," Berkeley Revolution, August–September 1970, https://revolution.berkeley.edu/gay-sunshine/.

108. Stubbs email, February 16, 2021.

109. Stubbs email, July 7, 2020.

110. Stout, "Emergence (see?)," vol. 2.

111. Stout email, July 3, 2020; Stout, "Emergence (see?)," vol. 2.

112. "Pittsburg State University: A Brief History," Pittsburg State website, https://axe.pittstate.edu/_files/documents/PSU_aBriefHistory.pdf. Kansas State College of Pittsburg was renamed Pittsburg State College in 1977.

113. Email conversations with Michael Stubbs, John Bolin, and Steven Weaver, October 13 and 14, 2020.

114. Weaver interview; handout from "1970: The Year the Rocked KU: Lawrence Gay Liberation Front," Spencer Online Exhibition, https://exhibits.lib.ku.edu/exhibits/show/the-year-that-rocked-ku.

115. "LGLF News: Its Objectives," *Gay Liberation News*, November 17, 1972, Queers and Allies Files.

116. Two excellent resources are Arthur W. Chickering and Linda Reisser, *Education and Identity*, 2nd ed. (San Francisco: Jossey-Bass, 1993), and Marsha B. Baxter Magolda, *Making Their Own Way: Narratives for Transforming Higher Education to Promote Self-Development* (Sterling, VA: Stylus, 2001).

117. D'Augelli, "Identity Development," 393–403, esp. 394; Fassinger, "Lesbian, Gay, and Bisexual Identity," 405–411.

118. Rick Mayes and Allan V. Horwitz, "DSM–III and the Revolution in the Classification of Mental Illness," *Journal of the History of the Behavior Sciences* 41 (2005): 252, 258.

119. Stubbs interview; Sharon Mayer, interview by author, August 28, 2019; *Lawrence Gay Liberation News*, September 15 and October 13, 1972, Queers and Allies Files.

120. Kathy Hoggard, interview by author, July 12, 2013; *Lawrence Gay Liberation News*, September 15, 1972.

121. Mayer (August 28, 2019) and Stubbs interviews.

122. *Gay Liberation News*, November 17, 1972, Queers and Allies Files; Hubbell and Stubbs interviews.

123. Dennis Dailey, interview by author, May 22, 2013; Mayer (August 28, 2019), Stubbs, Weaver interviews.

4. Lawsuits and Leadership

1. The request for recognition was resubmitted on March 3, 1971, and Chalmers rejected it on March 22, 1971. Documented in Civil Action T-5069, December 15, 1971, Queers and Allies Files.

2. Barry Albin, interview by author, June 28, 2013.

3. David H. Stout, "Emergence (see?)," vol. 2 (unpublished manuscript, 6 vols., November 25, 2011), University Archives; Albin interview.

4. Jack Klinknett, interview by author, September 11, 2013.

5. "Kunstler, William Moses," Civil Rights Digital Library, n.d., accessed March 11, 2020http://crdl.usg.edu/people/k/kunstler_william_moses_1919/; "Disturbing the Universe," a film on William Kunstler's life, *POV*, PBS, June 10, 2010, http://archive.pov.org/disturbingtheuniverse/.

6. "Law Forum to Feature Kunstler," *UDK*, April 21, 1971; "Gays to File Soon," *UDK*, September 8, 1971; Albin interview; Chuck Ortleb, interview by author, August 2, 2021; Steven Weaver, interview by author, May 18, 2020; Reginald Brown, interview by author, May 27, 2020.

7. Lee Hubbell, interview by author, March 8, 2013; Ortleb interview, August 2, 2021.

8. Beth Sullivan and Sarah Marloff, "The History of the LGBTQ Movement in Austin," *Austin Chronicle*, August 9, 2019, https://www.austinchronicle.com/news/2019-08-09/the-history-of-the-lgbtq-movement-in-austin/. Some have mistakenly referred to this as the first national Gay Conference, but in fact the first took place in November 1970 in Minneapolis, organized by FREE.

9. Articles 8, 10, and 20 of the KU Code of Student Rights and Responsibilities;

sections 1, 3, 11, and 20 of the Kansas Bill of Rights; and the First, Fifth, Ninth, and Fourteenth Amendments of the US Constitution.

10. *Up Front: The Official Newsletter of the Lawrence Gay Liberation, Inc.* 1, no. 1 (1973), Queers and Allies Files.

11. "Gay Lib Hires Kunstler," *LDJW*, July 22, 1971.

12. Ortleb quoted in Phillip Brownlee, "Barred from Justice," *UDK*, October 30, 1995.

13. "Gay Lib Hires Kunstler."

14. Information from Keith Spare in this section is from his unpublished manuscript, "Prairie Fairie" (August 1, 2020), provided to the author by email, October 27, 2020. Included here with permission.

15. Keith Spare, email to author, October 27, 2020.

16. Richard Linker, document sent via email, June 3, 2020; Peter Felleman, interview by author, June 3, 2020.

17. Linker document. Genderfuck involved mixing both men's and women's clothing items to challenge gender norms—discussed in more detail later in chapter 4.

18. Richard Linker, interview by author, June 5, 2020; Spare, "Prairie Fairie."

19. Linker document.

20. Felleman interview.

21. Bolin journal entry dated June 30, 1971, in his possession; shared with author October 12, 2020. Used with permission.

22. Linker document.

23. Peter Tachell, "The Gay Liberation Front's Social Revolution," *Guardian*, October 12, 2010.

24. Bolin email, May 11, 2021.

25. Women also dressed in drag, adopting male clothing and other aspects of masculine appearance.

26. "Genderfuck" applied specifically to men; there was not an equivalent style for women.

27. John D. Skrentny, *The Minority Rights Revolution* (Cambridge, MA: Belknap Press of Harvard University Press, 2002), 182–183.

28. Hubbell and Albin interviews; Bob Friedland, interview by author, July 29, 2020.

29. Sharon Mayer, interview by author, August 28, 2019; Michael Stubbs, interview by author, May 6, 2020; Linker email, June 3, 2020; Felleman interview.

30. LGLF members may have also been involved in this event in 1972; there were conflicting memories among those interviewed.

31. Felleman and Mayer (August 28, 2019) interviews.

32. Patrick Dilley, *Queer Man on Campus: A History of Non-Heterosexual College Men, 1945–2000* (New York: RoutledgeFalmer, 2002), 183–185.

33. The KU Information Center, established to control rumors during the height of protests in the 1970s, was the campus communication hub and had its "finger on the pulse" of what was happening on campus. It served as an important resource until July 2022, when it was closed.

34. This slogan was adopted by the Women's Movement in 1969 from an article by Carol Hanisch, "The Personal Is Political," February 1969, http://www.carolha nisch.org/CHwritings/PIP.html.

35. *UDK* articles include "Enrollment Reflects Changing Direction of University," September 7, 1971; "Few File for Assembly Positions," September 14, 1971; "Greek System Still Thriving," September 3, 1971.

36. Hal Ritter, "Gay Lib Issue Highlights Third Student Senate Term," *UDK*, March 14, 1972.

37. "Gay Lib Appeal for $600 to Go before Senate," *UDK*, September 13, 1971; Ron Womble and Mary Ward, "Senate to Hold Hearings on Fee Poll, Gay Libs," *UDK*, September 16, 1971.

38. "No Decision Made on Gay Lib Funds," *UDK*, September 22, 1971; "$600 from Gay Libs Wouldn't Be Fees," *UDK*, September 23, 1971.

39. Nancy Archer, Cathy Fuller, and Margi Ford, letter to the editor, *UDK*, October 4, 1971; Mike Willome and Rich Olmstread, letter to the editor, *UDK*, October 4, 1971; Alan Moser and Carl Munger, letter to the editor, *UDK*, October 5, 1971.

40. "No Decision Made."

41. Denis J. Brothers, letter to the editor, *UDK*, September 29, 1971.

42. Mike McGowan, letter to the editor, *UDK*, October 11, 1971.

43. Many referred informally to LGLF as Gay Lib.

44. Jan Kessinger, "Student Senate Approves $600 to Gay Lib Front," *UDK*, September 30, 1971.

45. "Chancellor Vetoes $600 for Gay Lib," *UDK*, October 6, 1971.

46. "Gay Lib Party under Review by KU Group," *LDJW*, September 30, 1971.

47. "400 at Benefit Dance for Gay Lib Front," *UDK*, October 4, 1971; "Green Light Given—Dance on for GLF," *LDJW*, October 1, 1971; *Gay Oread Daily*, October 1, 1971 (provided by John Bolin).

48. "Green Light Given"; *Gay Oread Daily*, October 1, 1971.

49. The Rock Chalk Café was a local bar that was popular among activists, hippies, and counterculture members. See also Mark Dent, "Soon to Close Bar Has Rich Campus History," *UDK*, December 5, 2007.

50. *Gay Oread Daily*, October 1, 1971. An example of "petty details" was concern that the words "Gay Liberation defense fund" were larger in size than "Women's Coalition."

51. "400 at Benefit Dance."

52. Women's Coalition untitled handout, October 1, 1971, Queers and Allies Files.

53. "400 at Benefit Dance."

54. T. Dean Caple, "Kunstler Says He'll File Suit This Month," *UDK*, November 3, 1971.

55. "Gay Lib May File Suit Nov. 1," *UDK*, October 21, 1971; "Gay Front Gets Date for Hearing," *UDK*, January 19, 1972; Harry Wilson, "KU Gay Lib Encouraged by Favorable OU Ruling," *UDK*, September 19, 1972.

56. Hubbell interview; *Lawrence Gay Liberation Front News*, April 7, 1972, Queers and Allies Files; Paul Sherbo, "Dances Provide Money for Gays," *UDK*, February 26, 1976.

57. "Gay Lib May File Suit."

58. Don Levy, "Gay Liberation Decides to Wait Before Seeking Recognition Again," *UDK*, November 6, 1973.

59. "StudEx OK's Register Plan," *UDK*, February 21, 1972.

60. William Balfour to Robert Zumwinkle, January 10, 1972, Balfour/Alderson Files.

61. "Gay Lib Front to Appeal for University Recognition," *UDK*, February 22,1972.

62. "StudEx Register Proposal Criticized by Both Sides," *UDK*, February 23, 1972.

63. David Ambler, interview by author, May 24, 2013.

64. The group announced their new Kansas Union office in *LGLF News*, April 7, 1972, and commented on being charged for office rental and monthly phone costs. Other references to recognition of the group appear in "StudEx Proposal to End Difficulties of Recognition," *UDK*, February 14, 1972; Wilson, "KU Gay Lib Encouraged."

65. "Kunstler, GLF to Talk Nov. 1," *LDJW*, October 22, 1971.

66. "KU Gay Liberation Front Entitled to Recognition," *LDJW*, August 28, 1970.

67. "Gay Lib Recognized at Nebraska, Colorado," *UDK*, October 6, 1971.

68. "Gay Front Gets Date."

69. "Gay Lib Suit against KU to Enter Court Today," *UDK*, January 26, 1972. See also "Gay Lib May File Suit."

70. "Gay Liberation Files Suit to Force KU Recognition," *LDJW*, December 16, 1971.

71. Marti Stewart, "Six Faculty Members Coplaintiffs in Gay Lib Case," *UDK*, February 9, 1972.

72. "Gay Liberation Attorneys Fail to Show Up," *Topeka Daily Capital*, January 27, 1972.

73. "Gay Lib Suit."

74. Robert C. Clark, "Kunstler Barred from US Court," *Kansas City Star*, January 27, 1972.

75. "Topeka Judge Bars Kunstler," *LDJW*, January 27, 1972; "Kunstler Barred from Courtroom," *Parsons Sun*, January 27, 1972.

76. Lew Ferguson, "Court Prohibits Kunstler from Representing Gays," *Wichita Eagle*, January 28, 1972.

77. Bill Tuttle, interview by author, March 21, 2013.

78. Civil Action #T-5069.

79. Rod Hardy, "Gays' Legal Committee Discusses Appeal Tactics," *UDK*, February 18, 1972; "Kunstler Barred."

80. Civil Action #T-5069; *Lawrence Gay Liberation Front News*, April 7, 1972, Queers and Allies Files.

81. Civil Action T-5069.

82. "Topeka Judge Bars Kunstler."

83. "Gay Front Loses Suit; May Decide to Appeal," *UDK*, February 14, 1972; "Judge Rules against KUs Gay Liberation Front Plea," *Salina Journal*, February 13, 1972.

84. "Kunstler Incurs a Judge's Wrath," *New York Times*, January 28, 1972; "Great Put Down," *Parsons Sun*, January 28, 1972; "Miller Applauds Barring of Kunstler," *Wichita Eagle*, January 29, 1972.

85. Paul Carttar, "Two Centuries Later," *LDJW*, February 4, 1972.

86. "Gay Liberation's Request Denied," *Topeka Daily Capital*, February 12, 1972.

87. Joe Zanetta and Rod Hardy, "Gay Lib Appeal Delayed: ACLU Supports Kunstler," *UDK*, March 7, 1972.

88. Dilley, *Queer Man on Campus*, 175.

89. Amy Best, *Prom Night: Youth, Schools and Popular Culture* (New York: Routledge, 2000), 6–9, 10–11, 142–159; Jonathan Zimmerman, "The Prom: An American Relic," *Chicago Tribune*, May 8, 2013.

90. Dilley, *Queer Man on Campus*, 175.

91. Patrick Dilley, *Gay Liberation to Campus Assimilation: Early Non-Heterosexual Student Organizations at Midwestern Universities* (New York: Palgrave Macmillan, 2019), 237.

92. Bolin email, July 21, 2021. Bolin had recorded the dance income in his log.

93. Greg Kuplen, "Local Gay Lib Changes Name," *UDK*, April 11, 1973; Greg Bashaw, "Gay Disco Turns to Fantasy," *UDK*, October 25, 1976.

94. Hubbell email, June 2, 2021.

95. Weaver and Linker interviews; Joe Lordi, interview by author, August 26, 2020.

96. Linker document.

97. Linker document.

98. Leonard Grotta, interview by author, March 13, 2013.

99. Bob Warren, interview by author, July 21, 2020.

100. Bashaw, "Gay Disco."

101. Brown interview; Martha Boyd, interview by author, September 16, 2019; Kathy Hoggard, interview by author, July 12, 2013; David Radavich, interview by author, March 15, 2013; Jim Pettey, interview by author, September 4, 2020; Mayer interview, August 28, 2019.

102. Dilley, *Queer Man on Campus*, 175.

103. Bashaw, "Gay Disco"; Linker document.

104. "Thieves Grab Gay Lib's $75," *UDK*, April 27, 1972; Pettey interview.

105. Cathy Sherman, "Senate Postpones Decision on BSU Budget Allocation," *UDK*, April 27, 1972.

106. "Lawrence Gay Liberation Front Emergency Position Paper," April 28, 1971, Queers and Allies Files; "Thieves Grab."

107. Pettey interview; Pettey email, June 28, 2021.

108. David Dillon, interview by author, April 1, 2013.

109. Chuck Ortleb, personal communication, December 5, 2014.

110. Pettey interview; Pettey email, May 26, 2021.

111. "Emergency Position Paper."

112. Randy Schuyler, "Gays Present Requests to Balfour," *UDK*, April 28, 1972. Punctuation as in original. No data is provided to support this "second largest minority" statement.

113. Written in pen on the original document, which can be found in the Queers and Allies Files.

114. KU hired the first full-time staff member to coordinate LGBTQ programs and services in 2014. "Department History," Women, Gender, and Sexuality Studies website, https://wgss.ku.edu/department-history.

115. Balfour quoted in Schuyler, "Gays Present"; "Emergency Position Paper."

116. Schuyler, "Gays Present."

117. "Suggested Tasks for a Student Research Assistant during Summer 1972 Semester," n.d., Balfour/Alderson Files.

118. "Position Paper on Library Material on Gay Liberation," n.d., Balfour/Alderson Files.

119. "Affirmative Action Board Proposal: Provisional Affirmative Action Plan, Modifications Proposed by the Lawrence Gay Liberation Front," November 8, 1972, Balfour/Alderson Files.

120. Schuyler, "Gays Present."

121. Mona Dunn, "Student Shouts Turned to Murmurs," *UDK*, April 21, 1972.

122. Rod Hardy, "Gays Talk of Guilt, Fears," *UDK*, February 23, 1972.

123. Stout, "Emergence (see?)," vol. 2.

124. Stout email, September 3, 2020.

125. Hubbell and Radavich interviews; Dennis Dailey, interview by author, May 22, 2013; Stout, "Emergence (see?)," vol. 2.

126. Hubbell interview.

127. Radavich interview; Donna Shavlik, interview by author, April 22, 2013; Timothy Miller, interview by author, August 22, 2013.

128. "Lesbian Group Seeks Community," *UDK*, October 19, 1973.

129. Quotations and information from Lynn Schornick are from a document sent by Lynn Schornick to the author via email on January 16, 2020 (included with permission).

130. Lynn Schornick email, May 24, 2021.

131. Lynn Schornick document.

132. David H. Stout, "The Lawrence Gay Counseling Service" (unpublished manuscript, April 25, 1975), Queers and Allies Files; Radavich interview.

133. Stout, "Emergence (see?)," vol. 3.

134. Details about the service are also outlined in a letter from Radd to the Personnel of Other Helping Organizations, July 5, 1972, Balfour/Alderson Files.

135. Radavich interview.

136. Radavich and Dailey interviews.

137. Radavich interview.

138. Stout, "Lawrence Gay Counseling"; Radavich interview.

139. Kuplen, "Gay Lib Changes"; Stout, "Lawrence Gay Counseling"; Stout, "Emergence (see?)," vol. 3; Radavich interview.

140. Stout, "Emergence (see?)," vol. 3; Stout email, July 7, 2020.

141. Stout, "Lawrence Gay Counseling"; Stout, "Emergence (see?)," vol. 2; Radavich interview.

142. John D'Emilio and Estelle B. Freedman, *Intimate Matters: A History of Sexuality in America*, 2nd ed. (Chicago: University of Chicago Press, 1988), 323–324; Rick Mayes and Allan V. Horwitz, "DSM–III and the Revolution in the Classification of Mental Illness," *Journal of the History of the Behavior Sciences* 41 (2005): 258–259.

143. Grotta interview.

144. "Position Statement on Homosexuality and Civil Rights," American Psychiatric Association, 1973, https://ajp.psychiatryonline.org/doi/abs/10.1176/ajp.19 74.131.4.497; Mayes and Horwitz, "DSM–III," 259; https://www.nytimes.com/19 73/12/23/archives/the-issue-is-subtle-the-debate-still-on-the-apa-ruling-on.html.

145. Stout, "Lawrence Gay Counseling"; Stout, "Emergence (see?)," vol. 3; Bashaw, "Gay Disco."

146. Stout, "Lawrence Gay Counseling."

147. David Radd, "Dear Helping Services Personnel" letter, Balfour/Alderson Files.

148. Stout, "Lawrence Gay Counseling."

149. Jean Ireland and Todd VanLaningham to David Ambler, November 9, 1977, Queers and Allies Files.

150. "Gays Celebrate Freedom Day," *UDK*, June 27, 1972. It was celebrated in other countries on June 24, but in the United States it was celebrated on June 28, the anniversary of the Stonewall uprising.

151. Kuplen, "Gay Lib Changes."

152. Dilley, *Gay Liberation to Campus Assimilation*, 139–141, 207, 212, 223.

153. "Gay Group to Publish Voter Guide," *UDK*, June 26, 1972.

154. Connie Parish, "Real Estate Agency in Lawrence Picketed by Gay Liberation Front," *UDK*, June 27, 1972.

155. Kansas Human Rights Commission, Kansas Act against Discrimination (KAAD) and Kansas Age Discrimination in Employment (KADEA), updated July 2012, 4, 7, http://www.khrc.net/KHRCStatuteBookUpdatedEffective07-2009.pdf.

156. Parish, "Agency Picketed."

157. Parish, "Agency Picketed."

158. Ralph Gage, "Local Demo Proposals Get Varied Reactions," *LDJW*, April 12, 1972; *Lawrence Gay Liberation News*, April 26, 1972, Queers and Allies Files.

159. Gage, "Local Demo Proposals"; *Gay Liberation News*, no. 3.

160. "Gay Liberation Seeks Reversal," *LDJW*, February 23, 1972. Filed in the Tenth Circuit Court of Appeals in Denver.

161. Wilson, "Gay Lib Encouraged."

162. Grotta email, September 2, 2020.

163. "Kunstler Requests Court Order KU Gay Lib Okay," *LDJW*, November 17, 1972.

164. Sherry Mallory, "The Rights of Gay Student Organizations at Public State-Supported Institutions," *NASPA Journal* 34, no. 2 (1997): 82–90; Don Levy, "Gay Lib Ponders Court Ruling," *UDK*, October 25, 1973.

165. *Up Front: The Official Newslettre of the Lawrence Gay Liberation, Inc.*, 1, no. 1 (1973), Queers and Allies Files.

166. "State of Kansas Articles of Incorporation, Lawrence Gay Liberation Inc.," April 2, 1973, Balfour/Alderson Files; Greg Kuplen, "Local Gay Lib Changes Name," *UDK*, April 11, 1973.

167. Albin interview.

168. Jack Baker to Leonard Grotta, June 15, 1972, Balfour/Alderson Files.

169. Stout, "Lawrence Gay Counseling."

170. Email from Nancy Reddy, Kansas Secretary of State Office, August 25, 2020.

171. "Gay Liberation to Reapply for University Recognition," *UDK*, October 30, 1973 (quotation from group member Denis Brothers).

172. Clark, "Kunstler Barred"; Levy, "Gay Liberation Decides to Wait."

173. "Still Radical after All These Years: At 74, William Kunstler Defends Clients Most Lawyers Avoid," *New York Times*, July 6, 1993.

5. "There Are a Lot More Homosexuals at the University Than We Thought"

1. Arthur Levine, *When Dreams and Heroes Died* (San Francisco: Jossey-Bass, 1980), 5, 9–13, 21–26, 103–105, 113–115; Robert A. Rhoads, *Freedom's Web: Student Activism in an Age of Cultural Diversity* (Baltimore: Johns Hopkins University Press, 1998), 5, 55.

2. Helen L. Horowitz, "The 1960s and the Transformation of Campus Cultures," *History of Education Quarterly* 26, no. 1 (1986): 34–38, quotations on 34 and 35; Helen Lefkowitz Horowitz, *Campus Life* (Chicago: University of Chicago Press, 1987), 261–268; Rhoads, *Freedom's Web*, 55–56.

3. John D'Emilio and Estelle B. Freedman, *Intimate Matters: A History of Sexuality in America*, 2nd ed. (Chicago: University of Chicago Press, 1988), 323.

4. David Olson, "Academic Emphasis Worries Some Students," *LDJW*, December 26, 1977.

5. Sara Holland, "B-School Suffers Overpopulation," *UDK*, June 18, 1974.

6. Susan B. Twombly, "'Lift the Chorus Ever Onward': Leading the University," in *Transforming the University of Kansas: A History, 1965–2015*, ed. John L. Rury and Kim Cary Warren (Lawrence: University Press of Kansas, 2015), 56–57; John Rury, "Introduction: Decades of Transformation: Fifty Years of KU History," in Rury and Warren, *Transforming the University of Kansas*, 10.

7. Twombly, "Lift the Chorus," 56–57.

8. Anita Knopp, "Groups to Study Morals," *LDJW*, March 15, 1974.

9. Debbie Bauman, "Gay Liberation Gives Hope to Homosexuals," *UDK*, December 10, 1975.

10. Marian Horvat, "College Students Favor Sexual Freedom, Poll States," *UDK*, June 18, 1974.

11. Richard Linker, interview by author, June 5, 2020.

12. While the name of the group changed to Lawrence Gay Liberation, Inc., in the summer of 1973, many continued to refer to the group by its original name, LGLF.

13. Bob Friedland, interview by author, July 29, 2020; Bob Friedland, email to author, July 13, 2021.

14. Charles Outcalt, "The Lifecycle of Campus LGBT Organizations: Finding Ways to Sustain Involvement and Effectiveness," in *Working with Lesbian, Gay,*

Bisexual, and Transgender College Students: A Handbook for Faculty and Administrators, ed. Ronni L. Sanlo (Westport, CT: Greenwood, 1998), 332.

15. "Editorial Statement," *Wheat Dreams* 1, no. 2 (July 1975): 1, Queers and Allies Files.

16. Jan Hyatt, "Area Gay Group No Longer Political," *UDK*, February 6, 1975.

17. Hyatt, "Area Gay Group."

18. There were early members who might in current times use the term "non-binary" to describe themselves, but there was not a term at that time for this category.

19. Bauman, "Gay Liberation"; Stout, "Emergence (see?)," vol. 2; Randy Schuyler, "Gays Present Requests to Balfour," *UDK*, April 28, 1972; "Lawrence Gay Liberation Front Emergency Position Paper," April 28, 1971, Queers and Allies Files.

20. John D'Emilio, *Sexual Politics, Sexual Communities: The Making of a Homosexual Minority in the United States, 1940–1970*, 2nd ed. (Chicago: University of Chicago Press, 1983), 228–229; Terence Kissack, "Freaking Fag Revolutionaries: New York's Gay Liberation Front," *Radical History Review* 62 (1995): 125–126, 228–229; Lillian Faderman, *Odd Girls and Twilight Lovers: A History of Lesbian Life in Twentieth-Century America* (New York: Columbia University Press, 1991), 204–212.

21. Beth Bailey, *Sex in the Heartland* (Cambridge, MA: Harvard University Press, 1999), 196.

22. Greg Bashaw, "Gay Disco Turns to Fantasy," *UDK*, October 25, 1976.

23. David Stout email, April 24, 2015.

24. Ruth Lichtwardt, "A Stroll Down Gayhawk Lane Part II: "Private Activities, Habits or Proclivities," in *Gay and Lesbian History at the University of Kansas*, ed. David D. Barney (Lawrence: University of Kansas, 1992), 1, University Archives; Patrick Dilley, *Queer Man on Campus: A History of Non-Heterosexual College Men, 1945–2000* (New York: RoutledgeFalmer, 2002), 181.

25. Bauman, "Gay Liberation"; Paul Sherbo, "Dances Provide Money for Gays," *UDK*, February 26, 1976: Ruth Lichtwardt, "A Stroll Down Gayhawk Lane: 1976–1986: The Dance and Go to Sambos Years" (Part I), in Barney, *Gay and Lesbian History*, 1.

26. David H. Stout, "The Lawrence Gay Counseling Service" (unpublished manuscript, April 25, 1975), Queers and Allies Files; Stout, "Emergence (see?)," vol. 3; Schuyler, "Gays Present"; "LGLF Emergency Position Paper"; Dennis Dailey, interview by author, May 22, 2013.

27. Stout, "Lawrence Gay Counseling"; Marshall Fine, "Gay Lib Event May Be at KU," *LDJW*, September 18, 1975.

28. Von Ende to Shankel and Balfour (memo), October 23, 1975, Balfour/Alderson Files.

29. Von Ende to Shankel and Balfour.

30. "Gay Rights, Women's Rights Debated," *LDJW*, December 13, 1977.

31. Robert Carlson and Herbert B. Moser to Dr. Harold M. Voth, February 28, 1975, Balfour/Alderson Files.

32. Jim Conley to Dr. Harold M. Voth, n.d.; William Bradley Jr. to Dr. Harold M. Voth, n.d., both in Balfour/Alderson Files.

33. Shankel to Dykes, July 10, 1975, Balfour/Alderson Files.

34. Balfour to von Ende (memo), October 24, 1975, Balfour/Alderson Files.

35. Materials about the conference, including the conference agenda, from the McKinney Collection, box 20, folder 32. See also "Gay Lib Event"; Todd VanLaningham and Jill Ireland to David Ambler, November 30, 1977, Queers and Allies Files.

36. Kansas Coalition for Human Rights by-laws from the McKinney Collection, box 20, folder 32. See also "Gay Lib Event"; VanLaningham and Ireland to Ambler.

37. Leonard Grotta, interview by author, March 13, 2013; Barry Albin, interview by author, June 28, 2013.

38. Steven Weaver, letter to the editor, *UDK*, February 23, 1976.

39. John Beisner and others mentioned that Wear Blue Jeans if You're Gay Day took place during the 1974–1975 academic year also. Beisner did not remember much, if any, advertising. Further information could not be located in the *UDK* or other media.

40. Rutgers Center for Social Justice Education and LGBT Communities website, http://socialjustice.rutgers.edu/about-us/history/.

41. Leon Unruh, "Gays Ready for Skirmish Despite Ads," *UDK*, October 13, 1979.

42. Chris Caldwell, interview by author, October 23, 2013.

43. Unruh, "Gays Ready for Skirmish."

44. Rick Thaemert, "Walk in a Gay Person's Jeans" (editorial), *UDK*, October 31, 1977.

45. Stephen J. Hill, letter to the editor, *UDK*, October 19, 1977.

46. Unruh, "Gays Ready for Skirmish."

47. Louis Camino and Kathy Petrowaky, "Jeans or No Jeans, Gay Day Overlooked," *UDK*, November 15, 1978.

48. Joe Bussell, letter to the editor, *UDK*, November 9, 1978.

49. Julie Freeman, letter to the editor, *UDK*, November 8, 1978.

50. "Festival for Gays Set," *UDK*, October 22, 1978.

51. Todd Zwahl and Kim Gilbert, letter to the editor, *UDK*, October 30, 1979.

52. Email to author from Kay (formerly Kim) Gilbert, October 5, 2021.

53. "Affirmative Action to Be Topic of Workshop," *UDK*, September 30, 1977.

The *Bakke* case had gotten attention on campus, prompting GSOK to join with other campus groups to sponsor an all-day workshop exploring this and other affirmative action issues in the fall of 1977.

54. National Archives, "Teaching with Documents: The Civil Rights Act of 1964 and the Equal Employment Opportunity Commission," http://www.archives.gov/education/lessons/civil-rights-act/.

55. John Younger, "February Sisters: A Historical Summary," March 1, 2012, https://wgss.ku.edu/february-sisters; Kelly C. Sartorius, *Deans of Women and the Feminist Movement: Emily Taylor's Activism* (New York: Palgrave Macmillan, 2014), 164–168; Kathryn Nemeth Tuttle, "A Seat at the Table: Student Leadership, Student Services, and the New Empowerment," in Rury and Warren, *Transforming the University of Kansas*, 270–273.

56. Bailey, *Sex in the Heartland*, 127–129; Sartorius, *Deans of Women*, 164–168; Tuttle, "Seat at the Table," 270–273. The other demands included creating a campus day care center, hiring female senior administrators, creating a women's studies program, addressing inequitable employment practices, and establishing a full women's health program.

57. Sartorius, *Deans of Women*, 164–168; Tuttle, "Seat at the Table," 271–273.

58. Kathryn Nemeth Tuttle, presentation to University Women's Club, February 8, 2021, https://youtu.be/GeWTndA29LM.

59. Jewell Willhite, "An Interview with Shirley Domer," Oral History Project, KU Retirees Club, September 17, 1997, http://www.kuonlinedirectory.org/endacott/data/OralHistoryTranscripts/DomerShirley.pdf; Sartorius, *Deans of Women*, 164–168; Tuttle, "Seat at the Table," 270–273. Shirley Gilham's last name changed to Domer in 1976.

60. Sartorius, *Deans of Women*, 167; Linda Schild, "Affirmative Action Aided by New Timetable," *LDJW*, September 27, 1973; Younger, "February Sisters."

61. Schild, "Affirmative Action."

62. "Grievance Plan Omission Questioned," *LDJW*, August 11, 1977; Jeffrey S. Byrne, "Affirmative Action for Lesbians and Gay Men: A Proposal for True Equality of Opportunity and Workforce Diversity," *Yale Law and Policy Review* 11, no. 1 (1993): 61–64; James W. Button, Barbara A. Rienzo, and Kenneth D. Wald, *Private Lives, Public Conflicts: Battles over Gay Rights in American Communities* (Washington, DC: Congressional Quarterly, 1997), 26, 64; John D. Skrentny, *The Minority Rights Revolution* (Cambridge, MA: Belknap Press of Harvard University Press, 2002), 324–326.

63. The following quotations and summary are from "Affirmative Action Board Proposal: Provisional Affirmative Action Plan, Modifications Proposed by the Lawrence Gay Liberation Front," November 8, 1972, Balfour/Alderson Files.

64. "Affirmative Action Plan Reviewed by Dykes," *UDK*, September 16, 1977.

65. US Equal Employment Opportunity Commission, The Rehabilitation Act of 1973, http://www.eeoc.gov/laws/statutes/rehab.cfm.

66. "2 Students May File HEW Complaint," *LDJW*, January 23, 1975.

67. "Affirmative Action Plan Reviewed"; Deb Teeter, letter to the editor, *UDK*, September 19, 1977.

68. "Affirmative Action Plan Reviewed"; "Grievance Plan Omission Questioned."

69. "Affirmative Action Plan Reviewed."

70. "2 Students May File."

71. "Grievance Plan Omission Questioned."

72. Delbert Shankel to Todd VanLaningham, February 1977, KU Executive Vice Chancellor's Office Records, Shankel, Del, Chronological Correspondence, November 1976–June 1977, University Archives. The term "sexual preference" was commonly used in the 1970s and is included here when it is part of a direct quote. Otherwise, the more current term, "sexual orientation," is used.

73. "Affirmative Action Plan Reviewed."

74. "Grievance Plan Omission Questioned."

75. Dykes to VanLaningham, KU Chancellor's Office Records, Archie Dykes Correspondence, 1977, Student Senate—XYZ General, General—V Folder, University Archives, Kenneth Spencer Research Library, University of Kansas, Lawrence.

76. Melissa Thompson, "Dykes Approves Grievance Policy," *UDK*, December 13, 1977. The KU Medical Center and the Wichita campus were not included in the plan—it applied to the Lawrence campus only.

77. Thompson, "Dykes Approves."

78. Brian Settle, "Gay Leader Criticizes Latest Affirmative Action Plan," *UDK*, January 19, 1978.

79. "Affirmative Action Hazy about Sexual Preferences," *UDK*, September 29, 1978; see also Settle, "Gay Leader Criticizes"; Thompson, "Dykes Approves."

80. "Affirmative Action Hazy."

81. "Grievance Plan Omission Questioned."

82. Twombly, "Lift the Chorus," 57; Burdett Loomis, "The University and Government: Managing Politics," in Rury and Warren, *Transforming the University of Kansas*, 94, 97. Other administrators also supported this assessment.

83. "Affirmative Action Hazy."

84. In 1998 President Bill Clinton signed into law Executive Order 13087 in which sexual orientation was added to the EEOC Affirmative Action Guidelines, prohibiting employment discrimination based on sexual orientation and granting individuals the right to file discrimination complaints at their place of employment

(http://www.eeoc.gov/laws/executiveorders/13087.cfm). Key KU administrators/ faculty involved with these guidelines verified the date that sexual orientation was added to the KU nondiscrimination policy. Personal communication with Saida Bonifield (December 8, 2014), Jeannette Johnson (December 15, 2014), and John Younger (December 15, 2014).

85. Linda Stewart, "Structure Said to Cause Student Senate Problems," *UDK*, October 19, 1977.

86. "Senate Rejects Chance," *UDK*, October 4, 1977.

87. "StudEx Register Proposal Criticized by Both Sides," *UDK*, February 23, 1972.

88. Allen Holder, "Students Gain Voice in Funding Decisions," *UDK*, October 25, 1977.

89. "Senate Rejects Chance."

90. Todd VanLaningham to David Ambler, October 28, 1977, Ambler Correspondence Files.

91. Holder, "Students Gain Voice."

92. David Ambler, interview by author, May 24, 2013.

93. Holder, "Students Gain Voice."

94. "Senate Shows Sense" (Comment), *UDK*, November 21, 1977. It is important to mention that an unsigned Comment represents an opinion held by all of the *UDK* editorial staff.

95. "Senate Shows Sense."

96. Kansan Editorial Staff, "Fund Gays on Merit" (Comment), *UDK*, February 13, 1978.

97. "Funding Change Proposal Passes," *LDJW*, September 24, 1977.

98. Kansan Editorial Staff, "Fund Gays on Merit."

99. Mark Olson, "Candidates Back Gays for Funding Changes," *UDK*, February 12, 1979.

100. "Fund Limits Disputed," *UDK*, February 13, 1978.

101. Olson, "Candidates Back Gays."

102. Olson, "Candidates Back Gays."

103. "Gay Services of Kansas Recognition Application," 1979, Ambler Correspondence Files.

104. Ann Eversole to GSOK, n.d., Ambler Correspondence Files.

105. "Kim Gilbert to Dean Caryl Smith" (letter), December 20, 1979, Ambler Correspondence Files.

106. Shankel to Chancellor Dykes (memo), n.d., Ambler Correspondence Files.

107. David Ambler to Chancellor Dykes (memo), April 3, 1980, Ambler Correspondence Files.

108. Ambler to Dykes.

109. Ambler to Dykes.

6. "We Are Here and We're Not Going Away"

1. Joe Prados, letter to the editor, *UDK*, October 14, 1971. Other key resources have been particularly helpful for this section: Patrick Dilley, *Gay Man on Campus: A History of Non-Heterosexual College Men, 1945–2000* (New York: RoutledgeFalmer, 2002); Patrick Dilley, *Gay Liberation to Campus Assimilation: Early Non-Heterosexual Student Organizations at Midwestern Universities* (New York: Palgrave Macmillan, 2019); Ruth Lichtwardt, "A Stroll Down Gayhawk Lane: 1976–1986: The Dance and Go to Sambos Years" (Part I) and "A Stroll Down Gayhawk Lane: Part II, Private Activities, Habits or Proclivities," in *Gay and Lesbian History at the University of Kansas*, ed. David D. Barney (Lawrence: University of Kansas, 1992); Stacey Reding, "Fighting 'Fagbusters': Gay and Lesbian Services of Kansas' Struggle for Recognition" (unpublished research paper, spring 2003), Queers and Allies Files; William M. Tuttle Jr., "KU's Tumultuous Years: Thirty Years of Student Activism, 1965–1995," in *Transforming the University of Kansas: A History, 1965–2015*, ed. John L. Rury and Kim Cary Warren (Lawrence: University Press of Kansas, 2015); and author interviews with Bill Tuttle (March 21, 2013) and Paul Lim (June 24, 2013). Both Dilley and Lichtwardt were former members and held leadership roles in the group; Reding was a KU student during the 1980s; and Tuttle and Lim were KU professors and allies.

2. Lichtwardt, "Stroll Down Gayhawk Lane I," 1.

3. Sara Kempin, "Senate Bill to Finance Gays Angers Some," *UDK*, April 14, 1983; Lichtwardt, "Stroll Down Gayhawk Lane II," 3.

4. "Kansas Dept. of Revenue, Alcohol Beverage Control; History and Overview of the Regulation of Alcohol in Kansas," http://www.kslegislature.org/li_20 18/b2017_18/committees/ctte_h_fed_st_1/documents/testimony/20170117_01.pdf. Congress passed the National Minimum Drinking Age Act in 1984. States that allowed persons under twenty-one to purchase alcohol would be punished by a 10 percent reduction in federal highway funding. This law did not address the consumption of alcohol, only the purchase. Some states, however, went further, banning consumption of alcohol by those under twenty-one. Kansas was among this group, banning alcohol consumption, including 3.2 beer, by those under twenty-one in 1985.

5. Lichtwardt, "Stroll Down Gayhawk Lane II," 2.

6. Lichtwardt, "Stroll Down Gayhawk Lane II," 2–3, Kempin, "Senate Bill."

7. Lichtwardt, "Stroll Down Gayhawk Lane II," 2–4; Reding, "Fighting 'Fagbusters.'"

8. Lichtwardt, "Stroll Down Gayhawk Lane II," 3-4; Tuttle interview.

9. John D'Emilio and Estelle B. Freedman, *Intimate Matters: A History of Sexuality in America,* 2nd ed. (Chicago: University of Chicago Press, 1988), 354-355; James W. Button, Barbara A. Rienzo, and Kenneth D. Wald, *Private Lives, Public Conflicts: Battles over Gay Rights in American Communities* (Washington, DC: Congressional Quarterly, 1997), 70-71; Lichtwardt, "Stroll Down Gayhawk Lane II," 3-4; Tuttle interview.

10. "Deaths," *KU's Oread Magazine,* June 7, 1996, 8.

11. Joe Lordi, interview by author, August 26, 2020.

12. James Kinsella, *Covering the Plague: AIDS and the American Media* (New Brunswick, NJ: Rutgers University Press, 1989), 25-34.

13. Lichtwardt, "Stroll Down Gayhawk Lane II," 3-4; Reding, "Fighting 'Fagbusters'"; Tuttle, "KU's Tumultuous Years," 251-252. On the national climate see D'Emilio and Freedman, *Intimate Matters,* 354-356; Button et al., *Private Lives,* 70.

14. Cindy Holm, "Senators Vote to Not Finance Gay Services," *UDK,* April 11, 1984.

15. Holm, "Senators Vote"; Reding, "Fighting 'Fagbusters.'"

16. Lichtwardt, "Stroll Down Gayhawk Lane II," 3; Reding, "Fighting 'Fagbusters'"; Tuttle, "KU's Tumultuous Years," 252.

17. Doug Hitchcock, "KU Administrators Hope Steps Will Stop Intolerance," *LDJW,* November 12, 1984 (quotation); Lichtwardt, "Stroll Down Gayhawk Lane II," 3; Reding, "Fighting 'Fagbusters.'"

18. Bruce Honomichl, "Attitude Behind 'Fag Busters' Harmful," editorial, *UDK,* October 1, 1984; Tom Rodenberg, letter to the editor, *UDK,* October 1, 1984; Lichtwardt, "Stroll Down Gayhawk Lane II," 3.

19. Hitchcock, "KU Administrators."

20. Lichtwardt, "Stroll Down Gayhawk Lane II," 3; Reding, "Fighting 'Fagbusters'"; Tuttle interview; Ruth Lichtwardt in "51 Years OUT: LGLF—The Beginnings," panel, October 20, 2022, https://mediahub.ku.edu/media/t/1_tyj8d2zu.

21. Lindsy Van Gelder and Pam Brandt, "AIDS on Campus," *Rolling Stone,* September 25, 1986, 89.

22. Reding, "Fighting 'Fagbusters'"; "Gay and Lesbian Services of Kansas Office Manual," n.d., Queers and Allies Files.

23. Lichtwardt, "Stroll Down Gayhawk Lane II"; Tuttle, "KU's Tumultuous Years," 252-253; Tuttle interview.

24. Hitchcock, "Administrators Hope" (quotation); Tuttle, "KU's Tumultuous Years," 252-253.

25. Tuttle interview; Lichtwardt, "Stroll Down Gayhawk Lane II," 3-4.

26. D'Emilio and Freedman, *Intimate Matters,* 354-356; Button et al., *Private Lives,* 70-71.

27. Lichtwardt, "Stroll Down Gayhawk Lane II," 2–4; Reding, "Fighting 'Fagbusters'"; Dilley, *Queer Man on Campus*, 174.

28. Lichtwardt, "Stroll Down Gayhawk Lane I," 1, 2–4, and "Stroll Down Gayhawk Lane II," 2–4; Dilley, *Queer Man on Campus*, 177–180; Reding, "Fighting 'Fagbusters'"; "GLSOK Peer Education Guidelines," n.d., Queers and Allies Files. While the sheet was undated, the use of the GLSOK. name indicates that it was created on or after 1981 when the group changed its name.

29. Lichtwardt, "Stroll Down Gayhawk Lane II," 3.

30. Button et al., *Private Lives*, 10–14, 27, 73; John D. Skrentny, *The Minority Rights Revolution* (Cambridge, MA: Belknap Press of Harvard University Press, 2002), 174–178, 182–188.

31. Robert A. Rhoads, *Freedom's Web: Student Activism in an Age of Cultural Diversity* (Baltimore: Johns Hopkins University Press, 1998), 7.

32. Chris Hampton, "What Is This Word 'Queer,' Anyway?," *Vanguard* [KU Queers and Allies newsletter], September 1997, Queers and Allies Files.

33. Dilley, *Gay Liberation to Campus Assimilation*, 206–225.

34. Dilley, *Queer Man on Campus*, 181.

35. "Fred Phelps Visits KU with Anti-Gay Message," *UDK*, September 30, 1992; Dilley, *Queer Man on Campus*, 177–183.

36. "'Equal' Wins Ordinance Amendment," *UDK*, April 26, 1995; Mark Fagen, "Simply Equal Celebrates Victory," *LJW*, April 26, 1995.

37. Dilley, *Queer Man on Campus*, 184.

38. John D'Augelli, "Lesbians and Gay Men on Campus: Visibility, Empowerment and Educational Leadership," *Peabody Journal of Education* 66, no. 3 (1989): 126–127.

39. Information gathered from email conversation with then SGD director Ash Wilson, January 4, 2023, and many KU websites, including the SGD, Office of the Provost, Office of Student Affairs, and Women, Gender, and Sexuality Studies Department, to name a few.

40. SpectrumKU Facebook page, 2015 (no longer available), https://www.facebook.com/SpectrumKU.

41. From the SGD website (2020), https://sgd.ku.edu/spc.

42. From the updated SGD website (2022), https://sgd.ku.edu/recurring-events.

43. Ron Gans, interview by author, June 4, 2020.

44. Phillip Brownlee, "Barred from Justice," *UDK*, October 30, 1995; Hubbell interview.

Conclusion

1. David Stout, Joe Prados, Lee Hubbell, Leonard Grotta, Reginald Brown, and Ruth Lichtwardt in "51 Years OUT: LGLF—The Beginnings," panel, Oc-

tober 20, 2022, https://mediahub.ku.edu/media/t/1_tyj8d2zu. All quotations from the panel are from this source.

2. "Liberate LFK: The Past, Present and Future of LGBTQ+ Activism at KU," December 10, 2021, https://www.youtube.com/watch?v=Ripqo1FsOrw&t=2s.

3. D. A. Graham, email to author, January 3, 2022.

4. Both David Stout and John Bolin commented on this in their writings and interviews.

5. "Liberate LFK."

6. Interviews with John Beisner (June 13, 2013), Ann Eversole (April 26, 2013), Dennis Dailey (May 22, 2013), David Awbrey (June 10, 2013), John Bolin (March 13, 2021), Reginald Brown (May 27, 2020), and others.

7. David H. Stout, "The Lawrence Gay Counseling Service" (unpublished manuscript, April 25, 1975, University of Kansas), Queers and Allies Files.

8. Kristen A. Renn, "LGBT Student Leaders and Queer Activists: Identities of Lesbian, Gay, Bisexual, Transgender and Queer Identified College Student Leaders and Activists," *Journal of College Student Development* 48, no. 3 (2007): 326–328.

9. Allen Holder, "Students Gain Voice in Funding Decisions," *UDK*, October 25, 1977.

10. David H. Stout, "Radical Means: Their Implications to Social Workers Striving to Change the System" (unpublished manuscript, November 1, 1972), Queers and Allies Files.

11. Jeffrey P. Moran, "In the Trenches of the Sexual Revolution," review of *Sex in the Heartland*, by Beth Bailey, *Reviews in American History* 28, no. 2 (2000): 299.

12. Dailey, Warren, and Davis interviews; Lillian Faderman, *Odd Girls and Twilight Lovers: A History of Lesbian Life in Twentieth-Century America* (New York: Columbia University Press, 1991), 213.

13. Chris Caldwell, interview by author, October 23, 2013.

14. Warren interview; Barry Albin, interview by author, June 28, 2013; Bob Friedland, interview by author, July 29, 2020.

15. Peter Felleman, interview by author, June 3, 2020; Caldwell interview.

16. Weaver and Warren interviews.

17. Radavich, Awbrey, Leat, Haenisch interviews.

18. Jan Hyatt, "Area Gay Group No Longer Political," *UDK*, February 6, 1975. See also Robert A. Rhoads, *Freedom's Web: Student Activism in an Age of Cultural Diversity* (Baltimore: Johns Hopkins University Press, 1998), 182–183.

19. Beth Bailey, *Sex in the Heartland* (Cambridge, MA: Harvard University Press, 1999), 216–217; David H. Stout, "Emergence (see?)," vol. 2 (unpublished manuscript, 6 vols., November 25, 2011), University Archives.

20. Anthony R. D'Augelli, "Identity Development and Sexual Orientation: Toward a Model of Lesbian, Gay, and Bisexual Development," in *ASHE*

Reader on College Student Development Theory, eds. Maureen E. Wilson and Lisa E. Wolf-Wendel (Boston: Pearson, 2005), 394.

21. Martha Boyd in "51 Years OUT: The Power of Connections," panel, October 21, 2022, https://mediahub.ku.edu/media/t/1_kmoyjb59.

22. Kathy Hoggard, interview by author, July 12, 2013.

23. David Hudnall, "C. J. Janovy's *No Place Like Home* Unearths the Forgotten Stories of the Fight for LGBT Rights in Kansas," *Pitch*, March 13, 2018, https://www.thepitchkc.com/cj-janovys-no-place-like-home-unearths-the-forgotten-sto ries-of-the-fight-for-lgbt-rights-in-kansas/.

24. "Fred Phelps Visits KU with Anti-Gay Message," *UDK*, September 30, 1992. Rebecca Barrett-Fox has written an excellent book on this group. See *God Hates: Westboro Baptist Church, American Nationalism, and the Religious Right* (Lawrence: University Press of Kansas, 2016).

25. David Stout, email, December 6, 2021; Brown quoted in Matthew Petillo, "Lawrence Gay Liberation Front 51st Anniversary Celebration Attracts Protestors," *UDK*, October 28, 2021.

26. Anonymous comments in this section come from responses on the event feedback form.

27. Niya McAdoo (@KUPresident), Twitter, October 20, 2021, 11:07 p.m.

28. Petillo, "Lawrence Gay Liberation Front 51st Anniversary."

29. "Liberate LFK."

30. Stout email, December 6, 2021.

31. "Liberate LFK."

32. Michael Stubbs email, February 12, 2022.

Appendix B: The Power of Connections: Lawrence Lesbian Communities in the 1970s

1. Deb Holmes, interview by author, October 28, 2019.

2. See chapter 1 for more detail.

3. Laurie Stetzler email, January 21, 2013.

4. David H. Stout, "Emergence (see?)," vol. 2 (unpublished manuscript, 6 vols., November 25, 2011), University Archives.

5. Michael Stubbs, interview by author, May 6, 2020; John Bolin, interview by author, March 13, 2021.

6. Stubbs email, September 14, 2020.

7. Stout, "Emergence (see?)," vol. 2.

8. David Radavich, interview by author, March 15, 2013; "Purple Gaze," *Vortex* 3, nos. 4–5 (1970): 9.

9. Sharon Mayer, interview by author, August 28, 2019.

10. Lee Hubbell, interview by author, March 8, 2013; Bob Warren, interview by author, July 21, 2020.

11. Kathryn Clark, interview by author, February 13, 2020. Quotations and information in this section are from this interview unless otherwise noted.

12. Clark email, February 18, 2020.

13. Rich Crank Oral History, interview by Tami Albin, digital transcript, "Under the Rainbow: Oral Histories of Gay, Lesbian, Bisexual, Transgender, Intersex and Queer People in Kansas," December 7, 2008, Lawrence, Kansas, http://hdl .handle.net/1808/6893.

14. Sarah Evans, *Personal Politics: The Roots of Women's Liberation in the Civil Rights Movement and the New Left* (New York: Knopf, 1979), 196, 225, 228, 231; John D'Emilio and Estelle B. Freedman, *Intimate Matters: A History of Sexuality in America*, 2nd ed. (Chicago: University of Chicago Press, 1988), 315–317.

15. Terence Kissack, "Freaking Fag Revolutionaries: New York's Gay Liberation Front," *Radical History Review* 62 (1995): 111–120; Alice Echols, "'We Gotta Get Out of This Place': Notes toward a Remapping of the Sixties," *Socialist Review* 22, no. 2 (1992): 9–33.

16. Lillian Faderman, *Odd Girls and Twilight Lovers: A History of Lesbian Life in Twentieth-Century America* (New York: Columbia University Press, 1991), 204–214; Beth Bailey, *Sex in the Heartland* (Cambridge, MA: Harvard University Press, 1999), 190–191.

17. Kelly C. Sartorius, *Deans of Women and the Feminist Movement: Emily Taylor's Activism* (New York: Palgrave Macmillan, 2014), 110–111, 120.

18. Stout, "Emergence (see?)," vol. 2; Hubbell interview; Chris Caldwell, interview by author, October 23, 2013; Sartorius, *Deans of Women*, 120; Martha Boyd, interview by author, September 26, 2019.

19. Stephanie Blackwood, interview by author, October 16, 2019; Kala Stroup email, February 8, 2021, Kala Stroup, interview by author, October 30, 2019.

20. Rusty L. Monhollon, *This Is America? The Sixties in Lawrence, Kansas* (New York: Palgrave Macmillan, 2004), 195.

21. Sartorius, *Deans of Women*, 136, 139–140.

22. Peggy C. Scott, "Participants Trace Women's Groups' Past," *UDK*, October 19, 1973; Kathryn Nemeth Tuttle, "A Seat at the Table: Student Leadership, Student Services, and the New Empowerment," in *Transforming the University of Kansas: A History, 1965–2015*, ed. John L. Rury and Kim Cary Warren (Lawrence: University Press of Kansas, 2015), 270; Sartorius, *Deans of Women*, 139–140.

23. Monhollon, *This Is America?*, 195; Tuttle, "Seat at the Table," 270; Bolin interview.

24. Clark interview; Kathy Hoggard, interview by author, July 12, 2013; Boyd interview, September 16, 2019.

25. Profiles of the University of Kansas, Office of Institutional Research and Planning, October 1977. Of the 23,446 students enrolled in the fall 1977 semester, the number of nonwhite students was quite small: 714 African American; 137 American Indian; 134 Asian/Pacific Islander; and 259 Hispanic.

26. Deb Holmes in "51 Years OUT: The Power of Connections," panel, October 21, 2022, https://mediahub.ku.edu/media/t/1_kmoyjb59; Deb Holmes email, February 4, 2021.

27. Article was written and signed by Patti Spencer and the women at the December 2 Coalition meeting, *Women's Coalition Newsletter*, December 6, 1971, Queers and Allies Files.

28. Scott, "Participants Trace"; Monhollon, *This Is America?*, 207.

29. "Lesbian Group Seeks Community," *UDK*, October 19, 1973 (quotation); Randy Schuyler, "Gays Present Requests to Balfour," *UDK*, April 28, 1972. For more information, see chapter 4.

30. Susan Davis, interview by author, November 18, 2019 (quotation); Debbie Bauman, "Gay Liberation Gives Hope to Homosexuals," *UDK*, December 10, 1975; Mayer interview, August 28, 2019; Elizabeth B. A. Miller, "Women Helping Women: The Battered Women's Movement in Lawrence, Kansas. A Case Study" (master's thesis, University of Kansas, 2006), 32, 65. The café was on Fourteenth and Massachusetts Streets, adjacent to the popular downtown area.

31. Holmes interview; Polly Pettit, interview by author, June 26, 2021; Clark email, February 18, 2020 (first quotation); Davis interview (second quotation).

32. *Lavender Luminary*, February 1975, Queers and Allies Files.

33. The terms "lesbian feminist" and "feminist lesbian" were both used in the 1970s. The more commonly used term is "lesbian feminist" and is used here, except when in a quote.

34. Carol Gwinn, "Lesbian Feminist Sees Mother-Daughter Split," *UDK*, February 25, 1974.

35. Kissack, "Freaking Fag," 121–123; Faderman, *Odd Girls*, 212. Early on this movement was called the Lavender Menace as a tongue-in-cheek reference to Betty Friedan's use of this term to describe lesbians.

36. Faderman, *Odd Girls*, 237–239.

37. D'Emilio and Freedman, *Intimate Matters*, 317–318, 321; Echols, "We Gotta Get Out"; Bailey, *Sex in the Heartland*, 190–191.

38. This information was provided to the author in confidence, so names are not cited.

39. Sherie M. Randolph, *Florynce "Flo" Kennedy: The Life of a Radical Black Feminist* (Chapel Hill: University of North Carolina Press, 2015), 2–8, 10, 189, 223; Marilyn Hayes, "Zealous Feminist Talk Sparks Spirited Rally," *UDK*, May 2, 1976.

40. Martha Boyd in "51 Years OUT"; Davis and Mayer (August 28, 2019) interviews.

41. Holmes, Davis, Clark interviews; Tonda Rush, interview by author, November 19, 2019; Kathryn Lorenzen, interview by author, March 4, 2021.

42. David Chartrand, "Music Collective a Voice Aimed at Women," *LDJW*, February 12, 1977.

43. Lorenzen, Holmes, Davis, Clark interviews. Lorenzen will be referred to by her current name unless there is a need to do otherwise.

44. Lorenzen interview; Chartrand, "Music Collective."

45. Laurie Mackey, "The Kansas State Fiddling and Picking Championships 1981–1990: A Lawrence Community Nourishes Kansas State Fiddling and Picking Championships," http://www.kansasfolk.org/stories/sp00304.htm.

46. Chartrand, "Music Collective." He had failed to include a reference to the influence of notable "girl groups" of the 1960s that evolved from R&B, pop, and rock, such as the Supremes, Martha and the Vandellas, and the Ronettes. African American women, who were generally absent in white mainstream pop, elevated the role of women in music, although their influence was often ignored. They were instrumental in paving the way for groups that followed.

47. Chartrand, "Music Collective"; Holmes and Clark interviews. Julia Deisler went by Julie and Tamara Perkuhn went by Tammy in the 1970s. They will be referred to by their current names unless there is a need to do otherwise.

48. For more information on Scalet and her legacy, see Kansas Music Hall of Fame website, https://www.ksmhof.org/2008-inductees/#beth_scalet; artist profile on Broadjam, https://www.broadjam.com/bio/bethscalet.

49. Kathryn Lorenzen email, August 10, 2021; poster obtained from Deb Holmes via email, April 6, 2020.

50. Lorenzen interview; David Olson, "Women's Conference Opens," *LDJW*, May 31, 1979.

51. Bonnie Morris, "How Should We Archive the Soundtrack to 1970s Feminism?," *Smithsonian*, March 30, 2018, https://www.smithsonianmag.com/arts-culture/how-should-we-archive-soundtrack-1970s-feminism-180968637/.

52. Blackwood interview; Blackwood email, February 8, 2021; Kate Drabinski, "The History of Baltimore's Lesbian Bar Scene," *Baltimore Sun*, July 19, 2016.

53. Hoggard interview, July 12, 2013.

54. Holmes interview.

55. Jolene Babyak email, November 1, 2019; Tedde Tasheff, interview by author, August 29, 2013; Pettit interview; Clark email, February 18, 2020.

56. See chapter 5 for more about the relationship between the LGLF and Dykes.

57. Leonard Grotta, interview by author, March 13, 2013; Hoggard interview, April 2, 2021. Others who sponsored the group included Ralph Buzzi, who owned an insurance firm, and Toc Tickner, owner of a North Lawrence bar, Ichabod's.

58. Hoggard interview, April 2, 2021.

59. Clark interview; Babyak email; Hoggard interview, April 2, 2021.

60. Clark interview; Blackwood email, July 3, 2020.

61. Debi Licklider, "Workshop Day Planned," *LDJW*, July 12, 1975; letters to the editor, *LDJW*, from Mrs. Barbara Hanna, July 18, 1975; Nancy Hartman, July 22, 1975; Deb Holmes, July 22, 1975.

62. Hoggard interview, April 2, 2021; Hoggard interview, July 12, 2013.

63. While interviews with many Creamers and Chickens team members point to these being two separate teams, there is not total agreement about this. Boyd, who played with the Creamers, recalled that as the Creamers were dwindling after their unsuccessful year in the more advanced league, they evolved into the Apple Valley Chickens. Stephanie Blackwood, who played with the Chickens, and Kala Stroup, who sponsored them, disagreed. They remembered two teams, with the Chickens being a newly created all-lesbian team and not an extension of the Creamers, a feminist and lesbian team.

64. Stroup and Blackwood interviews.

65. For more information, see "Catt Rules in Topless Case," *Lawrence Journal-World*, October 22, 1976.

66. Boyd interview, September 16, 2019.

67. Tonda Rush, "Womenspace's Evolution Gradual," *LDJW*, August 28, 1976; Davis interview. The account and quotations from Davis are from this interview unless otherwise noted. The media and others referred to it as "Womenspace," but the name identified by Susan Davis, "Womanspace," is the correct one and will be used in this book.

68. Rush, "Womenspace's Evolution."

69. Rush, "Womenspace's Evolution"; Davis and Clark interviews; Holmes email, February 4, 2021.

70. Rush, "Womenspace's Evolution."

71. Boyd (September 16, 2019) and Clark interviews.

72. Boyd (September 16, 2019), Blackwood, Davis, Rush, Clark interviews.

73. See chapter 2 for additional information.

74. Boyd interview, September 16, 2019.

75. Boyd (September 16, 2019), Holmes, Clark interviews.

76. Blackwood, Clark, Boyd (September 16, 2019) interviews.

77. Boyd (September 16, 2019) interview.

78. Clark email, February 13, 2020.

79. For more detail about Ling and his properties, see chapter 2.

80. Clark in "51 Years OUT."

81. Blackwood and Lorenzen interviews.

82. Ann Eversole, interview by author, April 26, 2013; Caldwell interview; Trip

Haenisch, interview by author, October 25, 2013; Chad Leat, interview by author, October 2, 2013.

83. Blackwood interview; Blackwood email, February 8, 2021.

84. Blackwood interview.

85. More detail is provided in chapter 5. See also Jan Hyatt, "Area Gay Group No Longer Political," *UDK*, February 6, 1975.

86. Debbie Bauman, "Gay Liberation Gives Hope to Homosexuals," *UDK*, December 10, 1975; Hoggard interview, July 12, 2013.

87. Stroup interview.

88. This account is from Judy Browder, email to author, January 29, 2021.

89. Judy Browder, interview by author, February 1, 2021.

90. Miller, "Women Helping Women," 26 (quotations), 73, 79–80; Amber Fraley, "Wonderfully Assertive and Proactive," *Lawrence Magazine*, Winter 2002, 35–36.

91. Miller, "Women Helping Women," 21, 26, 47, 92 (quotation).

92. Willow Domestic Violence Center website, https://www.willowdvcenter .org/.

93. Sartorius, *Deans of Women*, 112–117; Bailey, *Sex in the Heartland*, 197–198.

94. Hoggard interview, April 2, 2021.

95. Sartorius, *Deans of Women*, 112–117.

96. Hoggard interview, April 2, 2021. Other administrators who were identified as particularly supportive were Ann Eversole and Lorna Grunz Zimmer.

97. Hoggard (April 2, 2021) and Pettit interviews.

98. Hoggard (April 2, 2021), Boyd (September 16, 2019), Eike interviews; Sartorius, *Deans of Women*, 114; Bailey, *Sex in the Heartland*, 197–198.

99. Pettit interview. A copy of *No Pat Answer* is located in the KU Spencer Museum archives.

100. Hoggard interview, July 12, 2013; Eike email, January 29, 2021; Pettit interview (quotation); Pettit email, March 4, 2022. A copy of this video is located in the KU Spencer Museum archives.

101. Hoggard interview, July 12, 2013.

102. Sexual Trauma and Abuse Care Center website, http://stacarecenter.org/, especially the About Us page, http://stacarecenter.org/about-us.

103. Holmes interview.

104. Holmes interview; Holmes in "51 Years OUT."

105. Holmes interview. The "Me Too" Movement was created in 2006 by Tarana Burke to focus on the experience of sexual violence survivors and provide a platform to raise awareness and push for change, particularly for historically excluded survivors. In 2017, actor Alyssa Milano took it to the next level, urging people to bring their stories of abuse to social media. The #metoo hashtag went viral, bringing the issue into the mainstream and causing national exposure, discussion,

and the censure of many in positions of power, particularly entertainment executives and actors. See https://metoomvmt.org/get-to-know-us/history-inception/ for more information.

106. Rush interview.

107. Blackwood interview; Blackwood email, February 10, 2021.

108. US Department of Education, Office of Civil Rights, Athletics, https://www2.ed.gov/about/offices/list/ocr/frontpage/pro-students/issues/sex-issue04.html.

109. Women's Sports Foundation, "Title IX and the Rise of Female Athletes in America," September 2, 2016, https://www.womenssportsfoundation.org/education/title-ix-and-the-rise-of-female-athletes-in-america/.

110. Two of the many articles detailing Washington's accomplishments: Bill Rhoden, "A Fruitful Past but a Shaky Future," *Ebony*, August 1977; University of Kansas Women's Basketball, https://kuathletics.com/kansas-dedicates-marian-e-washington-womens-basketball-suite/. Washington's skills and accomplishments are legendary. She was a member of the US women's Olympic handball team; the first of two African American women to play on a US national team (1969–1971); the first to serve as the head coach for a US international team (1982 US Select); and the first to coach on an Olympic women's basketball staff.

111. Blackwood interview; Blackwood email.

112. Blackwood email.

113. Blackwood interview; Blackwood email.

114. Boyd interview, August 28, 2019.

115. Hoggard interview, April 2, 2021.

116. Laurie Stetzler, [untitled], *Vortex* 3, no. 7 (December 1970).

117. Holmes in "51 Years OUT."

118. Hoggard interview, April 2, 2021.

Appendix C: Gay Activism on Campuses across the State in the 1970s

1. Beth Bailey, *Sex in the Heartland* (Cambridge, MA: Harvard University Press, 1999), 179.

2. Kansas State University website, https://www.k-state.edu/about/history-traditions/.

3. C. J. Janovy, *No Place Like Home: Lessons in Activism from LGBT Kansas* (Lawrence: University of Kansas Press, 2018), 141.

4. David H. Stout, "Emergence (see?)," vol. 2 (unpublished manuscript, 6 vols., November 25, 2011), University Archives; Lee Hubbell, interview by author, March 8, 2013; David Awbrey, interview by author, June 10, 2013.

5. Spare generously shared information from his not-yet-published book,

"Prairie Fairie" (unpublished electronic manuscript, August 1, 2020). It has been a key resource in recounting this history and provided much of the detail used here.

6. "Making History: Kansas City and the Rise of Gay Rights," a project of the University of Missouri–Kansas City's Public History class, which debuted as a traveling exhibit in 2017: https://info.umkc.edu/makinghistory/the-phoenix-socie ty-for-individual-freedom/.

7. Carolyn Szczepanski, "KC's New Gay and Lesbian Archive of Mid-America Remembers a Pioneer Town," *Pitch*, June 3, 2010, https://www.thepitch kc.com/kcs-new-gay-and-lesbian-archive-of-midamerica-remembers-a-pioneer -town/.

8. Discussed at greater length in chapter 4.

9. UFM website, https://tryufm.org/50th-anniversary/. This organization now goes by "the UFM Community Center," eliminating the gendered reference, "Man."

10. Helen L. Horowitz, "The 1960s and the Transformation of Campus Cultures," *History of Education Quarterly* 26, no. 1 (1986): 20; Spare, "Prairie Faerie."

11. Information about Robert Sinnett was retrieved from https://www.pen wellgabeltopeka.com/obituary/77171.

12. Spare email, August 1, 2020.

13. The information and quotation are from a 1971 paper that Keith Spare wrote for a "Topics in Psychology" class he took with Bob Sinnett, "Homosexuality at Kansas State University" (reprinted in part in "Prairie Fairie").

14. Dan Biles, "Manhattan Gays Seek Awareness," *K-State Collegian*, September 17, 1973.

15. Biles, "Manhattan Gays Seek Awareness."

16. Spare email, July 13, 2021; David H. Stout, "The Lawrence Gay Counseling Service" (unpublished manuscript, April 25, 1975), Queers and Allies Files. Spare questioned if these presentations occurred, but LGLF members recalled them.

17. Joe Lordi, interview by author, August 26, 2020. He retrieved this information from his 1970s log.

18. Mona Dunn, "Student Shouts Turned to Murmurs," *UDK*, April 21, 1972; Stout, "Lawrence Gay Counseling."

19. WSU website, https://www.wichita.edu/innovationcampus.

20. Janovy, *No Place*, 82–83.

21. Robert Teutsch, "A Contextual History of LGBTQ Student Groups at Wichita State University, May 2016, https://wichita.campuslabs.com/engage /organization/spectrum. This article has been invaluable in providing historical information on gay organizing on the WSU campus.

22. McKinney quoted in Teutsch, "Contextual History."

23. Teutsch, "Contextual History."

24. Teutsch, "Contextual History."

25. These organizations include Gay and Lesbian Resource Association (1984–1987); Students for Education on Liberal Concerns (subsumed GLRA) (1987–1989); Responsible Active Gays (1989–1991); ACT-UP, WSU Chapter (1990–1991, when it evolved into a community organization, ACT-UP Wichita); Choices (1991–1993, renamed 10 Percent); 10 Percent (1993–2001 or 2002); Transgender Union (1991–1992); *That* Gay Group! (2000–2014); Spectrum: LGBTQ & Allies (2014–present).

26. "Explore TTC's History," Emporia State University website, https://www.emporia.edu/teachers-college/about-college/history-college/.

27. James W. Button, Barbara A. Rienzo, and Kenneth D. Wald, *Private Lives, Public Conflicts: Battles over Gay Rights in American Communities* (Washington, DC: Congressional Quarterly, 1997), 2, 64, 132, 139–142; Karen L. Graves, *And They Were Wonderful Teachers: Florida's Purge of Gay and Lesbian Teachers* (Champaign: University of Illinois Press, 2009), 120–121, 141, 143; Deb Holmes, interview by author, October 28, 2019; Amanda Machado, "The Plight of Being a Gay Teacher," *Atlantic*, December 16, 2014, https://www.theatlantic.com/education/archive/2014/12/the-plight-of-being-a-lgbt-teacher/383619/.

28. Casey Cagle, "Meet the Historical Storyteller of Emporia, Kansas," March 5, 2017, *Prairie Earth* blog (link no longer available); Roger Heineken document sent by email, July 4, 2020.

29. Lordi interview.

30. Heineken emails, June 24, 2021; July 4, 2020 (quotation).

31. Heineken email, July 4, 2020.

32. Heineken email, July 4, 2020.

33. Delbert Shankel to Chancellor Dykes (memo), May 27, 1980, Ambler Correspondence Files; "Gay Lib Organizations at Regents Schools" survey, Balfour/Alderson Files.

34. The document, "Timeline of LGBTQ+ Student Organizations," was provided by Rebekah Curry, Public Services Supervisor, University Libraries and Archives, Emporia State University, via email, January 5, 2021.

35. This included restricting those under twenty-one from consuming beverages greater than 3.2 percent alcohol content and restricting public consumption outside of membership clubs.

36. Heineken email, July 4, 2020.

37. The university adopted its current name in 1977.

38. Heineken email, July 4, 2020.

39. "Pittsburg State University: A Brief History," Pittsburg State University website, https://axe.pittstate.edu/_files/documents/PSU_aBriefHistory.pdf.

40. "Gay Lib Organizations at Regents Schools," n.d., Balfour/Alderson Files; Steven Cox emails, July 12 and 20, 2020.

41. Dunn, "Student Shouts"; Stout, "Lawrence Gay Counseling Service."

42. "History of FHSU"; Fort Hays State University website, https://www .fhsu.edu/about/fhsuhistory/.

43. Brian Gribben email, July 20, 2020.

44. Shankel to Dykes memo; "Gay Lib Organizations."

45. Henry Schwaller email, July 29, 2020.

46. Hubbell interview; Stout, "Emergence (see?)," vol. 2.

47. Reginald Brown, interview by author, May 27, 2020; David Radavich, interview by author, March 15, 2013.

48. Sam Zeff, "How K-State Became One of the Best Places for LGBT Students in the Country," KCUR, November 13, 2017, https://www.kcur.org/edu cation/2017-11-13/how-k-state-became-one-of-the-best-places-for-lgbt-students-in -the-country; QueerCat Newsletter, Fall 2019–Spring 2020, https://www.k-state .edu/lgbt/alumniandgraduation/lavnewsletter/LGBT%20Newsletter%202019 _2020.pdf; Spectrum Center website, https://www.k-state.edu/lgbt/contactabo ut/about.html; Campus Pride Index, https://www.campusprideindex.org/.

49. "Campus Pride's 2023 Best of the Best LGBTQ-Friendly Colleges and Universities," https://www.campuspride.org/2023bestofthebest/.

Bibliography

Interviews and Personal Communication

Interviews and Personal Communication Conducted by the Author

NOTE: All of these interviews were conducted in person or by phone (by phone if no further information is listed). All were digitally recorded and are in the author's possession, unless otherwise noted.

Barry Albin, June 28, 2013.

David Ambler, May 24, 2013, Kansas Memorial Union, University of Kansas, Lawrence.

David Awbrey, June 10, 2013.

Jolene Babyak, November 1, 2019. Interview conducted by email.

John Beisner, June 13, 2013.

Stephanie Blackwood, October 16, 2019.

John Bolin, March 13, 2021.

Saida Bonifield, December 8, 2014. Strong Hall, University of Kansas, Lawrence.

Martha Boyd, September 16, 2019. Kansas City, Missouri.

Martha Boyd, February 18, 2021.

Denis J. Brothers, August 20, 2013. Interview conducted by email.

Judy Browder, February 1, 2021.

Reginald Brown, May 27, 2020.

Mert Buckley, June 27, 2013. Interview conducted by email.

Chris Caldwell, October 23, 2013.

Kathryn Clark, February 13, 2020.

Dennis Dailey, May 22, 2013. Kansas Memorial Union, University of Kansas, Lawrence.

Susan Davis, November 18, 2019. Lawrence, Kansas.

David Dillon, April 1, 2013. School of Business, University of Kansas, Lawrence.

Casey Eike, August 25, 2013.

Ann Eversole, April 26, 2013. Kansas Memorial Union, University of Kansas, Lawrence.

Peter Felleman, June 3, 2020.

Bob Friedland, July 29, 2020.

Ron Gans, June 4, 2020.

Leonard Grotta, March 13, 2013.

Brandon Haddock, June 11, 2020.

Trip Haenisch, October 25, 2013.

Kathy Hoggard, July 12, 2013.

Kathy Hoggard, April 2, 2021.

Deborah Holmes, October 28, 2019.

Lee Hubbell, March 8, 2013. Lawrence, Kansas.

Jeannette Johnson, December 15, 2014.

Jack Klinknett, September 11, 2013. Lawrence, Kansas.

George Laughead, October 18, 2013. Kansas Memorial Union, University of
     Kansas, Lawrence.

Chad Leat, October 2, 2013.

Steve Leben, October 4, 2013.

Paul Lim, June 24, 2013. Lawrence, Kansas.

Richard Linker, June 5, 2020.

Joe Lordi, August 26, 2020.

Kathryn Lorenzen, March 4, 2021.

Niya McAdoo, November 9, 2021. Kansas Memorial Union, University of
     Kansas, Lawrence.

Sharon Mayer, August 28, 2019. Lawrence, Kansas.

Sharon Mayer, October 9, 2019. Lawrence, Kansas.

Michael McConnell, April 15, 2021.

Timothy Miller, August 22, 2013. School of Religion, University of Kansas,
     Lawrence.

Chuck Ortleb, December 5, 2014. Personal communication via phone (not
     recorded).

Chuck Ortleb, August 2, 2021.

Jim Pettey, September 4, 2020.

Polly Pettit, June 28, 2021.

Joe Prados, April 2, 2013.

David Radavich, March 15, 2013.

Jim Rhatigan, July 11, 2020.

Tonda Rush, November 19, 2019.

Lynn Schornick, January 16, 2020. Personal communication via email.

Del Shankel, March 14, 2013. Haworth Hall, University of Kansas, Lawrence.

Donna Shavlik, April 22, 2013.

Frank Shavlik, July 3, 2013.

Christine Smith, June 17, 2013. Lawrence, Kansas.

Keith Spare, June 2, 2020 through July 13, 2021. Personal communication
     via email.

Kala Stroup, October 30, 2019. Nunemaker Hall, University of Kansas, Lawrence.

Michael Stubbs, May 6, 2020.

Tedde Tasheff, August 29, 2013.

Bill Tuttle, March 21, 2013. Lawrence, Kansas.

Bob Warren, July 21, 2020.

Steven Weaver, May 18, 2020.

John Younger, December 15, 2014. Wescoe Hall, University of Kansas, Lawrence.

Other Interviews (not conducted by author)

Albin, Tami. "Under the Rainbow: Oral Histories of Gay, Lesbian, Bisexual, Transgender, Intersex and Queer People in Kansas." Lawrence, Kansas. https://ku scholarworks.ku.edu/handle/1808/5330.

Crank, Rich. Oral history in Albin, "Under the Rainbow." December 7, 2008. http://kuscholarworks.ku.edu/dspace/handle/1808/6893.

"An Interview with Shirley Domer." Interviewed by Jewel Willhite, September 17, 1997. Oral History Project, KU Retirees Club. http://www.kuonlinedirectory .org/endacott/data/OralHistoryTranscripts/DomerShirley.pdf.

Stout, David. Interviewed by Tami Albin, digital video recording, November 1, 2010 (in author's possession).

KU Archival Material

Note: Archival files that are referred to frequently have been given a reference title for ease of reading.

Ambler Correspondence Files

Office of Student Affairs Files, Ambler Correspondence Files, Gay Services, Box 12. University Archives, Kenneth Spencer Research Library, University of Kansas, Lawrence, Kansas.

Balfour/Alderson Files

Office of Student Affairs: Balfour/Alderson: Correspondence: Financial Aid-Housing (CWC), Box 5, Folder "Gay Lib." University Archives, Kenneth Spencer Research Library, University of Kansas, Lawrence, Kansas.

McKinney Collection

Bruce McKinney Collection, Kansas Collection, Box 20, Folder 32, 1977. University Archives, Kenneth Spencer Research Library, University of Kansas, Lawrence, Kansas.

Personal Papers of William Balfour

William M. Balfour Collection. University Archives, Kenneth Spencer Research Library, University of Kansas Libraries.

Queers and Allies Files

Student Organizations Records, Queers and Allies Chronological Records, Box 1. University Archives, Kenneth Spencer Research Library, University of Kansas, Lawrence, Kansas.

Books and Articles

Allen, Samantha. *Real Queer America: LGBT Stories from Red States*. Boston: Little, Brown, 2019.

Armstrong, Elizabeth A. *Forging Gay Identities*. Chicago: University of Chicago Press, 2002.

Armstrong, Elizabeth A., and Suzanna M. Crage. "Moments and Memory: The Making of the Stonewall Myth." *American Sociological Review* 71 (October 2006): 724–751.

Bailey, Beth. *Sex in the Heartland*. Cambridge, MA: Harvard University Press, 1999.

Barney, David, ed. *Gay and Lesbian History at the University of Kansas: Lawrence Gay Liberation Front, 1971–1975; Gay Services of Kansas, 1976–1980*. Lawrence: University of Kansas, 1992.

Barrett-Fox, Rebecca. *God Hates: Westboro Baptist Church, American Nationalism, and the Religious Right*. Lawrence: University Press of Kansas, 2016.

Baxter Magolda, Marcia B. *Making Their Own Way: Narratives for Transforming Higher Education to Promote Self-Development*. Sterling, VA: Stylus, 2001.

Beemyn, Brett G., ed. *Creating a Place for Ourselves: Lesbian, Gay and Bisexual Community Histories*. New York: Routledge, 1997.

———. "The Silence Is Broken: A History of the First Lesbian, Gay, and Bisexual Student Groups." *Journal of the History of Sexuality* 12, no. 2 (April 2003): 205–223.

Beemyn, Genny, and Susan Rankin. *The Lives of Transgender People*. New York: Columbia University Press, 2011.

Best, Amy. *Prom Night: Youth, Schools and Popular Culture*. New York: Routledge, 2000.

Bronson, Ken. *A Quest for Full Equality*. May 18, 2004. https://www.lib.umn.edu/sites/www.lib.umn.edu/files/2021-11/quest-copy.pdf.

Button, James W., Barbara A. Rienzo, and Kenneth D. Wald. *Private Lives, Public*

Conflicts: Battles over Gay Rights in American Communities. Washington, DC: Congressional Quarterly, 1997.

Byrne, Jeffrey S. "Affirmative Action for Lesbians and Gay Men: A Proposal for True Equality of Opportunity and Workforce Diversity." *Yale Law and Policy Review* 11, no. 1 (1993): 56–64. https://digitalcommons.law.yale.edu/ylpr/vol11 /iss1/3.

Carter, David A. *Stonewall: The Riots That Sparked the Gay Revolution.* New York: St. Martin's, 2004.

Cass, Vivienne C. "Homosexual Identity Formation: Testing a Theoretical Model." *Journal of Sex Research* 20, no. 2 (1984): 143–167.

Chauncey, George. *Gay New York: Gender, Urban Culture, and the Making of the Gay Male World, 1890–1940.* New York: Basic Books, 1994.

Chesebro, Jim. "The First National Gay Lib Convention: One View from Minneapolis." In Ken Bronson, *A Quest for Full Equality*, 51–60.

Chickering, Arthur W., and Linda Reisser. *Education and Identity.* 2nd ed. San Francisco: Jossey-Bass, 1993.

D'Augelli, Anthony R. "Identity Development and Sexual Orientation: Toward a Model of Lesbian, Gay, and Bisexual Development." In Wilson and Wolf-Wendel, *ASHE Reader on College Student Development Theory*, 393–403.

———. "Lesbians and Gay Men on Campus: Visibility, Empowerment and Educational Leadership." *Peabody Journal of Education* 66, no. 3 (1989): 124–142.

D'Emilio, John. *Sexual Politics, Sexual Communities: The Making of a Homosexual Minority in the United States, 1940–1970.* 2nd ed. Chicago: University of Chicago Press, 1983.

D'Emilio, John, and Estelle B. Freedman. *Intimate Matters: A History of Sexuality in America.* 2nd ed. Chicago: University of Chicago Press, 1988.

Dilley, Patrick. *Gay Liberation to Campus Assimilation: Early Non-Heterosexual Student Organizations at Midwestern Universities.* New York: Palgrave Macmillan, 2019.

———. *Queer Man on Campus: A History of Non-Heterosexual College Men, 1945–2000.* New York: RoutledgeFalmer, 2002.

Duberman, Martin. *Stonewall.* New York: Penguin, 1993.

Echols, Alice. "'We Gotta Get Out of This Place': Notes toward a Remapping of the Sixties." *Socialist Review* 22, no. 2 (1992): 9–33.

Evans, Sarah. *Personal Politics: The Roots of Women's Liberation in the Civil Rights Movement and the New Left.* New York: Knopf, 1979.

Faderman, Lillian. *The Gay Revolution: The Story of the Struggle.* New York: Simon & Schuster, 2016.

———. *Odd Girls and Twilight Lovers: A History of Lesbian Life in Twentieth-Century America*. New York: Columbia University Press, 1991.

Fassinger, Ruth E. "Lesbian. Gay, and Bisexual Identity and Student Development Theory." In Wilson and Wolf-Wendel, *ASHE Reader on College Student Development Theory*, 405–411.

Fellows, Will. *Farmboys: Lives of Gay Men from the Rural Midwest*. Madison: University of Wisconsin Press, 2001.

Ginsberg, Allen. "Gay Sunshine Interview." *College English* 36, no. 3 (1974): 392–400.

Gitlin, Todd. *The Sixties: Years of Hope, Days of Rage*. New York: Bantam, 1987.

Graves, Karen L. *And They Were Wonderful Teachers: Florida's Purge of Gay and Lesbian Teachers*. Champaign: University of Illinois Press, 2009.

Gray, Mary L., Brian J. Gilley, and Colin R. Johnson. *Queering the Countryside: New Frontiers in Rural Queer Studies*. New York: New York University Press, 2017.

Hoeflich, Michael H. "In Piam Memorial—Francis Heller." *Kansas Law Review* 61, no. 5 (June 1, 2013): 913–921.

Horowitz, Helen L. *Campus Life*. Chicago: University of Chicago Press, 1987.

———. "The 1960s and the Transformation of Campus Cultures." *History of Education Quarterly* 26, no. 1 (1986): 1–38.

Howell, Martha, and Walter Prevenier. *From Reliable Sources: An Introduction to Historical Methods*. Ithaca, NY: Cornell University Press, 2001.

Janovy, C. J. *No Place Like Home: Lessons in Activism from LGBT Kansas*. Lawrence: University of Kansas Press, 2018.

Johansen, Bruce. "Out of Silence: FREE, Minnesota's First Gay Rights Organization." *Minnesota History* 66, no. 5 (2019): 186–201.

Johnson, Colin R. *Just Queer Folks: Gender and Sexuality in Rural America*. Philadelphia: Temple University Press, 2013.

Katz, Jonathan N. *Gay American History: Lesbians and Gay Men in the U.S.A.* Rev. ed. New York: Penguin, 1992.

Kinsella, James. *Covering the Plague: AIDS and the American Media*. New Brunswick, NJ: Rutgers University Press, 1989.

Kissack, Terence. "Freaking Fag Revolutionaries: New York's Gay Liberation Front." *Radical History Review* 62 (1995): 104–134.

Levine, Arthur. *When Dreams and Heroes Died*. San Francisco: Jossey-Bass, 1980.

Levinson, Sandra, and Carol Brightman. *Venceremos Brigade: Young Americans Sharing the Life and Work of Revolutionary Cuba*. New York: Simon & Schuster, 1971.

Lichtwardt, Ruth "A Stroll Down Gayhawk Lane. 1976–1986: The Dance and Go to Sambo's Years." In Barney, *Gay and Lesbian History at the University of Kansas*.

————. "A Stroll Down Gayhawk Lane, Part II: Private Activities, Habits or Proclivities." In Barney, *Gay and Lesbian History at the University of Kansas*.

Lieberman, Robbie. *Prairie Power: Voices of 1960s Midwestern Student Protest*. Columbia: University of Missouri Press, 2004.

Loomis, Burdett. "The University and Government: Managing Politics." In Rury and Warren, *Transforming the University of Kansas*, 81–114.

————. "Lesbian, Gay, Bisexual, and Transgender Student Organizations: An Overview." In Sanlo, *Working with Lesbian, Gay, Bisexual, and Transgender College Students*, 321–328.

Mallory, Sherry. "The Rights of Gay Student Organizations at Public State-Supported Institutions." *NASPA Journal* 34, no. 2 (1997): 82–90.

Mayes, Rick, and Allan V. Horwitz. "DSM-III and the Revolution in the Classification of Mental Illness." *Journal of the History of the Behavior Sciences* 41 (2005): 249–267.

McCarn, Susan R., and Ruth Fassinger. "Revisioning Sexual Minority Identity Formation: A New Model of Lesbian Identity and Its Implications for Counseling and Research." *Counseling Psychologist* 24 (1996): 508–534.

McConnell, Michael, with Jack Baker. *The Wedding Heard 'Round the World: America's First Gay Marriage*. Minneapolis: University of Minnesota Press, 2016.

Miller, Elizabeth B. A. "Women Helping Women: The Battered Women's Movement in Lawrence, Kansas—A Case Study." Master's thesis, University of Kansas, 2006.

Monhollon, Rusty L. *This Is America? The Sixties in Lawrence, Kansas*. New York: Palgrave Macmillan, 2004.

Moran, Jeffrey P. "In the Trenches of the Sexual Revolution." Review of *Sex in the Heartland*, by Beth Bailey. *Reviews in American History* 28, no. 2 (2000): 298–302.

Outcalt, Charles. "The Lifecycle of Campus LGBT Organizations: Finding Ways to Sustain Involvement and Effectiveness." In Sanlo, *Working with Lesbian, Gay, Bisexual, and Transgender College Students*, 329–338.

Pardun, Robert. *Prairie Radical: A Journey through the 60s*. Los Gatos, CA: Shire, 2001.

Randolph, Sherie M. *Florynce "Flo" Kennedy: The Life of a Radical Black Feminist*. Chapel Hill: University of North Carolina Press, 2015.

Renn, Kristen A. "LGBT Student Leaders and Queer Activists: Identities of Lesbian, Gay, Bisexual, Transgender and Queer Identified College Student Leaders and Activists." *Journal of College Student Development* 48, no. 3 (2007): 311–330.

Rhoads, Robert A. *Freedom's Web: Student Activism in an Age of Cultural Diversity*. Baltimore: Johns Hopkins University Press, 1998.

Rury, John L. "Historical Research in Education." In *The Handbook of Comple-mentary Methods in Education*, edited by Judith L. Green, Gregory Camilli, and Patricia B. Elmore, 323–332. Washington, DC: Routledge, 2006.

———. "Introduction: Decades of Transformation: Fifty Years of KU History." In Rury and Warren, *Transforming the University of Kansas*, 1–39.

Rury, John L., and Kim Cary Warren, eds. *Transforming the University of Kansas: A History, 1965–2015*. Lawrence: University Press of Kansas, 2015.

Sanlo, Ronni L., ed. *Working with Lesbian, Gay, Bisexual, and Transgender College Students: A Handbook for Faculty and Administrators*. Westport, CT: Green-wood, 1998.

Sartorius, Kelly C. *Deans of Women and the Feminist Movement: Emily Taylor's Ac-tivism*. New York: Palgrave Macmillan, 2014.

Sievers, Sharon. "Gay and Lesbian Research in the 1980s: History and Theory." *Radical History Review* 50 (May 1, 1991): 204–212.

Skrentny, John D. *The Minority Rights Revolution*. Cambridge, MA: Belknap Press of Harvard University Press, 2002.

Stein, Marc. "'Birthplace of the Nation': Imagining Lesbian and Gay Commu-nities in Philadelphia, 1969–1970." In Beemyn, *Creating a Place for Ourselves*, 253–288.

Tuttle, Kathryn Nemeth. "A Seat at the Table: Student Leadership, Student Ser-vices, and the New Empowerment." In Rury and Warren, *Transforming the University of Kansas*, 263–308.

Tuttle, William M., Jr. "KU's Tumultuous Years: Thirty Years of Student Activ-ism, 1965–1995." In Rury and Warren, *Transforming the University of Kansas*, 227–262.

Twombly, Susan B. "'Lift the Chorus Ever Onward': Leading the University." In Rury and Warren, *Transforming the University of Kansas*, 43–80.

Wilson, Maureen E., and Lisa E. Wolf-Wendel. *ASHE Reader on College Student Development Theory*. Boston: Pearson, 2005.

Wolf-Wendel, Lisa, Susan B. Twombly, Kathryn Nemeth Tuttle, Kelly Ward, and Joy L. Gaston-Gayles. *Reflecting Back, Looking Forward: Civil Rights and Stu-dent Affairs*. Washington, DC: National Association of Student Personnel Ad-ministrators, 2004.

Index

Abington Bookstore, 31
acceptance, 10, 43, 76, 138, 212; lack of, 15; social, 150, 212
accountability, 147, 185, 207
ACLU. *See* American Civil Liberties Union
activism, 4, 7–8, 23, 74, 80, 81–86, 123, 154–156, 163–164, 187–188, 190, 197–198; antiwar, 49; campus, 69–70; civic, 127; civil rights, 55, 120, 229, 252; decline of, 147; early, 160–161, 207; gay, 12, 22, 45, 53, 63, 89, 152, 165, 166, 261–265; growth of, 127, 198, 269; lesbian, 255; lessons from, 204–219; LGBTQ, 5, 6, 10, 210, 218, 271; LGLF, 160–161, 190–191; New Left, 35; political, 27, 159; redefining, 250; resurgence in, 198; student, 46–54
ACT-UP Wichita, 326n25
Adam, Margie, 241
Advocate, 83
affirmation, xvi, 12, 50, 51, 128, 154, 232, 276
affirmative action, 175, 311n53; challenging, 9; federal, 178, 180; plan, 147, 176, 177, 178, 179, 180
Affirmative Action Advisory Board, 178, 180
"Affirmative Action Board Proposal" (1972), 176
Affirmative Action Handbook, 179
Affirmative Action Office, 176, 179, 253
Affirmative Action Review Board, 177
African Americans, 49, 51, 123; discrimination against, 119–120; petition by, 39–40; protesting treatment of, 36–37
AIDS, 9, 193, 197, 220, 273; deaths from, 194, 289n9; hateful response, 196; vigils, 199

"AIDS on Campus" (*Rolling Stone*), 196
Albin, Barry, 17, 22, 28, 33, 69, 119, 120, 159, 170, 223, 259; civil rights and, 85; on coming out, 139; cruising and, 44; on dances, 143; Kunstler and, 121
Albin, Tami, 7, 280n13
Alderson, Donald, 6, 66, 186, 224, 232; homosexuality and, 44
Allen, Samantha, 6
Alumni Association, 67
Ambler, David, 182, 184, 190, 196, 207, 224; on Alderson, 186; Caldwell on, 187; Dykes and, 188, 189; letter to, 153; obstacles for, 186–187; Shankel and, 189; Student Affairs Office and, 187; Student Senate and, 186
American Bar Association, 120, 135
American Civil Liberties Union (ACLU), 55, 70, 119, 120, 121, 128; conferring with, 73; lawsuit and, 137; resolution by, 137
American Field Service, 19
American Psychiatric Association (APA), 90, 152, 259, 273
anonymity, 32, 34, 55, 89, 142, 150, 266
antigay attitudes, 2, 3, 24, 44, 77, 170
antiwar movement, 11, 24, 37–38, 49, 53, 68, 121
APA. *See* American Psychiatric Association
Apathy Coalition, 184
Apple Valley Chickens, 244, 322n63
Apple Valley Farm, 244
Arabian Nights (bar), 33
Archie's Dykes, 232
Archives, KU, xvii
Armstrong, Elizabeth, 20
Associated Women Students (AWS), 233

Athletics Department, KU, 118

Austin, Riley, 62

awareness, 74, 180, 265; campaign, 190,
212, 268, 310n39; political, 82; public,
205; raising, 20, 172, 173, 247

Awbrey, David, 23, 30–31, 35, 68, 225,
289n15

Babyak, Jolene, 226, 242, 243

Bailey, Beth, xvi, 6–7, 167, 261

Baker, Jack, 30, 69, 71, 100 (fig.), 227,
299n100; gay liberation and, 85; incorporation and, 158–159; marriage of, 84

*Bakke vs. Regents of the University of
California* (1978), 175, 178, 311n53

Baldwin, Joe, 197

Baldwin United Methodist Youth
Fellowship (UMYF), 121

Balfour, William, 66, 68, 69, 72, 170, 177,
179, 224, 235, 253; harassment and,
146; lawsuit and, 134; letter from,
132; LGLF and, 67, 71; meeting with,
146–147; noncommittal response from,
71; Stout and, 70; suggestions from,
145; support from, 151

Bank (bar), 33

Bankston, Diana, 252

Baptist Campus Ministry Center, 264

Barlogas (bar), 272

Barnett, Gina, 266, 267, 268

Bee Gees, 220

Beemyn, Genny, 4, 6, 280n3

behavior: mainstream vs.
nonconforming, 124, 169, 177, 213, 249

Beisner, John, 139, 160, 171, 173, 205, 225,
310n39

Berlin, Margaret, 185, 225

Best of the Best LGBTQ Campuses, 276

Bierstube pub, 31, 125

Big 8 Conference, 133

Big 8 Gay Federation, 85

Bigotbusters, 195

bigotry, 175, 195, 197, 235

Biles, Dan, 264

bisexual, xxiv, 149, 198; term, xxiii

Bjornsen, Lars, 83

Black, Beth, 251

Black Panthers, 25, 81

Black Power, 273

Black Student Union (BSU), 39, 49, 51, 144

Blackwood, Stephanie K., 110 (fig.), 118
(fig.), 226, 233, 241, 243, 244, 256, 257,
258, 322n63; unspoken acceptance
for, 250

Blevins, Jon, 72, 223

Board of Trustees (APA), 152

Body Shop, 45, 62, 65, 93 (fig.), 96, 124;
sexual connotation of, 28

Bolin, John, 12, 16, 24, 45, 60, 78, 81, 82,
93 (fig.), 96 (fig.), 97 (fig.), 101 (fig.),
102 (fig.), 122, 123, 124, 216, 223, 283n45,
285n83, 286n104, 292n62, 298n83; on
AFS application, 19; articles by, 58; on
counterculture gays, 59; dance income
and, 304n92; on gay issues, 25; on GLF,
50; on Lawrence, 83–84; LGLF and,
41; as a role model, 210; poster by, 103
(fig.), 106 (fig.); Urban Plunge and, 26,
27; Venus and, 29; Women's Coalition
and, 230

Bottleneck (bar), 193

Bowman, Marilyn, 68

Boyd, Martha, 15–16, 33, 110 (fig.), 117
(fig.), 217, 226, 237, 243, 247–248, 259,
287n115, 322n63; activism of, 229; on
Blackwood, 244; on coming out, 16; on
harassment, 18, 19; Stroup and, 233

Boys in the Band, The (movie), 89

Bretz, Lynn, 113 (fig.), 226, 239, 240, 243

"Bride of Frankenstein," 28

Bride of Venus, 28, 29–30, 91, 124

Brink, W. J., 156

Brothers, Denis J., 129, 223

Browder, Judy, 226, 251, 252

Brown, Reginald Thomas (Reggie), 45,
49, 99 (fig.), 108 (fig.), 111 (fig.), 120,
165, 202, 211, 216, 220, 221, 223; BSU
and, 144; gay people of color and, 52;
on GLF meeting, 63; guerrilla theater
and, 155; LGLF and, 51, 79–80; on protestors, 219; and speakers' bureau, 76

Brune, C. J., 23, 226

Bryant, Anita, 170

Bryant, Jo, 253

BSU. *See* Black Student Union
Bubb, Henry, 25
Buckley, Mert, 225
Budig, Gene, 196, 224
Burge, Frank, 138, 145, 224
Burgess, Robin, 45, 52, 73, 82, 223
Burke, Tarana, 323n105
Business School, KU, 163
Buzzi, Ralph, 321n57

Caldwell, Chris, 14, 173, 183, 210, 225; on
    Ambler, 187; self-acceptance and, 211
Camino, Louis, 174
Can-Can Dance, 140
Canterbury House, 148
Carttar, Paul, 136
"Cause for Concern" (McCool), 35
Center for Constitutional Rights, 120
Center for Sexuality and Gender
    Diversity (SGD), 200, 201, 276
Chalmers, E. Laurence, 37, 40, 49, 67, 68,
    119, 120, 128, 129, 163, 175, 176, 224, 270;
    "duping" charge of, 130–131; lawsuit
    and, 133, 134; Templar and, 136–137;
    Women's Coalition and, 130
Chartrand, David, 239
Chesebro, Jim, 69, 100 (fig.)
Chicago Seven, 3, 120
Children of Sappho, 265, 269
Chisholm, Shirley, 236
Christian, Meg, 238
Christianity, homosexuality and, 152
Christopher Street, 194, 211
Christopher Street Day celebration,
    154, 206
City Human Relations Ordinance, 199
City of Lawrence League, 241, 242
civil rights, 3, 11, 35, 37, 38, 53, 81, 90,
    120, 121, 163, 186, 187–188, 197–198, 207,
    209, 229; focus on, 47, 133, 236, 252,
    269; importance of, 189; issues, 147;
    national, 49; violation of, 85, 137
Civil Rights Act (1964), 175
Civil Rights Council, KU, 36, 119, 283n43
Civil Rights Movement, 198
Clark, Kathryn, 23, 110 (fig.), 118 (fig.),
    207, 226, 236, 243, 246; on dances,

142; on discovering identity, 230–231;
    gatherings by, 237–238; on lesbian
    community, 248, 249; Ling and, 27;
    Womanspace and, 247
Clinton, Bill, 312n84
Cobb, Robert, 196
Come Out (poster), 139
coming out, 16, 62–63, 67, 137; gay
    community and, 138; reticence for, 139.
    See also outing
Commission on the Status of Women
    (CSW), 73, 147, 174–175, 233; WC and,
    234; Womanspace and, 245
commune houses, 247, 259
community: building, 35, 235–238;
    campus, 91, 146, 276; changing, 204;
    engaging, 87–90; lack of, 84; support
    from, 47, 48. *See also* gay community;
    lesbian community
Compton's Cafeteria, 20
Congress of Racial Equality, 283n43
connections, 2, 138, 217, 247; building,
    235–238; importance of, xvi–xvii;
    intergenerational, 210; making, 20–23
consciousness, 183; gay, 22; individual/
    collective, 48; lesbian, 258–260;
    political, 127
consciousness raising, 50, 80, 212; gay
    liberation groups and, 75; LGLF and,
    75–76
conversion therapy, 153
counseling, 50; funding for, 143, 153;
    LGLF and, 148, 149; peer, 90–92;
    services, 147–154, 212
counterculture, 39, 41, 49, 51, 58, 59, 61,
    270, 302n49
COVID-19 pandemic, 201, 279n4
Cox, Steven, 274
Crage, Suzanna, 20
Cramer, Toni, 116 (fig.), 251
Crank, Richard, 54–55, 231
Crofoot, John, 67
Cronkite, Walter, 120
cruising, 31, 44
CSW. *See* Commission on the Status of
    Women
Cuevas, Joe, 201

cultural change, 2, 11, 23, 161, 163, 168, 205, 207, 235
culture, 12, 14, 126, 171, 183; campus, 74, 208; community, 204; drug, 21; gay, 9, 20, 126, 169; guilt and shame, 13; heteronormative, 198; heterosexism and, 20; homophobic, 13; identity and, 35; lesbian, 9; university, 207

Dailey, Dennis, 148, 206, 210, 214–215, 224; GCS and, 153, 154; support/therapy from, 14–15; on validation, 216
dance clubs, 140
dances, 4, 9, 129–130, 160, 212, 220, 232, 239; advertising, 141; counseling/education programs and, 143; early, 140, 221; funding from, 193, 304n92; gay community and, 141; gay liberation and, 34, 130, 143; Halloween, 109 (fig.); impact of, 137, 143, 216; at K-State, 265; LGLF and, 9, 137–143, 144, 221, 239, 276, 284n58; music and, 140–141; political overtones for, 139; popularity of, 140, 168; poster for, 103 (fig.), 106 (fig.), 107 (fig.); robbery at, 144–147; at WSU, 266
D'Augelli, Anthony, 13, 15, 90
Daughters of Bilitis, 53
Davis, Michael, 170, 178, 180, 184
Davis, Susan, 46, 111 (fig.), 112 (fig.), 116 (fig.), 210, 214, 217, 226, 237, 238, 239, 251, 259; dances and, 142; house of, 249; Womanspace and, 245–246
Days of Rage, 39, 60, 94 (fig.), 95 (fig.)
Dean of Women's Office, 15
Defense, Department of, 198
Deisler, Julia (Julie), 111 (fig.), 112 (fig.), 226, 239, 321n47
D'Emilio, John, 2, 4, 61
DeYoung, Kathy, 250
Diagnostic and Statistical Manual of Mental Disorders (DSM), 273; removing homosexuality from, 152, 270
Dilley, Patrick, 6, 7, 54, 63, 199, 223, 314n1
Dillon, David, 144–145, 225
discrimination, 21, 22, 37, 129, 145, 176, 181–182, 200, 230, 271; condemning, 152; covert, 214; dealing with, 21,
146, 178–179, 255; double, 254–258; employment, 155, 156, 312n84; ending, 156, 177, 179; housing, 146, 155, 204; measures against, 198; protesting, 154–156; racial, 119–120, 197, 257; reverse, 175, 178; sexual, 155, 180, 197
District Court, US, 133, 134
diversity, 63, 64, 20, 265
Dole, Bob, 169, 284n54
Domer, Shirley. See Gilham Domer, Shirley
Douglas County Democrats, 156
Dowdell, Rick "Tiger," 45, 95 (fig.), 290n27; death of, 39
drag, 140, 156, 301n25; bars, 26; as political statement, 124
Dreiling, Norbert, 156
DSM. See Diagnostic and Statistical Manual of Mental Disorders
Duncan, Robert, 31
Dutton, Judy, 252
Dykes, Archie, 72, 164, 170, 177, 180, 224, 242, 272, 275; on academic perfor-mance, 163; affirmative action plan and, 178; Ambler and, 188, 189; griev-ance procedures and, 179; GSOK and, 186; Midwest Gay Conference and, 168, 169; political landscape and, 189

Ebert, Bill, 25, 68, 69, 72
Echols, Alice, 283n45
Ecumenical Christian Ministries, 291n34
Edmonds, Mark, 155, 156
Edmonds Real Estate, 155
education, 23, 50, 90; focus on, 47, 165; minorities/women and, 175
educational programs, 9, 123, 160, 190; dances and, 143; early, 74–80; expanding, 127; Education Amendments (1972), 257
EEOC Affirmative Action Guidelines, 312n84
effeminacy, 19, 212–213
Eiges, Sandy, 251
Eike, Casey, 226, 234, 243, 253, 254
Elbaz, David, 101 (fig.), 102 (fig.)
Eldridge Hotel, 31
electroshock therapy, 152, 153

Embry, Dennis, 134
employment, 198, 204; discrimination in, 155, 156, 312n84; minorities/women and, 175
Emporia State University (ESU), 79, 80, 237, 297n70; gay/lesbian community at, 270–273; gay rights at, 276
engagement, 87–90; civic, 37, 127; community, 74, 160; political, 60
Equal Employment Opportunity Commission Affirmative Action Guidelines, 180
equal rights, 157
Equal Rights Amendment (ERA), 229, 243
equality, 10, 21, 177; lobbying for, 128; social, 192; under the law, 50, 192
equity, 10, 49, 47, 170, 187, 188, 198, 203, 208, 220, 233; gender, 57, 167, 229; racial, 271
ERA. *See* Equal Rights Amendment
Esquire, 12–13
Establishment, 13; challenging, 207–210
ESU. *See* Emporia State University
ethnicity, 171, 255
Eversole, Ann, 187, 189, 224, 323n96
Executive Order 13087 (1998), sexual orientation and, 312n84
Exposure to Repression, Oppression, and Suppression (EROS) Plunge, 26–27

Fagbusters, 195, 196
Fall Festival, 173, 174
fan girls, 244
Farmboys (Fellows), 6
FBI, infiltration by, 82
February Sisters, 176, 234–235; Womanspace and, 245
Felleman, Peter, 28, 29, 30, 88, 101 (fig.), 102 (fig.), 122, 123, 125, 223, 285n83; on Stubbs, 86
Fellows, Will, 6
feminism: lesbianism and, 248, 251, 320n33; radical, 252; socialist, 243
Feminist Party, 236
feminists, 206, 236, 245, 247; agenda for, 234, 250; community, 249, 253, 254; houses for, 249; portrayal of, 232;

support for, 260; welcome for, 260
"51 Years OUT!: Celebrating Gay Liberation History of KU and Lawrence," 108, 110 (fig.), 111 (fig.), 202–203, 212, 218, 219, 220, 221; impact of, 204–205
Fight Repression of Erotic Expression (FREE), 20, 69, 82, 83, 84, 101, 300n8
Finance Committee, 195, 196
First Amendment, 18, 135
First Fridays, 235
First National Gay Liberation Convention, 82
Fischer, Holly R., 111 (fig.), 112 (fig.), 113 (fig.), 116 (fig.), 226, 239, 240
Fleming, Constance, 226, 244, 245
Flowers, Ron, 223, 250
Foolkiller folk music community, 239
Forer, Norman, 196
Fort Hays State University (FHSU), gay/lesbian students at, 274–277
Fourteenth Amendment, 135
Fowler, John, 31
Francke, Ann, 235
Franklin, Aretha, 238
fraternities, 14, 78
FREE. *See* Fight Repression of Erotic Expression
Freedman, Estelle, 4
Freedom Coalition, 194–195, 199
Freedom Day, 154
Freedom Fighters, 3
Freedom Riders, 120
Freeman, Julie, 174
Free State narrative, 21
Free University, KU, 167, 263
Friedan, Betty, 320n35
Friedland, Bob, 14, 111 (fig.), 165, 166, 202, 211, 215, 223; on harassment, 18; suicidal thoughts and, 17
funeral procession, 95 (fig.)

GALA. *See* Gay and Lesbian Awareness Week
Galvin, Earl, 86, 101 (fig.), 102 (fig.)
Gans, Ron, 32, 33, 55–56, 201, 214, 223; on coping, 15; suicidal thoughts and, 17

Gardenhire, Gary, 227, 266, 267, 268
Garrett, William, 39
Gaslight Tavern, 31, 45
gay, xxiv, 149, 198, 254; appearing, 169;
    being, 63, 74, 80; normal and, 213; term,
    xxiii, 54
Gay Activist Alliance (GAA), 61
Gay and Lesbian Academic and Staff
    Association, 194
Gay and Lesbian Awareness Week
    (GALA), 174, 175, 197, 199, 289n15
Gay and Lesbian Resource Association
    (GLRA), K-State, 326n25
Gay and Lesbian Services of Kansas
    (GLSOK), 194, 196, 197, 199, 216n28;
    funding for, 195; opposition to, 195
gay bars, 16, 26, 141
gay commune, 2430
gay community, xxiii, 7, 9, 27–28, 50–51,
    55, 73, 84, 129, 145, 147, 166, 171, 173, 177,
    184; AIDS and, 194; building, 43, 143,
    161, 191, 192, 229; campus/national
    issues affecting, 172; coming out and,
    138; dances and, 141; friendships in,
    22; frustrations/fears/triumphs of, 8;
    hostility toward, 81; music and, 239;
    revolt by, 20; stereotypes and, 214;
    support for, 234
Gay Conference, 86, 120, 300n8
Gay Counseling Service (GCS), 9, 152,
    161, 168, 190; approach for, 149–150, 153–
    154; establishment of, 148, 156; funding
    for, 153; hotline by, 150; referrals to, 151
gay grapevine, xiv, 151
Gay Hot Line, K-State, 264
"Gay Is Good" (Weaver), 91
gay issues, 25, 130, 173, 186, 261
gay liberation, 6–7, 8, 10, 22, 27, 43–44,
    48, 54, 61, 67, 84, 85, 125, 129, 131, 132,
    154, 155, 156, 160, 163, 169; dances
    and, 34, 130, 143; development of,
    82–83; function of, 73; as grassroots
    movement, 41; hostility towards, 81;
    lesbians and, 234; recognizing, 290n27;
    recommended reading list on, 145–146;
    rise of, 4
Gay Liberation Front (GLF), 48, 49, 53,

55, 58, 61, 66–67, 69, 83, 86, 101, 102, 171,
    174, 206, 219; definition of, 50; early
    days of, 222; meeting, 63
Gay Liberation Front-New York (GLF-
    NY), 21, 41, 46, 54, 101, 124, 216, 235,
    298n83; beginnings of, 61; New Left
    and, 80
gay liberation groups: consciousness-
    raising groups and, 75–76; formation
    of, 58; recognition for, 133
Gay Liberation to Campus Assimilation
    (Dilley), 6
gay men, xxiv, 2, 122; climate for, 21;
    hostile culture for, 296n64; lesbians
    and, 3, 78; subordination of, 124; in
    women's movement, 230
Gay Oread Daily, 130
gay people: biblical take on, 122; Black,
    51; of color, 51, 52; discrimination
    against, 182; minority of, 145; police
    and, 33; travels of, 86
Gay People of Emporia, 272
gay pride, 70, 154–156
Gay Pride Week, 154, 174, 194
Gaypril, 200
gay rights, 35, 183, 186, 192, 199; fighting
    for, 191, 276; issue of, 155, 197–198;
    resolutions, 156
gay rights groups, xiii, 56, 57, 69, 81;
    student/community, 60; tension in, 63
Gay Services of Kansas (GSOK), 170,
    178, 179, 182, 183, 184, 186, 187, 189–190,
    198, 275; appeal by, 188; collaboration
    by, 174–175; described, 168; fall
    festival and, 173–174; funding for,
    181, 193; leadership of, 180; Midwest
    Gay Conference and, 168, 169; name
    changes for, 167, 190; presence of, 192;
    recognition for, 171–172; support of, 185
"Gay Sexual Awareness" (course), 167
gay students: challenges for, 19–20;
    problems of, 147; public perceptions
    of, 11–13
Gay Sunshine, 85
Gay Women's Caucus, 76, 148, 235
GCS. See Gay Counseling Service
gender, xiii, 77, 137, 220, 257;

conceptualization of, 138; debates over, 122; expressions of, 138; harassment and, 19; power and, 19; redefining, 212–214

gender expression, 29, 212, 213, 214

genderfuck, 122, 124, 301n17; term, 301n26

gender norms, 125

Gilbert, Kim (Kay), 175, 185, 223

Gilham Domer, Shirley, 176, 179, 253, 311n59

Gilley, Brian J., 6

Ginsberg, Allen, 26, 31

GLAAD, xiv

GLF. *See* Gay Liberation Front

GLF-NY. *See* Gay Liberation Front-New York

Glover, Mike, 170

GLSOK. *See* Gay and Lesbian Services of Kansas

Graham, D. A., 203

Granada Theatre, 89

Gray, Mary L., 6

Greek system, 14, 78, 118, 127, 233, 238, 249, 250

Grey, Rod, 26, 29

Gribben, Brian, 274

Grier, Ed, 32

grievance procedures, 178, 179

Grist, 31, 286n104

Grotta, Leonard, 56, 79, 108 (fig.), 111 (fig.), 127, 156, 202, 205, 213, 215, 220, 223, 242; anonymity and, 150; on dances, 140; early life of, 1–2; hearing and, 157; on Klinknett, 157

Group W, 175

Gruber, Charles, 157, 226

GSOK. *See* Gay Services of Kansas

Guidance Bureau, KU, 151

guerrilla theater, 120, 155

Haddock, Brandon, 227, 263–264

Haenisch, Trip, 16, 142, 205, 218, 225; on activism, 206; on gender presentation, 213; relationships for, 17; on shame, 14, 15

Hammond Park, 273

Hanna, John, 195

harassment, 20, 146, 179, 193, 195; gender and, 19; homophobic, 194; lesbian, 19; police, 18; verbal, 196

Harper, Michael, 163, 225

Harper, Nan, 253

Harris, Katherine, 110 (fig.)

Hayes, Marilyn, 251

Headquarters Counseling Center, 79, 148

Healey v. James (1972), 158

Heineken, Roger, 227, 271, 272, 273

Heller, Francis, 68

Henry, Pat, 226, 246, 252, 253

heteronormativity, 84, 137, 138, 172, 200, 215

heterosexism, xxiii, 24, 164, 166, 199, 211, 231, 232, 254; cultural norms and, 20; hidden curriculum of, 13

heterosexuality, 91, 173, 176–177, 213

Highberger, Boog, 225

Highfill, Julie, 26

Hill, Steven, 173

Hippie Haven, 27, 40, 93 (fig.), 100 (fig.), 247

hippie houses/communes, 27–28, 30

Hoffman, Abbie, 136, 273

Hoggard, Kathy, 1, 46, 115 (fig.), 126, 224, 241, 243, 244, 251, 253; on dances, 216; softball and, 242

Holmes, Deborah S. (Deb), 78, 110 (fig.), 111 (fig.), 112 (fig.), 113 (fig.), 123, 226, 234, 239, 240, 243, 244, 255; demonstrations and, 228; feminism and, 229

Holy Cow Creamers, 114, 115, 242–244

homophobia, 12, 13, 22, 45, 77, 90, 136–137, 156, 159, 161, 193, 194, 218, 232, 241, 264, 269; confronting, 20, 56, 70, 254; impact of, 18; internalization of, 205, 258; lesbians and, 254–258; pervasiveness of, 257

homosexuality, 5, 12, 13, 33, 42, 47, 68, 161, 164, 259, 261, 263, 273; acknowledging/accepting, 21–22; Christianity and, 152; conceptualization of, 166; confronting, 260; Cubans and, 26; disapproval of, 44; Emily Taylor's support of, 232; healthy/positive/normal, 48; illegality of, 190; as mental illness, 91, 152; narratives about, 154; ostracism for, 25; religion and, 121, 152; self-realization of, 149; talking about, 11–12

"Homosexuality in America" (*Life*), 12
homosexual: term, xxiii
homosexuals, 54, 71, 149, 158; freedom for,
    50; healthy, 49; organization for, 133;
    rights/liberties of, 50, 169
Honomichl, Bruce F., 195
Hood, Mil, 111 (fig.)
Horowitz, Floyd, 70, 71, 72, 119, 137, 224
Horowitz, Helen, 163
"Hot to Trot" (dance), 107; poster for,
    106 (fig.)
Houck, Kemp, 134
House Judiciary Committee, 85
housing, 156; discrimination in, 146, 155,
    204; LGLF and, 86
Howell, Martha, xv
Hubbell, Lee, xvii, 16, 22, 80, 111 (fig.),
    124–125, 138, 140, 148, 152, 155, 156, 202,
    205, 223, 230; acceptance and, 76; on
    Alderson, 44; gay culture and, 126;
    Lawrence and, 34; LGLF and, 57, 64,
    127, 201; on proclaiming identity, 139;
    recognition and, 159; on rights, 48; on
    tolerance, 164
Human Relations Committee, 178
human rights, 119, 124, 178
Human Sexuality Committee (HSC), 78

"I Am Woman" (Reddy), 240
Ichabod's (bar), 321n57
identity, 48, 51, 63, 70, 80, 89, 161, 171, 199,
    205, 236, 249; Christian, 42; culture
    and, 35; denial of, 43; embracing,
    74; exploring, 201; gay, 25, 26, 59, 77,
    80, 151, 171, 213, 214–217; gender, xiii,
    214; hidden, 14, 143, 258, 271; lesbian,
    214–217; politics and, 25; proclaiming,
    139; racial, 51; sexual, 154, 241, 271;
    typologies, 54
Imber, Steve, 195–196, 197, 225
"In Celebration of the First
    Amendment" (dance), 137
inclusion: fighting for, 175–180;
    LGBTQ, 265
inequity, 39, 206–207, 236, 269
Information Center, 46, 91, 126, 176, 253,
    302n33

International Women's Day, 96 (fig.)
Intrafraternity Council, 146
Ireland, Jean, 153
Isaacs, Chris, 134
isolation, 17, 21, 210; feelings of, 15, 42, 127,
    191, 214, 276; overcoming, 126

Jackson, Gary, 49, 290n27
Jacobsen, David, 142
Janovy, C. J., 6, 218
Jewel Box (bar), 33
Johnson, Colin R., 6
Johnson, Jill, 236
Johnson, Karl E., 71
Johnson, Michael, 185, 223
Johnston, Pamela, 252
Journalism School, KU (William Allen
    White School of Journalism and Mass
    Communications), 203, 237
Just Queer Folks (Johnson), 6

Kansas Act against Discrimination
    (44–1001), 156
Kansas Bureau of Investigation, 38, 40, 55
Kansas City Screw, 292n64
Kansas City Star, 33
Kansas Coalition for Human Rights, 170
Kansas Drag Showcase, 200
Kansas Gay Political Conference, 170, 275
Kansas Humanities Council, 254
Kansas Music Hall of Fame, 240
Kansas Public Radio, 203
Kansas State College of Pittsburg. *See*
    Pittsburg State University
Kansas State Teachers College (KSTC).
    See Emporia State University
Kansas State University, 296n69; gay
    activism at, 261–265; gay/lesbian
    students at, 262, 264; gay rights at, 276
Kansas State University Activities
    Board, 265
Kansas State University Selective
    Service Information and Counseling
    Program, 263
Kansas Union, 31–32, 39, 58, 69, 87, 101,
    104, 108 (fig.), 109 (fig.), 138, 166,
    181, 200, 202, 205; beer sales at, 193;

conference at, 170; congregating at, 34; dances at, 4, 129–130, 137, 140, 142–143, 193; LGLF and, 131; protests at, 218; renting policies for, 146; reservations office at, 66; restrooms at, 44, 66

Kansas Vocational Rehabilitation, 151

Kanter, Gary, 82, 223

Katz, Jonathan Ned, 4, 5

"Keep the Scene Clean," 102, 125

Kelly, Valerie, 252

Kennedy, Flo, 236, 237

Kennedy, John F., 162

Kent, Marilyn, 226, 239, 243

Kent State University, 25, 182

King, Billie Jean, 256

King, Martin Luther, Jr., 120, 162

kiss-ins, 126, 199

Klinknett, Jack, 119–120, 121, 133, 157, 217, 218, 226; decision and, 137; lawsuit and, 134, 135

Kohler, Will, 12

KPR Presents, 203

Krassner, Paul, 24

K-State Collegian, 264

K-State LGBT Resource Center, 265

Kunstler, William, 3, 104 (fig.), 105 (fig.), 120–121, 128, 157–158, 227, 237; lawsuit and, 133, 134; Oldfather and, 135; strategy and, 131; style of, 160; Templar and, 134, 135

Kuromiya, Kiyoshi, 86, 101 (fig.), 102 (fig.)

KU-Y (YMCA and YWCA), 175

Laflin, Molly, 115 (fig.), 226, 243, 253

Lake Henry, 31

Landman, Vicki Larason, 253

Lane, Rachel, 219–220

Lathrop, C., 118 (fig.), 226

Laughead, George, 225

Lavender Graduation, 200

Lavender Luminary, 235

Lavender Menace, 320n35

Lawrence Chamber of Commerce, 102, 125

Lawrence Daily Journal-World (LDWJ), 57, 67, 133, 136, 163, 169, 239

Lawrence Gay Liberation, Inc. (LGL, Inc.), 158, 162, 166, 171, 190, 308n12; GCS funding and, 153

Lawrence Gay Liberation Front (LGLF), xiv, 5, 16, 18, 54, 58, 67, 72; accomplishments of, 207; approach of, 74, 159, 165–167; campus life and, 141; conflict related to, 127–133; constitution of, 192; division within, 73, 209, 218; founding of, 3, 8–9, 11, 28, 35, 36, 40, 4246, 65, 70, 82, 184, 229; gay/lesbian services and, 50; gender imbalance in, xvi, 231; growth of, 119; history of, 6, 7, 8; influence of, 6, 51, 203, 275–277; inner/outer circles of, 62; lawsuit by, 129–130, 132–137, 154, 208, 234; lobbying by, 152; materials about, 88–89, 90; members of, 9, 10; name change for, 165, 167, 308n12; newsletter, 49, 91; presentation requests and, 77, 79–80; role of, 73, 261; Solidarity Statement of, 290n27; structure of, 54–58; struggles of, 62–63; support for, 53, 129; support from, 20, 127, 129; tactics of, 160–161; writings/publications of, xv

Lawrence High School, 45, 52, 54, 77

Lawrence Lesbian Alliance (LLA), 172, 235

Lawrence Liberation Front, *Oread Daily* and, 57

Lawrence Women's Music Collective, 30, 111 (fig.), 112 (fig.), 113 (fig.), 116, 203, 216, 237, 238–241, 246, 254, 259; members of, 239

Law School, KU, 119, 176

LDJW. See *Lawrence Daily Journal-World*

leadership: hybrid, 207–210; LGLF, 10, 63, 231, 265; shared-gender, 231

League for the Practice of Democracy, 283n43

Leat, Chad, 14, 206, 213, 225

Leben, Steve, 73, 181, 182, 183, 186, 208, 225; proposal by, 184

Leffel, Rusty, 36, 225

lesbian, xxiv, 74, 198, 254; issues, 186; rights, 192; services, 50; term, xxiii

Lesbian, Bisexual and Gay Students of Kansas (LesBiGay OK), 198, 201

lesbian communes/houses, 217, 237, 247–258

lesbian community, 7, 9, 55, 129, 171, 215, 236, 239, 248, 249, 253, 258–260; building, 237–238; frustrations/fears/triumphs of, 8

lesbian feminist, xxiii, 9, 211, 241; term, 320n33

lesbian history, 4

Lesbian Nation, 236

lesbians, 30, 51, 247; children and, 231; climate for, 21; of color, 232; cross-race conversations and, 234; gay liberation and, 234; gay men and, 3, 78; inclusion of, 233; LGLF and, 229; needs of, 20; support for, 260; welcome for, 3, 260

lesbian students: challenges for, 19–20; problems of, 147

LesBiGay OK. *See* Lesbian, Bisexual and Gay Students of Kansas

Levertov, Denise, 31

Levine, Arthur, 162

LGBTQ, 2, 254; advocacy, 199, 201; center, 202, 276; history, 4–8, 219; issues, 5, 13, 200, 203; movement, 221–222; revolution, 11; rights, 200, 204; services, 9; term, xxiv

LGBTQ students, 90, 200, 201, 263, 274, 277; activism of, 208; stereotypes of, 207

LGL, Inc. *See* Lawrence Gay Liberation, Inc.

LGLF. *See* Lawrence Gay Liberation Front

LGLF News, 90, 303n64

Lichtwardt, Ruth, 108 (fig.), 111 (fig.), 168, 196, 197, 202, 224, 314n1

Lieberman, Robbie, 5

Life magazine, 11, 13

Lim, Paul, 22, 30, 32, 52, 141, 193, 224; on AIDS epidemic, 194

Ling, Daniel, 27, 226, 249

Linker, Richard, 21, 28, 31–32, 45, 46, 49, 57, 98 (fig.), 101 (fig.), 91, 122, 123, 167, 224, 285n83; on challenging status quo, 125; on harassment, 18; LGLF and, 41, 85; on music/dances, 140–141; on presentations, 77; strategy and, 131; Venus and, 29

Lipper, Fred, 26

LLA. *See* Lawrence Lesbian Alliance

Lone Star Lake, 154

Lordi, Joe, 31, 194, 211, 224, 272; on cruising, 18; on dances, 143, 276; on group dynamics, 62; log by, 288n2

Lorenzen, Kathryn (Kathy Buehler/KB), 111 (fig.), 112 (fig.), 113 (fig.), 226, 239, 249; on Scalet, 240

Maher, Michael, 69, 134

Malcolm X, 162

Manhattan Gay Consciousness Group, 264, 265

Manhattan Gay Liberation Front, 264

Marquis, Donald, 134

marriage, 148, 149, 151, 231; license, 69, 84; same-sex, 84, 85, 139, 197–198

Martha and the Vandellas, 321n46

Martin, John R., 120, 227; human rights and, 159; LGLF and, 136, 160; recognition and, 136

Mary Hartman, Mary Hartman (television show), 109

masculinity, 19, 77, 232, 301n25; label of, 214

Mattachine Society, 20, 35, 53, 61, 269, 289n15

Mayer, Sharon, 23, 30, 60, 202, 224, 230; on gay liberation, 125; LGLF and, 46; sexism and, 232

McAdoo, Niya, 212, 219, 225

McCollum Hall, 125

McConnell, Michael, 20, 30, 69, 227; on convention, 82; LGLF and, 84–85; marriage of, 84

McCool, John H., 36

McCrary, Jim, 31, 286n104

McGowen, Mike, 129

McKinney, Bruce, 266, 267, 268, 271

"Me Too" Movement, 255, 323n105

Medical Center, KU, 78, 151, 275

Meigs, Janean, 116 (fig.)

Meko, Jim, 69

Memorial Stadium, 38, 94

Menninger, Karl, 152

Menninger Clinic, 151, 169

Menninger Foundation, 33, 78, 152

Mental Health Clinic, KU, 151

mental illness classification, 79, 90, 91, 148, 152

mentors, 210–212
microaggressions, 17
Midwest Gay Conference, 168–171
Miller, Elizabeth, 252
Miller, Timothy, 22, 37, 225
Miller, Vern, 72
Minority Opinions Forum, 85
Mirror Store, 32
misogyny, xvi, 232, 256, 258
Mitch's (bar), 241
Monhollon, Rusty, 21, 39
Moody, Rick, 26, 29, 96 (fig.)
Moran, Jeffrey, 209
Moratorium March, 81
Morgan, Robin, 176, 245
Morris, Bonnie, 240
Mose, Felix, 196
MPLS Free, 69
Multicultural Student Movement, 198
music, 238–241; dances and, 140–141

Naramore, John, 26
National Gay Liberation Alliance, 69
National Minimum Drinking Age Act
    (1984), 314n4
National Newspaper Association, 256
National Organization for Women, 232, 236
National Women's Studies Association
    Conference, 240
Navratilova, Martina, 256
Near, Holly, 241
New Adult Community, 50, 284n63
"New Homosexuality, The" (*Esquire*), 1213
New Left, 5, 23, 57, 232, 252; activism of,
    35; agenda of, 208; GLF-NY and, 80;
    influence on, 47
New Right, 194
News Bureau, KU, 289n15
Newton, Huey, 297n80
New Year's Eve ball, riot at, 20
New York Native, 194, 211
Nichols, Jane, 226, 242, 243
No Pat Answer (film), 254
No Place Like Home (Janovy), 6
nonbinary: term, 309n18
nondiscrimination policy, 180, 275,
    313n84

normalizing gay experience, 4, 57, 217
Norris, Nancy, 109 (fig.)
North American Conference of Homo-
    phile Organizations (NACHO), 262

Off the Wall Hall, 193, 239
Oldfather, Charles, 40, 135, 225
Olivia Records, 240–241
Oread Daily, 57, 292n62
Oread neighborhood, 23, 27, 246, 247,
    249, 252
organizations, 64, 133, 184, 219; early,
    46–54; gay, 8, 24, 65, 138, 185, 188,
    268–269, 270, 275; gay rights, 85, 268–
    269; grassroots, 82; homophile, 262;
    lesbian, 185, 188; LGBTQ, 3; LGLF, 8,
    54–58; male-dominated, 251; registered,
    9, 188; strategies for, 60
Ortleb, Chuck, 28, 144, 145, 194, 210–211,
    224; Kunstler and, 120, 121
Ottawa University, 151, 152; LGLF
    and, 275
outing, 57, 60, 61. *See also* coming out
Outober, 200

Panhellenic Council, 146
Panthers' Constitutional Convention, 83
Pardun, Robert, 23
patriarchy, 231; inequality and, 236
People's Constitutional Convention, 81
Perkuhn, Tamara (Tammy), 111 (fig.), 113
    (fig.), 226, 239, 240, 321n47
Perrin, Dick, 153, 155, 165, 166, 213, 224
Pete's (bar), 33
Petillo, Matthew, 220
Petrowaky, Kathy, 174
Pettey, Jim, 89, 145, 213, 224, 262; attack
    on, 144; on marriage, 84
Pettit, Polly, 226, 242, 243, 253, 254
Phelps, Fred, 199
Phillips, Scoop, 262, 263
philosophical splits, 59–64
Phoenix Society for Individual
    Freedom, 262
picnics, LGLF, 30, 154
Piekalkiewicz, Maura, 252
Pike, Mary Lisa, 252

Pioneer Cemetery, 194

Pittsburg State University, 34, 87–88, 296n69; gay/lesbian students at, 273–274; LGLF and, 274

police, 39, 40; gay people and, 33; harassment by, 18; raid by, 33

policy change on campus, 192; call for, 144–147

political action, 49, 61, 80, 155, 157, 265; advocating, 59–60

political agenda, 50, 157

political climate, 161, 170

politics, 59, 265; anti-, 166; direct-action, 23; gender-bending, 124; identity, 25; LGLF and, 250; progressive, 21; radical, 23, 24; Yippie, 214

Pooh Corner, 97, 98, 100 (fig.)

Poppe, Ann, 134

"Position Paper on Library Material on Gay Liberation" (LGLF), 147

Position Statement on Homosexuality and Civil Rights (APA), 152

Potter's Lake, 58

Prados, Joe, 34, 49, 50, 52, 99 (fig.), 111 (fig.), 126, 138, 155, 202, 224, 780; on bars, 33; lawsuit and, 134

Prairie Power, 5, 23

Prairie Power (Lieberman), 5

prejudice, 18, 19, 50

presence, 126; creating, 87–90, 205–207

Prevenier, Walter, xv

Pride celebrations, 154–156, 174, 194, 268

Pride Index, 276

protests, 22, 125, 126, 197, 199, 219, 228; antigay, 218; anti-ROTC, 198; antiwar, 94 (fig.); civil rights, 38; discrimination, 154–156; feminist, 229; KU and, 35–40

Provisional Affirmative Action Plan, 176

Purple Fist (Purple Hands Protests), 58, 292n63

queer: term, xxiii, 48, 198, 199

Queering the Countryside (Gray, Gilley, and Johnson), 6

Queer Man on Campus (Dilley), 6

Queers and Allies: LesBiGayTrans Services of Kansas, 198, 200. *See also* SpectrumKU

Racialesbians, 236

racism, 39, 45, 49, 50, 58, 65, 82, 137, 234, 241, 257; lesbians of color and, 232

Radavich, David (David Radd), 53, 54, 76, 77, 140, 147, 148, 150, 151, 214, 224, 230; conversation with Brian, 66–67; on Lawrence, 127; Menninger and, 152; on mental illness, 79; name change for, 291n40; resignation from GCS, 152; return to GCS, 153; on support, 215

Radical Fairies, 85

radicalism, 23, 24, 59–60, 208, 209

Raitt, Bonnie, 238

Rape Victim Support Service (RVSS), 251–254

Rawat, Prem, 29

Real Queer America (Allen), 6

recognition, 65, 132, 133, 171–172, 180–181; bifurcated, 192; denial of, 70–74, 218; gaining, 159, 160, 191, 270; LGLF, 42, 136, 157, 158, 159–160, 204, 208; organization, 177, 185; policy for, 188

Reconstruction, 26–27, 57, 292n64

Reddy, Helen, 238, 240

Redhead (bar), 33

Regents, Kansas Board of, 68, 132, 169

registration process, 56, 66–70; changes to, 180–190

Rehabilitation Act (1973), 177

religion, 121–123; homosexuality and, 121, 152

Religion Department, KU, 164

religious Right, rise of, 197

Renn, Kristen, 63

Responsible Active Gays, WSU, 326n25

Rhatigan, James, 227, 266–267, 270

Rhoads, Robert, 198

Rice, Nick, 40, 45

Riseman, Elaine, 44, 45, 56, 66, 82, 147, 150, 151, 224, 230, 231; graduation of, 168; on homosexuality, 79; leadership of, 63; LGLF and, 74, 87; resignation from

GCS, 152; return to GCS, 153; Stout and, 61
Rivera, Sylvia, 61
Roberts, Oral, 42
Roberts, Randy, 274
Robinson, Bill, 164
Rock Chalk Café, 30, 40, 125, 130, 302n49
role models: becoming, 210–212; gay/lesbian, 212
Rolling Stone, 82, 196
Rolling Stones, 141
ROTC, 38, 198
Rumpel, Craig, 275
Rural Free Delivery (RFD), 85
Rush, Tonda, 226; Kennedy and, 237; organizing and, 46; on sexism, 256
RVSS. *See* Rape Victim Support Service

safety network, 216, 277
SafeZone, 200
Sambo's Restaurant, 125
same-sex couples, first, 85
San Francisco Examiner, 292n63
Scalet, Beth, 240
Scally, Jim, 194
Schick, Kathy, 226, 243
Schornick, Lynn, 148–149
Schorr, Ronald W. W., 134
Schwaller, Henry, 274–275
SDS. *See* Students for a Democratic Society
self-acceptance, 16, 43, 50, 154, 210, 211, 215
SenEx. *See* University Senate Executive Committee
Senior High Institute, 228
Seventeenth Street Collective (NYC-GLF), 298n83
Sex in the Heartland (Bailey), 6–7
sexism, xvi, 19, 45, 49, 58, 65, 82, 174, 206, 231, 232, 251; lesbians and, 254–258; pervasiveness of, 257
sexual acts: criminalization of, 70, 294n16
sexuality, 29, 50, 54, 58, 78, 137, 148, 154, 232, 236, 259, 266; attitudes about, 164; awareness of, 149; conceptualization of, 138; cultural discourse about,

199–200; expression of, 138; redefining, 212–214; repressing, 27
Sexuality and Gender Diversity Faculty Staff Council, 200
sexual orientation, xiii, 19, 28, 42, 124, 133, 147, 148, 166, 179, 185, 199, 214, 220, 254, 257, 262, 271; discrimination and, 155, 177, 180; employment discrimination and, 312n84; evolving conceptualization of, 201; as protected class, 180; religion and, 121; shame about, 2; as social construction, 5; term, 312n72
sexual proclivities, term, 136, 189
Sexual Trauma and Abuse Care Center, 254. *See also* Rape Victim Support Service (RVSS)
SGD. *See* Center for Sexuality and Gender Diversity
SHA. *See* Student Homophile Association
shame, 14, 17, 43, 126, 191, 259; internalization of, 2
Shankel, Del, 72, 168, 170, 180, 225, 272, 275; affirmative action plan and, 178; Ambler and, 189
Shapiro, Dave, 171, 172
Shavlik, Donna, 125, 225
Shavlik, Frank, 66, 225
Shearer, Mike, 43
Shelton, Bob, 196
Sievers, Sharon, 4
Simons, Dolph, 67
Simply Equal Amendment, 194, 199
Sinnett, Robert, 263
Sister Kettle Café, 235
Skidmore, Arthur, 68, 134
Skrentny, John, 11
Smith, Caryl, 188, 225
Smith, Christine Leonard, 34, 140, 226
SNCC. *See* Student Nonviolent Coordinating Committee
social change, 22, 48, 82, 163, 252
social connections, 32, 165, 259
social issues, 2, 11, 23, 37, 47, 48, 65
social justice, 25, 49

Social Welfare School, KU, 148, 151, 251
Society for Individual Rights, 81
sodomy laws, 67, 160, 294n16
softball, 237, 241–245, 259
Solidarity Statement (LGLF), 290n27
sororities, 118; lesbians in, 249, 250; as straight organizations, 14
sorority women, 233, 238, 249; lesbianism and, 250
South Farm, 117 (fig.), 248, 251, 254
Spare, Keith, 32, 227, 296n69, 301n14, 324–325n5, 325n13; on homophobia, 264; K-State and, 122, 262; LGLF and, 122, 262, 325n16; UMYF and, 121, 122
speak-outs, 37
speakers' bureau, 119, 123, 141, 147, 154, 166, 168, 175, 190, 228–229; establishment of, 76–80; presentations by, 212
Spearman, John, 39, 225
SpectrumKU, 200, 201
Spectrum: LGBTQ & Allies, 326n25
Spencer, Patti, 234
Sports Illustrated, 256
SPU. See Student Peace Union (SPU)
Sramek, Mark, 224, 250
stereotypes, 12, 89, 126, 207, 229, 248; challenging, 78, 220; gay/ lesbian, 211, 212–213, 214; gender, 77, 123–127; heteronormative, 123–127; homophobic, 207, 269; opposing, 217
Stetzler, Laurie, 45, 58, 224; LGLF and, 229; on revolution, 259–260
Stillwell, John Steven, 45, 83, 88, 97 (fig.), 102 (fig.), 122, 123, 166, 224, 285n83; articles by, 58; death of, 289n9; lawsuit and, 134; LGLF and, 41, 85; political activism and, 167
Stonewall uprising, 4, 20, 35, 53, 61, 82, 139, 154, 307n150
Storms, Michael, 153, 154
Stout, David H., xv, 16, 28, 45, 52, 54, 55, 56, 66, 82, 88, 96 (fig.), 111 (fig.), 120, 147, 148, 149, 150, 224, 230, 288n2, 296n68, 317n4; activist philosophy of, 208–209; Balfour and, 70; Body Shop and, 65; civil rights and, 85; coming out of, 42–43, 62; on dances, 221; early life of, 41–42; gay community and, 43, 44; gay grapevine and, 151; GCS and, 151–152; graduation of, 168; on homosexuality, 79; on Kansas Union, 34; Lake Henry and, 31; LGLF and, xiii, xiv, 48, 63, 67, 71, 72, 73, 87, 202, 231; protest and, 219; resignation from GCS, 152; return to GCS, 153; Riseman and, 61; sexual orientation and, 42; Shearer and, 43; suicide attempts of, 17, 42, 43, 63
Strong Hall, 62, 105, 244
Stroup, Joe, 244
Stroup, Kala, 206, 225, 244, 251, 322n63; Boyd and, 233; support from, 233
Stubbs, Michael, xv, 22, 24, 81, 85–86, 93 (fig.), 96 (fig.), 98 (fig.), 120, 124, 125, 202, 212, 224, 285n83, 298n83; articles by, 58; childhood of, 60; conventions/ events and, 86; on dances, 139, 141; on factionalism, 61; on gay liberation, 84; on LGBTQ movement, 221–222; LGLF and, 41; political action and, 25, 59–60; as a role model, 210; Urban Plunge and, 26–27; Venus and, 29; Women's Coalition and, 230
Student Affairs Division, Emporia, 271
Student Affairs Office, 187
Student Executive Committee (StudEx), 132
Student Government Association (SGA), WSU, 266
Student Homophile Association (SHA), WSU, 266, 267, 268
Student Mobilization Committee, 283n43
Student Nonviolent Coordinating Committee (SNCC), 242, 283n43
Student Organizations and Activities Office, 185
Student Peace Union (SPU), 283n43
Students Concerned about Higher Education, 35
Student Senate, 35, 38, 72, 130, 145, 173, 182, 183, 188, 194, 196, 199; Ambler and, 186; campus grievance with, 120; campus recognition and, 180–181; collaboration with, 190; decision-

making and, 68; funding from, 132, 138, 144, 186, 189, 192, 193; GLSOK and, 195; internal structures of, 181; LGLF and, 68, 70, 128, 129; proposal of, 184; recognition and, 73; women's center and, 234

Student Senate Executive Committee (StudEx), 68, 69, 119, 163, 196

Student Union Activities, 85, 237

Students for a Democratic Society (SDS), 5, 23, 24, 25, 283n43

Students for Education on Liberal Concerns, WSU, 326n25

StudEx. *See* Student Senate Executive Committee

Suffrage (music group), 240

suicide, 86, 272; attempted, 43, 63; considering, 15, 17, 42, 152

Summer, Donna, 220

Supreme Court, US, 158

Sweet Honey in the Rock, 34, 238

Taboo Topics, K-State, 263

Tachell, Peter, 124

"Tall Victor," 101 (fig.)

Tansy's Bookstore, 31

Tasheff, Tedde, 163, 164, 171, 225, 242; Shapiro and, 172

Taylor, Barbara, 26

Taylor, Emily, 114 (fig.), 232, 242; RVSS and, 253

Templar, George, 105, 227; Chalmers and, 136–137; Kunstler and, 134, 135; ruling by, 136–137

10 Percent, WSU, 326n25

Tent (bar), 33

Tenth Circuit Court of Appeals, 136

Terrace Lounge, 32, 33

Teutsch, Robert, 267

Thaemert, Rick, 172–173

That Gay Group!, WSU, 326n25

Thornton, Phil, 285n83

Tickner, Toc, 321n57

Title IX, 243, 257

Today's Student, 174

tolerance, 76, 164, 296n64

Tomlinson, Bob, 185

Tommy the Traveler, 56

"Too Hot to Stop" (dance), poster for, 107 (fig.)

Topeka, 25, 32, 33; gay community in, 43

Topeka High School, 77

transgender, xxiv, 198, 254; students, xxiii, 201

Transgender Union, WSU, 326n25

Transitional Care Services, 251–254

Trophy Room, 44

Tuttle, William (Bill), 38, 67, 135, 140, 196, 197, 225

"Two Centuries Later" (Carttar), 136

Tyson, Willie, 34

UDK. See University Daily Kansan

UFM. *See* University for Man Community Center

UMHE. *See* United Ministries in Higher Education

UMYF. *See* Baldwin United Methodist Youth Fellowship

"Under the Rainbow: Oral Histories. . ." (Albin), 7

UniCampus, 171

Union Operating Committee, policy change and, 131

Unitarian Church, 241

United Methodist Youth Camp, 121–123

United Methodist Youth Movement, 262

United Ministries in Higher Education (UMHE), 52, 54; name change for, 290–291n34

University Christian Movement, 26

University Daily Kansan (UDK), 27, 38, 43, 49, 57, 68, 69, 91, 127, 128, 129, 130–131, 132, 139, 164, 166, 172, 173, 174, 180, 183, 184, 186; classifieds of, 151; gay pride and, 154–155; GSOK and, 167–168; LGLF and, 2, 67, 133; Lone Star Lake picnic and, 154

University Events Committee, 130

University for Man Community Center (UFM), 262–263, 264, 265

University Leader, 274

University of Minnesota, 69; FREE and, 20, 82, 84, 101

University of Oklahoma Board of
   Regents, 157
University Senate, 120
University Senate Executive Committee
   (SenEx), 130
Up Front, 158
Urban Plunge, 26–27, 29, 60, 262, 284n63

VanLaningham, Todd, 153, 170, 173,
   174, 179, 180, 182, 224; human rights
   and, 178
Vector, 81
Velvel, Lawrence, 157
Venceremos Brigade, 25, 26, 60
Venus, 28, 86, 91, 93 (fig.), 97, 98, 124, 228;
   importance of, 29
Vietnam War, 23, 24, 45, 164, 273;
   opposition to, 37
violence, 39, 40, 55; domestic, 240, 247,
   252; sexual, 229, 252, 323n105; threat of,
   38, 196
visibility, 4, 13, 86, 87, 131, 136, 141, 161, 239,
   275; dances and, 139; impact of, 65, 205;
   importance of, 126; increased, 81, 158,
   165, 186, 190, 199, 207
Vogel, Carla, 195, 225
von Ende, Richard, 168
Vortex, 54, 57, 83, 91, 259, 292n64;
   launching of, 58; LGLF and, 58
voters' guides, 154–156
Voth, Harold, 169, 227

Warren, Bob, 34–35, 80, 87–88, 160, 202,
   206, 210, 224, 274; on dances/political
   overtones, 139; on gay liberation,
   214–215; on hard-core politicals, 59; on
   relationships, 211–212
Washburn University, 297n70; School of
   Law, 119
Washington, Marian, 257, 258, 324n110
Watergate scandal, 162
Watkins Museum of History, xv
Watson Library, 96
WBC. *See* Westboro Baptist Church
WC. *See* Women's Coalition
Wear Blue Jeans If You're Gay Day,

172–175, 190, 212, 268, 310n39; impact of,
   174; origins of, 172
Weaver, Steven, 22, 45, 83, 89, 91–92, 100
   (fig.), 120, 124, 131, 139, 160, 171, 204,
   206, 211, 215, 224, 232; articles by, 58; on
   collective action, 56–57; lawsuit and,
   134; on LGLF structure, 55; on Tasheff/
   Shapiro, 172
Wescoe, W. Clarke, 36–37, 38, 225
Wesley Center, 26, 234
Wesley Foundation, 148
Westboro Baptist Church (WBC), 218, 219
Wheat Dreams, 167
Wheel (bar), 256
When Dreams and Heroes Died (Levine),
   162
Wichita Gay Community Association, 266
Wichita State University (WSU),
   274; gay issue and, 261, 276; gay/
   lesbian students at, 266–268;
   nondiscrimination policy and, 275;
   organizing at, 325n21
Wilde, Oscar, 31
Willer, David, 134
Williamson, Cris, 238, 241
Willow Domestic Violence Center, 252
wine and cheese gatherings, 237–238, 241
Wolf-Wendel, Lisa, xiii
Womanspace, 116 (fig.), 215, 237, 251, 252,
   259, 322n67; described, 245–247
Women in Higher Education Office, 233
Women's Coalition (WC), 73, 76,
   129–130, 136, 146, 175, 215, 233, 235,
   237; counseling services and, 148;
   CSW and, 234; dance and, 130, 131;
   Gay Caucus of, 158; gay liberation
   and, 130; LGLF and, 145; poster by,
   103 (fig.); support services and, 251;
   Womanspace and, 245
Women's Division, Lawrence Chamber
   of Commerce, 102, 125
Women's Equity Action Coalition, 175
Women's International Year, 24
women's movement, 49, 229, 248, 252,
   302n34; gender/power and, 19
Women's Political Caucus, 253

women's rights, 11, 176
Women's Transitional Care Services (WTCS), 251, 252, 254
Woolworth's, 23, 124
Wright, John, 134
WSU. *See* Wichita State University
WTCS. *See* Women's Transitional Care Services

Yippies, 24, 124
"YMCA" (song), 220
Youth Camp, 123

Zimmer, Lorna Grunz, 323n96
Zwahl, Todd, 108 (fig.), 175, 185, 224